A PROGRESS IN
MOUNTAINEERING

CARN DEARG OF BEN NEVIS
Climbing the South Castle Gully

A PROGRESS IN
MOUNTAINEERING

SCOTTISH HILLS
TO ALPINE PEAKS

J. H. B. BELL

OLIVER AND BOYD

EDINBURGH: TWEEDDALE COURT
LONDON: 98 GREAT RUSSELL STREET, W.C.

FIRST PUBLISHED 1950

PRINTED IN GREAT BRITAIN BY
W. S. COWELL LTD, AT THE BUTTER MARKET, IPSWICH
FOR OLIVER AND BOYD LTD, EDINBURGH

FOREWORD

BY

F. S. SMYTHE

J. H. B. Bell and I are old friends and it gives me much pleasure
to write this introduction to his book, especially since he is both
a sound mountaineer, and a writer who is able to record
admirably his many and varied experiences on the hills and
mountains.

We first met at Wastdale and, as was fitting and proper,
began our climbing on the British hills. This is one of Dr Bell's
tenets, and there is no better preliminary training for mountaineering in the Alps than to wander in all kinds of weather
over the hills of Scotland, the Lakes, and Wales, and afterwards
learn to climb the crags.

Mark well what Dr Bell writes about the importance of small
beginnings. He tells you about the hills of his native land, and
then about his climbs in the Alps. I should like to cap his story
of our Jungfrau traverse with another and different story.

We had spent a very comfortable but expensive night at the
Jungfraujoch Hotel. Next morning we had to foot a thumping
bill, for prices in Switzerland for food and lodging are directly
proportional to the height above sea-level, and the Jungfraujoch
Hotel is the highest in Switzerland.

As we left the hotel I heard Bell muttering to himself about
the magnitude of the bill and it sounded like the distant rumblings of a thunderstorm.

The path we were on was cut across the steep snowslopes.
There we came upon a stout Teuton. He was edging sideways
like a crab along the path with shut eyes, digging his fingers into
the snow.

As we came up to him we heard him moan piteously:

'Schwindel! Schwindel! Furchtbarer Schwindel!' Quick as
a flash Bell turned to him and said: 'Ay, man you're right. It
was a swindle, a —— swindle!'

The most difficult and finest ice and rock climb we did, was
the ascent of the Aiguille du Plan by the Plan-Crocodile couloir

and the east ridge. I well remember the stoic fortitude with which he withstood a rain of ice fragments for hours on end as I cut the steps in the steep ice-slope leading to the ridge; then, on the ridge, his promptitude in levering away a large stone that had jammed my leg in a chimney, and, finally, his splendid lead up the rock pitches of the climb. Franz Lochmatter, who made the first ascent with his brother Joseph and V. J. E. Ryan in 1906, used to tell me when I met him subsequently that it was the finest rock climb he ever made.

I would like to conclude by wishing my old companion of the rope the best of good fortune. You will read his book with the same enjoyment that I do.

ACKNOWLEDGEMENTS

I have climbed with many friends, at home and abroad, who have helped by their comradeship, enthusiasm and example, in my progress in mountaineering and, therefore, to make this book. They cannot all be mentioned by name.

Nurtured in the *Scottish Mountaineering Club*, I owe a great debt to many of its members, past and present, particularly for the great work they have done in the exploration of the Scottish Bens and glens. This has been made available to all mountain lovers in the Club's series of Guide Books and in the pages of its Journal, which it has been my privilege to edit for several years. Other printed sources of my inspiration may be found in the Bibliography at the end of this work.

I am indebted to all who have contributed photographs whose names appear in the List of Illustrations, and also to the S.M.C. for the use of blocks. I owe the excellent drawings of technique, climbing incident, and of mountains where no photographs were available to Miss Joan Tebbutt, and the maps, along with several diagrams, to my wife. I understand very well how much care and insight have been expended on them.

For advice on certain points of technique I am grateful to Messrs P. J. H. Unna and John Wilson. Elsewhere I acknowledge the inspiration derived from the book by Mr W. H. Murray which has done much to foster interest in Scottish winter climbing. My thanks are due to the *Scots Magazine*, and especially to Dr J. B. Salmond, who first encouraged me to write on mountaineering for the public. The subject matter of Chapter XXI first appeared in that publication. In the compilation and arrangement of the book I have received much assistance from Messrs W. E. Forde and T. L. Jenkins.

Finally, I owe a debt of gratitude to my old friend, Frank Smythe, who has contributed the Foreword. At an early stage of my climbing career he introduced me to the joys of guideless mountaineering in the High Alps. His tragic death, early in

vii

1949, has left a great void in the ranks of British mountaineers, mountain authors, and photographers. I remember him as a staunch friend and comrade, and a continual source of inspiration and encouragement.

CONTENTS

PART IV

ALPINE MOUNTAINEERING TECHNIQUE

PART V

ALPINE EXPEDITIONS

ILLUSTRATIONS

PHOTOGRAPHS

MAPS

PART I

INTRODUCTION

CHAPTER I

PROLOGUE

THE object of this book is to conduct the reader along a progress in mountaineering, by encouraging him to start on the nearest hill, even although it is no more than a thousand feet in height. Mountain climbing is the finest of open-air pursuits, which, if properly pursued, may become a lifelong enthusiasm, filled with the spirit of exploration and the joy of adventure.

There are two aims which can and should be followed at the same time. The first is to climb our own British hills in all seasons and weathers, and by all manner of routes; to begin with by the easy ways up slopes of grass, heather or other rough ground and, at a later stage, by the more difficult routes over rocks or winter slopes of snow and ice. The second, and larger aim, is to acquire such a varied and thorough technique in British mountaineering as will enable the possessor to go exploring and climbing on the greater mountains of the world with a fair measure of confidence and safety, and without the assistance of professional guides. There is no doubt that this aim can be realised, within certain limits, by those who have tackled every variety of problem, both in summer and winter conditions, which is presented to them by British, but more particularly by Scottish mountains.

Mountains are far more numerous, more variegated and higher in Scotland than in England. Scottish mountains carry much more snow in winter and do so for many months, depending of course on the height and bulk of the mountain mass. For adequate practice in snow and ice climbing, Scottish experience, and plenty of it spread over several winters, is vitally important, because the major technical problems on larger mountains, such as the Alps, have far more to do with snow and ice than with difficult rocks. Even with a satisfactory all-round Scottish experience the British-trained mountaineer will have much to learn when he tries his luck on Alpine peaks. His education and basic experience will be sound, and he will know enough to

3

enable him to make a start in one of the easier districts of the Alps, where he will very soon gather such other experience as and when he requires it. The ample opportunity for climbing on many different kinds of rock, much of which bears hardly any mark of previous exploration, is another valuable feature of Scottish mountains, as it helps to develop initiative and judgment in the mountaineer.

The above considerations have, in effect, determined the plan of the book, and the author makes no apology for treating the Scottish Bens at such considerable length and leaving a much shorter section for the larger problems of the Alpine peaks. The reason is, of course, that the earlier section must carry most of the technique and the basic principles which will, later on, be used in the Alps.

If the reader does not think that England and Wales are receiving fair treatment let him look at a physical map of the British Isles and remember that rock climbing is only one facet of the larger mountaineering. England has more of the men and Scotland has more of the mountains. They should know each other better. If anything more need be said on the subject let the reader refer to the chapter on English Rock Climbing, in which the author disclaims any ability or competence to give an adequate treatment, but offers a respectful tribute to the pioneers of Lakeland and North Wales, who have brought the art of rock climbing to a higher level of competence combined with safety than anywhere else in Europe, and have maintained its sporting character by a healthy refusal to countenance the use of ironmongery and mechanised methods.

The book contains only six chapters on pure technique—hill walking, rock climbing, snow and ice climbing, and Alpine technique. These are, of necessity, very condensed. They may be read as they stand or referred to as required. The rest of the book, founded mainly on the personal experiences of the author, is intended to be a readable commentary on these chapters, but, so far as Scotland is concerned, it does not pretend to describe the full extent of the climbing possibilities. It does endeavour to sample the main varieties of mountain, district and climbing problem.

There are many omissions, several of which are conspicuous.

Knoydart
Loch Nevis looking westwards to the island of Eigg. A typical West Highland
landscape

The blackest, sullenest loch that fills
The ocean rents of these gnarled hills.
PRINCIPAL SHAIRP

Glasgow climbers rightly extol the merits of their Arrochar
Alps and the severe rock climbs available on that delightful
little peak, the Cobbler. It is even more serious to neglect the
main mass of the Central Grampians, many of which provide
excellent winter climbing and some of them extremely difficult

cliffs of mica schist, the commonest rock in the Scottish Highlands. There is no mention of that grand hill, Garbh Bheinn of
Ardgour, and nothing of that magnificent belt of hill country
from Beauly to Loch Carron. These are grave omissions, and
it would appear as if the rock climber had made serious en-
croachments on the all-round mountaineer. The author can
only plead that, hitherto, most books about the Scottish Highlands have been written by Englishmen who have spread the
idea that there are many mountains in northern Scotland which
are excellent for high-level walking, but who have not discovered
that these same mountains provide magnificent scope for first-
class climbing. The first Scottish mountaineer to give effective
publicity to the technical excellence of the Scottish Bens, both
in summer and winter, is my friend Mr W. H. Murray. His
book, *Mountaineering in Scotland*, has been a source of inspiration
to me, and I have endeavoured to extend the field over a
number of districts which he has not covered.

Let me add one more word of advice to the younger mountaineers, straight from my own experience. Do not imagine that
hill-walking requires no technique. It requires much more than
you imagine, and you will continue to learn all sorts of odd,
useful things for many years. Do not try to take a short cut to
the greater thrills of severe rock climbing. Hill walking is true
mountaineering, however the hard-bitten rock-climber may
regard it. Walking is the head and corner stone of all mountain
climbing, whether we are dealing with the little thousand-foot
hill near our homes or taking part in an assault on an unclimbed
20,000-foot giant of the Himalaya. In certain kinds of weather
and atmospheric lighting the one can look almost as beautiful
and impressive as the other.

Titles are seldom crisp, concise and enlightening. It is hoped
that the book will not prove to be an ill-matched union of
personal experience on the Scottish hills with a few ascents in
the High Alps. Neither part aspires to any degree of complete-
ness, but the idea of a progress in experience leads from the one
to the other, and the Alpine expeditions are only a higher stage
in the evolution of the complete mountaineer, who, in whatso-
ever country he may reside, ought to proceed onwards from the
foothills to the greater ranges beyond and above them. It is

surely better that he should lay the foundations of his experience among his native hills and by his own effort and initiative.

The rest of this section is a brief account of three expeditions. They are not chosen for their difficulty and excitement, but because they are good examples of different types of problem. There is nothing more beautiful than a Scottish snow climb on a perfect winter day, more engrossing than a hard and difficult rock climb or more exacting than the ascent of a great Alpine peak. It is hoped that they may serve as an outline of what the mountains have to offer, the challenge they present to an active body and a sound mind and how it can be answered.

CHAPTER II

BEN CRUACHAN IN SNOW

MANY people imagine that hills can be climbed with enjoyment only in summer. They have heard of those tough eccentrics who go there in the depth of winter, lose themselves, it is to be hoped without fatal results, but, in any case, oblige rescue parties of police, shepherds and gamekeepers to go and look for them amidst snow drifts as high as a house. All this makes good reading in the newspapers and invites indignant comment from the armchairs by the fireside. The truth is that anyone who has enjoyed a perfect day on the snow-clad Scottish hills in winter has discovered a new experience, the exhilaration of which can hardly be matched by any mountain ascent at midsummer.

On the 3rd of January, 1936, three of us left Taynuilt in order to climb Ben Cruachan by an unusual approach from Glen Noe on its northern side. It was a day of bright sun, blue sky, hard frost and clear visibility. We were ferried across the mouth of the river Awe, and then followed a long and delightful track winding through the woods, high above Loch Etive. Far away, at the head of the loch, was the snow-capped dome of Ben Starav (3,541 ft.), gleaming in the morning sun. Just before the track left the margin of the loch I went in for my New Year swim from a grassy peninsula. Yes, it was cold, but invigorating. Only the mile or two at the head of the loch was actually frozen over! A grassy track now led us up Glen Noe, with a cheerful stream, interspersed with waterfalls, on our left. We walked on steadily until we had rounded the lower slopes of a bulky, grassy shoulder on our right, and we could look up a side glen and view the summit ridge of Ben Cruachan.

From the top of the Taynuilt, or westmost peak of Cruachan, a faint streamer marked the shadow line of the summit cone cast upon the slight haze on its northern side. A steep, snowy ridge descended directly towards us. Nothing was hidden; the ridge was certainly steep and possibly iced in its upper portion. The only question was whether we had time to traverse the

8

mountain before nightfall. In the early annals of the Scottish Mountaineering Club there is a record of a party of good men, well equipped with ice-axes and rope, who took eight hours to ascend this very ridge when the conditions were very icy. We were no better than our forerunners, but also there would never be a more perfect day for the job.

The approach to the ridge was easy, and so was the lower part of it. As we rose the snow became very much harder and the ice-axes were brought into use. At first it was only a question of steadying ourselves as we kicked steps in the frozen surface. Then that became impossible and we had to cut a slash through the hard crust, using the adze blade of the axe. Still, we made good progress. To the north the view became more extensive and splendid. Loch Etive was of a sombre green colour with a curious, mottled sheen several miles to the north where the loch was frozen over. To the east, the main summit of Cruachan was edged with a bright, fiery band of sunshine, amazingly remote and beautiful, rather like a picture of Siniolchun in the Himalaya with its translucent upper ridges of clear ice. Straight ahead, our own peak was wrapped in cloud.

As we ascended, the going became slower and more difficult. The icy patches became much more frequent, and steps had to be hewed out more laboriously with heavy blows from the pick of the axe. The ridge was broken up with ice-encrusted rocks and boulders, everyone beautifully cased in long, feathery, frost crystals. The course became tortuous among these outcrops, as we sought the easiest route towards our objective. There was little time to lose, so we pressed on as fast as we could. In that clear, exhilarating atmosphere it was good to be alive and we made light of the labour of step-cutting, warmed as we were by the exercise, but fanned and kept to it by the cold northerly breeze. For a long time the summit hardly seemed to come any nearer, but we scarcely noticed the passage of time. It is on such days that the steady rhythm of healthy muscular action promotes a calm serenity and enjoyment which are almost the greatest gains of mountaineering. It is not only a matter of bodily contentment; the mind is ever active on the problems of balance and route selection, whilst all the senses co-operate in absorbing the grandeur of the surroundings, the colours of mountain, snow and cloud, the crunch and tinkle of the passage over snow, ice and rock.

Then the cloud cap retreated before us and we suddenly found that we were close to the final peak. To the west the horizon fell away to the Sound of Mull and the islands. As we approached the top the last remains of cloud flamed up, a glorious crimson, in the gap between ourselves and the highest summit. We emerged into the last of the sunshine, close to the summit cairn of the Taynuilt peak, just before 4 p.m., and stayed to feast our eyes on the most perfect winter sunset of my experience.

The sun itself was surrounded by a coloured corona, quite a local phenomenon, for, with a shift of position of twenty yards, it almost vanished. At the cairn it did not exist: twenty yards to the east it was a complete ring of brilliant colours with the violet on the outside. The cause must have been a thin mist of very fine spicules of ice whirled up from the snowfields by the wind flurries. As the sun set, the colouring became more impressive than ever. Along the northern horizon the colours ranged from a gorgeous heliotrope through a liquid green to a pure, dark blue. These winter colours must be seen in order to be believed. Summer cannot vie with them in purity and intensity. I remember, on another New Year, looking eastward from the summit of Ben More at sunset. The whole length of Loch Tay, as well as the windings of the river Dochart, were a pure, luminous green surmounted by the russet lower slopes and the lovely pink of the snowfields of Ben Lawers.

Here the summit panorama was more varied and impressive. Beyond the head of Loch Etive were the cloud-capped tops of Bidean nam Bian, highest mountain of Argyll, only Ben Starav remaining clear. To the east, beyond the Drochaid Glas peak of Cruachan, was the snowy pyramid of Ben Lui. Far to the south were the hills of Cowal, with the serrated outlines of the Arran peaks on the right. Loch Awe was spread out beneath us as a dark, sinuous band. In the west lay Mull, with snow-streaked Ben More, surrounded by the fiery line of the Atlantic, which also enclosed the distant peaks of Rum, far to the north-west. Such brilliant colouring and visibility are characteristic of the West Highlands of Scotland in fine, frosty, winter weather.

It is the combination of pure colour, snowy mountains, loch and ocean which affords views which are unequalled for sheer beauty amidst ranges of much higher mountains, such as the Alps. There, the scale of the mountains and their abrupt grandeur and savagery of outline are far more awe-inspiring, but there are no expanses of water in the picture, nor does the dry climate lend itself so readily to the atmospheric perspective which enhances the appreciation of distance and the delicate gradations of colour.

My friend, Dr Myles, had already left the summit and it was time for McClure and myself to follow, racing down the easy western slopes. The snow was good and we enjoyed one or two excellent standing glissades, until we finished on the rim of the deep gorge of a stream, unfortunately on the wrong side. In the gathering twilight we reached the main road at the west end of the Pass of Brander, near Bridge of Awe. We made light of the three miles of walking to Taynuilt, well contented with our day and with the prospect of a good dinner. One cannot always remain on the heights; the inner man will not be put off with *the baseless fabric of this vision*, even if the memory of such days lives on through the years.

CHAPTER III

THE CENTRAL BUTTRESS OF BUACHAILLE ETIVE

IT was only after the opening of the new Glencoe road, about the year 1932, that rock climbing activity in the area became really popular and parties began to frequent the crags of Buachaille Etive Mor at most week-ends in summer, and gradually in winter as well. Many of the new-comers were tough in fibre, and they usually camped, even in winter time.

The 'bad' old days were very pleasant, however. Then one had the mountains to oneself and conditions at Kingshouse Inn were still primitive. From one's bedroom one could smell the bacon frying through a hole in the floor, which was better than a breakfast gong. In another it was said to be necessary to put up an umbrella in bed if the weather was wet, which was very often the case. Rock climbing on the Buachaille was little more advanced than in the days of the pioneers at the beginning of the century. The difficulty was not in making a new route on the crags, but in doing so with discrimination, owing to the lavish display of attractive alternatives. Many visits may be necessary for the working out of the best route on a crag, and a number of climbers may make their several contributions to one good discovery before it is perfected.

The rocks of the Buachaille, like most British crags, have the defect of facing northwards for the most part, receiving little sunshine to dry them after rainy weather. For winter climbing this is an advantage, as the frost helps to consolidate the snow, but in summer one prefers dry rocks and welcomes a little sunshine for the harder problems.

The Buachaille has also a south-easterly face, but the crags tend to be less continuous and are broken up into shorter sections. The actual climbing starts at a lower level and the separate sections can be linked up into a very long expedition, finishing close to the top of the mountain (3,343 ft.), and capable of yielding no less than 2,000 feeet of climbing when taken all together. Herein lies the attractiveness of Central Buttress for a long summer day's climbing. The original route on the Buttress was climbed in 1898. The difficulties were not great by modern standards. The Buttress is split into an upper and a lower section by a long rake, called Heather Terrace, sloping steeply upwards from right to left. The pioneers used this rake for linking up an approach on the north side with an easy scramble for a finish from the higher southern end of the Terrace. Practically nothing more was done on this face for about thirty years.*

In July 1929 Alexander Harrison and I enjoyed an excellent climb on the northern face of the Buttress, crossing the foot of Heather Terrace. We solved the final difficulties by ascending two consecutive chimneys, one of which I was only able to climb by using the shoulder of my friend as an essential foothold. We were fortunate in being able to finish the climb by nightfall, for we had only begun about 6 p.m. This upper section, some years later, was made much more direct by W. H. Murray and his party. In the summer of 1931 Colin Allan and I prospected the cliff a good deal farther to the left, hoping to make a direct route up the rocky wall to the upper end of Heather Terrace.

On the extreme left is a smooth, almost vertical wall of alternately bleached and blackened rock, sometimes termed the Waterslide, although very little water ever comes down it unless the weather is really wet. No one has ever climbed this wall directly to the top end of Heather Terrace, for the upper half is perfectly smooth and holdless. Of course, it is never safe to make a sweeping negative assertion in rock climbing. Modern climbers are not all averse to driving spikes into cracks and doing a certain amount of steeplejacking, and I may be wrong in thinking that it cannot be climbed by orthodox methods.

On a cold, windy day in November 1931 Allan and I started as near the foot of the alleged Waterslide as we thought feasible, climbed straight up for nearly 200 feet to a prominent little semi-detached pinnacle on the face and found that we could not proceed much farther in a direct, upward line. On that day we solved the problem by traversing along a ledge to the right and gaining Heather Terrace by a short, exposed chimney where the only available holds were lumps of frozen turf. Allan

* See Map A, p. 108; also Diagram p. 114.

gave a great lead in the second half of the climb up a severe wall about ninety feet high. On wet, cold rock, for it was raining by that time, his performance was outstanding. The middle thirty feet caused me some anxiety but little enjoyment as I followed him. We both considered that we had not exhausted the possibilities of Central Buttress, but we tacitly postponed all further proceedings until a warm summer day.

On a perfect, sunny day in July 1934 we had our opportunity. The party consisted of Colin Allan, Miss M. B. Stewart and myself. This time we confirmed the fact that we could not climb directly up the wall above our little pinnacle, but that a rising traverse to the left was quite feasible on small ledges until we reached a small recess in the cliff. The next short pitch* was delightfully steep and exposed, but there was a secure anchorage above. The rest of the climb was very steep, but no more than 'difficult' according to modern rock-climbing standards. We finished at the upper end of Heather Terrace.

Colin and I, on a later occasion, were able to make a number of lesser variations on this route, but they make little difference to its character as a climb. The face is very steep but intersected by many cracks and ledges. The rock is very sound, and the combination of good rock with small holds, steepness, some degree of exposure and sunshine makes for delightful rock climbing. We lunched on the Terrace in a mood of self-satisfied, lazy contentment. But there was something of a different nature awaiting us before we managed to finish the climb. The upper cliff consisted of two tiers of rock, one above the other. The lower one was obviously easy, but the final wall of sixty to eighty feet was suspiciously smooth and steep.

After lunch, when we turned round again to face the rocks, that upper tier appeared to be not only vertical but somewhat undercut. Colin Allan, not being susceptible to such optical illusions, was eager to take the lead. We soon climbed to the base of the steep wall and I belayed his rope round a little spike of rock. After thirty feet or so his progress became very slow. He had started obliquely upwards to the left but was now almost above me, moving very carefully and exhibiting almost the

---

* Pitch = a difficult section. Usually there is an anchorage for belaying the rope which unites the party, at the end of a pitch.

whole of the soles of his boots to my upward gaze. Then he commenced to move upwards to the right, making for a sharp edge of rock. With a supreme effort he grasped it with both hands, kicked about with his feet and pulled himself up. Then he took a prolonged rest on his perch, without answering any of my anxious inquiries as to his present comfort or future prospects.

Evidently the next move was likely to be critical, so I was eventually summoned to join him. I have never climbed anything more strenuous. We called it Spillikin Pitch on account of a small thin flake of rock, sticking loosely in a crevice of a steep slab on the left. The Spillikin was irrelevant to the climb, as it was quite useless and off the best line. From Spillikin Slab I could find practically no holds on the last ten feet to the safe ledge, and I was grateful for the tension of the rope.

Colin now wished to climb a holdless, vertical, open corner of rock on his right, what rock climbers, whose terminology is often inexact and always limited, call an open chimney, about fifteen feet high. In order to do so he wished to stand on my shoulders. From my cramped position on the ledge the problem could only be solved after I had tied myself to a spike of rock at shoulder level, for Allan is no light weight. As he mounted up, the rope strained to meet the outward thrust, but Colin found a hold and climbed the pitch.

I had insisted on Allan removing his boots for the final move, so the next procedure was the hoisting of all the boots and sacks to the upper stance. Midge had been sunning herself all this time and passing occasional flippant remarks. It was now her turn to move up, which she did very neatly and quickly. On the last ten feet I gave her the benefit of a tight rope, but never an actual pull when she was moving. Clearly there must be enough holds for the negotiation of the pitch without strenuous arm pulling, granted sufficient balance and confidence. I was not to find the solution for several years. When it came to my turn to climb the last part I could not, of course, reach the essential hold in the open chimney, but I ascended the wall directly. There, the holds were just sufficient, so long as one knew where to find the crucial handhold for the right hand. As I was on a rope from above I could afford to take a chance and grab the unseen hold. At future visits I knew where it was and led the pitch unaided.

Spillikin Pitch has always interested me for the way in which it served as a test of climbing technique and a striking illustration that, in rock-climbing, the battle is not always to the strong. Allan found the pitch very severe and exhausting in 1934. In May 1935, along with Sandy Wedderburn, Allan failed to lead it at all. In July 1936, climbing with me, he again led it and I had a hard struggle as his second. In May 1945, I climbed Central Buttress with Ian Charleson as second. Commonsense, after such a lapse of time and the lack of climbing during the war years, should have prompted me to avoid the pitch, as there was an easy alternative way from Heather Terrace. Perhaps it was Ian's way of looking at it and saying that it did not seem so steep after all!

In any case I started up in stocking soles, going deliberately and slowly. I found two intermediate resting places. The Spillikin had disappeared, but I found another little flake of rock above the slab which I used as a temporary anchor for my rope, as, though not quite immovable, it was safe for a direct pull from below. I was feeling a bit stretched and tried to think out my moves as far as the safe ledge or mantelshelf. Could I get higher before attempting the irreversible movement of swinging across to the right and grasping the edge of rock? There was a footscrape and a small, steadying fingerhold. I was soon high enough to see, and almost to feel the necessary movement beforehand. I swung across; my right hand grasped the edge; my left followed immediately, stretching over far enough to gain a positive, pulling hold. I was up, slightly out of breath but with plenty of energy to spare.*

After Spillikin, the remainder of the climbing is fairly easy to the cairn on the summit of Central Buttress. For those who have a practical interest in C.B. but would prefer an easier alternative above Heather Terrace, I can recommend another route which is very steep, with good, small holds and an exhilarating sense of exposure. This route was worked out by W. M. McKenzie

---

* I was there again on 14th April, 1946, with my wife and my friend, John Wilson. The same tactics were again successful. My wife came up very neatly and enjoyed the pitch. John came up and said it was a horrible place!

in 1937. It starts from Heather Terrace about fifty yards to the right of our luncheon spot, by a steep ledge inclining upward to the left. Whoever can lead the route below Heather Terrace with ease and confidence should be able to lead this upper continuation to the top of the Buttress.

At the beginning of this account I alluded to the possibility of enjoying as much as 2,000 feet of rock climbing on the Buachaille. From the top of Central Buttress it is an easy, undulating scramble over D-Gully Buttress and Curved Ridge to the foot of Rannoch Wall. This is the eastern rampart of the famous Crowberry Ridge and a happy hunting ground for the modern rock gymnast. There are many routes on its apparently vertical precipice. There are also complicated traverses along intersecting ledges, so that one could spend a long day without repeating oneself. The best and most popular route is, however, by a conspicuous natural feature of the cliff, a long, steep groove, just round the lower corner from the orthodox classical route up the Crowberry Ridge.

This route, Agag's Groove, was first climbed in May 1936 by J. F. Hamilton, A. Anderson and A. C. D. Small, a group of members of the Junior Mountaineering Club of Scotland. It was an amusing day, for a competing party of the same energetic fellowship arrived at the rocks just a little too late. The easy rocks of the Curved Ridge made a perfect gallery (or dress circle) for the competitors, and it was a fine day. The venture was successful, and the name of the climb recalls the delicacy and exposure at the crucial pitch, which Hamish Hamilton led in stocking soles.

In April 1946 my wife demanded some more climbing after Central Buttress, so we ascended Agag's Groove, while John Wilson acted as photographer from several stances on the Curved Ridge. Until we got near the crux we moved fast, as the Groove, though very steep, has just sufficient good holds and stances on sound rock. At about 250 feet above the bottom there seems to be a bulging wall. The satisfying holds continue until one is just below the crux. This is quite short, but it is practically vertical. There is, however, no single movement which could not be reversed by a competent climber, without any undue effort, provided that he uses the holds properly. It

c

is a very difficult pitch, but, on account of its shortness and directness, is much less formidable than the ascent of Spillikin. My wife was exactly of this opinion, and came up very easily. All difficulty is not ended at the crux, above which there still remains about 100 feet of good, steep climbing on small holds, before one finishes on the easy, intermediate part of Crowberry Ridge. It is this combination of sound, steep rock with sufficient holds and considerable exposure* which has made Agag's Groove one of the most popular climbs in Glencoe. It is one of the best of modern Scottish rock-climbing discoveries.

There is another, less worthy reason for its popularity. There are perfect photographic stances on the Curved Ridge, from which the camera can depict the performers as veritable flies moving on a slightly roughened, vertical wall. The views are half profile and include the eastern edge of the Crowberry Ridge at its steepest as a presumptive vertical line for comparison. What luxury and satisfaction to look at the photographs and show them to one's friends!

We continued up the Ridge and over the Crowberry Tower, the rope being no longer necessary. A short, difficult drop took us to the Crowberry Gap and some easy scrambling to the summit of Buachaille Etive Mor. We were content to descend the mountain by easy scree slopes to Glen Etive with its perfect bathing pool, which can be refreshing and pleasant after a dry spell in hot weather at the end of April.

---

* *Exposure* results from a position where the holds are small and there is usually a big drop below. Difficulty is another matter altogether, and need not involve any danger. Both together may be a source of danger.

CHAPTER IV

THE ALETSCHHORN

THE Aletsch glacier is the largest and longest glacier in the Alps. Surrounding its upper basin are many of the greatest mountains of the Bernese Oberland. They are predominantly snow and ice mountains, and all the classical routes are by snow ways rather than rock ways. Lines of approach from Grindelwald and Lauterbrunnen, to the north, are generally difficult expeditions, but the railway which tunnels through the rocks of the Eiger and the Mönch to the Jungfraujoch (at 11,380 ft.), with its bizarre hotel projecting from the snow-draped cliffs of the Mönch like an outpost over the Jungfrau Firn, has enabled the climber to ascend several of these peaks by a much less toilsome way than was formerly possible.*

The Aletschhorn (13,720 ft.), is the second highest of the Oberland peaks. It is centrally placed in a great world of snow and ice, facing northward across the upper Aletsch glacier to the Jungfrau, eastward down the smaller Mittel Aletsch glacier to its junction with the larger stream of ice and southward to the Ober Aletsch glacier, which joins the great Aletsch not far above its termination in a great gorge above the Rhone valley, opposite Brieg and the Simplon tunnel. There are, therefore, many possible ways to the summit of the Aletschhorn, but the classical route is by the Ober Aletsch from the south.† It is not at all a difficult mountain, but the ascent is full of interest and may be regarded as a typical expedition on a great 4,000 metre snow peak.

In early August 1936 Professor H. W. Turnbull and I had been getting into training on some of the smaller peaks around Bel Alp, one of the most delightful Alpine centres, situated on the steep slopes to the north of Brieg at a height of 7,100 feet. We had experienced some bad weather, but this was slowly changing for the better. It was time that we attempted some-

---

* See Map F, p. 334.

† The first ascent of the Aletschhorn, in 1860, by Mr F. F. Tuckett and his guides, was from a bivouac on the Mittel Aletsch glacier, by the Aletschjoch and the S.E. ridge. Most of the early climbers, however, used the Ober Aletsch route.

thing worth while, and the only sensible plan was to go to the Ober Aletsch Hut in order to be able to seize our opportunity. An hour's walk along a good path took us to the Ober Aletsch glacier, which offers hardly any difficulties. It was an afternoon of casual showers of hail and snow, but the clouds were hardening and the bright intervals extending. After about three hours' walking from Bel Alp we reached the Ober Aletsch Hut (8,760 ft.), in good time for a comfortable meal. The evening sky and clouds betokened a fine day for the morrow.

The Hut is popular, as it lies on the route of the Beich Pass, connecting the Loetschenthal with the Rhone Valley. However, in mid-week it was not too full, and we were fairly comfortable. I always find it difficult to get much sleep in a hut when there is an early start in prospect and many people are lying side by side. The snorers, of whom there are many with the most diverse rhythms and harmonics, always seem to do rather better than the others. When, at length, the tumult had ceased and I was falling into a warm, delicious slumber, there was a nudge at my ribs and a voice whispered, 'We are half an hour late. It is three o'clock'. The strange thing about an Alpine start is that one is wide awake on the instant. The lack of sleep never seems to trouble one as soon as the first, unwelcome move has been made. Both Turnbull and I enjoyed our breakfast, slipped on our boots and left the Hut within the hour.

It was a cool, refreshing night of bright moonlight. The glacier was hard frozen and a pleasure to walk on. A few fleecy clouds raced across the sky, but there was no wind on the glacier. Our mountain was directly ahead of us, and we aimed at the foot of a long spur of rock running straight down from the summit to the glacier. We had decided to make use of the classical route, and it must have been on exactly such a perfect morning that Professor Tyndall made the ascent with the hotel porter from Bel Alp in August 1869. I cannot do better than quote his impressions of the scene, as described in *Hours of Exercise in the Alps*.

'Right before us was the pyramid of the Aletschhorn, bearing its load of glaciers, and thrusting above them its pinnacle of rock; . . . And amid them all, with a calmness corresponding to the deep seclusion of the place, wound the beautiful system

The South Face of the Aletschhorn
Dotted lines and arrows show ascending and descending routes. Part of descent is on slopes behind the mountain.

of glaciers along which we had been marching for nearly three hours. I know nothing which can compare in point of glory with these winter palaces of the mountaineer, under the opening illumination of the morning.'

We made our way off the glacier and on to the rocky spur without difficulty. As the sun slowly climbed the sky we made rapid progress to the end of the rocks, where we halted for our second breakfast at 7 a.m. Here we had a choice of routes, the more usual way which proceeds directly up rocky spurs with intermediate sections of snow to the summit, or the classic route across the snowfield to the right, making for a little snowy *col** on the south-east ridge of the mountain, which separated us from the basin of the Mittel Aletsch glacier. The latter route is, nowadays, seldom used, as the guides consider that there may be some avalanche danger at certain parts of it during unsettled conditions of weather and snow. We had no doubts at all on such a perfect day, after a hard night-frost.

Safety would be ensured by moving fast, and we were very

* *Col* is a saddle or depression on a ridge.

early. We had no intention of returning by the same route. We put on our *crampons** and maintained a good, steady pace in an upward direction over the convex, frozen surface, our objective being a sharp notch beneath the upper section of the summit ridge. We dodged a few crevasses without losing any time, and we crossed a *bergschrund†* without much difficulty. Finally, we came to fairly steep slopes of snow-ice, traversing across them, still to the right and upwards, linking with our route several islands of rock which protruded from the snow. The crampons enabled us to proceed with the minimum of step cutting. A final, steep rise brought us on to the ridge at 9 a.m., precisely to the notch at which we had aimed.

Without a halt we continued up the ridge, but soon came to broken rocks, half smothered in ice. This forced us to traverse on the south side as there was a cornice‡ on the other. As on most traverses we lost some time, but, later on, we were able to climb back to the crest of the ridge between steep ribs of rock, reaching the summit at 10.30 a.m.

It was bitterly cold, with a strong, north-westerly wind, but the visibility was perfect. Owing to its central situation the Aletschhorn commands one of the finest panoramas in the Alps. Especially impressive was the trio of Jungfrau, Mönch and Eiger to the north, across the vast snowfields and collecting reservoirs for the Great Aletsch glacier. Although the Aletschhorn is the second highest of the Oberland peaks it is sufficiently isolated and central to show everything from Mont Blanc in the south-west to the peaks of the Bernina in the east, without dominating such nearer summits as the Nesthorn, our next venture, or the Bietschhorn and the peaks of Kandersteg. The giants of the Pennine Alps were now seen in their true proportions, not as from Bel Alp where the Fletschhorn rivals or even surpasses the more distant and shapely Weisshorn. It is a typical, continental mountain prospect, with no hint whatever of the deep, warm trough of the Rhone Valley lying not so many miles to the south. To the mountaineer such a panorama,

---

* *Crampons*—spiked frames fitted to the boots for greater security on ice or hard snow.

† *Bergschrund*—a large 'crevasse' or chasm in a glacier, usually where the ice abuts on steep rocks.

‡ Cornice—overhanging eave of snow.

an ordered succession of glaciers, snowy and rocky ranges, entirely unrelieved by any hint of valley, lake or habitation can be intensely stimulating as well as satisfying. In my experience I should rate the view from the Aletschhorn more highly than those from the Jungfrau, Monte Rosa, the Matterhorn or from several of the Aiguilles in the neighbourhood of Mont Blanc.

After a brief halt we started downwards over steep, hard snow, making for the north-west slopes. The west ridge runs into steep, broken and difficult rocks, so we kept to the snow on the north side. Soon the slope began to bend over in a convex manner, becoming much steeper. We were keeping forty feet of rope between us and moving carefully. As the surface became harder we moved only one at a time. Then we came to a narrow slit, a rudimentary bergschrund, running for a long way across the face. Below it was a band of ice, into which the crampons hardly bit at all. The fierce, cold wind made the situation both precarious and unpleasant.

I halted, allowing Turnbull to proceed for a rope's length and entrench himself. Then I cut steps downward, an extremely fatiguing process when one is crouching and maintaining a precarious equilibrium on small, icy steps. At intervals I was forced to stand up straight, rest, and warm my hands which were only protected by mittens. Occasionally I used only the right hand, in order to give me a longer reach. The ice proved very hard and unpleasantly brittle. It was difficult to fashion a good step without splitting it. We were entirely in the shade on this steep, northern slope, and I feared that the axe might jump out of my hand, which was getting numb with cold. Several times this rope-length progress was repeated, but still my friend reported hard ice, even suggesting that we might be well advised to consider a return over the summit, for there was still a long, steep slope below us, which eased off towards a much crevassed snowfield at the bottom.

I could not plead that I had much positive experience, but I suspected that this belt of ice below the schrund could not be very wide, as the summer of 1936 was not remarkable for the lack of snow on the mountains. At any rate we decided to continue, and after two more stages of forty feet the crampons began to bite into the surface again, although we continued to move singly for some time longer. There was no more ice and all was well. Looking back from the saddle at the foot of the western ridge that slope looked appallingly steep. Perhaps it might have been better to have tackled the ridge itself, but I hardly think so. The Swiss Alpine Club Guide Book says that much step-cutting is required on it.

This descent had occupied us for more than two hours, and we were both thoroughly hungry. It was not possible to get out of the wind, but, at least, we sat down in sunshine and spent a pleasant half-hour over our lunch. On the ascent we had studied the way down the snow-field to the upper end of the Ober Aletsch glacier. There were many crevasses, but the inclination was not very great, and we had decided on our general line of descent. It is always best, whenever possible, to study the descent beforehand, for there is always a risk of a change of weather involving one in thick cloud or mist.

Professor Turnbull was leading and guided me by a zig-zag route between the crevasses and across not a few snow bridges which were becoming somewhat soft in the heat of the afternoon sun. We maintained a fairly tight rope between us. Nothing untoward took place, but I always consider that such a descent, in the languorous heat of the afternoon, is the least pleasant part of an Alpine expedition. The heat and glare, both from above and below, have a tendency to reduce one to a condition of careless somnolence, not an unusual sequel to an early start and a hard day's exercise. Yet it is a part of the expedition when constant vigilance is necessary, especially on the part of the leader. As we got lower the soft snow began to ball up on the spikes of our crampons, so that we had to halt repeatedly in order to free them. There was no actual danger, as the crevasses, though large, were perfectly obvious. At length we were able to discard the crampons and, still roped, glissade the last slopes to the level glacier.

We got back to the Hut at 3.30 p.m. and were delighted to meet two Swiss friends, Dr and Frau Stiefel, who regaled us with welcome mugs of tea. They had come up the glacier from Bel Alp. After this welcome interlude another two hours' going took us back to Bel Alp, in time for dinner. It was a grand expedition under perfect conditions, involving 5,160 feet of ascent and 7,100 feet of descent. We had the mountain entirely to ourselves, without any tracks of other parties on the snow-fields.

The Aletschhorn would, however, be rather a big proposition for a party of British-trained amateurs in their first Alpine season. Questions of route finding are involved on very considerable glaciers and snowfields. It may be perfectly true that a competent party, well trained in difficult snow and ice work on Scottish hills in winter conditions, would have no difficulties with problems of detail, but there would be considerable risk of mischance in doubtful conditions of snow and weather. Such a party could not possess the instinctive appreciation and intimate knowledge of the condition of the snow and the habits of the upper parts of Alpine glaciers, which alone would enable them to meet an emergency with confidence.

PART II

BRITISH MOUNTAIN
TECHNIQUE

CHAPTER V

HILL WALKING

IT seemed obvious to an older generation that getting to the top of a hill or mountain under ones' own power meant climbing, or even mountaineering in the case of a really big hill. Nowadays mountaineering has a definite technique. On the large scale it usually involves difficult passages over snow and ice or over rocks. In Britain, where we have no large mountains, the experts have made the most of our hills, and have devised difficult ways up the rock gullies and faces. Especially in England, among the *élite*, climbing is synonymous with rock-climbing and everything else is hill walking. Let us leave it at that, whilst inclining towards the broader meaning of the word. What seems perfectly certain is that the art of walking over rough, steep and difficult country is the only possible foundation for any kind of true mountaineering, and that its importance is increased and not diminished as we proceed from the lower hills to the greatest mountains of the world. This art should be well and truly learned on the easier and lower hills as a necessary stage in the education of the mountaineer. Moreover, it is surprising how one continues to improve, even after years of experience. This is one factor which makes the enthusiasm for mountaineering such a life-long treasure and delight. Speed belongs to youth, and many sports must be abandoned on that account in early middle age, but the hill climber improves his skill, preserves his fitness and learns to economise energy to such good purpose that he may still pursue his craft until long past the age of three score years and ten. Not a few of the stalwarts of the Alpine and Scottish Mountaineering Clubs are outstanding examples of this.

It has often been said truly that on the higher British hills and especially in Scotland, conditions may become wintry on almost any day of the year; so the hill climber, even in summer, must be prepared for cold winds, heavy rain and sleet, or even snowfall, as well as for finding the way in mist, cloud or storm.

We must now consider the equipment and technique which

are the minimum essentials for the purpose, and then give a
brief account of several expeditions involving no special difficulties. It is by means of such expeditions, and plenty of them,
that one learns hill sense, and does so much better and more
naturally than by starting out with the more exciting and
gymnastic problems of rock climbing. Far more mountain
accidents are the outcome of a lack of hill sense than of the
inability to cope with difficult technical problems of rock or
snow, which ordinary hill sense would have enabled the party
to recognize and avoid.

FOOTWEAR

Not all climbing boots are of good design, even those which are
expensive. Many are far too heavy and more heavily nailed
than is necessary. The welts are often too wide, and this is a
great disadvantage for dealing with rocks where the ledges may
be small and narrow. In order to appreciate this, one need only
consider the feet of such good climbers as red deer in Scotland
or *chamois* in the Alps. Their hoofs are very small. If they do
sink rather deeply into soft snow they can also extricate themselves easily, and they get good purchase on rock and scree.

The first essential is a well-fitting boot. It should be roomy
enough to hold two socks, as this helps to avoid sores and
blisters during long expeditions. The fit should be fairly tight
round the heel, but the toes should have some freedom to move
about. This helps the circulation and prevents cold feet and
frost bite in very cold weather. The soles should be fairly thick
and strong, when one traverses rough and rocky ground. The
uppers should incline to be soft and pliable, and should fit
closely round the ankle, so as to prevent the entrance of small
stones and grit. The double sock will help here. There is no such
thing as a perfectly water-tight boot, but good greasing of the
leather and a good sewn-in tongue are helpful. Shoes are not
suitable for serious hill climbing. The ankles are not protected,
either against impact with sharp rocks, often concealed in long
heather, or against the strains and twists which are unavoidable
during a fast descent of rough ground.

Nailing of boots for climbing and traversing our British hills,
especially in summer conditions, need only be fairly light.

Tackets are good enough for summer conditions. Clinkers round
the edges with hob-nails distributed sparsely in the centre of the
sole and heel are quite sufficient for all conditions except rock,
snow or ice climbs where there is some degree of difficulty, in
which case more specialised nails of an Alpine pattern may be
used more plentifully. It is now possible to obtain deeply corrugated, hard rubber soles and heels. Known as *Vibram* (Swiss) or
Itshide (British), they are excellent for rocks, steep slopes either
wet or dry, and even snow. They are much used in the Alps,
and have been used by mountain troops. For my own part, I
have, for many years, gone over the lesser grassy and heathery
hills, and some of the higher ones as well, in a pair of light boots
with Uskid rubber soles and heels. This is not to be recommended in winter. It teaches one to avoid slipping on steep
grass. In summer the main point is sufficient strength to give
long service and to protect feet and ankles. Lightly soled boots
cannot do so on rough ground. I once did a thirteen-hours'
traverse of five big peaks in the Cairngorms in rubber-soled golf
shoes. That was by mischance and not by intention: I am
unlikely to repeat the experiment.

Boots should be taken care of, when not in use. They should
never be dried in front of a fire. It is easy to burn and ruin
leather by overheating, even before it is dry. Dry them in the
open or in a very gentle warmth. Do not hand them over to
anyone else to dry. During a holiday they need not be dried at
all. It matters little if one must start walking in damp boots.
They soon warm up. New boots should be well oiled or greased.
This does not apply to the soles, however. It is quite a good plan
to treat the uppers both inside and out. Castor oil is good. So
are good greases, but mineral oils and greases are not good.
Polishes are out of place for climbing boots. After boots have
been made pliable they only require lesser and occasional treatment. They should be good for a week's hard use without
further attention. New boots should first be taken out on short
expeditions; if they get thoroughly wet it will help to mould
the boots to the feet. Keep the boots on trees when not in use.

CLOTHING

Two considerations must be borne in mind. Climbing and hill-walking involve extremes of muscular exertion and extremes of temperature. Great variations of temperature occur at all seasons, and not only during winter. Frank Smythe and I encountered a blizzard on the summit plateau of Ben Nevis on Easter Monday 1925, which may not have been at all abnormal, but Smythe was convinced that it could fairly be compared with some of the fiercest *tourmentes* on Mont Blanc. When we got down again we met nursemaids with infants in perambulators beside the Nevis Bridge at Fort William. It was then a mild, sunny afternoon with most of the higher hills shrouded in low cloud.

The guiding rules about clothing are clear and simple, but each must apply them in detail to suit personal preferences. Dress must be fairly loose, as light as possible to allow of maximum freedom of movement, but of strong texture so as to stand hard usage. The outer layer must be nearly windproof. To combat extremes of temperature one should carry spare woollies. A light Shetland pull-over can be remarkably warm as an under-garment, especially if it is tucked away into the breeches, when the additional warmth is next to the parts where it is most required. It is easy to carry several woollies in the rucksack. Walking breeches are best for hill-walking and scrambling, the plus-four type carrying needless cloth for soaking up water and shorts affording too little protection for severe conditions. As regards outer garments in general, the windproofness should not involve extra weight, nor should the cloth absorb much water when wetted, like corduroy. Strength and durability are most essential for the breeches when rock scrambling is part of the day's work, so that close-woven tweed or whipcord, or even strong cotton breeches may do very well. For the jacket a close-woven cotton gaberdine or windproof Grenfell cloth are best. Double texture is advisable, with a few, easily accessible pockets which can be properly fastened.

Woollen gloves and mits are excellent. If the weather is not too cold the mits (covering hands but not fingers) can be worn alone when scrambling on rocks. In really severe weather on the hilltops a woollen helmet is essential. It is my personal opinion that many of these extend too low down. If the collar of the jacket buttons round the neck this is unnecessary. Puttees used to be more common than they are nowadays. I find that old stocking uppers, worn over the stockings, are ample protection, even for deep snow.

On British hills it is futile to expect to get home dry on all or most expeditions. The best that can be done is to carry a light oilskin for protection above the waistline. Wind and rain often come together, and flapping garments are to be avoided. A good, capacious rucksack is necessary for spare clothing, food and other equipment. The Bergan, or steel-frame type, is comfortable to wear and cooler in hot weather, but a thorough nuisance for most forms of rock-climbing. Rucksacks seldom are, and need not be, entirely waterproof. It is easy to use oilskin bags inside them to protect what must be kept dry. Never carry more than is necessary, especially in the earlier stages of a hill-climbing career. Sometimes a lot has to be carried, if one is going on a trip lasting several days. In that case, the weight should be carried close to the back, but without causing discomfort by excessively tight straps. Energy is wasted and discomfort results from being forced into a stooping position. Otherwise, it is better to try and enjoy the complete freedom of the hills!

FINDING THE WAY

When visibility is good, finding the way over mountains is not difficult, for a route can be selected by the exercise of common-sense and deduction from past experience over that part which is seen, whereas the descent over the far side of the mountain, which is not seen, can be facilitated by the study of the map, or, at the worst, one can return by the same or part of the same route. Three things are therefore advisable: the habit of observing and memorising mountain form and the prominent features of a landscape, a general knowledge of the characteristic mountain and valley configuration of the district and the ability to read maps, whilst realising their shortcomings in matters of minor detail.

It is assumed that we are trying to find the easiest way, avoiding the passage over difficult ground or precipitous rocks. The best way to learn about the form and structure of hills and mountains is to select several of the smaller hills which are known to be easy; not too high, yet not without some steep and

D

rocky sections which can provide a spice of interest and difficulty for the expedition. One should make a study of such hills, climb them from different sides on days of settled weather, at first returning by the route of ascent, and later traversing the hill and descending by another way which had been previously examined from below or, better still, ascended. Thus one learns much about the structure of a hill or group of hills.

One will learn to observe, and will gain something like the experience of the earliest Alpine guides, who knew their own hills intimately from having gone over them many times, when hunting the *chamois* or exploring the rocks in search of valuable crystals and precious stones. These men were limited in their knowledge and outlook, but outstanding in hill-sense. Many of them became excellent, all-round mountaineers when they continued to climb with good amateurs who, better educated than themselves, could apply more scientific methods to the problems of orientation, weather and snow-craft. In these first expeditions one should rely on natural observation. At the end of the day the map should be used in order to elucidate obscure points, resolve difficulties and explain mistakes. Mountaineering is like other sports. One learns by mistakes, and it is better that these should be made in good weather and on easy ground, where the only penalty is some additional fatigue and loss of time. I have followed this plan from the beginning and have often reverted to it, purely for the delight of exploration, when I have found myself among homeland mountains with which I was not familiar. There were failures, but they were more than repaid by the lessons I learned. On the other hand, it must be admitted that some people never seem to acquire this 'bump of locality'. They ought to do both planning and execution with the constant help of guide book, map and compass, from start to finish.

My earliest explorations were mostly on a group of three minor hills in Fifeshire, the pleasant and isolated range of the Lomond Hills—East Lomond 1,471 feet, West Lomond 1,713 feet and Bishop Hill 1,492 feet. To the north the ground falls steeply to the low valley of the Howe of Fife, the southern slopes being much more gentle. There are drops of 500 and 800 feet respectively between the hills, and wide expanses of upper

1, 2, Twin Peaks of Cruachan　　　　　　　　　　　3, Ben Starav

CLOUD HORIZONS

New Year on the Clachlet

THE OCHILS IN WINTER ABOVE ALVA

moorland. The views are wide and satisfying, across the Firth of Forth to the south-east and a whole semi-circle of Highland hills to the north. I have crossed the hills alone in all seasons and weathers. On the somewhat featureless plateau of the Bishop Hill I have occasionally been at fault in a heavy mist when there was no wind to indicate direction. It is surprising, however, to what extent a sub-conscious sense of locality acts as a guide. I never once descended the southern side instead of the northern. I have seen the waning moon rising from the North Sea after midnight, close by the Isle of May lighthouse, and have picked out the snowy peaks of the Grampians, from Ben Vorlich to Ben Lawers, Schiehallion and Ben-y-Gloe, by the light of a February full moon from a vantage point close by the summit cairn of the West Lomond. These early ventures not only gave me hill-sense, for the West Lomond possesses some sizeable tiers of vertical, dolerite cliff on which I made my first attempts at rock-climbing, but also a growing desire to make a closer acquaintance with that boundless range of the Grampian summits to the north. Since these earlier days I have become equally familiar with the higher, more extensive but less shapely Ochil Hills to the east of Stirling, which again stand up as a frontier chain between the industrial plains and the northern mountains of Scotland.

Many of my earlier expeditions on larger mountains were carried out alone, before I had entered the ranks of the mountaineering fraternity, before I possessed a compass and when I had only the most elementary type of cycling map to indicate the locality of the mountain and its height. They were days of settled good weather. I cycled fifty-five miles before ascending Schiehallion and returned the same day. I was caught aloft by swirling cloud on Ben More (Perthshire), but could not see that there would be any difficulty in returning by the same eastern ridge to my starting point and bicycle by the Glen Dochart road. The ascent of Ben Macdhui by the Glen Derry track and Loch Etchachan gave me inspiring views across the Larig to the great corries of Braeriach and Cairn Toul. My first visit to Ben Nevis was by the pony track, at the age of sixteen, but was none the less exciting for all that. My base was at Newtonmore in Speyside. I left by bicycle at 6 a.m., and once or twice I nearly turned back on account of the strong west wind which faced me throughout the forty-seven-mile run to Fort William. But a little food works wonders. It took me exactly two and a quarter hours to climb the Ben by track from Achintee in Glen Nevis. In those days there was still a wooden hotel on the summit. Part of the way I talked to the pony-driver who escorted the supplies to the hotel. There was mist between 2,500 and 3,500 feet, but the top was perfectly clear, calm and sunny. I shall never forget that wonderful view, with the Glencoe hills (then unknown to me) and the twin Paps of Jura gleaming like dull gold beyond a shimmering sea.

Several years later I explored all the higher mountains of North Wales alone, enjoying myself on the perilous narrows of Crib Goch and the Gribin Ridge of Lliwedd. On the summits of the Glyders I was in cloud and nearly descended towards Pen-y-gwrd, but I recovered my bearings in time and completed the day's sight-seeing by descending to Llyn Idwal after an inspiring peep down the Devil's Kitchen. Abraham's *British Mountain Climbs* was leading me on towards the more exciting phases of the sport, but these random, early experiences did not make me a devil's advocate for solitary climbing. The practice has serious drawbacks and even more obvious dangers. Nowadays, there are far more opportunities for joining an inexpensive climbing club, or for graduating into such from friendships contracted whilst touring round Youth Hostels in mountain districts. Yet, when all is considered, it is a good thing to go alone on the mountains at times, even although it is advisable to confine such expeditions to lesser and easier hills. When we are alone the mountains can speak to us so much more intimately. Even a single companion may, to some extent, form a barrier—even a friend like-minded with ourselves.

ORIENTATION

Whenever conditions are difficult or confusing in unknown mountain country, and especially when it is possible that time will add to the difficulty, proper scientific means of orientation must be used by the party. These must be applied in a spirit of common sense and not in a slavish, unimaginative manner, according to rule and formula. All such methods are based on the use of map and compass, with due regard to the limitations of both and the nature of the ground.

It is not necessary to carry a heavy prismatic compass. Quite a light instrument will do, but it ought to have a floating dial and some form of damping, so that the direction line on the compass comes quickly to rest. This is most desirable, for, if one is overtaken by dense mist on a great mountain plateau as, for instance, on the Cairngorms, it may be necessary to steer by compass for hours at a stretch, and to check direction very often. The cheaper types of compass with rapidly oscillating needles are difficult and troublesome to steady. They waste time, although they ultimately give the same information. Whatever compass is used, the north point should have its direction checked beforehand. Remember that the compass points to magnetic and not true north. In Scotland (round about year 1948) the compass points about twelve degrees west of true north. This difference is the magnetic declination or variation, and is, at present, a slowly diminishing quantity from year to year. It also varies somewhat from place to place, as may be seen from large-scale maps of physical geography. Compass needles are affected by the proximity of all iron and steel objects such as ice axes, and still more by the magnets of photo-electric exposure meters for use in photography. Keep these at a distance, and keep the compass level whilst taking readings.

Now, as to maps. The best is the one-inch Ordnance Survey map of the district, but perfectly good work can be done with the half-inch to the mile map. Do not expect to find everything on a map. There may be lines of cliff, unmarked on the map, especially on the half-inch ones, and a suggestion of cliffs in other places where the ground, though steep, is quite practicable for a descent without any rock difficulties. On the one-inch map the main contours at intervals of 250 feet are said to be instrumentally determined and accurate, but the fifty-foot contours are sketched in. From the scale of the map and the distance apart of the contours one may form a good idea of the steepness of a mountain face, but where there are extensive rock buttresses, ridges and gullies one can form no conclusion of any value about details. Gradients calculated from an O.S. map are the ratios of height to distance moved on the horizontal, so that a

1 : 1 gradient means an angle of forty-five degrees. The ascent or descent of this might involve using the hands as well as the feet. A gradient of one in two is quite steep enough for descent by an inexperienced party.

One other point might be mentioned. The north and south line of the map is not everywhere parallel with its edges. Try this out for yourself. The difference is not great, and there is usually a true north line marked on the map, as well as a magnetic north line. The latter will vary slowly as the years pass. It is hardly ever feasible on mountain expeditions to take one's bearings or set one's course with great accuracy, for the course must be guided by the nature of the ground. However, it must be remembered that a variation from the desired course of, say three degrees, means a divergence of nearly 100 yards after proceeding one mile. This will make it clear that the magnetic declination must be allowed for, but a reading accurate to within five degrees or so is normally sufficient.

No great skill or long practice is needed for orientation by map and compass. There are, generally speaking, only three problems to solve, and the principle is the same in each case. (1) If we know our location on the map and we wish to go to another place which can be identified on the map, how shall we set the course? Use a celluloid protractor. If the place to which we are bound is on the east side of the north-south line, place the centre of the protractor on our own position on the map with the curved perimeter to the east side and the straight edge pointing due north, taking care to find the true north line of the map. Then a straight line from the centre of the protractor through the place we are aiming at will give, on the curved edge, the true bearing of our line of march. To get the compass bearing we must add to this the compass declination or variation. All bearings are counted in degrees from 0° to 360°, proceeding from north through east, south and west in succession. If we are aiming at a place to the west of the north-south line the position of the protractor is reversed, with the curved perimeter towards the west. Obviously, the magnetic variation must be subtracted in order to get the compass bearing from the true bearing.* (2) Having done this we take out the compass, set it

* This may give a negative result in particular cases. As this method gives

properly to magnetic north and take our course with the compass bearing which we have found, or we can orient the map correctly and use it to identify any other points on the map which are sufficiently prominent to be observed without any risk of error. (3) If we do not know our location on the map and we have a good view of identifiable surrounding objects, we can find our own location. Take a compass bearing on such an object, say a distant mountain top. Correct for magnetic variation so as to find the true bearing. Orient the map and, using this bearing, lay down a line, from any point of which the observed mountain top must show this bearing. Then take another mountain, if possible at a considerable angle from the first, preferably between 45° and 135° from the other, and take its bearing. Lay down the corresponding line on the map. Our own location will be at the point of intersection of these two lines. It will be obvious that the method fails if the two observed objects are either too close together or nearly at opposite points of the horizon.

Two other methods may be described, which are useful when we have no compass. The first utilises the position of the sun. We need a watch which shows correct time. British summer time must be allowed for. With correct solar time the sun souths at noon, is due east at 6 a.m. and due west at 6 p.m. Set the direction of the hour hand directly towards the sun, and the south line will be midway between that direction and twelve o'clock on the dial. Conversely, if we have a compass but no watch, the solar time can be estimated very nearly by taking the true bearing of the sun by compass. The sun travels through fifteen degrees in one hour. If we are on the mountains in a clear night we can get our bearings from the true north line to the Pole Star, easily identifiable from the characteristic setting of the stars in the two constellations of the Little and the Great Bear. If there is partial clouding and we are familiar with other prominent constellations we can often guess a good approxima-

bearings west of north, the interpretation is, of course, a small positive bearing east of north. To ensure uniformity in all cases it is best to count all bearings from 0–360° east of north, in which case the magnetic variation is always added to true bearing in order to get compass bearing. The same plan is applicable to problem (3). In many cases, of course, it seems more natural to use bearings west of north. So long as we know what we are doing it matters little, but is easier to adopt the official method when passing on information to others.

tion to the position of the Pole Star. Time can be gauged approximately by the rising and setting of other prominent stars or their passage across the south line or meridian, which varies with the month of the year.

ORIENTATION IN MIST OR STORM

Now we come up against real mountaineering difficulties in bad weather conditions. The all-important thing is to know our location before entering the mist, and to be careful, by compass steering, noting landmarks and, if necessary, by 'dead reckoning' not to lose that knowledge. It is useless to steer for a very distant objective in difficult mountain country. The direct route, although the shortest in space, may not be practicable as regards time, effort or difficulty. Suppose we are on a ridge which may be joined by side ridges. We are aiming at a more or less distant mountain top where there is a cairn that can be identified. The ridge proceeds straight for a mile, descends, then bends at an angle to the right and rises again. There is no straight line on the ridge from our present position to our objective. What we do is to lay down a course on the first straight section. In order to find out when to change our course, we can either estimate the probable time we shall take to cover the mile and reach the dip or saddle, or we can actually count the estimated number of paces to that point, preserving direction meanwhile and, of course, knowing the average length of our pace. This is called proceeding by 'dead reckoning'. On difficult ridges it is often necessary and can be very accurate. The late Mr J. A. Parker, of Aberdeen, civil engineer by profession, who climbed all the 3,000-foot peaks of Scotland, besides many mountains in the Alps and elsewhere, often employed this method with uncanny accuracy in very difficult weather conditions on Scottish mountains. It is worth learning and trying out in bad weather on a hill we know, or think that we know.

The same procedure should be followed on ridges where there are forks or side ridges at various points. Estimate the distance to the fork, following a bearing. Then take another bearing and proceed to the next landmark. A difficulty often occurs in such country. One finds oneself on an apparent ridge which ends in a cliff. Then one must go back to the fork and try again. Many

accidents and benightments have resulted from delay in facing
such a situation, and from proceeding on what is rightly suspected to be the wrong course, just because no one takes the
initiative and insists on a halt for reconsidering the position.
On a really narrow, twisting ridge the compass cannot help, nor
can it always discriminate between two possible ridges at a fork.
Local knowledge can, however, be amplified by the evidence of
the compass.

Summing up the position, the following points are the most
important if one is caught by mist or storm in unknown, and to
a lesser extent, in known mountain country.

(1) Locate position on the map before losing sight of surroundings.

(2) Accurate bearings, direction keeping and distance estima-
tion. Pacing is better than timing for the latter.

(3) If a party is involved in mist it is best to keep the steers-
man with the compass in the rear, so that he can keep the party
in line and check up the direction frequently. However, each
man should have a compass, and the leader should also use
his own.

(4) Always consult the compass at a halt, or at a cairn or
mountain top. As all ridges, even when they are smooth and
hump-backed, radiate from the summit it is of the highest
importance to take accurate bearings when leaving such a point.
Always mark the line of approach before halting. A map may
not always help with narrow, twisting ridges, but accurate
bearings do help in the long run.

(5) The compass is nearly always a reliable guide on Scottish
hills, except in a few cases where magnetic rocks vitiate its
readings, for instance, on the Cuillin gabbro of Skye.

(6) Narrow ridges limit possibility of error. It is at the broad
stretches of ridge and the wide *cols* or saddles between gently
sloping plateau mountains that difficulty is greatest. Be accurate
in such regions.

(7) Do not contour slopes in a mist. One loses direction and
may, sooner or later, be forced to climb up again to the ridge
crest. One can wander endlessly around the upper slopes of a
corrie in mist, and also encounter difficult ground.

(8) Mist exaggerates heights, depths and obstacles. Do not

retreat without a close-up attempt to proceed, if you know the course is right.

(9) If a ridge peters out in a cliff it is probably a 'false' ridge. Go back to the last forking point. This is quicker and safer than attempting to continue.

(10) There are two other aids to location and steering. The first is a pocket aneroid barometer. This can be very useful in mist for determining, in collaboration with the map, when a top or *col* has been reached. Over short distances and small differences of height a good instrument is fairly accurate. The other aid is wind direction. On open ridges and plateaux the direction of the wind is usually fairly constant for reasonable periods of time. On saddles between mountains, wind direction is of no value whatever as a guide. The hill contours modify it completely. In funnels and corries, and often on narrow ridges where there are cliffs and irregularities, wind direction is equally unreliable.

SOME USEFUL HINTS

Warmth. It is almost as bad to be overheated as to be chilled, and climbing is warm work. Better start off without too much clothing and carry spares in the rucksack. One soon warms up, and it is a bad plan to halt whenever anyone wishes to discard clothing. When a halt is made for food one should, especially in cool or windy weather, put on spare clothing at once and take it off after the meal, when one has gone far enough to warm up again. Digestion, in its early stages, takes away the heat from the skin: it absorbs bodily energy rather than supplying any.

Food and halts. It is a very good plan to train oneself to go without food for long periods, but a very bad one to start this on a long expedition. If conditions become cold and stormy food helps the morale of the party enormously. There are times when unexpected difficulties crop up along with the storm or blizzard, making a halt for food almost impossible. Then it may be a question of struggling on, so as to get clear of difficulties before nightfall. This is what tests the staying power of a party, and brings out the value of being able to do without frequent feeding. Even then, a little food, such as chocolate or dried fruit, may be kept ready to hand. Always keep a small reserve of food in a dry corner of the rucksack. It may as well be dry, as there is plenty of water on the hills! I have never found that alcohol was worth carrying, least of all in a dilute form, as an emergency reserve. Sugary foods are the best kind of reserve, but I do not think there are any general rules applicable to everyone. Personally, I dislike sugary foods in normal life, but feel the benefit of such immediately in conditions of hunger, fatigue and cold. When much energy is consumed, as in climbing, the work is done by the oxidation of carbohydrates, and the easiest way to carry them is in the form of bread, in as dry a form as possible. Other foods are chiefly useful for affording variety and palatability. For untrained men the other foods may be more essential. Rapid convertibility into energy is not necessary for a properly trained individual. The habit of using such foods is likely to be a disadvantage on really hard expeditions.

PLANNING AND TIMING THE EXPEDITION. Good preliminary staff work, with a clear knowledge of the objective and study of maps, is essential. The best rule for timing an expedition is Naismith's formula, originated by W. W. Naismith, the founder of the Scottish Mountaineering Club. He knew what he was talking about, as one of his exploits in the company of Gilbert Thomson, his friend and collaborator in the starting of the S.M.C.* will show. They started from Dalwhinnie, having arrived by the midnight train from Perth. They were bound for the Easter Meet of the Club, which was being held at Inveroran, Argyllshire, on the old Glencoe road. They reached their destination in the evening of the same day in good, going order, having climbed Ben Alder and traversed Rannoch Moor. Their achievement is best appreciated by studying the map and noting the roughness and undulation of the ground. Naismith's rule is to allow one hour for every three miles on the flat and an extra hour for every 1,500 feet climbed.

When applying the rule in practice the time for halts should be added, and a generous allowance made for any strong, adverse wind, and in winter for snow and bad ground generally. It is better to have plenty of time in hand and to make an earlier start than is really necessary. Most distances are under-estimated from the map, and mistakes in finding the way can consume a lot of time.

* Scottish Mountaineering Club.

CONDUCT OF PARTY. On any expedition where difficulties may be met, unless the party is composed of experienced men who know each other's capabilities, it is desirable to have a leader. He will lead by initiative, persuasion and general consent. The first thing to be done is to see that all necessary equipment is carried. There should be at least one map, compass, watch and torch or lantern. It may be better to have more than one. Someone should carry an elementary first-aid kit with a bandage or its equivalent, string, knife and some antiseptic; for there is always the possibility of an accident.

There should be no rushing at the hill. The pace should be comfortable for the slowest member of the party. Shorter steps are best when climbing, especially on uneven ground. Accurate placing of the feet is very important, on a rough, loose slope especially. Keep the foot as level as possible and save energy. A good pace will usually enable everyone to breathe through the nose and not with open mouth. This does not dry up the body so much nor accentuate thirst on a hot day. If conditions are difficult, and if possible at all times, the party should keep together. If a party splits up, each fragment should know the programme, route and destination of the others. In the event of a mishap it saves a lot of trouble if a search party has to go out later on.

If a party is overtaken by nightfall in cold and wet conditions some sort of shelter should be sought. Even although it proves inadequate, provided that it does protect to some extent from wind and rain, it is safer to stay there rather than venture down an unknown mountain face in darkness. If there is enough spare clothing and the party is in good health and training it is less dangerous (if dangerous at all) to remain there, moving arms and legs as much as possible during the night so as to keep the circulation going. Wind is the worst enemy and cold rain may be as bad. In summer and autumn a night's exposure on British hills is usually neither fearsome nor dangerous, especially if one has a reserve of food.

ACCIDENTS

To accidents involving mechanical injuries must be added those where a party or its members lose their way and, in consequence, suffer from exposure to cold and storm. The risk can always be reduced to minor proportions by observing the precautions advocated in this chapter, by careful training and all-round experience. The risks and inconvenience to a search party may be minimised if every party leaves information regarding its route, objective and destination before setting out on an expedition. Another rule which should always be observed is not to split up the party until all dangerous ground is left behind and the way back to civilisation is safe and well marked. When the party must be split up, each fraction should know the destination and route of the others. If these rules are followed the labour of a search party, if at all necessary, will be greatly simplified.

Now suppose that one member of the party is injured. Perhaps he thinks he can walk to safety and shelter. If there is any doubt as to his condition it is best to summon help. If possible, one member of the party should remain with the injured man, but this may not be possible (*a*) if there are only two, or (*b*) if there are three, but the route of descent is difficult or dangerous. Then the injured man must be left in a safe place, with as much shelter as can be arranged and with all available spare clothing and some food. Warmth and shelter are most important, because most mechanical injuries involve some degree of shock, and chilling is then particularly dangerous.

Only elementary first-aid should be applied by unskilled persons. This would include (1) stopping bleeding and cleaning and sterilising open wounds, (2) immobilising broken limbs, so that movement can do no damage and pain is minimised, and (3) applying warmth. Stimulants, such as alcohol, are generally harmful. Sugary foods are best, if possible supplied in a hot condition.

If other parties can be contacted it is essential to know the conventionally accepted signals and answers. The distress signal is made by whistle, waving flag or flashing light—six signals at intervals during one minute, one-minute's interval and then a repetition. The reply is similar, using only three signals (blasts, waves or flashes) instead of six.

There are, throughout the most frequented British mountain areas, organised first-aid and rescue posts under the control of climbing clubs which are affiliated to the British Mountain Rescue

Committee. Their organisation and equipment are described in a pamphlet published by the Committee and are also detailed in *Climbing in Britain*, edited by J. E. Q. Barford for the British Mountaineering Council and published by Penguin Books Ltd.

If official help cannot be secured by the messenger from the injured party the former must enlist such local assistance as he can find. It all depends on the location of the injured person or persons whether it is wise to conduct a rescue party by night. In any case, all necessary preparations should be made to start early enough, so that any difficult ground is reached with the first signs of daylight. In far too many cases accurate information is lacking as to the position of the party requiring help.

Do not send messengers in opposite directions to different valleys or villages about the same accident. This causes confusion, if not worse. Remember that, although the Rescue Committee is run by established climbing clubs, they are seldom called upon to help their own members or members of other clubs, but mostly for rash and unskilled novices who have not troubled to learn the rudiments of mountain craft before venturing into dangerous places. Difficult mountains are usually in sparsely populated regions, and the same people are called out, again and again, for this thankless task. Their time is valuable, and they are more than entitled to a recompense for their altruistic efforts. A similar consideration applies in the case of the local police officers.

MOUNTAIN FORM AND CHOICE OF ROUTE

Mountain form varies considerably in different districts. Experience and the map will show where the steep and difficult places are likely to be. There is nearly always an easy way. In fact, there is no British mountain, apart from a few peaks of the Cuillin range in the Isle of Skye, which has not a perfectly easy way to the top, usually more than one. A general rule is to select a ridge or shoulder for the ascent. It should not be interrupted by any walls or tiers of cliff, and it should not be separated from the summit by any considerable or steep gaps. Mountain faces are not so good for an easy route, as they frequently become

NOTE.—An excellent discussion on Mountain Accidents, by Dr D. G. Duff, occurs in the 1949 issue of the *S.M.C. Journal*.

Loch Eilt — The Road to the Isles

excessively steep, decorated with tiers of cliff (even although these may be climbable), and may often be covered with long slopes of scree (loose stones of all sizes).

Heather, growing over and concealing scree, is very trying ground, especially for descending. If one intends to traverse a series of peaks it is wise to make a preliminary reconnaissance and to note carefully what looks like offering an easy line of descent from the last peak. In general, if one has been unable to do this, it is always advisable to choose a route for descent which is nearly all visible from the top. This is a counsel of perfection, but, if most of the way is practicable, no single tier of cliff is likely to be so continuous as to prove more than a temporary nuisance.

Most troublesome of all Scottish peaks, in this respect, are the Torridon sandstone mountains of Wester Ross and Sutherland. The topmost slopes are often gently inclined heaps of angular quartzite scree, but the middle belt is composed of escarpments of red sandstone cliff, successive tiers which are often interlocked so as to form a baffling network of defences. In many cases, such as the Glen Torridon face of the long ridge of Liathach, there are perfectly easy ways down, but they are notoriously difficult to find from above.

Scree is unpleasant, hard on the boot nails, but easy to descend. As on other rough ground, one should dig the heels in and take plenty of time. In a few cases the scree is small and uniform. Then it is a pleasure to run down at considerable speed. There are some good slopes on the Glen Etive side of the Buachaille, from Stob Coire nan Lochan to Coire Beith, above Coire Lagain in Skye, and most frequently where there is trap rock. When approaching low ground look out for paths. They save much time. If there are no paths it is seldom advisable to follow a watercourse too closely. A stream may plunge over waterfalls and through deep gorges, with deep tributary gorges on either side. Likewise, it pays to keep on the higher ground and avoid the marshes and lush vegetation of the valley bottom. If large streams must be crossed it is usually worth while to aim for the bridges which are marked on the map. In wet weather even a moderate sized stream may be so swollen with rain as to be an impassable barrier.

There is no finer way of getting to know the country and the mountains than to plan an expedition over several peaks inter-connected by ridges. This is true exploration and mountaineering if one sets out with the necessary minimum of memorised map knowledge, and only carries the map in reserve as a last resort. The mountains will have different forms and present diverse problems. The scenery will be continually changing. Mistakes may be made, but they will be fruitful in after experience.

Several Scottish districts might be suggested as suitable for this sort of expedition: The Ben Lawers range north of Loch Tay; the Blackmount group south of Glencoe; the Ben Doran-Achallader range south-east of Rannoch Moor; the peaks of Mamore Forest between Loch Leven and Glen Nevis; the Ben Alder range west of Loch Ericht; many expeditions in the Cairngorms, which should not be tackled in winter unless well known; the Mam Soul group north of Loch Affric; the hills of Cluanie and Glen Shiel. There are many fine ranges, like the last two mentioned, north-west of the Caledonian Canal.

CONCLUSION

I shall conclude with a brief account of the sort of mistakes that are liable to occur when traversing easy mountains. On New Year's Day, 1935, Dr Myles, C. M. Allan, D. C. MacDonald and I set out to climb Ben Alder, having left a car at the eastern corner of Loch Pattack. The streams were in spate and we were unable to cross a main feeder of the Loch until we had gone far enough upstream to the fork where two equal streams joined to form it. We then decided to ascend the sharp little peak called Lancet Edge and to leave the main top of Ben Alder for another occasion. It was a pleasant, mild, sunny day, so mild that I went up the narrow ridge stripped to the waist. We lunched on the summit at 2.50 p.m. Allan thought that we ought to return by the same way, but Myles wished to go on to the summit of Geal Charn (3,688 ft.). This was in cloud and snow-covered. We reached it at 4 p.m.

We descended by an easy ridge into a narrow glen on the north-east side, where the map had led us to expect a path. Unfortunately, it was beginning to get dark and our only torch had a battery very near exhaustion. We knew our general direction, but I shall not weary the reader with our flounderings over endless peat hags as we struggled towards a faint, low gap in the hills to the east. Having crossed it we struck a faint track which gradually improved. Far ahead was a pale, grey blur which we hailed as Loch Pattack. But the car was on the far side of the Loch, and both incoming and outgoing streams were unfordable! The map, faintly illuminated by the orange glow of the dying torch, showed a bridge two miles lower down over the river Pattack. On we trudged in mist, rain and gloom, missing the path twice on account of two-way forks and having to retrace our steps. At length, when we felt sure that we had covered much more than the two miles, we cut straight across to the right and found the road on our side of the river. Weary and sodden, we regained the car at 8 p.m. We had failed by neglecting at least two vital considerations, probably because we were over-confident regarding the easy nature of the ground.

In early September 1941 I spent a week-end at Aviemore. Monday was a good day of strong, fresh, west wind and scudding cloud. I parted from my sister on the lower reaches of the Larig Ghru track, intending to climb Cairngorm and to meet her on my return journey on the Lurcher's Crag. She had map, compass and watch: I trusted to hill-sense. I enjoyed the bracing walk across the moors, crossing the northern corries of Cairngorm until I breasted the final slopes beyond Coire an't Sneachda. Then I passed up into the cloud and the full force of the wind. I lunched by the summit cairn (4,084 ft.). I intended to catch the 5.30 p.m. train south from Aviemore, the depressing alternative being a midnight train and hours of weary waiting at Perth. The correct thing to do was to return by the way I had come. I should soon have been beneath the cloud level with no further difficulties.

But I thought I might as well try to cross the high plateau over Cairn Lochan to the Lurcher's Crag. It was good going and I did find the top of Cairn Lochan. My direction guide was the wind and the declivity on my right. The wind is never very constant on high mountains, owing to the contours of the ground. In this case, as I discovered later on, the wind veered towards the south. Beyond Cairn Lochan I found a track,

E

marked at rare intervals by a series of stone men. There is so little up and down in this region that it is hard to decide where one is really going. I had not been in these parts for nearly twenty years. Then I came upon a wide, mossy hollow with a stream issuing from a spring in the moss. For the moment the place seemed vaguely familiar, but I could not recall the association. Then it recurred to me. I was convinced that I was at the source of the Feith Buidhe, a stream which ultimately plunges down to Loch Avon. I suspected that I was making for the top of Ben Macdhui.*

At any rate I acted on this supposition, swung to the right, crossed a gentle ridge and began to descend a steep, rough slope, broken by occasional small crags. At length the mist thinned out. Beneath me were two small lochans, which I soon recognised as the Pools of Dee. When I got down to them I felt pretty certain that I had lost my train in any case, so I stripped and plunged into the dark, icy water for a swim. After a yard or two the bottom fell away quite suddenly, just as if I had stepped off the edge of a wall. This is not an uncommon feature of the mountain lakes in the Cairngorm region. Then I turned northwards, crossed the wilderness of boulders at the head of the Larig Ghru Pass, 2,733 feet above sea level, and soon met a party who were ascending from the north.

They told me it was a quarter to four. I had still a sporting chance. I trotted and ran all the way to the crossroad to Loch an Eilein, beyond the iron footbridge put up by the Cairngorm Club, and found my sister awaiting me in a car at five o'clock. No one could be more surprised than I was at catching that train. It is a distance of five and a half miles from the top of the Larig to the footbridge. I had a good thirst when the train got to Perth. Things do not always end so pleasantly when one wanders about in the mist, without map or compass, on the summit plateaus of the Cairngorms.

* See Map C, p. 198.

A NOTE ON THE ANEROID BAROMETER

Care and the understanding of certain sources of error are necessary when using the aneroid for the determination of altitudes. For small differences of altitude this is not so important. The following are the principal points to consider: (1) Measurements cannot be at all reliable during variable weather with rapid fluctuations of the barometer. This can be determined by comparison of readings at the base and a higher station of which the respective heights are known from a trigonometrical survey; (2) Aneroid barometers, unless specially compensated, have a temperature error, which affects readings on the barometric (atmospheric pressure) scale as well as the altimeter scale. If the instrument is not compensated it must be checked for error against a standard; (3) Altimeter scales are logarithmic scales, of which the divisions get smaller as the altitude increases (as the pressure decreases). If altimeter and barometric scales are not moveable with reference to each other the zero altitude usually corresponds to a barometric reading of thirty-one inches. If the actual reading at the base is much less, as it usually is, the altimeter reading should be recorded relative to the known height above sea level of the base, and the difference used as a correction for all other heights. If the two scales are relatively adjustable it is still better to proceed thus from a zero of thirty-one inches, but the alternative plan of adjusting the altimeter scale zero by setting the scale to give the correct height of the base will give results which will not be greatly in error, for the scale error will tend to be neutralised by the next correction to be considered, though the compensation is seldom or never accurate; (4) The standard altimeter scale corresponds to a mean atmospheric temperature of 50°F. for British instruments. If the mean temperature of the high and low stations exceeds this the column of air between them is of lower density (in warm weather) and the altimeter difference will be too small. The reverse holds for cold weather. As atmospheric temperature normally falls in a regular manner with increase of altitude, a single temperature reading at the low level station is sufficient to determine the approximate correction. At 45°F. no correction is needed for 1,000 feet of rise. At 70°F. one must add fifty feet to altimeter reading per 1,000 feet of rise, and at 20°F. deduct the same amount; (5) Every aneroid has a greater or less time lag in acquiring its final correct reading. That means that one may have to wait a few minutes on the summit before the instrument reads the full height, and, of course, as one descends more quickly than one climbs, the time lag will be more pronounced. This error must be determined by experiment for each instrument.

See J. G. Inglis, 'Aneroid Barometers', *S.M.C.J.*, vol. 9, p. 243, also *S.M.C. General Guide*, p. 119.

CHAPTER VI

ROCK CLIMBING

SCOPE AND TRAINING

ROCK climbing is an integral part of mountaineering, but it is only a part. Mountaineering on the larger scale involves difficult questions of exploration and transport of supplies before the main climbing problems are even reached. Great mountains are usually covered with accumulations of snow and ice, particularly on their higher slopes. The bigger the mountain the more necessary to choose the easiest way of ascent, and the more likely that a route will be selected over glaciers, snow slopes and snow-covered ridges, with a minimum of difficult rock. Consideration must also be given to the all-important factors of time, weather, wind, cold and a rarified atmosphere. Any rock climbing must be done fairly quickly and should not be too difficult or strenuous. These considerations apply in a greater or less degree to the ascents of all big peaks in the Alps, Caucasus, Rockies or Himalaya. In the Alps the approaches are well known, marked by paths to a considerable height, and there are many high huts, conveniently situated so as to shorten the final ascent and enable more time to be spent on severe technical difficulties. Even in the Alps, however, severe rock climbs are unusual on the bigger peaks.

On British hills difficulty must make up for the lack of height, if the sporting possibilities of our lower mountains are to be exploited to the fullest extent. It may be assumed that many readers of this book aspire to guideless mountaineering in the High Alps as one of their objectives. For them, training in British rock climbing has considerable value. The earliest British mountaineers learned their rock climbing from Alpine guides. It was not specially difficult rock climbing in those far-off days. There is no longer any excuse whatever for British climbers going to the Alps without an all-round training in this branch of mountaineering.

There is evidently a need for two different sorts of training in rock climbing. The kind that will fit a man for dealing with the ordinary problems of rock-craft on the bigger mountains is more important from the mountaineering point of view. This would lay the greatest emphasis on the ability to move quickly and safely over moderately difficult rocks, sound or unsound, wet or dry or patchy with snow and ice, throughout a long and strenuous expedition which necessitates a certain amount of route finding, with little guidance from other parties or printed directions. Such a course of training, involving both ascent and descent, is indispensable for guideless work on the big Alpine peaks, and is the primary objective of this chapter. It can easily be achieved on British hills, but the Scottish mountains, on account of their greater number, height and variety of rock structure, are better adapted for this purpose than the more difficult and standardised routes in Lakeland and North Wales.

This is not a matter of difficulty or exposure; English rock climbing cannot be excelled anywhere in those respects. There is far more moderately difficult rock available in Scotland, so that long days can be spent on traverses over a great extent of climbable rock, demanding rapid and rhythmic movement of the whole party for many hours at a stretch, including many ascents and descents. During winter and spring months Scotland can offer on its higher mountains a typically Alpine alternation of snow, ice and rock, which is seldom available in England and never on the same scale.

This kind of training possesses certain other advantages from the aspect of safety. It is well known that accidents occur, very frequently, on the easier places, especially during the descent after a party has completed a difficult climb. The nervous tension is relaxed and succeeded by a reaction of comparative carelessness when there are still minor difficulties to be faced. On a difficult rock climb certain safety measures are always adopted.

Only one man moves at a time, and the rope which links the party together as one unit is firmly anchored to the rock. There is a tendency to accept these static devices as a complete guarantee of safety in themselves, with the after-effect of an unwarranted carelessness when the rope has been taken off and each member of the party moves off by himself. What is required is habitual awareness at all times on the mountains, developed in every member of the party and not only in the leader. This is best acquired on long expeditions where the degree of difficulty, never too great, varies continually. Where there is danger or difficulty for the weakest member of the party the whole party should be roped, but all moving together unless the difficulty is considerable. It will not be necessary to anchor the rope, in general, for the rope will only be required for checking a momentary slip and never an actual fall. It is by such training that a party will work together as a single team and acquire dynamic rather than static security. The real factor of safety will lie in the habitual awareness and response to difficulty on the part of each member. Like other habits, that of dynamic awareness and security will not be easily lost when the rope is taken off or when its use is no longer necessary.

Rock climbing is also an independent sport in its own right, quite apart from getting to the top of the mountain. As such, it is a valuable training for all forms of difficult mountaineering and makes full use of the sporting possibilities of our smaller British mountains. It trains a man to co-ordinate eye and limb, to observe and weigh up a situation and come to a decision. It trains him to know and examine himself and to know, as A. F. Mummery says, 'That the fingers of one hand can still be trusted with the lives of a party, and that the lower limbs are free from all trace of knee-dissolving fear'. But it is much wiser to learn how to move safely over complicated hill country and over long stretches of moderately difficult rock first of all, without taking a short cut to the greater thrills of the more severe climbs.

Both varieties of training have their place in utilising to the fullest extent the potentialities for healthful sport and recreation of our British mountains. Expeditions of both types will be described in this book. They will be mainly Scottish for the following reasons: (a) The greater extent and variety of Scottish mountains; (b) Scottish rock-climbing development has been slower and more recent than English; its achievements and possibilities are less well known. A comparative chapter on the author's experience of English and Welsh climbs has been included, so as to link up the Scottish descriptions with English recognised standards of performance. There is only one art of rock climbing, and its present level of excellence in Britain derives mainly from its historical development in England.

It is an open and unprofitable question, whether rock climbing or snow and ice climbing requires more training and experience. There is, even in Scotland, far more opportunity for the former. Even in winter and spring the standard of the latter varies enormously from one year to another. Rock-climbing routes can be approximately graded and standardised for length, difficulty and exposure, assuming reasonable weather and dry rocks. This cannot be done for snow climbs. Rock-climbing guide books can thus be fairly accurate and reliable.

Careful training and much experience behind good leaders on different mountains and types of rock can improve the standard of performance of an indifferent climber over a period of many years. The very best rock climbers are born rather than made. They have a natural balance and neatness of movement, using the feet to do the work rather than pulling with the arms. They move deliberately from hold to hold, economising energy, and co-ordinating eyes and limbs with a cat-like grace of rhythmic movement. They never land in positions from which they cannot safely retreat. Consequently, they move safely at all times. Not all these characteristics are born in a man, certainly not the latter ones. They are acquired by practice and training, not without observation and common-sense. For good mountaineering, on all but the hardest routes, they can be acquired in sufficient degree by most persons who have enough enthusiasm, patience and perseverance. They may never become outstanding leaders, but they can be safe and reliable seconds.

Many books have been written with elaborate chapters on equipment, procedure, safety devices and refinements of technique. These have their place and are valuable for reference, as experience is gained. Much of this information is unnecessary in the initial stages, where a good leader is worth more than many text-books. If one is overmuch encumbered by detail it is possible, and not unlikely, for one to develop a cramped and mechanised style of climbing. The novice should endeavour to acquire a free style of movement and balance, along with the habitual self-reliance and awareness which are the hall-mark of the capable rock climber, as of most other sportsmen.

Emergency safeguards are needed for difficult rock climbing, yet, by themselves, they cannot help a man to climb well, still less to lead well. The first rule of climbing is that the leader must never fall off: its observance depends on his own powers and nervous co-ordination. Earlier expeditions are best confined to a wide variety of different types of rock of moderate difficulty, including some really long climbs on mountain ridges in all sorts of weather. At the same time, good practice on much harder problems of a shorter type can be obtained, preferably near ground level, where there is little danger in the event of a fall or slip.

EQUIPMENT

Much of the equipment is the same as for hill walking. Rock climbing, especially for a party larger than two, is often a slow business, so it is very important to pay due heed to clothing and warmth. Gloves, in many places where hand-holds are small, cannot be worn, but mittens or fingerless gloves can give most of the needed warmth and protection. Keeping the hands warm makes climbing much safer, as the awareness of small and unseen holds is greatly improved.

Footwork is of even greater importance. For all kinds of rock in all sorts of weather nailed boots are the most suitable foot-gear. Too much stress need not be placed on particular types of nailing, nor should the nailing be too heavy. Wing nails spaced round the edges of sole and heel, properly secured through the welt, are sufficient, along with thinly spaced muggers on the inside area. Tricouni nails are also good. I prefer a combination of both types. Remember that most reliance will be placed on the nails at the inside edge of the toe. On difficult, slabby rocks rubbers or plimsolls are a great advantage. They grip over the whole surface. They are not good for training purposes, as one tends to get a false sense of security, attempting things beyond one's ability without the careful placing of feet which is essential with nailed boots. There is no gainsaying their value, lightness and comfort on difficult rocks in *dry* weather. It is now possible to buy boots with corrugated rubber, nail-like soles and heels.

They are hard wearing and said to be very good on every surface except wet ice or slimy rock.* These *vibram* soles have been
much used in the Alps, and a similar material called *Itshide* is
obtainable here. Rope and cloth-soled shoes and boots are used
on difficult Alpine rock. They are better than rubbers on wet
rock, but stocking soles† grip better than any of these, unless the
feet get so cold as to lose sensation. Smooth rubbers can be very
dangerous on wet rock. Whatever one uses it is important to
remember that on small holds one must grip with the edge of
the boot. Wide and overlapping welts are therefore bad.

The climbing rope is an essential factor of safety for all climbing on difficult rock. It unites a party, not only physically but
morally, into a single team for purposes of mutual aid and
security. By its means a capable leader can enable less competent, but still reliable members of the party to achieve an
interesting and difficult expedition, which they could not safely
carry out by themselves. It is a curious fact that the confidence
and security of the leader are increased by the presence and
moral support of others less capable than himself. This additional security is obtained by the proper use of the rope. At
difficult places only one man moves at a time, the rope and the
other members of the party being anchored to a secure piece of
rock. When the leader moves he, too, is secured. Since he is
above the anchor, in the event of a slip on his part, he can still
fall past it until the rope draws him up. The safety of the leader
is, thus, less than that of the others, but it is a real factor of
safety. The three requirements are (1) a good leader who does
not fall, (2) a good rope, (3) a good rock anchor, properly used.

British ropes of hemp or manila from a reputable maker are
good and reliable. Climbing rope is generally available in three
weights—full, three-quarters and line. Three-quarters is quite
heavy enough for general use, and suitable for beginners who
are unlikely to do any severe or exposed climbs. Full weight may
not give any extra security on a long pitch, on account of the
drag of the extra weight on the leader, which can have an

---

* I have found *Itshide* excellent and hard wearing for rock climbing in summer
conditions. On moderately wet but clean rock it is still good, especially if the rock
is rough. On very smooth, very wet and on slimy or lichen covered rock, it may
be extremely unsafe.

† Only one ply, for double socks may slip over each other.

adverse effect on his balance, all the worse if the rope becomes wet. Whatever rope is used, it should be frequently examined for flaws, cuts or weak places.

Ropes can be frayed, and even cut, by sharp rocks, but damage due to excessive strain or bad conditions of drying or storage can only be detected by untwisting parts of the rope and noting the condition of the inner surface of the strands—whether they are frayed, broken or discoloured. That should be done at regular intervals and a suspect rope discarded altogether. Note that surface wear must always be greater on a thinner rope. The frictional strain or abrasion is carried on a smaller area, and the proportion of abraded rope must be greater than in the case of a heavier rope. This is particularly applicable to nylon rope where a thinner quality will be used on account of its greater strength. When examining a rope it is well to make sure that the ends are properly whipped. This is quite a simple operation and should be learned. It is always necessary where a rope is cut with the object of making separate loops for special purposes, e.g. roping down from a difficulty. Ropes are measured by circumference and not diameter. This is easy to do by wrapping a thin string round for a dozen turns or so and then measuring. Full weight rope would naturally be used to protect a leader on severe routes with considerable exposure, especially in trying out new routes.

New ropes tend to kink, especially when wet, but they should not be unduly stretched. Severe stretching takes the life or elasticity out of a rope. Without elasticity the rope cannot absorb the energy of a falling man without suffering a severe strain; it is no longer a factor of safety. Long experience of rock climbing, where I have very often been leading, has inclined me to prefer a light weight of rope. The advantages are most marked on long, difficult climbs with a long run-out of rope between positions of security, and where rucksacks and boots may have to be hauled up separately on the rope. When a retreat by means of the doubled rope is necessary one must carry a long, spare length of line for the purpose.

The newest variety of climbing rope is nylon, which is still very expensive. Weight for weight it is much stronger and more elastic than manila. Owing to its chemical constitution it hardly loses any strength when wetted, absorbs less water and should kink less than other ropes. It is very smooth, but this does not appear to be a handicap in use. I have little experience of its wearing properties.* Its lightness and strength make it very popular.

Each climber is attached to the rope by means of a waist loop, secured by a knot. Three considerations are important about knots. They must not slip under strain. It should be possible to undo them easily, even if the rope has been under strain when wet. The knot should not weaken the rope unduly. The usual British climbing rope is made up of three strands twisted together with a right-hand lay, which means that the rope resembles a standard British screw with a right-hand thread. It appears in more than one climbing text-book that one should be careful to tie knots with the lay of the rope, but there is no agreement about this, and the matter is really of minor importance; although something may be inferred from the fact that hawsers of large diameter are usually compounded of lesser ropes in such a way that the twist of the constituent ropes is the same as that of the constituent strands of the latter. The strength of most knots is not much more than half the strength of the original rope, but some are better than others, the important consideration being that the free ends of the rope which emerge from the knot should not, when under tension, be bent at an acute angle; for shearing strain under a shock is always greater at a sharp bend where the separate strands of the rope will not share the strain equally.

It is sometimes necessary to join two ropes. The proper knot should be used for the purpose. The join should not, if avoidable, be made on the rope to the leader, as, in the event of a fall, that rope would suffer a severe strain. Neither should the join be effected by a middleman wearing two waist loops, one on each rope. This might subject him to a severe twist in the event of an accident.

Some people find it difficult to learn how to tie knots. For them simplicity is essential at first. The easiest way is, un-

* Nylon is liable to deteriorate if exposed to temperatures of 400°F or over. It melts at 480°F. The chief danger is when a running rope rubs on a stationary one, generating surface heat on the latter by friction. Apart from this risk it is reported to wear satisfactorily.

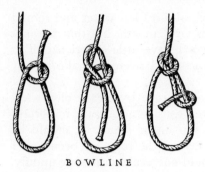

BOWLINE

MIDDLEMAN'S

FISHERMAN'S JOINING KNOT

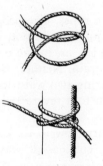

CLOVE HITCH

Useful Knots

doubtedly, to tie on with an ordinary overhand knot on the doubled rope, either close to the end or at the middle, as required. It does not slip, but, if considerable strain comes on the knot, especially when it is wet, it may be exceedingly difficult to untie. Unless it is well made and carefully tightened it may slip to a slight extent.

Therefore, it is better not to rest content with this knot, but to take the little extra trouble to learn the best ones for each purpose. They are as follows: For the end man the Bowline; for a middleman the Bowline on a Bight is best but uses extra rope, as the climber has a double waist loop; the Middleman knot uses less rope and is satisfactory in general, though it may tighten a little under strain. Two ropes should be joined with the Fisherman's Joining Knot, made with the free ends of both ropes, on the same lines as the Middleman Knot is made on a double rope. The Clove Hitch is useful for hauling spare gear separately up a pitch.*

* A pitch is a difficult section on a climb. There are usually secure positions, both above and below.

Plenty of information about knots can be obtained from other climbers and from various books. It is sufficient here to include illustrations of those mentioned. The Admiralty *Manual of Seamanship*, Part I (H.M.S.O.), describes many others. For instance, the double sheet bend is a good alternative to the fisherman's joining knot. When using the bowline one should remember to lock it with a half hitch or an overhand knot on the waist loop. It is also useful to know how to make a triple bowline, which is the most comfortable way of lowering an injured person.

It pays to keep the rope tidily coiled when not in use, to keep it as dry as possible and not to tread on it when in use. It may be necessary to take kinks out of the rope after uncoiling. Generally, the extra twists have been imparted during the coiling process. By coiling with alternate turns in opposite directions, with a figure of eight formation, it is possible to make a coil without this defect.

If the last man must be hauled up a pitch he should tie on about four feet from the end of the rope and make a small loop at the very end, into which he can insert a foot, using it as a stirrup rope. By standing in the loop and raising himself somewhat he can frequently succeed in grasping a higher hold and so help himself and those above. The alternative is for the man above to lower a rope with a loop at the end, for use as a separate stirrup rope. The man below will then transfer his weight alternately from one rope to the other, the man above taking in the slack of one rope while keeping the other tight, and not being obliged to actually lift his friend, which he might not be able to do.

Stirrup Rope

Each member of the party should carry a rucksack for spare garments, food, rubbers if desired and other necessaries. A heavy sack interferes with balance and free movement. Rucksacks are a pest in chimneys. A spare length of rope or line is useful in case of a forced descent on the doubled rope. As mentioned in the section on 'Safety in Climbing', it may also be useful to carry a short length of line with a loop spliced on at both ends and a snap-link or *Karabiner*, which is an oval, steel link, a straight part of which is hinged, can be opened for clipping on to a rope or another ring, but is kept shut by a spring. Along with this one may carry a *piton* (ring-spike, or peg), which can be securely driven into a crack in the rock as an artificial anchor for the rope. These are emergency items of equipment.

TYPES OF ROCK CLIMBING PROBLEMS

Rock climbing routes, as a rule, should follow some properly defined natural line and must be neither too easy nor impossibly difficult. On great mountains, such as the Alps, it may be a difficult matter to reach the summit by any route whatever, and especially if the intention is to follow a particular ridge or face of the mountain. We must then select the easiest route on that ridge or face and surmount any difficulties we meet. On British mountains there is always an easy way, unless in severe conditions of weather or snow and ice, so the climber sets himself the problem of getting up the cliff within narrowly defined limits.

Even so, he is often following a line of structural weakness, a sort of breach in the natural defences of the crag. There are many such features available. One cannot climb a smooth, vertical face of rock. The angle must slope back to some extent. There must be terraces or ledges for occasional resting places. There must be miniature ledges or cracks in the face, to be used as footholds or handholds.

In the early days, climbing routes followed two types of rock feature as a rule; ridges and gullies. The first projects from the face and the second cuts back into it, both lying at an easier gradient than the face itself, even although each may have occasional steps or vertical sections. Such steep sections are known as *pitches*. Climbing routes described in guide books are usually split up into a succession of pitches, not necessarily all natural ones. The next development was to attack still narrower rifts, known as *chimneys*, which could usually be bridged between back and foot or back and knee. If these became too narrow, admitting only a foot or a hand, they were still useful as lines of ascent and known as *cracks*. In chimneys and cracks support could be obtained by friction and jamming against the retaining walls. The climbing was often very strenuous, but balance was not always so important as strength and endurance.

At a later stage of development it was discovered that lateral support was not essential, but that an improved balance would enable one to climb near-vertical walls with tiny holds and steep slabs with hardly any holds at all. This was not done so much by strenuous arm pulling, but rather by neat foot-work, good balance and accurate co-ordination of eye and limb. The result was the discovery and execution of many new and exceptionally difficult rock climbing routes on crag faces which the older climbers had only favoured with a glance before pronouncing them to be impossible. Let us review the different sorts of rock climbing problems. The novice will have his preferences, but should try and gain some degree of proficiency at all of them. On many of the greatest and longest climbs, British and Alpine, one may encounter all or most of these types in a single day's climbing on one mountain.

Arêtes or *Ridges* of any length and difficulty are not common in Britain. Most of them, having stood the rough and tumble of ages of geological denudation, are of fairly sound rock. They are the natural routes between peaks. The best known and most attractive ridges, only difficult for short stretches at a time, are to be found on the Cuillin Hills of the Isle of Skye, and are of very sound rock. Other examples of the horizontal type are the Aonach Eagach in Glencoe, the A'Chir in Arran and the Crib Goch ridge of Snowdon. Steep lateral ridges, abutting against a mountain face, are commoner and afford very good climbing. Sometimes they are called buttresses and partake of both architectural habits. A buttress has often a narrow ridge on part of its upward sweep, generally near the top. The Amphitheatre Buttress of Craig yr Ysfa (North Wales) and the knife edge of Scafell Pinnacle (Cumberland) are instances of this. There are many in Scotland, such as the Tower and Observatory Ridges on Ben Nevis, the Crowberry Ridge in Glencoe, the upper part of Rosa Pinnacle in Arran, and the Eagle Ridge of Lochnagar. The latter has several long, steep, narrow and difficult sections and is probably the finest example of a steep and difficult British ridge. Wind can be a serious menace on an exposed ridge.

Ridges are often blocked by steep, or vertical sided gaps, steep walls and towers, known as *gendarmes* to the climbing fraternity. Contrary to civilian traffic regulations the best plan is to attack the policeman boldly and climb over him—unless there happens to be a clear way round on either side. It is seldom wise to recoil from such difficulties, for a traverse below the obstacle often lures one on to very unsound rock, on to smooth slabs or round a corner on a narrow ledge which frequently thins out to vanishing point over a vertical cliff. Another great advantage of sticking to the crest of a ridge is that there are nearly always good projecting rocks available for holds, or as hitches and secure anchors for the climbing rope.

Gullies are natural lines of weakness on a cliff face. The average gradient is usually less than that of the face itself. But there are compensating disadvantages, for the rock has usually been hollowed out because it is less resistant, and consequently, less sound than that of the surrounding walls. Much loose rock remains in the bed of the gully. It is, therefore, a bad plan for two

Surmounting a Chockstone

parties, or even one large party, to be climbing in a gully at the same time, for the upper members, however careful they may try to be, are likely to drop stones on the people below. Even a small party of two or three ought to keep close together. Pitches occur in gullies where a boss of rock has resisted the weathering agencies and stands up as a wall, or where a great block, with or without a few smaller ones, has jammed at the narrow part and serves as the roof of a cave. As gullies are natural watercourses such caves are often wet with slippery, moss-covered walls. They present difficult problems. Sometimes one wall can be climbed with foot and handholds until one is high enough to get an arm across the top and pull up on the edge of this boulder, called the *chockstone* (although this word is mainly applied to blocks in chimneys which are usually much narrower). Then a mighty heave and wriggle will land the climber on the roof.

Gully climbing was a very early development in English rock climbing. On Scafell, Deep Ghyll and Moss Ghyll; on Pillar, Walker's Gully; and in Wales, the Great Gully of Craig yr Ysfa were climbed. It is not to be thought, on that account, that gully climbing is inferior or out of date. The three longest Scottish gullies, the Waterpipe in Skye, the Chasm of Buachaille Etive and the Clachaig Gully in Glencoe are all splendid climbs. The rock is not very good in the Waterpipe, but the Chasm offers all types of pitches of increasing difficulty in a long day's climbing, and the rock is sound. The Ben Nevis gullies, which are high up on a north-east face and snow-filled for many months, have much decayed and unsound rock and are not to be recommended as rock climbs.

Chimneys are much narrower and steeper than gullies. They often overhang altogether in places, but may, nevertheless, offer practicable means of ascending vertical steps on a face, or even on a ridge. Where there are adequate holds on the back or side walls, and if the chimney is wide enough, the method of climbing is straightforward, either facing in or sideways. In other cases one must wriggle upwards between the walls with back on one wall and knees or feet on the other. In very wide chimneys the necessary span must be between feet and hands. Such procedure is known as 'backing up', in general. Energy can be saved by using the palms of the hands behind the hips as a help in lifting the body. It is important to rest wherever possible, as it may be necessary to economise energy for a

Backing Up

F

final strenuous effort in the nature of an arm pull, where the chimney is closed at the top by an overhanging chock-stone. Chimney climbing can be very tiring work.

The following are good rules which are worth observing at all times:

(1) Use all available holds on the walls, and use them for resting places.

(2) Don't get too far inside a chimney, especially if it narrows at the top. One has less freedom of movement and the apparent, additional safety is more than counterbalanced by a strained position. Positive holds on the walls cannot be properly used in a narrow space.

(3) Always economise energy and keep a reserve for the final movements which may be very strenuous. Keep enough energy for a safe retreat, if necessary.

(4) Make sure about the final holds, e.g. behind the chock-stone, before making any irreversible move towards them.

(5) Climb chimneys with the feet and body muscles, and as little as possible by pulling up with the arms to high handholds.

Chimneys and cracks on faces are normally of fairly sound rock, although this depends entirely on the prevailing rock structure. They are not so often wet, and usually provide belays for the rope. In many cases the leader can anchor himself firmly by wedging across the chimney. Even although these places may overhang, the in-cut nature of the holds makes them less dangerous than difficult and strenuous.

Cracks and Corners. A crack is simply a very narrow version of a chimney. Sometimes both feet and arms can be used. In narrow cracks only one arm and perhaps a toe can be inserted, while the other foot finds a few minute holds on the outside face. Sometimes the hand or fist can be inserted in a crack as a wedging hold for steadying purposes, or even for taking part of the weight of the body while raising a foot. Crack climbing can be very strenuous. The 'Lay-back' is a useful but exhausting method of climbing steep cracks with a sharp edge, when they split the angle of an open corner. The climber grips the edge, using feet or knees against the smooth rock face. Considerable pressure is often necessary and the position is tiring to hold. As in climbing a vertical steeple-jack's ladder, the arms must

be kept straight so as not to tire them
out prematurely.

Open corners on vertical rock can
be exceedingly strenuous and difficult. Both in cracks and corners the
utmost use must be made of any kind
of footholds, even when only the toes
can be inserted at an unnatural
angle. Hands should only be used for
preserving balance and not so much
for lifting. Both hands can sometimes
be inserted side by side in a vertical
crack, pulling against each other on
opposite sides, but only for short distances.

One final aid may be occasionally
useful in a crack of varying width.
This is to carry up a suitable stone
which can be wedged in the crack as
an artificial *chockstone*. That is a last
resort for solving an intractable prob-

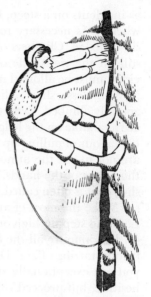

The Lay-Back
*Climbing Corner and use of
Thread Belay*

lem. I have known of a case where it had been inserted and
had come loose on a future occasion when used by another
party. Test them always.

Slabs. Steep, smooth slabs offer difficult problems. Any roughness, proturberances or cracks are a great boon. It is here that
rubbers and stocking soles are particularly useful. Just as on
steep snow and ice one should remember that the danger is not
one of falling backward but slipping forward and downward.
The best posture is the nearest to the upright, using foot friction,
arms outstretched with fingers caressing the rugosities of the
rock, so as to preserve the balance and maintain the maximum
friction. One must not cling to the slab or lie along it. When the
rock is rough it is amazing how steep slabs can be climbed. The
upper part of the south-west route on Pillar and Mallory's Slab
on Sron na Ciche (Skye) are examples. The Long Climb (later
described) on Ben Nevis gives grand practice on steep, smooth
slabs.

Face Climbing. Many of the foregoing types of problem occur as incidents on a steep, face climb. The crucial difficulties arise where it is necessary to effect a lodgment on an overhanging sill or ledge. Climbers often talk of overhangs where the face is still on the right side of being vertical. So much imaginative vision must be allowed in the description of a new, severe climb! Nevertheless, short, slightly overhanging walls of rock are actually climbed. Everything depends on what sort of handholds are available on the ledge above. If these are positive and in-cut the labour of pulling up with the arms is so much lighter. If they are not in-cut the utmost use must be made of friction against the palms of the hands. In the case of an overhang, or mantel-shelf as it is often called, the important principles are as follows: (1) Make the most of any footholds, however rudimentary. (2) Learn to step up high on one foot whilst preserving the balance. (3) Reconnoitre all the holds, plan the necessary moves and rest before starting off. (4) Don't try and pull up with one arm unless you are exceptionally strong. (5) Once you have started don't hesitate, but proceed rhythmically and quickly until you are in safety. (6) Be well anchored by your second whilst moving.

If you can climb up securely to a position of equal height, or slightly above the mantelshelf, a few feet on either side of it, this may be the best way of reaching it by a traversing move. Such a move may be irreversible, meaning that you are likely to fall off if you don't succeed. It is, therefore, all the more necessary that it should be carefully planned and exactly executed. The final crossing may be effected by a hand traverse with the whole weight of the body hanging from the fingers. This type of gymnastic problem is best practised on a suitable boulder where there is no danger. It is often very useful on a difficult rock climb.

Many of the hardest British rock climbs are face climbs. They do not, on that account, call for the greatest strength and endurance. Good balance, good planning and hold selection and rhythmic movement count far more than rush tactics and pulling strength.

Traverses link upward movements, avoiding overhanging sections of cliffs. Here again, good balance and rhythm are essential. All movements on a traverse ought to be reversible. The art of interchanging the position of the feet is indispensable. Ledges have a habit of petering out when explored round corners on a cliff. One must be able to retreat at all times.

Combined Tactics is a method for assisting the leader from below by other members of the party, so as to enable him to overcome a specially difficult problem. So long as difficulty overcome is not succeeded by greater difficulty unforeseen or actual danger in the manoeuvre, the method is often justified by results. In that respect it bears a distant relationship to the practice of jumping for holds! The procedure is justifiable, if (1) the leader is competent and reliable, (2) those below have a perfectly sound stance and anchorage, and (3) it is reasonably certain, so far as one can see, that if the leader is so assisted he will be able to get up the pitch, and will not find himself in just as difficult a position afterwards. The third condition means that the immediate difficulty appears to be the only bar to success or a safe retreat later on. My own experience of combined tactics is scanty but justified by success. On the Knife Edge Arête in the Amphitheatre on the west face of Aonach Dubh, Colin Allan pushed me up so far that he was still taking a good deal of my weight on his outstretched left hand when I finally got good, pulling holds on a smooth scoop of rock. But Colin was exceptionally strong and I was a lightweight. I was once the victim when offering a shoulder to a friend who fell off. Luckily, it was only on a biggish practice boulder.

SAFETY IN CLIMBING

Although safety in climbing depends primarily on good balance, mental as well as physical, the standard of security can be considerably raised by careful and intelligent management of the rope which unites a climbing party into a single team and the proper use of such fixed anchors or belays as the crag or mountain offers for securing the rope. The principles described in this section are applicable with appropriate modifications, to a descending party and also to progress on steep snow and ice, although these aspects of climbing technique are described elsewhere.

Wherever possible, having regard to the competence of the party and the degree of difficulty and exposure involved (which are by no means the same thing), the members of the party will move together, linked by the rope which unites them morally as well as physically. This is the case for moderately difficult climbing, the adverb applying to the ability of the least skilled member. The party will be always on the alert, each member being prepared to check a slip on the part of anyone else. The leader must adjust his pace according to the nature of the ground and keep an eye on the movements of the second. Each man minds the rope leading to the man in front, carrying a short loop of rope in his hand, so as not to jerk him. In the event of a short difficulty the leader may use a hitch for the rope by passing it over a convenient spike of rock, progress becoming one-man-at-a-time until the difficulty is passed. This method is particularly applicable to long climbs, where the standard varies a good deal and there are long, moderate sections. It always applies to much of a long Alpine expedition where time must be economised. Practice in this method is essential on British climbs, as it forms habits of precision and co-operation. It is especially desirable for moderately easy descending routes, speed and safety in descent being an important branch of the larger mountaineering.

When ascending, the most competent man leads, and, if the party exceeds two in number, the next skilled man comes second. On a really difficult climb a party of three is quite big enough, especially if one man is comparatively unskilled. For the descent the best man comes last, and his second in skill goes first as pathfinder. The first principle of safety is that the leader shall not fall, which means that he should not be attempting something which is beyond his proved ability, having regard to three criteria: (a) his previous standard of safe performance, (b) the conditions of the climb as regards cold, wet rocks, etc., (c) the leader's actual health and climbing form at the time. No mechanical safeguards applied according to formula can secure a party for long if the leader does not measure up to these standards. The rest of the party, within their competence, must be perfectly reliable. No one must loosen stones which might fall on a member below.

Where a difficulty is encountered which may put a strain on the capacity of the least skilled member, the linking rope must be anchored securely to a fixed point on the rock face, and only one member of the party move at a time. The distance moved corresponds to that between two convenient anchorages, usually called belays, although a secure stance may often serve equally well. This determines the minimum length of rope between two climbers, exclusive of their waist loops. It can usually be estimated for any particular climb, either from guide books or from the nature of the rock. On difficult climbs it may, at times, exceed 100 feet. If too much rope is used it may prove a nuisance and embarrassment to the leader, especially on steep rocks with small stances. This must often be borne cheerfully, for the leader must have enough rope to reach a secure stance and a belay. It is not so important in the case of the rope linking the lower members of a party, if the leader, at least, is perfectly secure. Sometimes, on an unknown route, the length of the leader's rope can be adjusted before he embarks on an extra long pitch. In no case is it advisable for a man to be attached to two ropes by two waist loops. The ropes should be joined independently by the proper knot for the purpose, preferably not on the leader's rope.

On difficult rocks the problem of security differs according to whether it is the leader or someone else who is moving. In the latter case there is little, if any, shock on the rope if the person comes off or misses his footing. The case of safeguarding on a horizontal traverse will be considered later. Let us deal first with the safety of lower members of the party. Crags offer two kinds of security to the climber—spikes, flakes or jammed blocks to which the rope can be attached, and ledges or niches for holding the body. Climbers call them belays and stances respectively, and they would like to have both at the same time, in order to feel perfectly safe. Nature, as a rule, is not so obliging. There are more stances than belays. It is better to have a narrow stance and a secure belay than the other way round. The two methods of belaying reflect this niggardly attitude on the part of the rocks. If we seek the glory of overcoming difficulties what right have we to expect made-to-measure belays and stances just where they are required?

The simplest way for the leader to secure the second when the latter is moving up to him is to pass the moving rope round the fixed anchor, or belay, as he is taking it in. The anchor should, if possible, be at a convenient distance above him. He must use both hands, paying continual attention to the rope, keeping it reasonably taut, but allowing sufficient freedom for the man below to move without constriction. The term belay is of nautical origin and means the securing of a running rope by means of a cleat. The latter is thus equivalent to what the rock climber calls his belay. It may be a rock spike, a flake of rock, a jammed block in a crack or a sufficiently massive block on a ledge. Whatever it is, the belay must be tested before use by putting a strain on the rope in the direction from which the ultimate strain will come when it is used. The running rope should never be allowed to fray itself against a sharp edge of rock. This method of securing the progress of a lower climber

Direct Belay

is called the *Direct Belay*. When properly used it is perfectly satisfactory for its purpose. It is simple and saves time. It is particularly useful where there is only a narrow stance, perhaps somewhat constricted. It is therefore more generally applicable than more elaborate methods and may consequently allow the climb to be broken up into shorter sections, or run-outs of rope between halting places.

When using the Direct Belay for his second the leader can secure himself at the same time by taking one or two turns of his own rope round the belay, or even by tying himself directly to it by doubling the return rope from the belay, tucking it through his waist loop and tying the free loop with an overhand knot back on itself. This may be necessary and advisable in a difficult situation. When taking in the rope over the belay he may take a turn of the running rope round his hand when his second is at a difficult place.

Some anchors are not suitable for belaying with a thick rope. If the leader carries a longish loop of line and also a snap-link he will be able to attach himself much more quickly and safely in such a case, and especially so to a jammed stone in a crack. Many rock climbers carry a length of line with a loop spliced on at both ends. Although the sporting ethics of British climbing is against the use of fixed ring-spikes (pitons or pegs) driven permanently into the rock, the use of loops and snap-links is a reasonable way of gaining additional security and saving time.

Of recent years the *Indirect or Body Belay* has been generally favoured for the most difficult situations in rock climbing, even for safeguarding lower members of the party, but particularly for securing the leader. Here, the climber ties himself on to his belay, bracing himself against the rope coming from his anchor, and thus becoming a belay in his own person. He takes the rope running to the moving man under one arm, across his back and over the other shoulder, using both hands to hold it. For many stances it is better to pass the rope round the small of the back, as imposing less leverage in the case of a sudden strain. If the anchor is a good deal to one side the Indirect Belay may impose a bad lateral strain and the Direct method would appear to be

Indirect or Body Belay

preferable, but the Indirect Belay is much better if the anchor is inconveniently high above the stance.

The Indirect Belay is especially useful when there is a good stance. What should never be done in a difficult situation is for the leader to use this method for bringing up a second without using any fixed anchor, even when he has only a moderately reliable stance, merely trusting in his own strength and stability. This has been a fruitful cause of accidents. Where a man can wedge himself securely against the rocks he becomes, to all intents and purposes, a fixed anchor, and this warning does not apply. For safeguarding lower members of the party the choice between the Direct and Indirect methods of belaying depends entirely on the relative merits of the stance and belay of the leader. With a poor stance the Direct Belay is preferable; with a good stance a poor belay is not such a disadvantage, and the Indirect Belay will be used.

SAFEGUARDING THE LEADER

The leader cannot be secured absolutely, in all cases, against the results of a fall, because there is a limit to the strength of rope which can be conveniently used in rock climbing. There is also the question of the shock to the body of the leader, even if the rope does not break. If the second uses the body belay he is also subject to a similar sudden pull. This mechanical shock is determined by three factors: the velocity of the leader when the rope tightens on him, the rate at which the tension of the rope draws him up and, of course, the weight of the leader. In most cases, for a given vertical height of fall, the ultimate velocity, owing to friction on inclined ledges or slabs, will be a good deal less than would be the case with a clean drop, but it will be better to consider the latter contingency as an extreme case.

The kinetic energy of the falling leader must be absorbed somehow if he is to be stopped. This can be done in one of two ways, or by a mixture of both. If the second uses a body belay he may pay out extra rope to the leader in a controlled manner when the strain comes on him, acting as a sort of human brake on the rope, and thus converting the absorbed energy into heat, if this can be done at all in such an emergency. If a direct belay is used and there is no rendering or paying out of extra rope, then the rope itself must stretch without breaking, and so absorb the energy.

Climbing ropes of the best quality, although they have never been systematically tested for strength in the past, may soon be expected to conform to a specification which will include a strength test. In this test a gradually increasing load will be applied until the breaking point is reached, but this is not the same thing as a shock-loading test where the upper end of the rope is fixed and a given weight attached to the other end is allowed to fall freely, the load being increased in successive tests until the rope breaks. It has not proved to be easy to predict, from strength and stretch data under graduated loading, what results are to be expected from shock loading. It is certain, however, that the maximum tension in the latter case depends entirely on the elastic stretch of the rope under stress. It is only by stretching that the load on the rope can be brought to rest in a gradual manner. If it is stopped too suddenly the instantaneous tension on the rope is bound to exceed its breaking strength. Two other conclusions can be drawn, the one theoretical and the other as a result of experiment. The stretch of the rope under a given force is proportional to its length. If the climber has a clean drop his kinetic energy is proportional to the height through which he has fallen. The tension developed in the rope when his fall is checked must be nearly proportional to the ratio of these quantities (very approximately perhaps), and would be largely independent of the height fallen through. This curious result seems to be borne out by experiment. The other experimental conclusion is that a normal manila rope (full weight) may be expected to break if subjected to the shock of a ten-stone man falling clear for any substantial height, if the rope is rigidly attached to a rock belay above. If he uses nylon rope the leader has a much better chance of survival, even if the rope is much lighter and, in fact, of a lower breaking strength. This is because the stretch of nylon, under load, is so much greater than that of manila or hemp. (Other mechanical data and conclusions are relegated to a note at the end of this section.)

The direct belay cannot, therefore, protect a leader against the effects of a clear fall. We must, however, see that the rope is always kept in good condition and that its elasticity is unimpaired, for a rope which has been subjected to excessive tension never recovers its stretching properties. A rope should never be allowed to get wet when under tension, as is sometimes done in order to take the kinking habit out of new rope. An easier method is to soak the rope out in warm water for a few hours and then dry in the open air. Knots weaken the rope by anything up to fifty per cent, so it is well to avoid a joining knot between two ropes on the length which runs out to the leader. Nylon rope, although expensive, has great advantages over manila in respect of lightness, strength and stretch. Natural fibre ropes lose a good deal of strength on wetting, but nylon is hardly affected. As a thinner nylon will be used (than manila) it will suffer more from abrasion and should be inspected frequently.

We must now consider in what way the second can mitigate the shock on a falling leader and on his rope. It has been suggested that he can take in loose rope as the leader falls. This might be effective if the fall started as a gradual slide, but a moment's consideration will show that the attempt has no chance of success in the event of a clear fall and is almost certain to result in complete loss of control of the rope. An unobstructed heavy body falls sixteen feet in the first second and forty-eight feet in the next. The second's only chance is to brace himself firmly and hold on to the leader's rope. If once the rope begins to run through his fingers he can have little hope of recovering control. If he attempts to use his hands as a brake he will burn and lacerate them to such an extent as to make his efforts of no avail. It has been proposed that the second should wear special gloves for this purpose and should arrange the rope so as to use body friction as well. This is certainly the most hopeful way of solving the problem, for a gradual braking action will absorb energy and greatly relieve the tension on both rope and leader. It can be shown by calculation that the conversion of the energy of a ten-stone man falling through fifty feet would not result in the liberation of an excessive amount of heat if it were properly distributed. Interested readers can be recommended to study the practical methods of Mr K. Tarbuck* along these lines. He claims to be able, by his method, to check the fall of a leader without damage to either leader or second. Mr Tarbuck regards the conventional indirect belay as unsound. He uses nylon rope.

The above discussion assumes that the second man uses the body belay for the leader's rope. Even if the leader's rope does not break he may suffer a severe shock, mainly on his ribs, with a possibility of grave internal injuries, unless there is some method of braking to supplement the natural elasticity of the rope. In severe Alpine rock climbs the leader often uses some

* See *Rucksack Club Journal*, 1947, p. 234; *Wayfarers' Journal*, 1947, p. 50.

form of wide, strong, closely-fitting body-belt which helps to distribute the shock. A triple bowline waist loop (bowline tied on the doubled rope) will serve as a substitute.

It may also be advisable for the leader to secure his waist loop by another over one shoulder. If he falls upside-down this will prevent him from slipping out of his waist loop.

I cannot, think, however, that the indirect belay is applicable in all cases without discrimination. There is a tendency to assume a suitable arrangement of stances and belays that is seldom found on many rock formations which provide both sound and difficult climbing. There, it may be wise to use the direct belay and, if at all possible, to shorten the intervals between successive anchorages. A direct belay can provide additional friction, but can seldom be used for a gradual braking action on the leader's rope in the event of a fall. It is rather surprising that some climbing engineer has not yet offered an efficient braking device for use in association with a direct belay.

Good belaying should never be accepted as a palliative for bad climbing. The leader simply must not fall. If he, with his greater responsibility, takes an undue risk, he is not entitled to pass it on to the other members of his party. He ought to have a second who can back him up in a tight corner on a difficult climb, but then the second is almost a potential leader and would enable the former to use as short a run-out of rope as possible at a difficult place. There can be no fixed rule about it. It may be far safer for a first-class leader to use a long run-out in order to reach a perfect belay, particularly if the rest of the party are of mediocre ability.

The undiscriminating use of the indirect belay is all too likely to jeopardise the whole party if the leader falls. The second may often be caught off his guard and pulled out of balance, so that he loses control of the rope and allows the leader to fall to the full extent of the rope. Even if the rope does not break the leader may be injured or helpless, and the second, owing to the drag of the leader's rope, may be unable to move. In order to avoid this the second should tie on to his belay, using the rope which runs out to the leader. He then belays the leader in the usual way, using the body belay. If an accident happens and control of the leader's rope is lost, leaving the latter hanging at the end of his rope, the weight of the leader will come on to the belay directly and leave the second free to attempt a rescue by some other means. Such means are described in a later chapter, when discussing the method used for rescue from a crevasse (Alpine technique).

A brief account of one or two accidents which have actually taken place may serve to illustrate the points which have been discussed. No names are given, and the reader will draw his own conclusions. On one occasion I was the third member of a party on a severe rock climb where we had just completed a pitch of ninety feet. As the next and final pitch was little over ten feet I was, for the moment, a spectator coiling a rope. The leader was in a hurry to finish and he did not shorten his rope. He was held on an indirect belay, and the shock of his fall jerked the rope through the fingers of the second, who was dragged back against the belay after all the rope had run out. My spare rope was very useful. Fortunately, the leader had slid down steep slabs for the greater part of the run-out of over ninety feet. He was able to tie on the spare rope and co-operate in being rescued. The hands of the second were badly lacerated. We were lucky to get off so lightly. A direct belay on a short rope would have been perfectly satisfactory, as the leader rebounded from a platform at that level.

I remember another occasion when the leader fell outwards from a chimney, bounded off a ledge and fell down a wall for over 100 feet. His second had him on an indirect belay, was dragged forward and was left hanging, head downwards, over the wall, the rope breaking between first and second. Another party was near at hand and rescued the second. No other anchor could have been used. This illustrates the possible plight of the second man. In yet another case a leader came off on a severe climb and was held by his second, who was using the indirect belay. The leader was lucky, somewhat bruised, but able to climb up again. The second was badly burned on the hands and on the back of the neck. His condition was so bad that it was only with the greatest of difficulty that the leader was able to rescue the second and get him off the hill.

On a horizontal traverse the consequences of a fall, though exceedingly unpleasant as regards bruises, are much less serious, for there is not such a severe strain on the rope. It can be shown that the strain is almost independent of the horizontal length of rope which has run out. Here the risk is equal, as between the first and last man of the party. It is not advisable to take a novice on a climb involving a very difficult and exposed traverse, unless he can be placed between two experienced climbers.

There is yet another method by which the leader can protect himself on a severe pitch. He may be able to use belays as he passes them, either to secure himself while he is resting in an otherwise precarious position or as a safeguard while he advances. In the latter case he may untie and thread his rope behind a chockstone in a crack, or get the same result by the

Running Belay

use of his rope sling and a snap link. By using a *piton* or peg which, it is to be hoped, will be removed later on by his second, he may be able, on an unknown climb, to explore in safety until he has found the crucial holds to which he could not otherwise have ventured to trust himself. There is no justification for a leader to make use of *pitons* on an established route in order to compensate for his own deficiencies.

The use of the Running Belay for the leader is especially valuable when an exposed and difficult traverse completes a severe pitch to a secure anchorage. Sometimes a rope sling may serve the purpose, over a good spike belay, but careful consideration must always be given to the direction from which the shock would come on the belay in the event of a fall. The strain on the second will come in an upward direction, and he may not be so anchored that he can meet it. The strain on the rope may be greatly increased according to the acuteness of the angle of flexure at the running belay, and this would also apply to any rope loop which is used, or any snap-link.

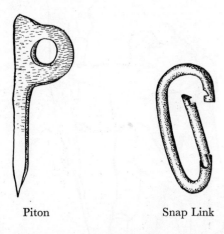

Piton   Snap Link

It would be out of place and would occupy too much space to discuss the general question of the propriety of the use of artificial aids and safeguards in British rock climbing. In an emergency, caused, for instance, by a minor accident or the sudden onset of bad weather, the use of *pitons* may clearly be desirable to facilitate the safe retreat of the party. On a new route the use of a single *piton* may make all the difference at the crux, and subsequent climbers may, with better knowledge, be able to do without it. The use of a whole string of *pitons* can never be justified on a British, sporting climb. It may be otherwise in the Alps, where guides must earn a precarious living by

EASTER ON THE MAMORES

taking all sorts and sizes of clients over dangerous places where they would be utterly unable to venture by themselves. When such safeguards have been employed without discrimination by foreign amateur climbers the results have been a number of spectacular ascents by the experts and an even greater toll of accidents amongst their less skilled successors.

NOTE ON THE STRENGTH OF CLIMBING ROPE

The British Mountaineering Council has recently issued a specification for climbing rope made of natural fibres (hemp or manila), which is mainly based on British Standard Specifications, but also includes other properties, laying particular emphasis on stretch and elastic recovery. For nylon rope there is, as yet, no agreed specification, but a forecast is made of desirable requirements. The following are approximate figures for the different weights of manila and nylon ropes which are commonly in use for climbing.

	Lbs./100 ft.	Circumference inches	Ultimate strength lbs.
Manila, full weight	$5-5\frac{1}{2}$	—	2,600
,, three-quarters	$3\frac{3}{4}$	1·25	1,850
,, half (line)	$2\frac{1}{2}$	—	1,250
Nylon, medium	$2\frac{1}{2}$	1·05	2,000
,, quarter	$1\frac{1}{7}$	·63	900

The stretch requirements for manila ropes include an ultimate extension of $12\frac{1}{2}$ per cent at breaking point and an extension of $6\frac{1}{4}$ per cent at one-quarter of break-loading, $4\frac{1}{2}$ per cent is non-recoverable. For nylon rope a stretch of 35–40 per cent at breaking point would be expected.

The behaviour of a rope under shock-loading cannot be predicted from the above figures, partly because load and extension are not in proportion and the rope does not behave like an elastic solid, but also because ultimate stresses due to shock waves have not been sufficiently studied.

An empirical formula has, however, been proposed which is alleged to give reasonably approximate results for the maximum, instantaneous tension under shock loading when the upper end of the rope is secured in a rigid manner. As may be expected, this tension is much reduced with a rope which has good stretching properties.

The formula for a full-weight manila rope, where the falling weight is 150 lbs., falling through a height of h feet, the length of rope undergoing stretch being l feet, gives the maximum tension as T lbs. weight.

$$T = 300 + 3,400 \, h/l$$

It is clear that the h/l ratio is of crucial importance, and if this is anywhere near unity the value of T is greatly in excess of the ultimate strength of the rope. It has also been proved that the insertion of a spring attachment just below the point of suspension will reduce the final value of T by as much as 30 per cent if the spring can furnish an additional extension of 15 per cent of the length of the rope.

For a medium weight nylon rope the constant 3,400 is replaced by the number 1,440. Even in this case the ultimate strength of the rope can be exceeded in certain circumstances, but the result is much better, owing to the extra large stretch of the rope. This has another result, in the form of considerable, vertical oscillations or waves after the shock, which may cause serious abrasion of the rope against any sharp edge of rock.

The above considerations suggest that, when the angle of the pitch being climbed is not near the vertical, as for instance on a steep, severe slab, there may well be sufficient friction available to justify the use of a direct belay for the second where there is a good one available but no corresponding satisfactory stance.

G

DESCENT

On British hills, where there is always an easy way down, we tend to neglect the technique of descending difficult rocks: on Alpine rock peaks there is usually no easy way and we may be forced to descend them. Even if we do not climb outside of Britain we may be faced with the same problem if we get stuck during an attempt on a new route, or if we are forced to retreat from a difficult position by the onset of bad weather or by a minor accident. If we have mastered the technique of descent, which is simply a matter of training and experience, we can retreat with confidence and in safety. Many accidents have been caused by incompetence and neglect, so far as this branch of climbing is concerned. The terrors of descending difficult rocks are partly imaginary and will disappear with practice. Some kinds of pitches are actually easier to descend than to climb up. This is often true of chimneys.

Wherever the difficulties are not too great one should face outwards. In so doing one does not feel as secure as when facing the rock and clinging to handholds. In the latter position, however, the extra security is static and often strained in character. When facing outwards one can see the next move, plan ahead and move continuously. That is dynamic security. The hands should be kept as low as possible. On more difficult rocks it is often possible to move downwards from a sideways position, getting the best of both worlds, so to speak. This may be very good for chimneys. Walls and face climbs are most difficult to descend, but the sideways position is helpful, and it is usually not too difficult to change the feet and face the other way when necessary. One should learn this useful art when climbing up, for it is no more difficult when descending. Neat footwork is especially useful on the descent.

Unless one is highly competent it is unwise to descend difficult rocks which one has not previously ascended, at least once. It may appear simple in the guide book, but one cannot expect to be able to identify and make use of all the small holds on a rock face during a descent unless one knows the feel of the climb beforehand from actual experience. Comparatively short sections of vertical cliff may present insuperable difficulties for a first descent and may yet be easily climbed by utilising one or two undercut fingerholds, or a combination of a very small foothold and a press-handhold just beneath a slight overhang. One solution of the difficulty is to lower a man on the rope, let him climb up again and persuade him to lower the others and finally climb down himself with the aid of his new-found knowledge. This is not guide-book knowledge, but acquired skill and tactile memory: it resides in the balance, finger tips and soles of the feet. The physiologists sometimes call it the *proprioceptive* sense, a sense of the relation of the parts of the body to each other, which is essential to balanced movement.

It is unnecessary to consider the problems of descent in detail. The motions of ascent are reversed; the maximum use must be made of friction. If motion is kept under control by friction gravity becomes an ally, and descent can be made an almost continuous succession of short moves, where no overhangs require to be negotiated. Thus, it is usually not difficult to descend steep slabs, as it is always possible to slide down the last few inches or more to a hold. Where there is any loose rock on a face great care should be exercised by everyone during the descent. The rope may dislodge stones on to the lower members of the party.

Security measures are practically the same for descending as for climbing, but the leader goes down last without assistance from the rope. The most experienced of the others will go first as pathfinder, under the direction of the leader if necessary. If a pitch is too difficult for the leader to climb down without assistance he must descend on the doubled rope. This *Roping Down* procedure should be learnt by all rock climbers. It is very much used in the Alps as a time-saver on long rock climbs. In the Chamonix district, for instance, the usual method of traversing the Grand and Petit Dru involves a long series of descents on the doubled rope, with convenient, fixed iron rings where necessary. Harold Raeburn, one of the pioneers of guideless climbing in the Alps, says in his book, *Mountaineering Art*, that roping down is unnecessary on this traverse. I cannot speak from experience about the Drus, but have found many other fixed rings on Alpine rock peaks where roping down was not really necessary. It is only needed for emergencies in British climbing, but the method, being simple and easily learnt, ought to be known and occasionally practised by all rock climbers.

A doubled rope or line is used, hanging from a fixed rock anchor which has no sharp edges, and where the rope will not jam after tension has been applied, as it must later be recovered by pulling a loose end from underneath. As this is not always possible it is better to use a separate loop of rope over the anchor or belay, through which to thread the doubled rope. The loop will not be recovered afterwards. Better cut it long enough to be able to use it double over the belay, so that the doubled rope is not jammed between loop and rock. Much time is saved if each member of the party ropes down, the weaker members being secured as well by the climbing rope, if a separate line is used for roping down.

One descends in a sitting position, facing the rock. The doubled rope comes down in front of the climber between his legs, is passed under and round one thigh (usually the right one), up in front across the chest, over the opposite shoulder and either down the back or round the neck and down in front. If the right leg is used the left hand grasps the rope from the belay at face level, and the right hand grasps the descending free rope. The climber can easily control the speed of descent by releasing rope with movements of the right hand. This is the safest and slowest method. If the rope passing upward from the thigh is merely passed through the crook of the right elbow then both hands can grasp the rope from the belay, and elbow motion controls the speed of descent in a freer and easier manner, though not so safely for a novice. Whatever method is used the climber should

Roping Down
Note dotted lines for alternative method

steady himself with outstretched feet against the rock face and make use of all the available holds. Needless to say, the doubled rope must be long enough to reach a safe stance below.

Roping down is a very dubious policy in descending an unknown face of rock, unless one is satisfied that there is only one impossible pitch and that the rest of the descent is feasible. If there are no natural belays it may be necessary to insert a *piton* into a crack in the rock, from which to suspend the rope loop. If there is only a short, awkward section the others can easily be lowered by the leader, who can often hang the doubled climbing rope over the belay, without unroping himself, and so descend past the difficulty, using both hands to hold the doubled rope. Practise the art of roping down on easy places to begin with, where there is no great drop. You will not then be alarmed if you spin on the rope whilst hanging freely.

BAD WEATHER,
WET AND GREASY ROCKS, ICE

Nailed boots are best for wet rock. Although stockinged feet grip well the feet become numb, with consequent loss of both sensation and security. The hands must also be protected, for which mittens are a great help. The worst kind of wet rock is that which grows a film of lichen. This becomes very slimy and greasy. Where there is vegetation on rock ledges it is loosened by wet, although it may have been quite feasible to use it when dry for swarming over a mantelshelf. It is no use saying that one should never climb on such rocks. Many excellent and sporting routes on British crags have short sections of this nature. Adequate practice will enable one to acquire a safe technique for the purpose. We must accept the rocks as the natural operations of geological processes present them to us. These considerations apply in equal measure to Alpine rock peaks, where unsound and shattered rock is exceedingly common on the loftiest buttresses and ridges. There is only one reliable method of dealing with unsound rock. Learn to recognise places which are suspect and test every hold before putting your weight on it. That does not mean pulling the hold out altogether. Many holds are sound enough under a straight downward pressure, but unsound for a pull from underneath, as there is nearly always an outward component in such a pull. One should, therefore, avoid pulling up with the arms on such rock but use press-down holds wherever possible. All this cannot be learned without much practice, which cannot be obtained on the well gardened and tested, standard routes. This is an essential element in the education of a rock climber who intends to pioneer new routes.

Wind is another factor which may increase the difficulty of rock climbs. The only plan is to avoid face climbs in a high wind. The chilling effect is as dangerous as the force of the wind. Rock climbing is still possible, and often fascinating in winter, when there is some snow or ice on the ledges. Then one should stick to the easier routes and an ice-axe should be used. It is awkward to carry, but it must always be securely held. On the whole, it is a nuisance when hung on the wrist by a sling.* It is often very useful as a prop when descending rocks of moderate difficulty, facing outwards. When the rocks are glazed with ice they should be left alone, as being too dangerous. A little snow on the ledges does not matter so much. This is further discussed when dealing with the climbing technique for snow and ice.

KINDS OF ROCK

The climber should aim at getting experience of many different kinds of rock. The standard routes on Lakeland crags, and generally, but not always, on Welsh crags, are on very sound rock. The Cuillins of Skye are composed of a very rough and sound, tertiary lava called gabbro, so sound as to inculcate bad habits of stretching up and trusting to arm pulls, but dykes of trap rock occur in many places which are not nearly as sound. Ben Nevis offers excellent prophyrite in many places, but unsound trap rock in others. Glencoe offers a similar variety. Granites vary a good deal. On Rosa Pinnacle, in Arran, the rock is magnificent and rough, but elsewhere the granite is not nearly so good. Cairngorm and Lochnagar granite weathers badly into rounded holds, and grows a patina of lichen which becomes slimy and difficult in wet weather. The great mass of

---

* Some climbers find that a light, rope sling, about three or four feet long, is both safe and useful.

the Scottish Highlands is composed of metamorphic schist which, when it forms bold cliffs, offers very few holds and even fewer belays. Schistose cliffs are usually either easy or impossibly difficult. They tend to develop overhangs and thin horizontal ledges. In the north-west of Scotland little known but very interesting climbing can be obtained on any of three superimposed geological formations; the oldest of British rocks, Lewisian gneiss, at the bottom; a rough, red Torridon sandstone above it and Cambrian quartzite on top. The Torridon sandstone forms great walls of cliff, very like tiers of masonry. It is the most difficult of all good, British climbing rock, usually perfectly firm, but offering only rounded holds and hardly any belays.

What determines the suitability of rock for climbing purposes is not so much the chemical composition but the texture and jointing, and especially the lie of the bedding planes. For easy climbing these planes should slope downwards towards the mountain and away from the climber. He thus climbs over their sharp edges without great difficulty, even though the general inclination of the face is very steep. The opposite kind of slope resembles that of the roof tiles of a house and offers much more difficulty with a lower gradient. All rocks, even igneous ones, have some system of three dimensional joint planes, not necessarily at right angles to each other. Some interest in the geological structure of mountains and a natural gift for observing these details will stand a climber in good stead if he is looking out for new rock routes in unknown mountain country.

SUMMING UP

This chapter may be fitly concluded by a few general remarks which apply to a party engaged on a serious rock climb. Some of these, although mere commonsense, are apt to be neglected.

(1) The leader should see that all equipment is in order before the start. This includes reserves of food and clothing, torch and spare rope.

(2) It is often better to face a night's exposure in safety than to court an accident by proceeding. One should keep the vital organs warm and move the limbs at intervals.

(3) A difficult rock climb is no place for one who is unfit or

unwell. The leader must not attempt what he has good reason to suspect may be beyond him, as judged by his climbing form and the conditions of weather and rock on the day in question.

(4) One expert should not take two novices on a very difficult route.

(5) Many accidents occur on moderate rocks after the tension is over. Keep alert. Do not split up the party until all are on easy ground.

(6) Do not hesitate to retreat in good time, so long as a way is available and within the powers of the party, if the leader has any doubt of his ability to complete the climb.

(7) Evidence of someone having been on a route before (e.g. nail scratches) is no proof that a feasible route exists.

(8) Wear the rope, even on moderate rocks, if the least skilled member needs it. That preserves morale, prevents accidents, and may even save time!

(9) Large parties are usually a danger or a cause of delay and exposure to cold and falling stones. The same holds good for two parties on the same climb.

(10) If 1, 2, 3 are listed in order of competence the correct order for an ascent is 1, 2, 3, for descent 2, 3, 1 and for a traverse 1, 3, 2.

(11) Don't dislodge stones. In loose gullies, especially when descending, let there be only one small party with its members close together.

(12) Test all holds and belays before using. Prefer press holds to arm pulling.

CHAPTER VII

SNOW AND ICE CLIMBING

ALTHOUGH it is often possible to climb snow-covered hills in North Wales and Cumberland the experience obtainable there cannot hope to compare with what is available for months during a normal winter on the higher Scottish hills, either as regards extent of snow, variety of conditions of snow and ice, or real approximation to the snow and ice problems of the high Alps. In this chapter we shall discuss snow and ice craft, as applicable to Scottish hills.

Snowfall on the higher hills, not a mere sprinkling but sufficient to offer difficulties to the climber, can be met at most times of the year except for about three or four months in summer. Serious snow difficulties are unusual before December, and there may be none at New Year. All except north faces and corries may be nearly clear by the end of March. That is unusual, but it all depends on the winter's weather. At the other extreme there may be brief storms and blizzards at the height of summer, so that reserves of clothing are necessary at all times.

Many types of snow surface are encountered on Scottish hills —deep, powder snow; the same covered with light, breakable crust; deep, wet snow; half compacted snow where steps can be made by kicking with the toes; very hard snow, on which the boot makes no impression; and all varieties of ice, varying from hard-frozen material which still retains air space to the dense, solid, black, brittle ice, formed directly from water trickling over rocks and freezing as it flows. This is the hardest type. As it is also brittle the art of cutting steps in it with the ice axe is both a strenuous and a skilled occupation. An intermediate stage, still retaining some air-space, is tough, glutinous and awkward to cut. Such tough snow-ice appears to be formed in a moist climate. It is most unusual in the Alps.

EQUIPMENT AND ITS USE

Even when steps can be kicked up a snow slope it is advisable that every member of the party should carry an ice axe, and, whenever the slope is really steep, that the party should be roped together. There are many opinions about the best form and dimensions of the ice axe. The shaft should be of fairly straight-grained, tough wood, usually ash. The length depends on the climber's stature. An ice axe is used for more than one purpose. For step cutting on hard ice on steep slopes a short axe is easier to use. As a steadying safeguard when traversing narrow ridges, or on rocks partly covered with snow, a longer axe is more useful. When glissading down long snow slopes in an erect position the long axe is best. A good compromise for a man five feet six inches tall would be thirty-four inches to thirty-six inches from head of axe to end of steel spike. For such an axe the length of the pick should be about seven inches, only slightly curved downwards at the end, and the length of the adze four and a half inches. The shaft should be of oval section, so that it will not turn round in the hand when cutting steps. The head should be of tough, mild steel, hard enough but not brittle, as it is sure to strike a

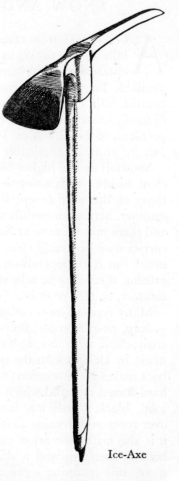

Ice-Axe

rock some time. Spike and ferrule ring are best separate. A sling for wrist attachment is useful, made of some strong, woven material. This is useful for carrying at occasional difficult places on rocks. It is better not to fix any ring or screws on the shaft, as is sometimes done when the sling has a sliding ring attached. A practical method is to use a cord as long as the axe with a wrist loop. This may prevent accidental bodily injuries during a slip. It is good to train oneself to scramble over rocks whilst retaining the axe in one hand. An axe can be very useful as a forward steady, when descending moderate, snow-covered rocks, frozen turf and so on. Other methods of carrying an axe whilst climbing difficult rocks can be devised—on a small loop of line attached to waist, on the rucksack, etc.—but security is essential.

For severe winter climbing on steep ice and icy rock it is a great help to carry an additional short axe. The author uses a slater's hammer with shortened shaft and shortened hammer, of the following approximate dimensions—length of shaft thirteen inches to fifteen inches, length of pick six inches, shortened hammer head two inches to three inches.

SNOW SLOPES

The correct way to climb difficult snow and ice can be learned on steep, open snow slopes, but not too steep to begin with. Open snow slopes do not, in general, lie at an angle exceeding forty-eight degrees. It is wrong to take the novice, as a subordinate member of a roped party, on very difficult winter climbs. He may become timid and adopt a posture of clinging to the slope. Climbing steep snow or ice is rather like climbing a steeplejack's ladder. The jack does not cling to the ladder with bent arms—a fatiguing and ill-balanced posture. Instead of that he keeps his arms straight and walks up erect, hanging slightly outwards, but with little strain on the arms, which slide along the trams. No illustration is an exact parallel. The points to note are balance and mobility.

On steep snow and ice one may slip *downwards*: when one falls it takes place *upwards* against the slope. The slip is what one must guard against, and there is only one reliable method. Keep the arms, considered as extended by means of the ice axe, without strain, at all times ready to correct any momentary lack of balance or the beginnings of a slip. That is all they have to do. Keep the centre of gravity above the base line joining the feet. It is a small but sufficient base, from which all movements must be made. This demands an erect position, with as little bending at knees or hips as may be absolutely necessary to preserve flexibility. This rule holds good, as far as possible, for any kind of climbing on snow and ice, whether one is ascending, traversing, descending or glissading. Avoid all tendency, from fear or misplaced caution, to lean inwards towards the slope. The proper use of the ice axe, apart from cutting steps or belaying a moving member, is as a steadying arm or lightly used prop against the slope above one—not as a prop below or a tie above. This avoids tension or cramp of the muscles, and makes for flexibility, alertness and security. It is best learned on short slopes, not too steep at first, where unroped practice is safe if there is a good run-out of soft snow below, should one chance to slip. In positions of greater difficulty the ice-axe may be used properly as a tie with the pick secured above, but if erect, balanced movement is already habitual, the harder problems become much easier.

Open snow slopes can usually be climbed by kicking steps into them. The ladder of steps should go straight up the slope, as a rule, and the interval between steps should not be too great for the shortest man of the party. When the snow becomes harder the need for cutting steps can still be avoided by zig-zagging and kicking sideways. If there is any tendency to slip, the ice-axe should be driven in slightly above one, using the spike as a steady against the slope. Additional security and a resting place can be obtained by cutting an extra large step, or 'soup plate', at the corners of the zig-zag.

Snow Slope

As the slope steepens the party will be roped together, as for rock climbing, but all moving together, each man carrying a single loop of rope in the hand and watching the man in front, but not impeding or jerking his movements. Each man keeps his axe ready to fix in the snow, for use as a belay for the rope in the unlikely event of a slip. This is the only practicable method on long snow slopes, which are occasionally encountered in Scotland and frequently in the Alps. It saves vital time and makes for alertness and team work in the party. For belaying in snow the axe is thrust in deeply, somewhat above the climber, vertically downwards, and the rope is passed round the shaft at snow level. If the slope is extremely steep the axe shaft should be somewhat between the vertical and a line at right angles to the slope. The use of the body belay and the practice of tying on to the belay axe with a knot are both unnecessary and inadvisable.

A different situation arises if the snow is in bad condition, either dry, loose and powdery or wet and slushy. The surface layer does not then adhere properly to an underlying, hard, frozen layer, and there may be a danger of the top layer peeling off the underlayer, taking the party with it in a snow slide or avalanche. Only experience will show when the danger exists. It is common in the Alps and less likely in Scotland. Avoid such slopes, if possible. As a rule, they are only found in steep gullies, but they may occur as open, steep slopes, especially when a

Security on
Steep Snow

partial thaw follows a heavy snowfall. They may only occur in patches. When they must be climbed, security precautions should be taken. The leader, belayed by the rest of the party on sound snow, proceeds alone, removes loose snow and cuts steps into the firm layer underneath. He then brings up the other members, one at a time, from a secure, basin-like stance, with the rope secured over a well-sunk ice-axe. This takes a lot of time. It is often possible for the leader to proceed by kicking for twenty to thirty steps before digging out his security stance. It all depends on the conditions. Always, the belaying axe should be deeply driven into firm snow, and the rope to the others should pass over the shaft at ground level, so as to exert as little leverage on it as possible. Do not take a turn of the rope round the shaft. This would increase the strain on the shaft and the rope.

The procedure is the same where the second safeguards the leader. It differs from rock climbing practice for several reasons: (1) The rope can always run perfectly over an ice-axe shaft without fraying. (2) The position of stance and belay can always be selected, so that the belay is directly above the stance. (3) The main dangers to be avoided are those of pulling out the ice-axe and of the collapse of the leader's stance. These should form one unit. It is better and safer that the shock of a falling and sliding leader should be taken at ground level on a well secured axe than that it should exert a much greater leverage on the body of a climber who is only standing on the surface. If the latter is tied to his ice-axe as a belay it is obvious that the axe must be considerably above him, for the shock to come on the axe at surface level. If the strain comes too high up on the shaft of the axe there is danger of the shaft breaking or being pulled out. This main problem of security on snow and ice slopes has been dealt with at what may appear to be a disproportionate length, as rock climbing practice has tended to induce an altogether unwarranted belief in the all-round merits of the body belay. This does not hold good, as a rule, for snow and ice climbing.

GULLIES

Great difficulties are unlikely to be met on an open snow slope, but it is well to be prepared. Snow-ice* can lie at much steeper angles in a gully. Then the leader must cut steps all the way. It may be quicker to cut a ladder straight up, but the cutting position is easier for a zig-zag staircase. There are two further advantages. The chips from the steps will not constantly bombard the other members of the party. The zig-zag ladder will be much easier to descend, if a retreat is forced upon the party by unforeseen circumstances. In easy snow-ice one or two slashes with the adze will cut a good step; in really tough snow-ice many blows of the pick may be required. Seize the axe with both hands; do not swing it too far back; try to use the weapon in a balanced and rhythmic manner, so that the weight of the

* See Glossary at end of book.

axe and the blow fall at the right moment. Step-cutting may then be continued for long periods without muscular fatigue. A slight sway of the body, always in balance, will ease the work of arms and wrists. Only long, continued practice can make perfection. It all follows from an erect, balanced posture and rhythmic movement. The completed step should have a slight inward and downward slope, not too much or the steps may break away under the following members.

It takes a long time to learn to judge the different condition of the snow in varied situations and types of weather. It varies a good deal inside the same gully. There is often a hard channel in the centre, especially in late winter and spring. That is where masses of avalanche snow have slid down. It is often better to keep to one side and secure occasional anchorage by means of holds on the rocky walls, where possible. The altitude has a considerable effect, for the upper sections of the Nevis gullies are usually much harder than those on lower mountains. Where the angle is not severe and the snow is soft the weight of the climber will often compact it satisfactorily, even although he sinks in up to the knees.

Then it is quite a good plan to wriggle straight up the gully, making use of the maximum of body friction, and using arms and legs almost in the way that a swimmer does. Of course, the ice-axe must be thrust in deeply above the climber for security. The knees are very useful, although progress is rather a cold business. There is often a thin, top crust on the snow. No general rule can be given as to the safety of such snow slopes. Only experience and the compacting of the snow under pressure can serve as a guide. The expert will not be slow to give heed to any warning signs. Scottish snow is much safer in this respect than Alpine snow, but the safety does not last indefinitely when there is a heavy thaw, especially in spring time.

At the top of a gully there is often a great eave of overhanging snow, called a cornice. These may be very difficult to negotiate, so that gullies which are known to possess them should be avoided by beginners. Such gullies should always be avoided when there is a thaw, as large slices of the cornice must, sooner or later, break off and fall down the gully. Some Ben Nevis cornices may be as much as thirty feet high with an overhang exceeding ten feet. It will be appreciated that the fall of a sub-stantial part of such a cornice would sweep a party of climbers down the gully with it, not necessarily burying them, but very probably knocking them about severely, with possibly fatal results.

On most Scottish mountains there is some sort of a funnel at the top of a gully, and the cornice does not overhang all the way round, leaving, perhaps, only a short, vertical wall of snow at one corner. That is the place to seek an exit. Always get the rest of the party well secured just below the cornice. There is often a hollow lip underneath which affords secure anchorage in hard, old snow. The leader can then tackle the wall. He will need both hand and foot-holds, and may have to borrow someone's ice-axe to drive in horizontally, as an extra hold or step. The short, slater's hammer type of auxiliary axe is very useful. Climbing up the wall is then a matter of cutting holds for hands and feet and taking no undue risks. A certain amount of snow may require to be hacked away so as to make the angle easier

Surmounting a Cornice

SUMMIT CORNICE, BRAERIACH

near the top. The important thing is that the leader should be perfectly secured by the others, as cornices can always break away in slices.

A fatal error is for the leader to tackle the cornice at the end of a long run-out of rope. If he falls off he will have acquired considerable momentum when he shoots past the rest of the party, and the shock on the rope, when it tightens, may drag them all from their stances and pull out the belays. Something of this sort seems to have occurred, in April 1933, on the Castle of Ben Nevis to two English climbers of the front rank, the leader being badly injured and his second killed, as there were steep rocks some distance below.

On a few occasions cornices have been overcome by tunnelling operations. That may take many hours of hard work. On one occasion, at least, the party retreated and returned next day, when they completed the tunnel—hardly a practicable method for everyday use! Never risk an attempt to tunnel through a cornice unless you are certain that it is composed of old, compacted snow and that the weather is good and frosty. Such an attempt on a Ben Nevis cornice in the Spring of 1949 resulted in the break-away of a huge slice, the party being swept down a steep gully with one fatal injury and another lesser casualty to its members.

RIDGES

Snow-covered ridges offer exhilarating, sporting and variegated routes. Ridges which are narrow and difficult as summer rock climbs are usually still more difficult, and often impossibly so, in hard, winter conditions. The chief difficulties can be discussed under three headings: a thin film of ice on the rocks, known as *verglas* in the Alps; ice or icy crust on the crest or flanks of the ridge; cornices projecting from the ridge on either or both sides. Double cornices are exceedingly uncommon on Scottish ridges.

Very little need be said about *verglas*. It is an exceedingly dangerous condition, as the film is too thin for steps to be cut in it, and usually consists of dense, black ice. It is found when ridges have been stripped of snow by a thaw wind, wetted with rain and refrozen. Steep rocks and ridges are best avoided under

H

such conditions. If the rocks are only partially iced and are mainly covered with snow-ice, well frozen to the rock, careful climbing and strict security measures, using rock belays, are essential.

On very narrow ridges, like the Cuillins in Skye, the crest may be a mass of ice, where there are *gendarmes* or rock towers which are usually climbed over in summer. The only alternative is then to descend and traverse the flank of the ridge. This may involve a lot of difficult step cutting in ice before the crest can be regained. In difficult spring conditions this is commonly found on the ridges of Ben Nevis. The rocks are often thickly encased in frost crystals, which must be cut away before holds and belays can be excavated. Such conditions can make the Tower and Observatory Ridges of Nevis exceedingly difficult and exciting expeditions, suitable only for a team of experts.

Cornices are a problem, only on very narrow ridges such as the Cuillin, Aonach Eagach and a few places on other mountains. Double cornices are said to have been found on the Aonach Eagach (Glencoe), but I have not experienced them there myself. Wherever there is reason to suspect the existence of a cornice the party must keep well back from the corniced edge. They may have to get off the crest altogether and traverse below it on the other side. The important thing to remember is that, if the cornice does break away, the line of fracture may be as far back as where the line of the steep snow slope below the cornice, when produced upwards, would cut the top snow surface. That may be some distance behind the overhanging edge. The safe procedure is always to anchor one member of the party in an absolutely secure position while the others are moving. Scottish snow is tough, except under conditions of a spring thaw, but precautions ought to be taken. If someone does fall through the cornice unexpectedly it may be necessary for the next person on the rope to jump down the other side of the ridge in order to save him.

Steep ridges can also be difficult after a considerable fall of dry, powder snow, which has not adhered to the old snow or rock beneath. Knowledge of the summer rock structure will be a good guide as to whether this powder snow is likely to slide off or not, but proper belaying measures are always essential in such places. A typical case is the Eastern Traverse round the Great Tower on Ben Nevis. Snow builds up in winter above some lower ledges until it lies against the upper cliff at a very steep and terrifying angle. Unless the snow is powdery and uncompacted it is, however, usually safe. The ledges form a good, incut base.

Traversing easy ridges under snow conditions is splendid practice for acquiring good snow technique. The party may not require to be roped at all. In most other cases, where the use of rope is advisable, the party can still move all together, and proper security measures can be taken, just as for narrow ridges on rocks. Sometimes rock holds can be used, but usually the ice axe can find a lodgment between the rocks.

STEEP ICE

Ridges and gullies vary considerably in gradient and are liable to contain vertical steps. If there is a sufficient stretch of gully at a gentle angle below the steep pitch, a winter snowfall may fill up the pocket completely until no pitch remains. For this reason No. 2 Gully on Ben Nevis offers a good, difficult winter climb, with no severe section or much alteration in gradient throughout, although it has one severe pitch in summer, when free of snow. Gullies can be more difficult in early winter, before there has been enough snowfall, for the same reason. Steep pitches on ridges are seldom or never marked in this way by accumulations of snow. There is too much wind. That is why ridges are usually much more difficult in snow conditions. The difficulty is at a maximum when the ridge has been partially cleared of snow by a thaw, followed by a spell of frosty weather. Conditions are even worse if a dry snowfall covers the icy surface.

All sorts of intermediate conditions are found according to the prevalent type of winter. It is therefore an essential part of winter climbing technique in Scotland to learn how to deal with steep ice. A common and very beautiful condition is encountered when all the rocks are heavily plastered with fog or frost crystals. This condition is more awesome than menacing, for the crystals are often easily detachable, leaving clean rock holds underneath. Fog crystals grow by vapour condensation on cold rocks, building up against the flow of the prevailing wind. They are normal on Scottish mountains in winter and may attain to huge dimensions.

Let us consider a steep ice pitch in a gully. The angle may not be far short of vertical. Hard snow-ice can lie in Scottish gullies at angles up to fifty-five degrees or so. I have verified this on different mountains with a clinometer.* The clear ice may lie at any angle, as it has been built up after a thaw by a trickle of water. Every safeguard is necessary when climbing steep ice, as there is seldom enough depth to get a satisfactory belay, even with the pick of the axe. The best plan is to bring up the rest of the party to the highest good anchorage where the axes can be deeply fixed for a secure belay. They should all reinforce each other, so that, if the leader falls and pulls out or breaks one ice-axe, the others will hold. A body belay can be used, but it offers no advantage as compared with the direct belay over the axe. The leader will find that the short axe is exceedingly useful. It gives him a secure hold with one axe whilst he is cutting holds, often above his head, with the other.

Cutting up steep ice is a very slow business. Steps and holds must be well fashioned and well spaced at very short intervals. The position is trying, and the leader may have to retire more than once for a rest, or the lead be changed. Blows of the axe have little force above the head of the leader, and ice is often brittle. Rhythm and balance are keys to success. If the pitch is a long one—over twenty feet—ice *pitons* could be inserted for security. I have found that nine to twelve-inch lengths of half-inch (outside diameter) steel conduit tube, such as is used for enclosing electric wiring, buffed sharp at one end, make excellent pegs for the purpose. They can be driven well in at a suitable angle, not too far off the vertical, and the rope can be slipped through a removable ring hanging on the peg. If one is very particular it is easy to drill a couple of holes opposite each other near the blunt end of the tube, through which a stout cross-wire can be fitted to prevent the ring sliding upwards and

* *Snow Angles.*—Zero Gully, Ben Nevis, April 1936. Below great ice-pitch 40° rising to 47°. Upper part below an ice-pitch, uniformly 56° for a long way. Final section under summit 51°. Centre post of Coire Ardair 42° low down, 48° below the basin underneath great pitch, 55° at foot of ice wall, over 70° on the wall. No one has yet climbed this wall (March 1948).

off the peg when the rope suffers a jerk. Such things are easy to carry and to replace.

A long run-out of rope may be necessary for climbing an ice-fall of this nature in a gully. The leader must finish the pitch and arrive at a secure anchorage with a good belay, either on rock or in deep, secure snow-ice, before bringing on the other members of the party. If the side walls of the gully are coated with frost crystals it is worth while to cut them away, wherever there is any prospect of discovering a crack which might serve as a belay for an ice-axe. Knowledge of the gully in summer conditions can be very useful. A leader negotiating an ice pitch must be sure of his holds and must think out his movements in advance. If he trusts entirely to one hold at any one time he cannot hope to correct a slip by grabbing something else. I have known an ice wall of fifteen feet in height which took over an hour to climb, and another case where a traverse across thirty feet of ice wall occupied nearly an hour and a half.

The same type of problem is encountered on vertical steps of a ridge, except that one is likely to be able to make more use of rock belays. One may also start up a snow slope which gradually steepens to ice, below a wall of cliff which one must circumvent. The final stage below the cliff is often broken up by outcrops of rock. The utmost use should be made of these for stances or belays. Fairly steep rocks may become coated with snow, partly thawed and refrozen, so as to yield a surface up which one may cut steps. It is a fascinating problem to convert known summer rock routes into practicable, if severe, winter climbs. So far, I know of no instance, in Scotland at least, where a winter route has been made where no summer route was known. The thing is certainly possible, for many gully pitches can be easier after a heavy winter's snowfall, but that applies to short pitches, and not to a complete route on a mountain.

It is extremely difficult for a solitary climber to check a slip on hard ice. It can only be done by immediate action. Throw yourself on your face, with pick of axe biting vertically into the ice, with all your weight on it. If the pick is sharp and it can be maintained in position you have a chance of stopping. Try it out first on a safe slope, or with someone else holding you at a rope's end.

DESCENT

Every climber should learn how to descend steep snow, and occasionally to descend short ice pitches which have already been ascended by the party. The general plan of descent is much the same as for difficult rocks. The expert descends last and his second in command acts as pathfinder, with the additional duty of seeing that any novice in the party secures himself at each stance, if the party is moving one at a time. The pathfinder must test the condition of the snow as he goes. There will be no question of persisting in a way of descent if there is any doubt about the security of the snow. This cannot, in all cases, be judged from above, and it is not sufficient to throw a stone into a gully in order to see whether it will start a snow slide or not. Less experienced parties, on this account, should either descend by the way they came up, or choose a way which is known to be safe from former experience. The first of these is the most educative plan. It is the best way to learn how to descend steep snow.

The steps used for the ascent can be utilised for the descent. If there is time available it is even better to cut a fresh staircase downwards. Every ambitious climber must learn to cut steps downhill. This involves a difficult balance and, in general, one-handed cutting. More blows will be required per step, as the force expended is less. It is usually necessary to cut downwards in a zig-zag, and it is well to cut an extra large stance at each corner. The last man must descend very carefully. It is always best to face outwards for the descent. With a zig-zag staircase it is at least possible to face sideways. Security measures are the same as for climbing up. Only in the case of a steep ice pitch would it be advisable for the last man to drive in a peg and descend with the safeguard of the rope from above, or by means of the doubled rope, using an extra length of line for the purpose. On ice pitches the party would have to face in, if using the steps constructed for the ascent, or double rope down from a peg in other cases. Such descents are only for a united team of experts. Common prudence would forbid them altogether unless the section below the ice pitch was known to be straightforward.

On a long slope of snow-ice the labour and time taken over a descent, if no steps are available, can be greatly curtailed by lowering all but the last man on the rope for short stretches, and anchoring the members securely below. Then the last man descends as safely as possible by short steps, digging in his toes and securing himself continually with the pick of his axe struck into the slope above. If the danger of a slip is less, the whole roped party can descend continuously in this way, as there is sure to be at least one pick securely fixed at all times. This applies to an experienced party and not to novices. It is not advisable if the hard slope ends lower down above a cliff. Experience, alone, will show what method is permissible, and that is why the actual descent of steep snow-ice is so necessary a part of an all-round technique.

GLISSADING

If the snow slope is not steep, is in good condition and has a perfectly gentle and easy run-out lower down, glissading (or sliding) is the quickest and most enjoyable mode of descent. Scottish snow gives, on the whole, better and more extensive practice than is available on the big Alpine peaks, where there are *bergschrunds* and *crevasses** in unexpected places. It is absolutely necessary that the final run-out should either be perfectly visible or known to be easy, as control may be lost during a fast glissade. If one glissades down a gully there should be no ice pitches, or one should be absolutely certain of being able to stop before reaching one. Neither should there be any ice-hardened avalanche runnels, where one would lose control. If the snow is too hard frozen no glissade ought to be attempted at all.

The standing glissade is far the best and easiest to control in good snow. The position is erect, with flexibility at the knees, in order to preserve balance when the surface is uneven and the speed varies accordingly. One foot has a slight lead, taking more of the weight, but the feet are kept fairly close together. Pace is regulated by digging

* See Glossary at end of the book.

Standing Glissade

in the heels for slowing up and pointing the toes downward to accelerate. The axe is not a prop for leaning on. It is used for steering, and as an emergency brake. Change of direction can usually be effected by the feet, and by altering the distribution of weight between them. Furrowed snow is difficult. Lean back slightly and use the axe a little more. Be very careful in gullies, especially if they narrow at any point, for there may be hard snow-ice at the narrows. If control is lost at such a place the climber may be flung helplessly on his back.

Sitting glissades may be possible when the snow is not good enough for a standing glissade. If the snow piles up underneath, a sideways roll will get you started again. Do not use the axe pick as a brake. Grip the shaft by the head with one hand and a bit lower down with the other. Press the spike backwards and downwards into the snow for steering or braking. Arch the body upwards between heels and axe for maximum braking power. If control is lost there is still some hope of regaining it if one turns face down and tries to brake with the full weight pressing the pick of the axe into the snow, but not too abruptly, or the axe may be wrenched sideways or lost altogether. That is another reason why axe shafts are made oval in section.

Sitting Glissade; Braking

Experience of glissading on one mountain and during one season is valuable for one's technique, but does not give all-round knowledge of possible Scottish snow conditions on other mountains or after a different kind of winter. The only safe plan is to keep the speed within control at all times. I learned this myself, with a few bruises and more good fortune, after a good many years of climbing. Roped glissading by a party is seldom satisfactory.

Remember that it is possible to start a snow slide or minor avalanche in a gully by glissading, where a slow, step-wise descent would be quite safe. The only good advice, in such a mishap, is to try and keep on the surface of the descending mass of snow. Adopting a swimming position is said to be best, but I have no personal experience of riding Scottish avalanches. If there is a gentle run-out the avalanche will come to rest of itself, but it may be much compressed and refrozen. I know of no Scottish records of climbers being buried in such cases, but I should imagine, from certain huge mounds of avalanche debris below certain gullies, that the risk is there. Dry, powder snow is not a serious hazard in Scotland. It is the wet snow avalanches, with or without falling cornices, during a heavy spring thaw, that are the real danger. Avoid gullies at such times.

Some Alpine climbers assert that Scottish avalanches are innocuous. They can be referred to the story of the 'Loss of Gaick',* when five persons were killed by an avalanche in January 1800. This avalanche came down a steep hillside during the night and destroyed the hut in which the men were sleeping. Accidents are not uncommon, however, and four people were carried down by an avalanche on an open hillside near Braemar, in January 1948. Several were detained in hospital.

* See *Guide to the Cairngorms*, p. 68.

PART III

SCOTTISH MOUNTAIN
EXPEDITIONS

WITH A SHORT, COMPARATIVE
CHAPTER ON ENGLISH ROCK CLIMBING

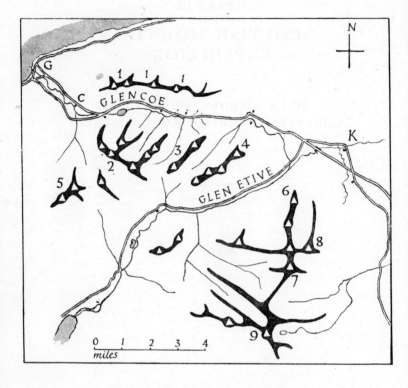

MAP A   GLENCOE AND BLACKMOUNT

	PEAKS	Height in feet
1,1,1	Aonach Eagach Ridge	3167
2	Bidean nam Bian	3766
	Ridge to N.W. goes over Stob Coire nam Beith	
	Ridge to N.E. over Stob Coire nan Lochan, and forks left to Aonach	
	Dubh and right to Gearr Aonach	
	The easterly ridge goes N.E. over Beinn Fhada	
3	Buachaille Etive Beag ridge	3,129
4	Buachaille Etive Mor ridge (climbs on N.E. peak) . . .	3,345
5	Sgor na h-Ulaidh	3,258
6	Sron na Creise	2,952
7	Clachlet	3,602
8	Meall a' Bhuiridh	3,636
9	Stob Ghabhar	3,565
K	Kingshouse Inn	
C	Clachaig Inn	
G	Glencoe Village and Hotel	

CHAPTER VIII

GLENCOE

I FIRST saw Glencoe in June 1919, when on a walking tour with a friend of my student days. We left our bicycles at Bridge of Orchy station to be forwarded to Tulloch by rail. Then we proceeded on foot along the old road by beautiful Loch Tulla and the Blackmount. Tom Lumsden was not a mountaineer, but he had a keen appreciation of the grand things of nature and delighted in hill walks over rough country. His clear and active mind derived contentment and fresh interest from the Scottish Highlands, although he was essentially a thinker in science and sociology. It was one of my regrets that I could never persuade him to take to rock climbing. Mountaineering has owed a great deal to men of his type, such as Forbes, Tyndall and many others.

We were fascinated by the noble outline of Buachaille Etive Mor, as we came down the long stretch of rough road past Black Rock cottage to Kingshouse, and even more as we continued past the Study and down the gorge of Glencoe, with the evening sunshine lighting up the Three Sisters and the cone of Stob Coire nan Lochan which, from that point of view, conceals Bidean nam Bian and dominates the wild grandeur of Glencoe. We slept at Clachaig that night, and next day, in the company of D. H. Menzies, who had just returned from climbing in the Cuillin, traversed the three high tops of Bidean. It was a perfect introduction to the mountains of Glencoe, and I have never forgotten it.

In the years which have followed I have spent numberless week-ends on these mountains. Their charm has never palled, either in summer or winter. It might be some rock-climbing problem on Buachaille Etive, some snow and ice expedition up the gullies or ridges of Bidean, some days that were failures owing to storm and rain, or simply to an ill-planned piece of exploration: yet every occasion contributed something of interest, enjoyment and permanent value. There were delightful summer camps in Glen Etive, the best of them when we used

sleeping sacks without tents, or even a wet night in sleeping sacks under one of the bridges of the new Glencoe road in the gorge: there were delightful swimming pools in the Etive, in Loch Etive, in the gorge of Glencoe where the river is always cold and clear on the hottest day of summer, or in the little loch below Clachaig by the side of the old road. And there were amusing convivial gatherings in the old Clachaig Inn before it was modernised and made attractive to the touring motorist, and many more in Kingshouse under successive landlords. All these are delightful memories of the companionship and free-masonry of the mountains.

There were not so many climbers in Glencoe in the old days, especially in the winter months. The new road, completed round about 1931, conferred many benefits on the week-end climber, but I cannot help thinking that it has also taken some good things away, indefinable though these may be. At least in the depths of a snowy winter, nature reasserts her empire for a time, and one is content to reach the summits of Buachaille and Bidean by the simplest, time-honoured ways.

The Glencoe area, now owned by the Scottish National Trust, is by far the most accessible for Scottish climbing of reasonable length, variety and difficulty. It is not to be compared with the Cuillin or Ben Nevis, but it is a very good second. Its mountains, Bidean nam Bian (3,766 ft.), Buachaille Etive Mor (3,345 ft.), and the Aonach Eagach ridge north of Glencoe (3,167 ft.), all carry a good deal of snow in winter, especially in their northern

Glencoe

and north-eastern declivities. Glencoe has the distinction of possessing the two longest and finest British gully climbs—the Chasm of Buachaille Etive Mor and the Clachaig Gully of Sgurr nam Fiannaidh, both far superior to the Waterpipe Gully in the Cuillin. Best known to English climbers are, no doubt, the Crowberry Ridge of Buachaille, the Church Door Buttress of Bidean and the moist rift of Ossian's Cave, high above Loch Triochtain.

Especially during the last quarter of a century, the merits of Glencoe as a first-class centre, both for rock-climbing and difficult winter climbing on snow and ice, have become much more widely appreciated. In this chapter we shall indicate where the easier and safer rock climbs are to be found, a matter which is often neglected or cursorily handled in guide books which are written by experts for experts. As to the more difficult expeditions, one or two will be described which, in the author's opinion, are typical of the best which Glencoe has to offer, from the point of view of mountaineering value rather than exceptional difficulty.

STRUCTURE AND GEOLOGY

The geology of the Glencoe mountains is of great interest and has much to do with their excellent climbing possibilities. Here there is a great modification, in quite a small area, of the general character of the Highland rocks, away from the usual, metamorphic, ancient schists, owing to the intrusion of subsequent igneous rocks. In Glencoe there were many successive lava flows during the Old Red Sandstone period. They were of two types, andesites which flowed freely, and subsequently the more viscous rhyolites which formed thicker beds and which now afford excellent climbing rock. This rock occurs, not only in Glencoe on the upper tiers of cliff on the west face of Stob Coire nan Lochan and on Stob Coire nam Beith, but also on Buachaille Etive Mor where it forms the best climbing rock of the district. The latest lavas are typified in the hornblende-andesite found near the summit of Bidean nam Bian. Simple mountaineers call it trap rock when they climb the Church Door Buttress of Bidean or some of the cliffs on the north-east face of Stob Coire nan Lochan.

Geologists speak of the Cauldron Subsidence of Glencoe. It is no longer a subsidence, as the rocks within the area have been more resistant to the erosive action of time than the surrounding masses. Hence they, nowadays, stand up as mountains. The area is bounded by an oval-shaped geological fault, about eight miles long by five across. Inside are the volcanic lavas, as well as some agglomerate or consolidated volcanic ash: outside are the old schistose rocks. Along the fault line is a granite intrusion, pushed up in a molten state by the subsiding core. The granite is still found on An t-Sron.

It is well, however, to remember that the present-day contours of the mountains have been developed long since the time when the foundation rocks were laid. In the tertiary period, long afterwards, there was probably a river running from Ardgour, in the west, across the present site of Loch Linnhé, through Glencoe and eastwards to Rannoch Moor. It is likely that the glen was carved out by this river, although the drainage is now divided by the watershed west of Altnafeadh. In the more recent, quaternary age there has been much glacial erosion, as elsewhere in Scotland, leaving moraines and rock-basin lakes like Loch Triochatan.

Even although the contours have been so vastly altered since the Old Red Sandstone age, it is worth while for climbers to consider that the igneous rocks then extruded now form the actual core of the Glencoe peaks and the cliffs on which they climb. The excellence of the rock depends on the composition,

BIDEAN NAM BIAN

texture and system of joints developed while the original lavas cooled. As the forces of erosion must also be guided by the original characteristics of the rocks it follows that the present-day outlines of the mountains are, to a large extent, determined by these ancient volcanic upheavals.*

EASY WAYS AND EASY ROCK CLIMBS

The Glencoe area provides excellent opportunities for climbing of all grades of difficulty, both in summer and winter conditions. The mountains and the types of rock are sufficiently variegated. Climbing is available on ridges, gullies, chimneys and faces. There is ample opportunity in winter for testing one's ability on all kinds of snow and ice, though not so good as on Ben Nevis, where the snow and ice persist later into the spring, owing to the greater height of the mountain.

Before doing any difficult rock climbing or any serious winter climbing it is well to be familiar with the appearance and lay-out of the prominent ridges, crags, gullies and corries in snowless conditions. This can usually be combined with some easy rock climbing. In fact, it ought to be. The first thing is to learn the easy ways off the mountain, in case bad weather or nightfall should overtake the party.

There are two useful, easy lines of descent from Buachaille Etive Mor. A descent to Glen Etive is started by following the ridge southwards from the cairn on Stob Dearg until it begins to bend steeply down to the right towards the next saddle. An easy scree slope runs down towards Glen Etive for a long way, but one must avoid a steep section near the bottom, either by the corrie on the left (the shortest way to the road) or, still easier, by the right. For the descent to the Glencoe road one turns right off the top ridge, making for the top of the easy shoulder opposite Altnafeadh. A more direct route towards Altnafeadh would be down the Great Gully, which offers only moderate difficulty in summer, but may be very difficult in winter. This route is not so easy as the other.

Next, one should memorise the main features of the crags facing north and east. The key landmark is that conspicuous pinnacle, the Crowberry Tower, just north of and below the

* See Prof. E. B. Bailey, *S.M.C.J.*, vol. 22, p. 116.

I

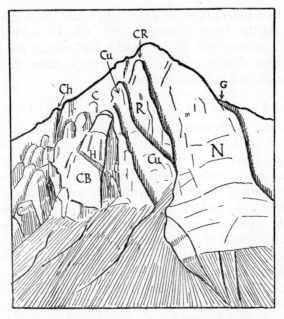

Stob Dearg, Buachaille Etive Mor

G	Great Gully	CB	Central Buttress
N	North Buttress	H	Heather Terrace (or Ledge,
CR	Crowberry Ridge		as in Glencoe Guide Book)
R	Rannoch Wall	CC	Collie's Route
CuCu	Curved Ridge	Ch	Chasm

summit. It stands out best from the Glencoe road about halfway from Kingshouse to Altnafeadh. The Tower crowns the steep mass of rock known as the Crowberry Ridge. Most eastern climbing routes converge on the Crowberry Tower. It is well to recognise it from Glen Etive also. With the help of a sketch diagram of the climbs they can all be picked out by their position relative to the Crowberry Ridge. Towards Glencoe there are in succession the long, deep Crowberry Gully, the broad, impressive North Buttress and the Great Gully. There are now quite a number of routes beyond this. In the opposite direction from Crowberry Ridge we have the Easy Gully flanked on its left by Curved Ridge, the easiest continuous rock climb on the mountain which, once climbed, can be later used as a practice route for descent. Proceeding, we come to D Gully and D Gully

Buttress, which merges on its left with a very steep, narrowing face on a broad base, traversed at mid-height by a heather terrace running steeply up to the left. This is Central Buttress which affords some good, difficult routes on the sunny side of the mountain. The main landmark on the Glen Etive face is farther south. It is a long, steep cleft, splitting the face for a height of about 1,800 feet and known as the Chasm. Any easy descent must be well to the south of the Chasm.

We may now come to close quarters with the mountain. The Curved Ridge is the best objective. The line of approach should be chosen so as to avoid any tier of rocks or steep slabs. This is not difficult, but it is advisable to locate any prominent landmarks, so that a retreat, if necessary, may be executed safely and easily. There is a little steep section at the base of Curved Ridge which is taken on the Crowberry Ridge side. This approach will give one an idea of where to start a climb on the Crowberry Ridge on another occasion, and also how to cross Crowberry Gully, if bound for North Buttress. The Curved Ridge is very steep in parts, but has good holds and belays. Its upper end is just below Crowberry Tower, and the way to the summit lies short of the Tower Gap and to the left. It is easy to find and to follow. It is a very good idea to use the Curved Ridge as a line of descent. It teaches the party how to use the rope properly without wasting too much time. Only on the steep bits should it be necessary to belay each member of the party and move one at a time.

The next climb chosen might well be North Buttress. It is a broad buttress, and several routes are possible. One must get on to it low enough, before the Crowberry Gully becomes too deep. A good route goes up a sort of ridge near the edge overlooking that gully, but the most interesting way is nearer the middle of the buttress, involving some very steep rock and good practice in short clefts and chimneys. The rock is sound and there are adequate belays.

In cold weather, when northerly winds prevail, the Glen Etive face of the mountain is more attractive. The original rock-climbing route on the mountain, Collie's Route, first done in the year 1894 by Professor Norman Collie, is interesting and fairly easy. First identify the Central Buttress, of which the lower rocks are conspicuous on the left, by reason of a vertical, streaky-looking cliff of alternately bleached and blackened rock. It is often called the Waterslide, though it is not usually wet. To its left is a sort of stepped ridge, a series of rocky buttresses one on top of the other, rather like a giant staircase. Collie's Route started on the left of the lowest buttress and then followed the crest of the ridge. It is an excellent route of moderate difficulty, but a start can also be made on the right. Choose the easiest way on the lower crag, or serious difficulty may be encountered.

There is much broken rock between Collie's Route and the Chasm. The North Wall of the Chasm gives some good sections on moderate rock, with grass and heather in between. Higher up, one can work back towards the upper part of Collie's Route. As this face of the mountain is less definite it offers good opportunities for easy route selection. The novice may also feel attracted to Sron na Creise on the opposite side of Glen Etive. On the side facing Kingshouse one can enjoy 250 feet or more of pleasant climbing on two buttresses and in two gullies, but there is some unsound rock. The Sron offers good gully climbing in snow conditions. There is one other part of the Buachaille which offers good practice. These rocks are situated opposite Altnafeadh at the western end of the mountain, and one can start at a fairly low level. They are convenient to Lagangarbh Hut (belonging to the S.M.C.). The easy ways can be picked out on the spot. They are not easy to describe in detail.

Now for Glencoe proper. One of my earliest rock climbs was the traverse of the Aonach Eagach Ridge which walls in Glencoe on the north side. The entertaining section is narrow and short, but it is good practice to try everything as it comes, including the *gendarmes* which block the ridge at the narrowest part. They can be passed on easy ground, if necessary. One impulse must be sternly repressed—to seek a way down to Glencoe before all the difficulties are well past. This applies particularly if one is going eastward, when it is necessary to get past Am Bodach, in order to make sure of an easy descent to the Glen above the Study. I ought to know something about this ridge, as E. A. M. Wedderburn and I traversed it by night, by the light of the harvest moon in September 1937. The moon chose to obscure itself behind some dense clouds as we were approaching the narrow section, so we sat down and smoked a contemplative pipe. It was a delightful excursion. As a snow expedition it can be very difficult. There is not much good rock climbing on the north side of Glencoe.

On the south side is Bidean nam Bian (3,766 ft.), the highest peak of Argyllshire, with its cluster of subordinate peaks and ridges. Before doing any rock climbing one should traverse these ridges. Starting from Clachaig, the route should be over An t'Sron (2,750 ft.), Stob Coire nam Beith (3,621 ft.), Bidean and then a choice between the eastern or northern ridges. Each has its merits. The shorter expedition crosses over Stob Coire nan Lochan (3,657 ft.), then downwards by a long ridge to Aonach Dubh (2,849 ft.), which overlooks Loch Triochatan. The best descent is from the col before reaching Aonach Dubh, by the easy Dinner Time Buttress, between two gullies, into lower Coire Beith. There is a little rock to avoid, here and there.

If one goes east from Bidean the route is longer, over Stob Coire Sgreamhach (3,497 ft.), and then sharp left over the very long ridge of Ben Fhada (3,120 ft.), the northerly nose of which overhangs the gorge of Glencoe. It should be mentioned that between Stob Coire Sgreamhach and Ben Fhada there is a col with a sharp drop just above it. This is best avoided by descending the slope on the east side before coming to the rocky descent. It is best to leave the crest and descend the easy, eastern slopes before reaching the Nose, to the boggy glen of the Larig Eilde. A descent can also be made to the valley on the left, but this should be done much earlier. Most climbers call this the Hidden Valley, as its lower end is blocked by a huge, V-shaped accumulation of boulders which conceal and isolate this charming little valley most effectively. A beautiful meadow, with a huge boulder eminently suited for practice climbing, makes it an ideal spot for camping. There are a few, deep caves amongst the boulders, which are perfectly dry, even in wet weather. The final descent to the Coe is on the left side of a deep, tree-clad gorge. In wet weather the fording of the Coe may be a problem. It is best to go well down-stream from the gorge until the river becomes broad and shallow.

If the ridge-walk just described is taken in the opposite direction some excellent rock scrambling can be enjoyed by going straight up the nose of Ben Fhada above the gorge of the Coe. There is a choice of routes of varying difficulty. It is a good place for practice, and also for judgment in selection of route, so that one may not land into difficulties. There should be no fear of that, however, as everything is in full view from below. The middle one of the Three Sisters, Gearr Aonach, consists of an upper and a lower cliff of good, red rock. This is also suitable for a climb of moderate difficulty, and was, in fact, climbed by Naismith's party in Easter 1898, and again descended by a parallel route. It is worth while to repeat their climb.

On the face of the westerly Sister, Aonach Dubh, is a curious fissure, like a narrow, lofty portal into the interior of the mountain, called Ossian's Cave. The poet is unlikely to have visited the place at all, but it was climbed by Nichol Marquis, a shepherd, in the early nineteenth century. It is easy to ascend a long, steep, inclined grassy ridge to the left of it, and then to work across a watercourse to another inclined terrace, leading up to the right below the cliff on which the Cave is situated. The final 100 feet, Ossian's Ladder, is not so easy. The rock holds are masked by vegetation, often very wet, and the descent can be awkward and difficult, as there are no good belays for a rope. The Cave is an impressive eyrie, with a steep, stony floor, and very uncomfortable. It does not go far back, and is usually wet. It contains a metal box for visitors' cards. It is not to be recommended as an expedition, as accidents have occurred. Parties have been stuck there for the night and rescue parties called for. By following the terrace below the Cave for a considerable distance to the right it is quite easy to work one's way through the broken, upper crags on to the summit of Aonach Dubh.

Better rock for moderate climbing is available on the buttress to the right of Dinner Time Buttress, overlooking Coire Beith, but not on the lowest tier of rock. There is some very good rock on the middle and upper tiers, the approach being by the gully to the right of Dinner Time Buttress. There are many interesting possibilities and a few, good routes a good deal farther to the right on these same tiers of rock. In fact, one would never expect from below to find a huge amphitheatre of steep crags in that quarter. Most of the climbing, as well as the approaches, are difficult.

Stob Coire nam Beith
A A   Arch Gully   C C   Crack Climb
1, 2, 3, 4 Buttress Climbs
The chimney shown between CC and 4 is Deep-cut Chimney

The best place of all for good, moderate rock climbing is on the northern face of Stob Coire nam Beith, the grand, pyramidal, rocky peak which fills the skyline above Coire Beith, as seen from the foot of Loch Triochatan. It is a large face of rock and demands some study, but the diagram will help. First identify the long Arch Gully near the left edge of the continuous rocks. The Arch is not easy to see unless one is close under it. The two buttresses on either side of Arch Gully give good, longish, moderate rock climbs. The Crack Climb, to the right of these, is excellent, but a good deal more difficult. My earliest climb on these cliffs was No. 4 Buttress (long before the numerical nomenclature was adopted). I had a novice with me, and the buttress gave us an excellent, easy climb. The buttress is on the right of the Deep-Cut Chimney. After the first stretch to the right one follows the crest to the left, and the route can be considerably varied. The upper rocks of the Stob turn out to be quite easy, and all the rock is very sound. The Arch Gully is moderately difficult up to the base of the final obstacle, a severe triple chimney, over 100 feet high, which was first climbed by Colin Allan and myself in November 1933. The pioneers, led by Mr G. D. Abraham, avoided this pitch by climbing out of the gully on the right-hand side, and so gaining the upper rocks fairly easily.

The eastern side of Stob Coire nan Lochan offers one moderate, classic rock climb. This is the middle, north-eastern buttress, called Raeburn's Buttress. It could be taken as a sequel to a climb on Aonach Dubh. One starts up to the right, from the bottom of the deep gully between the central and southern buttresses. This is stepped trap rock with one or two small chimneys. Above this one is faced with the steep upper wall, one part of which is rather difficult, where one has to traverse left along a thin flake and climb on to a shelf above, with very little in the way of holds. The climb finishes easily enough. Raeburn's Buttress makes an excellent and very difficult climb under snow conditions.

NOTE.—A perusal of the *Glencoe Rock Climbing Guide* will indicate quite a number of newer routes of moderate difficulty, but most new climbs have a tendency towards the severe standard. In this Guide Raeburn's Buttress is named Centre Buttress, Coire nan Lochan.

MORE DIFFICULT ROCK CLIMBS

A few years ago it would have been little exaggeration to say that the Crowberry Ridge of Buachaille Etive Mor, the Church Door Buttress of Bidean nam Bian and the traverse of the Aonach Eagach Ridge were the only Glencoe climbs which were known south of the Border. Nowadays, thanks to a great spurt of exploring activity on the part of a growing number of younger Scottish climbers, the attractions of Glencoe as a first-class climbing centre are more widely recognised. It is, therefore, unnecessary to describe these older, classical routes. Those who have proved their ability to climb the routes already described can extend their experience to the Crowberry Ridge and the Church Door Buttress, and should even be able to descend the former in its original or simplest form (omitting the Abraham traverse or the variation by Speirs) with comparative safety.

Apart from medium length face climbs, of which one of the best examples, Agag's Groove, has already been described in an introductory chapter, Glencoe is outstanding in possessing two of the longest and grandest gully climbs in Britain. The Chasm of Buachaille Etive Mor is described in a separate chapter. Clachaig Gully, at the foot of Glencoe, has been dealt with by W. H. Murray,* the leading spirit in its first ascent in 1938. These two gullies, strongly contrasted in character, are of fairly equal climbing height, about 1,500 feet or so. Most climbers who are familiar with both of them would, I think, consider that the Chasm is the harder and more variegated climb. The rock scenery is very grand and the rock remarkably sound, but the existence of more frequent avenues of escape offends some climbing purists. The standard of climbing increases in severity as one ascends.

Clachaig Gully has been a challenge to rock climbers since Norman Collie led the first party to the attack in 1894. Until the successful ascent by Messrs W. H. Murray, A. M. McAlpine, W. G. Marskell and J. K. W. Dunn in May 1938, all previous parties appear to have been stopped by what is now known as the Great Cave Pitch. The pioneers climbed this by a severe route, involving a very difficult traverse, on small holds, on a vertical cliff, high above the pool at the foot of a waterfall. In 1940 I climbed it with John Wilson and Douglas Laidlaw, and we found that, by climbing somewhat higher up steep slabs on the right, the traverse to a grassy niche, from which it was easy to reach the lip of the fall and the top of the pitch, could be made much easier and safer. The hardest pitch of the gully is Jericho Wall, some distance higher. The only severe part is, however, near the bottom. The rock on the upper part is not all sound, and the leader should go fairly high to a good belay and stance. Accidents have occurred when this has not been done. John Wilson, my wife and I revisited the gully on 27th October, 1946, a day of hard frost, when the ascent occupied us for six hours. We were of opinion that the Chasm provided more and better climbing, as there were long stretches of very moderate difficulty in the upper part of Clachaig Gully. The latter is, however, an excellent, hard climb, the difficulties commencing about 700 feet above the level of the road. In early summer the profusion of trees, shrubs and ferns in the lower part make it an

* *Mountaineering in Scotland* by W. H. Murray (Dent, 1947).

attractive expedition of an unusual type, but the actual climbing is mostly on very sound rock. The gully carries much less snow in winter than the Chasm, and is usually somewhat drier than the latter. Escape routes are neither frequent nor easy.

Two other gullies should be mentioned. Crowberry Gully on Buachaille Etive is only formidable as a winter route, but offers a good climb of sustained interest in summer. The hardest gully on Buachaille is a narrow rift between North Buttress and Cuneiform Buttress, the latter offering a very difficult climb as well, especially if the exit is effected by the upper chimney. The crux of Raven's Gully which was first led by John B. Nimlin in June 1937, occurs at the fourth pitch. It is in the form of an overhung cave with smooth, vertical sides, and is usually regarded as a problem in combined tactics for a party of three, one of whom belays the others from a recess at the back of the cave. Nimlin, however, accepted no such assistance. I have not tackled the pitch myself, but have seen two very good climbers fall off it, on separate occasions, when I was securing them at the back of the cave. The gully has many good pitches, but none to compare with this in severity.

Shadbolt's Chimney, near Ossian's Cave, on the face of Aonach Dubh, is almost the only classical route which has maintained its place, when judged by modern standards of difficulty. It was climbed in June 1908 by A. C. McLaren and L. G. Shadbolt. The lower section is a smooth, strenuous, orthodox chimney. The middle is a steep face with thin ledges and small holds leading to the crux, which is a short, severe chimney with a welcome belay at the foot. When I climbed it in 1927 I was much impressed by the steepness and difficulty of the face, but very little other climbing seems to have been done there by the modern school.

Colin Allan and I had several happy hunting grounds on the rocks of Bidean nam Bian and its subordinate ridges. We enjoyed several excellent climbs in the Amphitheatre, high up on the western face of Aonach Dubh, and at least one good day on the lower, north-east nose of the same peak. In 1931 we made a direct route up the centre of Diamond Buttress, which faces Church Door Buttress across Central Gully, beneath the summit of Bidean nam Bian. The lower rocks of this 550-foot cliff are somewhat loose, but the interest of the climb continues until within fifty feet of the top, including the ascent of a prominent pinnacle, which is severe. On the upper section there are too many easy ways of escape to one side or the other, but the nature of the rock, hornblende andesite, does not favour continuity of difficulty. We never had any success on the rocks below Aonach Eagach.

The modern school of difficult climbing in Glencoe has shown a tendency to concentrate on the Rannoch Wall and the walls of the North Buttress of Buachaille Etive. Many of these newer climbs are severe in standard and on very sound rock, but there have also been discoveries in several other places.

CHAPTER IX

RANNOCH AND GLENCOE IN WINTER

SOME of the best winter climbing on the Scottish mountains is available in the Rannoch, Blackmount, and especially the Glencoe areas, often as early as December and always in the early spring. After a heavy snowfall there is often very good weather, most convenient of all if the roads are clear and the snow has become hard and icy on the mountains. There is climbing of all grades of difficulty—easy mountains such as Clachlet and Stob Ghabhar, grand, long ridges such as those of Bidean nam Bian and the Buachailles Mor and Beag, but also difficult gullies and even face climbs on rocks which, although easy in summer, are now transformed into complicated problems of a high Alpine standard of difficulty.

Let us begin with basic mountaineering, getting to the top of the mountain by an obvious, natural route and, if possible, traversing several peaks in the day's expedition. A grand range for this purpose is the arc of hills bordering Rannoch Moor on the south-eastern side. On February 6th, 1937, I motored to Bridge of Orchy, climbing Ben Ledi on the way. Four of us gathered there and spent the night at the hospitable cottage of Mrs Morrison, close to the railway station. Sunday dawned clear and cold, with cirrus clouds above and some stratus in the valleys. We left early by car for Achallader farm. Our objective was Ben Creachan (3,540 ft.), a few miles to the north-east. After leaving the railway line, where it passes through the lovely old pine wood of Crannach, we struck upwards across the moor. At first the way led through the thinning forest, with alluring glimpses of the sun-kissed summit line of Ben Achallader. Then we, too, were in sunshine, which was so hot that we stripped to the waist. High up on the slope we arrived at a frozen loch below the upper crags. The surface was a curious mixture of contorted waves of snow and ice. It seemed compact, and we crossed it on foot, although two of us crashed in at the last step before landing on the far bank. There we split into two parties, each choosing our own gully for the ascent.

The climbing was not difficult, though we had a few steps to cut on an awkward, rocky traverse below the narrow part. Near the top we were again forced to cut steps, as the final slope was icy, leading up to a small cornice, which we climbed at one point where it was vertical but not under-cut. As we stepped on to the ridge the view was magnificent to the east, down the valley of Glen Lyon to the gleaming snow-caps of the chain of Ben Lawers. We turned to the left to the summit of Ben Creachan. Visibility was perfect in all directions. Creachan is an outpost above the south-eastern corner of Rannoch Moor. The desolation of this huge expanse was beautifully variegated by its many sheets of water and the encircling snowy mountains. We looked down upon Lochs Lyon, Rannoch, Ericht, Laidon, Ba and Tulla. Bidean nam Bian was somewhat hidden by the Buachaille, and the peaks of Mamore Forest set off the commanding outline of Ben Nevis. To the south-west were the peaks of Ben Cruachan.

The rest of that day was good, hard ridge walking. The wind was easterly and most invigorating. It was a day when it was good to be alive. Life pulsed within, at every step over these crisp, icy ridges. We passed easily over Meall Buidhe, climbed up to twin-topped Ben Achallader (3,404 ft.), and then swept downwards to a low saddle, only to climb again steeply to the summit of Beinn an Dothaidh (3,283 ft.). By this time the wind was much colder and clouds were rising in the west. Far to the south we could see the serrated outlines of the peaks of Arran in the Firth of Clyde. Old friends, such as Bens Vorlich, More and Stobinian, Cruach Ardrain and Ben Lomond came into view as we progressed along the ridge. The ever-changing prospect of the surrounding hills and valleys is, indeed, the major charm of ridge walking.

We were now racing down to the last gap before the final 1,000-foot slog to the last summit of the day, Ben Doran (3,524 ft.). Fighting against time as we were, it was hard, hard work. We only reached it long after sunset, with the snow whirling about us in the icy blasts of the east wind. In the haste of our exertions we had taken no notice of the changes in the mountain scene about us. All was now a patchwork of deathly cold hues of grey and livid blue, with one last coppery vestige of departed day over Ben Cruachan. We hurried back to the saddle and were down the short, rocky funnel and on to the moor before night swallowed us up. Our last flounderings over the ridges of heather and peat were directed by one bright light which emanated from the kitchen of Mrs Morrison. Arriving about a quarter past six we were soon enjoying a huge meal before a comfortable fireside. Next day I went over our route on the map and found that we had traversed fourteen miles and climbed 5,800 feet during the eight and a half hours of our outing. If the Scottish mountains grant even one occasional day so delightful and invigorating, the rest of life becomes eminently worth while.

To those who visit these hills, but are more interested in improving their technique in snow and ice gullies, I would recall another day in December 1938 when I climbed from Bridge of Orchy with W. H. Murray. We walked to the beginning of Crannach Wood and made for the northern corrie of Achallader, where we climbed the mountain by hard frozen snow slopes and a rocky gully crowned by a steep cornice. Having traversed Achallader we enjoyed a fast descent to the recesses of the north-western corrie of Ben Dothaidh and ascended the latter mountain by the narrow, steep gully which finishes just to the right of the main summit. This gave us some excellent step cutting in the upper part, and much variation is possible. If there is plenty of snow it is possible to glissade from the top of Dothaidh for about three-quarters of the way down to the railway, using one of several shallow gullies of no great steepness. This expedition took us about eight hours.

Now let us take a shorter day, from Kingshouse Inn. Again in severe mid-winter conditions, John Wilson and I crossed the moor to the foot of Sron na Creise (2,952 ft.), which we ascended by one of its steep gullies. This gave us a good spell of step-cutting in snow-ice, finishing very steeply with a short, difficult eight-foot pitch in a rock chimney, where wedging tactics were necessary in order to get above a chockstone. Then we emerged into brilliant sunshine on the ridge and strode along briskly towards the higher tops. A few streamers of cloud played hide and seek among the peaks of Cruachan to the southward. Only the higher mountains protruded through the level sea of wavy cumulus cloud on that perfect January day. We went on to the summit of Clachlet (3,602 ft.) and then returned, dipped to a saddle on a ridge and gained the highest top, Meall a'Mhuiridh (3,636 ft.) before returning to Kingshouse in the late afternoon.

Looking southwards towards Stob Ghabhar from the Clachlet, I recalled one of my earliest snow expeditions in 1923 when a party of us walked up Coire Ba and enjoyed a good climb on the northern buttress of Sron a'Giubhas, a northern outlier of Stob Ghabhar. The main attraction of Stob Ghabhar is, however, a short but exceedingly steep, rocky gully, close under the summit on the north face, known to climbers as the Upper Couloir. It is only about 200 feet in height, but comprises two difficult pitches, the upper of which is often very icy. In 1923 we found it too difficult for us and retreated by the way we had come. In 1927 it was the scene of an accident which just missed being a very serious affair. Two parties were on the climb at the same time. The second man of the upper party had just warned the leader, who was precariously poised on ice steps near the top of the upper pitch, that he was not securely placed and could not hold him if he fell. The second party was watching the proceedings from a lower stance. At that moment the leader of the first party slipped, with the result that the whole party went hurtling down the icy snow slopes. As the Couloir is very narrow they cannoned into and detached the other party as they shot past. Two axes were torn from their moorings in the snow and the third, having to take all the strain, broke in two. Fortunately, all the victims came to rest in soft snow before reaching the edge of a lower line of cliffs. Most of the men suffered sprains and bruises, but only one casualty had to be carried down to the road through the long hours of a miserable, wet and stormy night.

It was, of course, quite wrong for two parties to be on such a climb at the same time. The primary fault, however, was the lack of a secure belay for the second whilst the leader negotiated the severe ice pitch. Even although a longer run-out of rope would be necessary the invariable rule must be to have a secure belay in such a situation. It is difficult to comment fairly on the breaking of an ice-axe. The shaft may have been faulty, but it is all too probable that the tightening rope exerted its leverage on the axe at some distance above the snow level. In snow and ice climbing the rope should be laid round the axe shaft at ground level, and kept there.

On New Year's Day, 1936, I climbed the Couloir with A. McClure. We found the first pitch fairly easy. The upper pitch promised better prospects on the right, but when McClure tried that route he found dry, incoherent snow lying on thinly glazed rock. So the next attempt was made up an icicle-fringed wall in the left corner. I remember getting good holds at crucial points behind thick icicles. The upper part of the pitch was very slow work, as every foot- and hand-hold had to be chipped in hard ice. There is one comforting feature about this Couloir. If conditions are hard and icy at the crux one is almost certain to meet with a straightforward slope of perfectly secure, hard snow above the vertical section. Short as it is, the Upper Couloir of Stob Ghabhar must always be treated with respect.

Other straightforward winter expeditions are the traverse of the parallel ranges of the Buachailles of Etive and the traverse, in varied combinations, of the peaks of Bidean nam Bian. So far as my own experience goes I have usually aimed at combining such an expedition with a preliminary ascent, by a route involving some degree of technical difficulty, to the main ridge or one of the peaks. That is not so easy in the short days of December or January, but, in March and April, several hours of good and interesting climbing can be followed by some delightful ridge walking in the later afternoon and early evening. There is no more delightful finish or rounding off to an interesting climb.

On several occasions Colin Allan and I have finished a climb with a snow bath on the summit plateau of Stob Coire nam Beith (3,621 ft.), a fitting sequel to our labours in an ice gully or on a rocky face, for there are many practicable winter routes on the rocks of Stob Coire nam Beith, which, though easy in summer, are interesting and difficult when sheathed in snow and ice. To the critical but uninitiated reader a snow bath under such conditions may appear to be an extreme of asceticism or bravado, according to his attitude of admiration or cynicism. In fact, it is neither the one nor the other. It is far less of a shock to roll about in deep, powdery snow on a calm, sunny afternoon than to dive into ice-cold water, and enormously less than the revolting chill of the domestic cold bath, which rudely

BUACHAILLE ETIVE MOR

shatters the peaceful rhythm of the nervous system after a warm and comfortable sleep. In any case, whoever indulges in a snow-bath on a mountain crest will continue his progress along the ridges with renewed zest and vigour.

Another easy but rather long winter expedition is the traverse of the twin ridges of the Buachailles Mor and Beag. When Allan and I did so on a day of hard frost in early April we started off with the ascent of the North Buttress of Stob Dearg of the Buachaille Etive Mor. From the southern summit of the ridge, Stob na Broige (3,120 ft.), we should normally have glissaded nearly all the way to the Larig Gartain (1,600 ft.), between the ridges of Mor and Beag. The snow slopes were so icy that we were compelled to use a more cautious mode of descent, proceeding step by step and hooking in the snow-ice above us with the picks of our axes. A standing glissade would almost certainly have got out of control, tossed us on our backs and battered us about all the way to the saddle. One should always be on one's guard against such a contingency. We adopted the same tactics for the descent from Stob nan Cabar, our last peak for the day, at the northerly end of the Buachaille Beag.

According to the text-books one should usually be able to check a slip on snow-ice (or even ice, in the opinion of some optimists!) by holding the pick of the axe down against the surface with the whole weight of the body. This may be so at the very start of the slide. It is only necessary to reflect that the braking force must be steadily applied, that the results will vary inversely with the square of the speed and that irregularities of the surface must give rise to side thrusts which are likely to defeat our best efforts to maintain the pick in the braking position. The divergence between static rule and dynamic experience should beget a wise degree of caution when glissading on snow-ice.

When traversing the Bidean ridges there are several places where splendid, safe glissading is usually feasible into the corries, but one must be assured of a clear run-out of gentle snow slope at the lower end of the glissade. Standing glissades are preferable to sitting, for control is easier and visibility better. It is best to choose the line by a previous inspection from below. Glissades into Coire Beith are usually feasible from the top of Stob Coire

K

nan Lochan, from the col between it and Bidean nam Bian or from the col between Stob Coire nam Beith and Ant'Sron. They are not advisable from the Glencoe ends of ridges running down to the Three Sisters. There are also one or two good lines to the head of Coire nan Lochan and to the head of the Hidden Valley between Stob Coire nan Lochan and Beinn Fhada, but there are bands of cliff at various places, and one ought to be sure of one's ground.

MORE DIFFICULT CLIMBS

The Aonach Eagach ridge, bounding Glencoe on the north, is the best long traverse of the district under hard winter conditions. It is excellent practice for Alpine work. I have been on it in early April when conditions were all that could be desired. Sandy Wedderburn and I ascended the long gully which sweeps down from the ridge to Glencoe and is bounded on the east side by that impressive, rocky nose called 'The Chancellor'. After a little rock-work near the foot the gully provided a long, uneventful plug up a steep, hard snow slope. The view from the crest of the ridge through the jaws of the Chancellor gully provides a grand setting for the Bidean ridges when they are plastered with snow and ice. To the north-west were the jagged, golden outlines of the Cuillin ridges of Skye. Ben Nevis towered over the Mamores and the Aonachs.

The narrow part of the ridge exacted great care and a fair amount of step-cutting, for there were cornices above the cliffs, now on one side and now on the other. W. M. McKenzie has described conditions when there has been a double cornice at one part. It would then be necessary to traverse along the steep slopes below the cornice, sometimes a long and difficult task. Even with a single cornice one should keep very well away from the edge. This, again, is good experience for Alpine work. Except at the narrow section we had no serious difficulty, and it is unlikely that any sections of hard ice will be found in a normal Scottish winter. Such a ridge gives excellent practice for a roped party to move continuously, unless at positions of difficulty where the rope must be secured over an ice-axe and the party move one at a time.

Now for a good gully climb. On 15th March, 1936, Allan and

I were joined by John Dow and R. L. Beveridge, who wished to ascend the long, steep gully between the Central (Raeburn's) and South Buttresses of Stob Coire nan Lochan, at the head of the corrie between Aonach Dubh and Gearr Aonach. After an early lunch we started up this 500-foot gully. The first pitch was well smothered in snow. It demanded step cutting of a relatively simple type. Soon we came to the real crux, a formidable wall of ice which was not far short of vertical. This statement has no real, physical significance. It simply means that a climber, whose balance is reasonably good, would be unable to climb such a pitch without cutting both handholds and footholds in the ice, and that he would feel, most of the time, as if he were perched on a steeplejack's ladder, hanging a little backward from his hands. This does not actually imply verticality, as ice steps are both narrow and slippery. But the position is both difficult and tiring to hold for any length of time. Allan did most of the leading. I followed and improved the steps.

He started from under the vertical wall of rock on the left and worked his way up in a rising line, linking up a series of narrow ice pockets and ledges towards the equally perpendicular right wall, and finally reaching the top of a steep, rocky shelf, dripping with icicles. For about 150 feet the difficulty was continuous. It was a grand lead and a strenuous piece of work, as we all recognised when it came to our turn to follow. Then we struck an excellent, steep slope of hard snow-ice at a uniform gradient, which was only varied by one or two minor ice pitches. We made good progress in spite of the hard labour of cutting steps; and the small cornice at the top gave us very little trouble, as it thinned away at one corner into a low wall. I am told that there has been, of recent years, a considerable rock-fall in the gully, so that its climbing qualities are modified. W. H. Murray informed me that, in the early part of the year 1947, the ascent was very severe and icy. W. H. Tilman, the Himalayan climber and explorer who accompanied him, was much impressed by the strenuous and severe nature of Scottish winter climbing.

The quality of such a climb must depend on the type of weather during a period, measured sometimes in terms of weeks rather than days, before the ascent takes place. The Central Gully of Bidean nam Bian is perfectly easy in summer, but Colin

Allan and I enjoyed a hard, icy ascent in December. In early January we could make nothing of the South-Central Gully of Stob Coire nan Lochan, on account of much new and powdery snow which was not consolidated to the ice-crusted rock underneath. The Curved Ridge of Buachaille Etive, though an easy route for descent in summer, can be an exceedingly hard climb under severe, winter conditions. Exceptionally heavy snowfalls may often fill up pitches in gullies, leaving steep, uniform slopes of snow, which, after thawing and re-freezing, are excellent for climbing. A much lesser snowfall, followed by a short thaw and a prolonged frost, can convert a gully floor into a thin ribbon of ice. This happened in March 1947 to the Great Gully of Buachaille Etive, which is not normally a hard winter climb. Herein lies the charm and adventure of winter climbing. It is not repetitive work: guide book directions are only of minor value: the work demands initiative and intelligent forethought.

Again and again I have come to realise the benefit of my Scottish winter experience, which cannot be gained by a few casual visits to the hills at Easter time, for climbing in the Alps in summer; especially after bad weather, when ridges and faces, normally easy, are plastered with new snow or icy crust. Naturally, the conditions are very different. Alpine bad weather is usually succeeded by days of brilliant sunshine, and the new snow is quickly stripped from the rocks. In a Scottish winter or early spring the sun has little power, especially on northerly faces.

It may now be of interest to describe two face climbs, chosen because they are by no means difficult in summer conditions. In April 1939, in company with Alex. Small and Miss J. McNeill I climbed Raeburn's Buttress* on Stob Coire nan Lochan. The day was not particularly cold, but snow was plentiful and great quantities had to be cleared off the ledges in order to make secure stances, so that it took us about an hour to climb sixty or seventy feet; for this was a stepped face of rounded trap rock with very few belays. Having ascended by a loose, open chimney we were faced by an oblique upward traverse where the condition of the snow, betwixt frost and thaw, was somewhat unsound, with a tendency to slide. Avalanches were unlikely owing

---

* In *Glencoe Rock Climbing Guide* called Centre Buttress, Coire nan Lochan.

to the rough, bouldery nature of the underlying rock, but it was well to be careful. Then we got on to a hog-back ridge where it would have been possible to retreat into the north-central gully, which is always an easy way of ascent. The mist thickened as we approached the steep, upper wall of the buttress. When Raeburn's party first climbed the buttress in April 1907 there was no snow at this stage. I had climbed it myself with Colin Allan in 1935 under good conditions, but now I had grave doubts about the short, difficult section at the foot of the wall.

We passed a rock pinnacle by a series of steep ledges and gained a neck behind it. Then came the crux—a mantelshelf on the wall which overhung slightly but seemed to be free of ice. The solution was a low traverse of several yards to the left, an ascent behind a small flake and a strenuous pull up a corner to the ledge above. One more pull landed me on a good ledge with a satisfactory belay, but I was fortunate in the absence of ice on the crucial handholds, and I should never have attempted the move without previous experience of the landing under snow-free conditions. Difficult winter climbing can always be aided by knowledge of the mountain under summer conditions. That was the last difficulty, and we attained the summit ridge by 6 p.m., enjoyed a splendid glissade down the slopes into Coire Beith and reached the Glencoe road in less than an hour. Raeburn's Buttress must be a very tough proposition in real icy conditions earlier in the year. There is still time for me to return to it!

My other example concerns the oldest climbing route on the Buachaille, climbed by Dr Collie's party in March 1894. Like many other routes on Scottish mountains it is an old and superior vintage which is best tasted and savoured in very *dry* winter conditions. On 31st December, 1944, Ian Charleson and I were fortunate in getting a lift by car to the head of the Glen Etive road. The car was due to return to Crianlarich later in the day, and we were allowed from 11 a.m. until 4 p.m. to try our luck on the mountain. That was a short allowance of time, so that we had practically no halts, eating our sandwiches at any odd moment. The moor was frostbound and as hard as iron. It was a perfect winter day with bright sunshine and a light northerly air. The rock ledges were iced up to a considerable degree, and dry powder snow overlay the whole upper cone of the mountain.

My first, rather venturesome intention was the ascent of Central Buttress. It did not take us long to reach the base of the rocks at its southern end. Charleson started to lead the first pitch of the route which I had pioneered in 1934. When he was about thirty feet up I asked for his opinion on our prospects. The answer was just what I ought to have expected, 'Rocks about seventy-five per cent iced higher up, but I think I can go on'. As this part was, in summer, of a very moderate standard of difficulty I could easily guess what the really steep section of the climb would be like. Our prospects on Central Buttress were negligible, so we decided to retreat and try something easier. To the left of the sheer cliff was a snowy gully leading to a little saddle which gave access to Collie's route. We decided that here lay our only chance of reaching the summit of the Buachaille.

From the saddle we ascended as directly as possible, using short traverses where this was necessary for avoiding the difficulties. This whole face is characterised by short, steep walls of rock separated by narrow, heather-covered ledges. The heather was most useful, as the dry powder snow which lay upon it protected the rock underneath from icing up. We kept no count of time. All I remember is that we never relaxed our progress. The pitches were never long ones, but some were sufficiently testing for all that. Uncertainty as to the outcome persisted until we were a little way above the level of the upper end of Heather Terrace on Central Buttress. The genial sunshine made all this clearing of snow from ledges and crawling over mantelshelves on our stomachs both endurable and entertaining. At length we reached a good horizontal terrace, bounded on the left by a vertical drop into a steep, narrow, curving, snowfilled gully.

The character of the climbing became safer and easier. We kept up the broken rock ridge with the gully on our left until we arrived at the base of an upper snow-field. We now looked upwards to the right across a snowy col to the Crowberry Tower, and to the left towards another skyline of snow. This snowfield is not directly underneath the summit rocks; above it lies another, descending from a saddle high up on the left and running down to the right to converge on the snowfield below the Crowberry Tower Gap. It was now close on 3 p.m. and, judging from summer experience with an allowance for winter conditions, we expected to reach the summit in about twenty minutes. We soon found our mistake, for we had to slash out steps practically all the way.

The snow structure varied a good deal. In places there was a polished, icy crust covering dry powder snow, a few inches in depth, which again covered a much harder, icy surface of old snow, thawed and re-frozen. This was the Scottish counterpart of what is known as wind-slab in the Alps; a very dangerous snow structure on steep slopes, as it tends to break up into cakes which readily avalanche. Probably it is more compact and stable in Scotland, but we took no risks where we found it, securing ourselves with the axes to the firm layer underneath. We cut straight up, and then to the right, to a little col which we crossed to the upper snowfield. Then we contoured to the left, cut straight up the slope to the skyline at the top, traversed beneath some rocks until we found an easy place to climb up between them, and finally reached the top of the mountain at 4 p.m.

The view was clear and splendid, except to the west where haze obscured the peaks of Rum and Skye. Nevis, the Mamores and the Aonachs were brilliant in sunshine.* Lochs Rannoch, Laidon and Ba were a wonderful translucent green, with the least hint of yellow. Bidean nan Bian looked a great mountain, majestic and aloof. It was typical, perfect winter colouring. We were very late and started to descend almost at once. On the convex summit ridge, frozen to the hardness of concrete and gleaming with icy plates, the going was difficult. At last we turned leftwards on to the easy boulder and scree slopes towards Glen Etive. The boulders were still ice-glazed and the snow crust broke under our weight at every step. Still, we raced down the familiar slopes and reached the glen road about 5 p.m. with about a mile and a half to walk, expecting that we should be soundly rated by our friends for being an hour and a half behind our trysted time. However, it turned out that they, too, were over an hour late, so that we were justified in pushing the attack to a finish and securing a perfect winter climb.

In this varied chapter on winter climbing in the Glencoe area

* The solar time was 3 p.m. on account of British war-time reckoning.

no attempt has been made to describe the most difficult expeditions of all; for the main purpose is rather to show the contrast between summer and winter climbing and to point out the likeliest routes and conditions for building up technique on varied types of problem. The hardest winter climbs of Glencoe have been well described elsewhere, for most of them have been carried out by a comparatively small group of Glasgow enthusiasts during the years since 1935. These men were content to face expeditions of anything up to twelve hours' duration and longer. Once they were benighted in December, half-way up the Garrick Shelf Route on the Crowberry Ridge, but they returned to the assault on another occasion and succeeded. Originally they were a group of the Junior Mountaineering Club of Scotland, but are now instilling new activity and enthusiasm into the younger men, being themselves in the ranks of the senior club (S.M.C.).

The two most graphic accounts are from the pen of Mr W. H. Murray, in articles which first appeared in the *Scottish Mountaineering Club Journal** and have subsequently formed the core of the first book which deals adequately with modern Scottish climbing, particularly under severe, winter conditions.† A general account of difficult winter climbing in the Glencoe area has also appeared in the 1947 issue of the *S.M.C.J.* from the pen of W. M. Mackenzie, who was one of the same, small group. These hard expeditions are only for parties in good physical condition, with a long record of Scottish snow and ice expeditions behind them. For such men, who know each other's capacity, the risks, such as they are, can be taken with a large margin of safety, even when the weather changes for the worse. Other parties must examine themselves and count the cost before embarking on the venture; but the rewards are great, especially if a man has the ambition to proceed to the greater Alpine expeditions without the aid of guides. Such a man, writes A. F. Mummery, 'gains a knowledge of himself, a love of all that is most beautiful in nature, and an outlet such as no other sport affords for the stirring energies of youth; gains for which no price is, perhaps, too high.'

---

* *Journal*, Vol. 21, p. 237, and Vol. 23, p. 1.
† *Mountaineering in Scotland* by W. H. Murray (Dent, 1947).

CHAPTER X

BEN NEVIS: ROCK

INTRODUCTION

AMONG Scottish mountains, especially from the climber's point of view, Ben Nevis* holds as much pre-eminence as does Mont Blanc above the other peaks of the Alps. Indeed, the parallel is remarkably apt. Both are great, dome-shaped mountains, with a relatively easy way up one side and very steep and formidable rocks on the other. Ben Nevis, owing to its greater height than most other Scottish hills, carries more snow in winter and spring, so that its steep, north-eastern aspect offers the most nearly Alpine type of climbing which can be enjoyed in Britain. At the same time the magnitude of its north-eastern cliffs and the excellent quality of the rock afford the longest and most difficult Scottish rock climbs in summer. No parallel should be overdone, but it is perhaps admissible, as has already been suggested and printed, to adapt the lines from Byron's 'Manfred' to Ben Nevis, although originally composed in honour of the great Alpine mountain:

> *Ben Nevis is monarch of mountains,*
> *They crowned him long ago,*
> *On a throne of rocks, in a robe of clouds,*
> *With a diadem of snow.*

The meteorological records accumulated during the twenty years from 1883 until 1904 at the old Observatory on the summit of Ben Nevis make very interesting reading. They are described by W. T. Kilgour in *Twenty Years on Ben Nevis,*† but nowadays the book is out of print and hard to come by. Temperature records show that the overall mean was 31·4°F. over the entire period, so that, if the same rate of temperature fall continued to hold good with increase in height, 1°F. per 275 feet of ascent above sea level, a permanent snow cap and a small glacier would certainly be in existence if the mountain were a thousand feet higher. The figures for the annual snowfall

---

* Ben Nevis (4,406 ft.), Mont Blanc (15,782 ft.)
† *Twenty Years on Ben Nevis* by W. T. Kilgour (Alex. Gardner, 1905).

at the summit are considerable. In any one year the maximum depth at the summit is usually attained between mid-March and mid-April, although maxima for the year have been recorded as late as the end of May. The greatest recorded depth amounted to twelve feet in each of the years 1884 and 1885, but it appears that the figure has been much less of recent years. Rainfall is also very great and amounted to an average of 157 inches over the twenty years, the rainfall at Fort William being very much less. There are, on the average, only 104 fair days per annum on the summit of the Ben.

In spite of this dismal picture climbers can take heart, for the months of April, May and June are very much drier than the others. It also follows that the best conditions for snow and ice climbing are normally prevalent during March and April, although first-class climbs are available much earlier and are sometimes possible in May. Indeed, the north-eastern gullies are very seldom clear of snow until much later, and, in most years, small snow patches do not melt completely before the late autumn supplies a fresh covering. The accumulation of snow and ice is usually enormous at the end of winter, the tops of the cliffs and gullies being decorated with huge cornices, which have been estimated to reach a thickness of from fifteen to twenty-five feet.

All kinds of snow conditions may be encountered when climbing gullies, ridges and buttresses, so that the quality, difficulty and duration of the climbs are such as to tax the powers of the toughest experts, and to compare very favourably with some of the great Alpine climbs. The geographical situation of the Ben, coupled with the mutations of its Atlantic type of weather, result in great precipitation combined with frequent changes of wind and temperature, and a consequent partial thawing and refreezing which produces the toughest quality of snow-ice on ridges and gullies. The flattish summit dome acts as a catchment area for snow, and the prevalent westerly winds blow a great deal of it over the edge of the cliffs, thus helping to pile up enormous amounts on sheltered ledges and in the gullies.

No one who has visited the valley of the Allt a' Mhuilinn, between Ben Nevis and its easterly neighbour, Carn Mor Dearg, on a fine day in early spring is likely to forget the splendour of the Nevis cliffs in their gleaming panoply of snow and ice. Finer still is the summit view from Carn Mor Dearg, especially if one can see it in early morning or late afternoon.

Ben Nevis could hardly offer such excellent snow and ice climbing if it did not possess a rugged outline with long, steep ridges and gullies. In addition, the quality of the rock is so good that it provides sound routes of all degrees of difficulty for the rock climber. The frontage of cliff from the saddle between Ben Nevis and Carn Mor Dearg to the north-westerly cliffs on Carn Dearg* is nearly two miles, and there are parts of the cliff as much as 2,000 feet in height. It will assist the reader at this stage to look at the diagram of the ridges and gullies of the north-east face of the Ben.

Most prominent in a good, distant view from the road over the moor between Spean Bridge and Loch Lochy, or from road and railway about two or three miles east of Fort William is the steep edge of the North-East Buttress, but most picturesque from the Mhuilinn Glen is the long, graceful sweep of the Tower Ridge, with a great 700-foot pyramid of rock as its base, named the Douglas Boulder after the best known editor of the *Scottish Mountaineering Club Journal* during the classical period of climbing exploration on the Ben. Below the base of the Boulder, at 2,000-feet elevation, is the Charles Inglis Clark Memorial Hut† of the Scottish Mountaineering Club. This was presented to the Club by Dr W. Inglis Clark, one of the most noted of these early explorers and photographers, in memory of his only son, also a keen mountaineer, who was killed in the 1914–18 War. The Hut was opened in 1929.

Ben Nevis is a curiously isolated mountain. Glen Nevis, which bounds it on the west and south, is a very deep valley, only rising to 400 feet above sea level at the exit of the Nevis gorge, seven miles from Fort William and due south of the summit of the Ben. The saddle between Ben Nevis and Carn Mor Dearg at the head of the Mhuilinn valley is 3,475 feet above sea level, and the foot of the Douglas Boulder is little over 2,000 feet in altitude. It is also of interest to note the contrast between the

---

* Carn Dearg is the north-west spur of Ben Nevis; Carn Mor Dearg is a separate mountain to the north-east.

† Usually named the C.I.C. Hut.

steep, prominent and rugged grey cliffs of the Ben and the reddish, uniform scree slopes of Carn Mor Dearg, so that one is prepared to find that the Ben is just as unique from the geological as from the mountaineering point of view.

It is, in fact, the central core of a series of lava flows, due to volcanic outbursts in that early epoch when the Old Red Sandstone was deposited elsewhere. Not all the intruded igneous rock is good for climbing, for Carn Mor Dearg itself consists of a granite intrusion which has nevertheless weathered away into scree slopes. The easy path up the western flank of Ben Nevis crosses part of this 'Inner Granite' of the Carn Mor Dearg formation below the site of the old half-way Hut. The core of Ben Nevis formed an area which collapsed into the molten 'Inner Granite', with faulting and injection of dykes round about itself. The result was generally a rapid cooling and solidification, producing a fine-grained durable rock which, although it was first of all at a low level, yet, on account of its resistance to the erosion and weathering of subsequent ages, now remains isolated as the highest point of Britain. This is another instance of the general principle that the Scottish mountains are not true mountains of uplift, but the resistant remains from the erosion of a plateau.

The volcanic outbursts were repeated at intervals over a considerable period of time, so that part of the climbing rock is andesite lava, some very fine-grained and some much coarser, whilst another part is a less resistant agglomerate, a fragmental type of rock which was laid down during the explosive phases. The climbing qualities of the rock are determined alike by their dip (direction and inclination of bedding of the different layers), manner of jointing and surface texture. In all these respects there is great variety on the Ben. The lie of the climbing routes and ledges, as well as their difficulty, bear witness to their geological diversity. The best of the rock, such as the cliffs on the Douglas Boulder, the rocks of the North-East Buttress below the First Platform and on its front facing Observatory Gully are excellent, although the smoother texture never makes the climbing so easy as on the rough gabbro of the Cuillin in Skye, where one can often glide up surprisingly steep slabs by friction alone. On the other hand, there are parts of the Ben where the rock is unsound and insecure trap, and extreme care is absolutely essential. Those impressive buttresses called the Comb and the Castle are of this type.

For all that the geologists can tell us it is much better to test the theory by a practical visit to the cliffs themselves, and to treat all rocks with care and respect. The most reliable faces have faults and trap intrusions here and there. These form lines of weakness and of unreliable rock, but they also give rise to easy ledges and chimneys which make several routes possible that would not otherwise have been so. It is well to remember that the processes of erosion and decay are proceeding today as they have done in all past ages, and that their effects are most manifest in such places as chimneys and gullies. Even an unusually heavy shower of rain can loosen stones high up on a cliff, especially if accompanied by a high wind. The pioneer party on the difficult Slav Route was immobilised for about an hour during such a squall at the difficult lower crux of the route. There were several stonefalls, although the month was September and there had been no previous night frost.

GRADED ROCK CLIMBS

The older school of British rock-climbers preferred routes along prominent ridges or up gullies. The gullies taught them to climb chimneys as well. A great advantage was that the routes were obvious natural features of a rock face, and consequently very easy to identify. So far as Ben Nevis is concerned, much of the early climbing was done by Easter visitors who were members of the Alpine Club. The gullies, therefore, were primarily of interest as snow and ice climbs and were seldom or never attempted or climbed in summer. This was, perhaps, just as well; for any gully which is snow-filled during a great part of the year is bound to be subject to intense weathering and decay, so that the virgin rock, apart from its covering of scree and rotten debris, is liable to be most unsound.

At least two of the Nevis gullies have proved exceedingly formidable, if not dangerous, as summer climbs. Gardy Loo gully, in its upper section, is one of the more difficult winter routes on the Ben. Dr Graham Macphee, who first climbed it in summer conditions in 1935, describes it as one of the hardest rock climbs on the Ben. It is also dangerous, owing to loose and unsound rock, some of which is very soft. I climbed it with George Dwyer in August 1940, and we were more impressed by the dangers and looseness than by its actual severity, though each condition reacts on the other. Certainly a large party should never climb such a place. This happened in 1944 when a friend of mine, who was not leading, had two stones dropped on him by other members of the party. I heard a similar account of the first summer ascent, the only one before this date, of No. 2 gully which has a very dangerous and severe pitch about half-way up. These considerations dispose of the Nevis gullies as desirable rock climbs for any but cranky experts, except for such easy ones as numbers 3 and 4 (and possibly Tower Gully), which can always be used as quick routes of descent. Of these, No. 4 is an excellent, fast scree run, rather severe on the boot nails, but useful in bad weather.

The ridges of Ben Nevis, however, are long and sound, and they are wonderfully well graded as regards difficulty. They form the best training ground for rock climbers. The novice is able, not only to learn the rudiments of the craft and the various types of difficulty, but he can also learn two things of supreme value to the mountaineer who intends, later on, to climb on greater mountains such as the Alps. On easy ridges, like the Castle Ridge and the Tower Ridge, he can learn to take his place, either as leader or follower, in a party which moves safely, and often continuously, whilst using the rope. Later on he can learn to descend such ridges in the same manner. That is how Ben Nevis serves to make climbers into real mountaineers. There is an excellent mixture of easy and difficult; and some degree of route finding is called for, especially during a descent.

The Castle Ridge is the easiest, but one can get into some very awkward places on the descent if one is not careful. The first ascent of the Tower Ridge is best made by approaching the gap between it and the Douglas Boulder from the Observatory Gully side. At a later stage the direct route up the face of Douglas Boulder—a grand climb of 700 feet on very steep and difficult but sound rock—may be made, and then also the Great Tower can be negotiated by one of the western routes. These routes demand some experience, good cragsmanship and dry

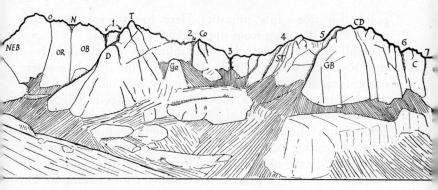

BEN NEVIS AND CARN DEARG*

GULLIES

o	Zero Gully	2,3,4	Gullies known by their numbers
1	(2 branches at upper End) Observatory Gully top left is Gardy Loo, top right Tower Gully	5	Carn Dearg Gully
		6,7	South and North Castle Gullies

RIDGES AND BUTTRESSES

NEB	North East Buttress	Ga	Garadh na Ciste
OR	Observatory Ridge	ST	South Trident Buttress
OB	Observatory Buttress	GB	Great Buttress of Carn Dearg
T	Tower Ridge	C	Castle
D	Top of Douglas Boulder	CR	Castle Ridge
Co	Comb		

SUMMITS

N	Ben Nevis	CD	Carn Dearg

CORRIES

Between T and CD is Coire na Ciste

The main valley above D is Coire Leis

Slopes of Carn Mor Dearg in foreground fall away gently into the Mhuilinn Glen

rocks. At a first ascent the easiest way should be followed on the ridge, avoiding the steepest part of the Little Tower on the left and passing the Great Tower also on the left by the Eastern Traverse. The Tower Gap beyond is fearsome looking, but has good holds.

By this time the rock-climber should have learned to proceed with care and security. Of the other ridges the North-East Buttress is not very difficult if one sticks to the proper route, except for the Mantrap near the top which is a short and

* See also "The Orion Routes", p. 268

polished problem in gymnastics. Here, too, the easy approach to the First Platform from upper Coire Leis is best.

Of all the Nevis ridges the best continuous rock climbing is on the Observatory Ridge. Its lower, slabby nose is a place where one can easily get into difficulty if one misses the central route which is marked by scratches. The upper ridge is delightfully narrow and airy, but not at all difficult. The rock is very sound throughout. The last of the ridge-like routes is the Observatory Buttress, shorter than the former, with a lower stepped portion with very good holds. A fault cleaves the buttress about the middle, and there is just one correct place for crossing it. The upper section is less determinate and is loose in places. A fatality occurred here a few years ago after the two members of the party had unroped. Apparently a block of rock came loose, but the angle of the face is not at all severe, and it is difficult to understand how the accident occurred. I have descended all these ridges, but would recommend careful route finding, especially in the case of Observatory Buttress. The descent of Observatory Ridge is the most interesting, but that too is a matter for experts, both as regards technique and route finding. Whoever leads a party in such an expedition should know the ridge from previously having ascended it, preferably more than once.

Now for the selection of several shorter rock climbs where the technique is more difficult. Nevis has many such, but only a few will be suggested, where the rock is particularly good and sound. Two such places are excellent for practice—the face of Douglas Boulder and the west face of North-East Buttress below the First Platform. The south-west ridge of Douglas Boulder, bounding the western gully from the Gap on the side of Coire na Ciste, is excellent and moderate. It also gives a quick route of descent for a skilled party. I have descended it alone from the Boulder summit to the scree at the foot of the rocks in eighteen minutes. The Direct route of ascent is graded as very difficult and follows an almost direct line from the lowest point of the rocks to the top, as viewed from a position in the Mhuilinn glen about 100 yards above the C.I.C. Hut. It is delightfully steep, yet the holds are positive and adequate and the belays good.

There are many routes of varying difficulty below the First

Platform on the west face of the North-East Buttress. Slingsby's Chimney is loose, especially near the top, and should be avoided. Raeburn's Arête is certainly the best approach to the Platform for experts. The rock is very sound, but there is much slab work, long runs-out of rope and few belays. My first ascent was by this route. I have ascended it several times, once at the beginning of May when many of the ledges still carried snow and some of the slabs had trickles of ice over them. It is a very difficult route for a descent, mainly owing to the featureless nature of the slabs which accentuates the difficulty of finding a route. Between Raeburn's Arête and Slingsby's Chimney are quite a number of recognised routes of varying degrees of difficulty and interest, but all on good rock. From these a choice can be made to suit the capacity of the party, but the routes lie fairly close together, and the directions of the Guide Book should be carefully followed if a certain standard of difficulty is not to be exceeded.

One excellent natural route of a more difficult character is No. 1 Route on Carn Dearg Buttress. It faces the C.I.C. Hut and looks most vertical and severe. But the rock is so sound and rough that steepness and safety go hand in hand for competent climbers. The classification is severe, but I think most climbers would now call it an 'amiable' severe. The buttress gets a lot of sunshine and is climbable early in the year; the rock is wonderfully rough. The direct Cambridge start is decidedly severe. Great care is advisable at the penultimate pitch above the big chimney.

Another excellent route is Raeburn's Buttress on Carn Dearg, with an awkward but not difficult approach and a final section which is airy and sensational, demanding considerable care. If one avoids the severe, lower crag, the South Trident Buttress is a delightful route, but the variations on the lower crag are both severe and exposed. I have mentioned the routes in the last two paragraphs as completing the training of the rock climber on Ben Nevis up to the stage when he may be able to tackle the hardest and longest routes, and as showing the immense possibilities of the Ben for turning out a finished rock climber, not only for the best British rock climbs but also for similar work in the Alps. There is also much trap rock on Ben

L

Nevis of varying degrees of soundness, but it is unnecessary to deal with it here.

MORE DIFFICULT ROCK CLIMBS

Detailed accounts of rock climbs have an unfortunate and monotonous habit of similarity, a mustiness of flavour and verbiage which is best confined to the guide books, unless the experience of the reader or some vivid incident can charm the dry bones into life. There are many excellent and very difficult rock climbs on Ben Nevis, and I have for many years been of the opinion that the climbing on that mountain is superior to that which can be enjoyed anywhere else in Scotland, not excluding the Cuillin range in the Isle of Skye. The face climbs are best of all, holding much in reserve for the initiative of future mountaineers. A separate chapter is devoted to some recent discoveries on the greatest of the Nevis cliffs, the tremendous face which sweeps down from the crest of the North-East Buttress to the inner reaches of Observatory Gully, where a small but nearly permanent snowbed persists throughout most of the summer. All that can be done here is to suggest a few other routes as a representative sample of the more difficult climbing available on the Ben.

In September, 1936, Colin Allan, Sandy Wedderburn and I found ourselves at the base of Rubicon Wall, which, at that date, was reckoned to be the hardest rock climb on the Ben. It is a steep wall of rock, flanking the lower half of Observatory Buttress, next to the precipitous, unclimbed gully between the latter and the face of Observatory Ridge, and was first climbed in 1933 by the party of Mr A. T. Hargreaves. We found it somewhat difficult to decide on the exact beginning or line of their route. Starting as close as possible to the gully we soon found ourselves on rather severe slabs. Sandy was in the lead until we overcame these and found a suitable niche, still close to the edge of the gully, in which we sat down to lunch. Colin then took over the lead, swarming up a flake on the right and continuing up another ninety-foot pitch of steep slabs with small holds. The steepness and difficulty continued all the way to the finish of the climb, when we found a small cairn, a few yards away on our right, which was clearly the end of the 1933 route.

This perfectly sound, exceedingly steep and difficult route can be highly recommended to a strong party, but there must be considerable scope for variations on this broad face, as none of the detailed accounts show good agreement with each other.*

Another interesting case of severe routes occurring close together on a Nevis cliff is the Bottom Tier of South Trident Buttress. It was first climbed by Dr G. Graham Macphee and G. C. Williams in June 1934. The next ascent was by W. G. McClymont and myself in May 1936, and we passed Macphee's cairn after our difficulties were ended. In September 1938 Wedderburn and I were limited by bad weather to ascending the Ben by the track, but our day was not wasted. The sun came out and we descended Observatory Buttress to the Hut, enjoyed an excellent meal and climbed back over the mountain by South Trident Buttress, using Macphee's route on the bottom tier. There does not seem to be much to choose between the two routes, as regards interest or difficulty.

In 1943 the location of most of the doubtful routes on Ben Nevis was investigated by B. P. Kellett. He had great difficulty in differentiating the 1934 and 1936 routes on the lower part of South Trident Buttress, although I had none at all in 1938. Kellett made the issue still more obscure by claiming a third new, severe route, distinct from the others. Quite apart from the perplexities and confusion of routes on the bottom tier the South Trident Buttress is one of the most interesting and satisfying climbs on Ben Nevis. The middle tier makes very good climbing, if taken as directly as possible, and the upper part, including the top tier, formerly known as the Pinnacle Arête of Carn Dearg, makes a delightful finish.

Most of the more recent, severe climbing on Ben Nevis has been pioneered by Mr B. P. Kellett, and the original accounts, from his pen and his diaries, have appeared in the *Scottish Mountaineering Club Journals* in the years 1944, 1946 and 1947. Kellett was an exceptionally able rock climber and his descriptions are meticulously accurate. It is tragic to reflect that he lost his life in a fatal accident on the Ben in September 1944. The available evidence tended to show that he was not, on that

* See *Mountaineering in Scotland*, p. 47, by W. H. Murray (Dent, 1947).

occasion, engaged in climbing anything new or specially difficult.

I had hoped to accompany him on several of his latest routes, particularly his Route 2 on the Great Buttress of Carn Dearg and one of his new discoveries to the left of the Orion climbs, but bad weather and wet rocks made this impossible. It is only fair to say that Kellett's climbing, for sheer daring, was often almost uncanny to watch. He led me up his Routes A and B on the North Buttress of Carn Dearg, and I have no particular wish to visit either place again. It is, of course, hard to disentangle one's impressions from subsequent tragic events. His account of the first ascent of Gardy Loo Buttress (between Tower and Gardy Loo gullies), matter of fact as it appears at a first reading, is enough to bring out a sweat on the brow and the palms of a reader who has seen the place and is aware of the previous unsuccessful attempts on this formidable and sinister cliff. He invited me to join him on a second ascent. It was a high compliment, but the onset of bad weather relieved me from facing a difficult decision!

CHAPTER XI

BEN NEVIS IN WINTER

INTRODUCTION

HE who has climbed Ben Nevis only in summer knows but half the story, for the old Ben puts forth his mightiest challenge when clad in all his winter armour of snow, ice and storm. During one of my early visits to the Alps with Frank Smythe, after a rather tough day when we were only too thankful to reach the hut, having climbed our mountain on a day of storm and bad snow conditions, he said to me, 'That shows the difference between the Alps and our British hills. You are glad to get to the top by any way whatever. These mountains really try to do you in'. The same thing applies to Ben Nevis in its most wintry garb.

It is no longer a case for relying on the directions from a Guide. Everything is changed. Places which were easy in summer are so smothered in snow, ice and frost crystals that the summer route is no longer recognisable. The Tower Ridge can be an easy way of descent in summer. I have left the summit at midnight in the month of July and chosen the Tower Ridge as an interesting and pleasant way down to the Clark Hut. In winter and spring, especially after an unusually heavy snowfall followed by alternate wind, thaw and frost, the ridge may be quite impossible to ascend, so that parties have to retreat or may be benighted through failure to realise soon enough what they are up against. At other times the weather may change rapidly during an expedition, and what appeared well-considered and practicable at the start may end in a protracted fight to avert accident and disaster.

Climbers who are members of the Scottish Mountaineering Club, or of certain privileged clubs, have the advantage of being able to start from the Clark Hut at the very foot of the crags, and thus making full use of the short winter days. In the pioneering days there was another haven of refuge open to those who succeeded in fighting their way through the difficulties and reaching the summit; as warmth, welcome and refreshment were usually available at the old Observatory. Now there is little comfort in the windy, derelict and ruinous remains of the old buildings, although some parties have tunnelled their way inside when entirely submerged in snow, and have lived there in comparative comfort during a New Year's blizzard. For it may prove to be the last, and apparently the easiest problem of getting down from the summit that spells disaster for an exhausted party in bad weather conditions.

On Easter Monday, 1925, Smythe and I fought our way to the summit by the track in a blizzard of blinding snow and spindrift. One must experience such a storm before one can hope to realise what it means. My companion considered that one seldom encountered any worse *tourmente* on Mont Blanc. We were comparatively fresh men in the middle of our day. What would such a blizzard have meant to a party which had been fighting their way, without respite, for many hours up ridge or gully? And they would have the additional hazards of gathering darkness and increasing cold. It is no wonder that there have been accidents and fatalities to winter climbers on Ben Nevis, perhaps more especially to those from south of the Border who have had no previous experience of Scottish snow conditions. The really surprising thing is that the tally of winter accidents on the Ben has been so light during the last twenty years. But the warning note should be sounded. The rate of accidents was on the increase before 1939, and the increase is likely to continue with the rise in popularity of winter climbing and improvement of communications.

Easter is the most popular time for English visitors, and much depends on the weather and snow conditions at that period. It must be firmly asserted that a few expeditions on the Alps in summer do not qualify a man for difficult winter conditions on Ben Nevis, and this is all the more true if the Alpine experience is of the guided variety. A great British mountaineer, H. W. Tilman, one of the first party to scale Nanda Devi (25,645 ft.), in the Himalaya, had a mishap on Ben Nevis in the spring of 1946, owing to bad weather conditions. Fortunately, there were no serious consequences, but Tilman remarked afterwards in conversation, that a man who could climb safely on Ben Nevis in winter conditions could climb anywhere. So it should not be considered out of the way to suggest that newcomers to Scottish snow might well confine their activities to lesser mountains or easier routes until they gradually acquire some experience of that mysterious entity, the condition of the snow. It is a matter which takes a longer time to learn than rock-craft, mainly because we can never reconstruct the conditions for ourselves, nor can our experience be perfectly translated into words.

My own introduction to snow climbing took place on Ben Nevis, on Easter Sunday 1922. I learned a great deal from an excellent leader, my friend Ernest Roberts, an experienced veteran of the Alpine Club, and for many years the editor of the *Yorkshire Ramblers Club Journal*. Roberts had previous winter experience of Ben Nevis and he understood the vagaries of Scottish snow. As we walked up the track from Achintee a perfectly regular snowline about the 1,500-foot level extended evenly along the hills surrounding Glen Nevis. A little snow fell, but, as we passed the Lochan Meall an t'Suidhe the air cleared and I had my first sight of the splendours of the north-east face of Ben Nevis in winter—great ridges sweeping up in whiteness to a mottled sky and gullies bulging with blue-green ice. It was not the same sort of snow that I had been accustomed to in the plains. It gave a different sort of crunch underfoot. When one looked down the hole made by an ice-axe the colour was a beautiful pale blue. One does not always see this effect, and I was lucky in my introduction to Scottish snow.

We lunched during a snow squall in the hollow of Coire na Ciste. It must have been about the site of the Lochan, but there was nothing visible except a snowy hollow with a small crag, and then steep slopes ahead. Soon we started off up these slopes below No. 2 Gully, for Roberts expected that we should be able to make our way up, although he could not foretell what sort of cornice there might be at the top of the gully. At first the snow was very soft, but it firmed up as the walls of the gully hemmed us in. As the gully narrowed it steepened, the snow becoming much harder. We could no longer kick steps. The axes, hitherto used in the manner of spiked walking sticks, were now to be applied to their main purpose. The surface was tough snow-ice, and Roberts proceeded steadily to cut a zig-zag staircase of steps. As he was not much taller than I the spacing suited me very well. At every turn of the zig-zag was a larger step, where he belayed me carefully over a driven-in ice-axe when I moved up to join him. Likewise, I safeguarded him when he moved in front.

At the steepest part we were assailed by a fierce wind, a sand-blast of icy spindrift, whirling round and coming at us from every quarter at once. Then there was a troublesome section where the snow was deeper and softer. I relied on the experience of the leader who considered that the snow was not badly com-pacted to the harder layer underneath. In any case, under the prevailing conditions, we could not have cleared the soft stuff and cut into the underlayer, for the steps would have filled up immediately. So we kicked out steps and adopted a style of crawling straight up the slope, helping ourselves with our axes held before us and driven deeply into the snow. In certain kinds of snow I have found this a very safe and useful way of climbing, but it is a good thing to test the cohesion of the soft surface snow to the underlayer. This can always be tried by one member of the party on the rope. With experience one gradually senses the reliability of the snow by the way it compacts or yields when sudden strain is put upon it.

At length we reached the foot of the steep funnel below the cornice at the top of the gully. We were again on hard snow-ice. It was an imposing cornice, overhanging considerably in a wide eave on the left, but not nearly so high and without any over-hang at the right-hand corner. Cornices are built outward by drifted snow from the plateau, and the prevailing thaw wind, when the drift snow adheres best, is from the south-west. Roberts made for the easier right-hand corner and was careful to cut good, solid steps. Below the cornice was a hollow lip, and I was left there, securely belayed, while the leader cut the last few holds on the vertical wall and pulled himself up. After securing himself he invited me to follow, and soon we were shaking hands over the success of a very good climb.

The scene was most impressive. For the time it had stopped snowing. Above and behind us were dark, snow-bearing clouds: a dazzling shaft of sunlight streamed up from below through a rift in the lower cloud—the reflection of the sun in the distant waters of Loch Linnhé. Roberts stood there sparkling and ice-bedecked in the sunbeams; exactly like a polar explorer with hair, moustache, eyebrows and woolly helmet all encased in ice. We moved off to the summit of the Ben. The old Observatory was thickly cased in snow with long frost crystals at all the projecting edges. Unlike cornices, these fluted ornaments of fern-like beauty are formed, not of drifted snow but of supercooled vapour. They build themselves outwards into the wind. They occur on all Scottish hills in winter, but are most beautiful and massive on the higher levels of Ben Nevis. We also admired the huge cornices at the mouths of Gardy Loo and Tower Gullies, particularly the latter; and Roberts recalled his last experience on the Ben when his party succeeded, after a hard fight, in storming Gardy Loo Gully.

We returned along the plateau and over Carn Dearg. Then we made for the top of the long funnel, occupied in summer by the Red Burn. Down it we enjoyed a magnificent standing glissade, for the condition of the snow was just right. After a short walk to the old Halfway Hut we brewed some tea with a small primus. Duly refreshed, Roberts led me over Meall an t'Suidhe and down by a steep and intricate route to Nevis Bridge and Fort William. Such was my satisfying first experience of Ben Nevis under snow and ice.

Next day we again set out for the Ben, but decided to attempt something nearer hand. We made for South Castle Gully on Carn Dearg. As the day was calm, crisp and clear, we thought that we might put it to a better use. Traversing out of the gully to the right we had little difficulty in securing a lodgment on the rocks of the Castle. In summer time this may be more difficult, but now very little rock was showing except at the sides of the gully. We gradually worked our way up the centre of the Castle, cutting a line of steps so as to link up the outcrops of bare rock. By this method it is possible to find good footholds and stances in the snow pockets amongst the rocks. It saves time and step-cutting. If the snow is in a doubtful state as regards avalanche danger this provides safe stances and additional security. I was already learning to reflect on such things and picking up a good deal of practical technique which proved invaluable to me later on, in the Alps. The immediate object was only to save time and labour, because the snow was icy and the rocks had conveniently bedded ledges.

It was interesting work and we made steady progress, although Roberts well knew that the most serious difficulties lay ahead, where the summit cliffs became much steeper and almost appeared to overhang. We came to a natural halting place which was a sort of narrow cave. The cornices at the edge of the plateau seemed to be little more than 200 feet above us. Roberts asked me to try leading up the next difficulty, but I was soon halted by chimneys of hard, black ice. The rock strata shelved outward and downward and the rocks were filmed with ice. After Roberts had inspected things for himself he thought for a little, shook his head and advised retreat. To attempt to force the issue might, he said, take many hours. So I learned the wisdom, and also the technique, of a timely retreat. Our steps were still good and usable, but we exercised great care on the icy parts. As we walked down the Mhuilinn glen a few hours later the Tower Ridge and North-East Buttress looked magnificent and austere in the evening light.

Next day we had to leave Fort William, but there was time for one more mountain. We left the train at Tyndrum and made our way up the Choninish glen to Ben Lui. I was appointed to lead up the Central Gully in the north-east corrie. The day was again perfect and I enjoyed myself. It was only necessary to cut steps in the narrow, upper section, where we climbed the steepest branch of the gully. Even so, Ben Lui (3,708 ft.), was very much easier than anything we had done on Ben Nevis, and the cornice was quite a simple affair. The extra 700 feet of height on Nevis makes all the difference in the world, especially as late in the spring as April, to the hardening of the snow, that peculiar process of transformation into snow-ice which is usually termed 'firnification' in the Alps. If the climbing was easier the view from the summit of Lui was unexcelled—embracing Loch Awe, Ben Cruachan, the Glencoe hills, Ben Nevis, Ben Lawers, Schiehallion and many other hills.

On Good Friday, 1925, I was with Frank Smythe at Fort William. We opened our campaign with the Castle. The snow was in excellent hard condition. Where Roberts and I had turned back three years previously Smythe and I had some intricate work on iced and snowy rocks with badly sloping holds.

Actually, there was little more than fifty feet of difficulty followed by an easy slope to a small cornice at the top, which was easily overcome. So I enjoyed my revenge on the Castle, but, from the summit of Carn Dearg, we were at once faced by the challenge of the Tower Ridge with hardly a spot of black showing above the level of the Douglas Boulder. On that perfect evening it appeared unearthly in its peaceful beauty but also, 'as the air, invulnerable'.

THE GULLIES

The Nevis gullies are most useful for learning about the condition of the snow, the icy channels which are the natural tracks for falling stones and fragments of cornices which have broken away and the way in which cornices build up, how to climb them or force a way through them. Apart from the two Castle Gullies which I have never climbed and of which the southern is usually considered to be the easier, there are four gullies which are not at all difficult, viz, Nos. 3, 4, 5 and Tower Gully. No. 5 has some short pitches at the narrow section, but these offer little trouble, as a rule. It has a very wide upper funnel, so that an exit can almost always be made at one point or another. I climbed it with R. M. McIntyre as a farewell climb on a Monday morning in April 1932. We left the Clark Hut at five a.m., had some trouble with deep snow and breakable crust in the middle section, but reached the top of Carn Dearg at seven a.m. There was a lip below the cornice at the top, fringed with a beautiful curtain of icicles through which we could see the morning sun shining brightly on the distant cone of Schiehallion. It seemed a shame to break the icicles and flog down the graceful snowy curves of the cornice.

Nos. 3 and 4 gullies are usually easy to descend, No. 4 being the easiest of all and least likely to give trouble with a cornice. It is curved at the top, but from below the curve it is generally safe to glissade all the way to Coire na Ciste. The same cannot always be said of No. 3, which is perfectly straight. If one descends No. 3 it is wise to be exceedingly careful until below the narrow, rocky portal at the foot of the upper funnel. There is often a considerable cornice at the top, but there are two upper openings, of which at least one may be practicable for starting a descent. In icy conditions No. 3 should be treated with great care, as there may be a polished, hardened avalanche trough between the portals. On a former occasion I was lucky to escape with a few bruises and bumps when a standing glissade got out of control. I retained my axe, but the spike is not a very powerful brake on a hard surface, whereas any attempt to use the pick on such a surface would simply jerk the axe out of one's hand altogether if, as is usually the case, the slide has developed a certain velocity before the remedy can be applied.* In a hard, icy condition of the snow which is not so bad as to necessitate the actual cutting of steps, the safest mode of descent is to stamp the feet down sideways, edging them into the surface, remain as upright as possible and secure oneself continually with the pick of the axe driven in forcibly slightly above, so that a slide will never start. This warning should apply to any Nevis gully, even to No. 4, during hard, frosty conditions, and sometimes to broad, open snow slopes as well. One should note that the top of No. 4 gully is at the lowest point of the rim of the plateau above Coire na Ciste and is next to the steep rise leading to the summit of Carn Dearg.

The only other Nevis gully which can be recommended for a practice descent, not without a little difficulty, is the Tower Gully, on the summit side of Tower Ridge. This gully is easy in summer, but it carries huge cornices in winter. Everything depends on the size and continuity of the cornice. If entry can be effected safely from above the party will probably be able to descend the rest of it safely. Below the upper part it is necessary to traverse obliquely downwards to the right, over a steep slope, in order to get on to the upper snows of Observatory Gully below the exit of Gardy Loo Gully. This may be difficult if the snow is in bad condition. Observatory Gully is steep, but has no pitches lower down.

On Easter Monday, 1929, on the occasion of the opening of the Charles Inglis Clark (C.I.C.) Hut by the Scottish Mountaineering Club, three of us walked to the summit of the Ben and made our way to the opening ceremony down Tower Gully.

---

* A fatality occurred in mid-winter during the war years on the steep snow slopes between the foot of No. 3 Gully and the Lochan Coire na Ciste. The cause was loss of control during a glissade on the frozen slope about nightfall.

Part of the old cornice had fallen in, affording us an easy entrance, and Charlie Parry cut the steps down the gully. There was a fierce, cold wind with blasts of spindrift. Lower down, where we had to turn to the right, great care was necessary owing to the masses of new snow. The mist swayed and eddied around us, but there were wonderful glimpses of distant mountains and of Loch Laggan, thirty miles to the east. Once past the dangerous slope we enjoyed a straight run on splendid snow down the entire length of Observatory Gully. Owing to the gentle run-out at the bottom we were able to glissade the whole way, in perfect control, to the Mhuilinn glen. We arrived at the Hut at 4.15 p.m., over an hour late, but still in time for the remains of the feast. But we were not too late for the delightful dinner that evening in the Palace Hotel, Fort William. Such a dinner, following a day on the hills by almost everyone concerned, was permeated by the true mountaineering spirit. Dr Inglis Clark, mountaineer, explorer and pioneer of Scottish mountain photography, had just come down from the opening ceremony, despite his age of over seventy years, and he gave us a delightful and colourful speech in praise of mountaineering and of Ben Nevis in all its many moods.

The Gardy Loo Gully is the most fearsome of the Nevis gullies when seen from above in winter. Its walls are not far short of vertical and it is defended by cornices where they are not so. The name dates back to the old Observatory days, when all manner of rubbish and discarded material was tipped over the side into the gully, just as in the narrow streets of old Edinburgh, when open gutters did duty for drains. The tipping of a bucket of dirty water from an upstairs window was usually preceded by a shout of 'Gardez l'eau' from above. These days are also in the past as regards Gardy Loo Gully, but rusty relics of old cans, pipes, bedsteads can still be found in the huge mounds of rocky debris at the foot of Observatory Gully, a tribute to the action of the geological forces of denudation within our own times.

Gardy Loo Gully is narrow and steep, but not over 250 feet in height. Half-way down is a natural rocky arch which is completely buried in snowy winters. When that is so the main difficulty is to climb the wall beneath it. When the archway is clear, there may be a severe ice pitch just above it. I have been three times up Gardy Loo in winter, but there was always room to crawl through the archway. My first ascent was on 31st December, 1928, with R. R. Elton. We had been ignominiously driven off the Tower Ridge by a gale of wind and ice-crusted rocks. The ice pitch above the Gardy Loo archway was a tough proposition. I found myself inside a little chimney curtained by massive icicles, and had to break out of it in order to climb up on the left to an ice slope. Twice I had to retreat, restore the circulation to numbed hands and straighten tense limbs, but ultimately I got through and cut substantial steps in the ice above. The icicles were sufficiently massive to confer some measure of security. When my friend came up there remained only a short, steep slope to the top, for the cornice had broken away to a short, vertical wall.

That was a day of unequalled visibility to the Cuillin of Skye, Rum, Mull, Jura and all the north-western peaks. We descended by the Arête and traversed the ridge to Carn Mor Dearg, just in time to view a sunset which was one mass of crimson glory in the west. On the following day, clad in shirt sleeves in warm sunshine, I ate my lunch on the top of Carn Dearg. The day was windless and the north-western hills were perfectly imaged in the calm waters of Loch Eil. In such days Ben Nevis can be truly Alpine and magnificent in its grandeur. Looking at the summit crags from the foot of Observatory Gully, before climbing Gardy Loo on the previous day, the racing clouds were flashing with silver and gold in the level sunbeams and bringing to mind Milton's lines on the 'crystal battlements' of Heaven. And we were setting out to storm these battlements.

My next ascent was on a gloomy April day in 1932. We vanquished the gully at dusk, and, amid the racing clouds of mist and spindrift, we had an anxious struggle to find and force our way down by the normally easy western slopes. To our shame, be it said, that not a man of the four of us carried a compass. We could only proceed with the utmost care, within sight of, but not too near the edge of the north-eastern precipice, until we reached the level plateau between Nevis and Carn Dearg. Then we turned to face the gale, and there was just sufficient mirk of twilight to enable us to distinguish several of the snow-covered cairns which mark the route of the old tele-graph line to the Observatory. That was the end of doubt and difficulty, as we raced down the slopes and saw the sombre gleam of the Lochan Meall an t'Suidhe far below us. We had emerged through the floor of the cloud. We were descending to the C.I.C. Hut, but, in the prevailing conditions, our circuitous route was much safer than attempting to descend by the Carn Mor Dearg Arête, which may be very difficult to locate and may even demand continuous step-cutting.

THE GREAT RIDGES

The best winter mountaineering in Scotland is on the great ridges of Ben Nevis. The Castle Ridge is the easiest, as it terminates nearly 1,000 feet lower than the others. The classic route is the Tower Ridge which, although fairly easy in summer, gives a very long and interesting climb under snow and ice. At mid-winter it is often impossible to climb the steep rocks of the Douglas Boulder by the direct route on account of ice on the narrow ledges. In spring the Boulder may be snow-free and offer a good, difficult introduction for the serious snow and ice work beyond. The Tower Ridge may be impossible in winter. In that case one can be certain that no other ridge will go, except perhaps the Castle Ridge.

My first attempt on Tower Ridge was with Frank Smythe at Easter, 1925, the day after we had climbed the Castle. Several parties belonging to the Scottish Mountaineering Club were on the mountain, as it was the occasion of the Easter Meet at Fort William. Only one party, who were bivouacking in the, now vanished, Half Way Hut on the western slopes, had gone very early to the Tower Ridge. As we halted, with a number of others, at a huge boulder above the Allt a'Mhuilinn, called the Luncheon Stone by the pioneers, we could see Rusk and Rutherfurd high up on the sunlit ridge. But alas! they were descending, which was a bad omen for us. We resolved to have a good rock climb to begin with and tackled the Douglas Boulder. It gave us good sport and we reached the summit cairn by three p.m. In those days there was no Clark Hut and we had walked from Fort William.

The day continued fine, so we both voted for giving the ridge a trial. The gap between Douglas Boulder and ridge is neither deep nor difficult. We encountered no serious difficulties beyond the gap until we approached the foot of the Little Tower, as the steep rock nose below it carried little snow. The Little Tower was a very different proposition. So smothered was it in snow and ice that we feared it might take hours to overcome by direct attack. We were not yet beaten, however. There was a way of descending on the side of Coire na Ciste, not a big descent, whereby we were enabled to reach a steeply sloping band or terrace which trended upwards in the direction of the Great Tower. This is known as the Secondary Tower Ridge, and we hoped that from it we could regain the main ridge just short of the Great Tower. Step cutting was necessary all the way. Smythe feared, with his Alpine experience, that such steeply inclined snow would be sure to peel off in a minor avalanche sooner or later. I assured him that he under-estimated its toughness and dourness (like the Scottish character). We continued and climbed steeply up the band, using side holds on the rocks on our left, where available. The move was successful and we were at the base of the Great Tower by five p.m.

The easiest way of circumventing this all but vertical boss of rock is by the Eastern Traverse, above Observatory Gully. It looked frightful: the idea of traversing a broad band of snow, as steeply inclined as a high angled roof, with a sheer drop over a cliff at the lower edge, gave us pause. Across Coire na Ciste, on the summit of Carn Dearg, a large group of mountaineers were observing our movements with interest. They were going down to Fort William for dinner, and here were we, at least half ignorant of what lay before us, but pretty sure that it was going to take a long time and much hard step cutting before we could even reach the easy summit slopes of the mountain. Could we make it at all before nightfall?

Smythe stepped out on to the steep band of snow. It was gratifyingly hard and firm. The mist closed in about us, hiding all but the frost crystalled cliff of the Tower and the line of footsteps, curving inwards to cross the top of a little gully and then outwards round the next bulge of the buttress. Things were not improving: here and there the snow was very thin and the axe struck bare rock, but there was always a way of some kind that

Winter

Summer

THE TOWER GAP, BEN NEVIS

led onward and upward. The snow was tough and sound; I will say that for it. Working hard and steadily, it took us an hour to regain the crest of the ridge beyond the Tower. It was now snowing gently, with nothing visible ahead but an awesome gap in the ridge in front of us, and then the great, white wall of the final rocks. We held anxious converse. The rocks were cased in frost crystals about a foot thick. We knew about the Tower Gap, but we had no idea of the difficulties beyond and we feared that there might be a cornice below the summit plateau.

In all prudence, or perhaps on account of our ignorance, retreat was the only sensible course of action. From the Tower Gap two chimneys descended into the mist in opposite directions. The one on the right I had read about. It was Glover's Chimney, a difficult climb in summer. We knew nothing of the other except that it must lead to Observatory Gully, and we could see nothing. The only sure way of retreat was the way by which we had come. Moving carefully, yet as quickly as possible, we retraced our steps round the Tower. There was no drifting snow and the steps were all good. I shall not detail that descent. The passage of time was only measured by the landmarks of our route. We were soon below the mist. As we got down the last of the rocks by the steep gully from the Douglas Boulder Gap to Coire na Ciste (for we knew too little of the topography of the Ben to select the easier gully leading towards Coire Leis) the setting sun coloured the summit snows of Carn Mor Dearg a deep crimson. Far below us the Great Glen was filled with a lovely violet coloured haze. It was one of those wonderful colour contrasts, soft yet brilliant, which are only seen in our Scottish Highlands in winter or spring, and almost unknown in the drier climate of the Alps.

We got off the rocks by eight p.m. and hurried down the glen in careless contentment. The last wisps of cloud were drifting over the summit of the Ben: the great ridges assumed a pale, spectral hue—intensely cold and aloof. We were profoundly thankful that we had beaten a timely retreat. The last peril of the day was when we were stumping dreamily towards Fort William along the railway track. A belated goods engine crept swiftly and silently up behind us, and we hastily jumped down

M

the embankment. At ten p.m. we met Mr J. A. Parker, President of the S.M.C., in the main street. He was unaffectedly glad to see us, and the word 'search party' was not even mentioned!

Needless to say, the challenge of the Tower Ridge, clad in full wintry armour (it had to be so for sporting reasons), was often in my mind. The next trial of strength was at Easter 1929. On the Saturday C. W. Parry and I had ascended Observatory Ridge and descended the North-East Buttress with comparatively little trouble on snow-free rocks in glorious weather. It snowed and blew all that night. We were staying at the Clark Hut, just before the formal opening. Smythe and Roberts were also there, so we set out, all four of us, for the Tower Ridge next day. In doubtful weather we took the easiest approach and gained the ridge beyond the Douglas Boulder Gap. As we got higher a proper blizzard set in. Ledges were all smothered in new snow, which had to be cleared as there was some ice underneath. It became unendurable and we retreated from the rocks of the Little Tower.

In 1932, a winter of ample snowfall, I tried again, in the company of Robert MacIntyre, of Perth. We motored to Fort William on a Friday afternoon early in April. We opened the campaign in a rather unorthodox way, going to the local cinema, where we saw a modern American version of something like Shakespeare's 'Comedy of Errors', under the title 'Lonely Wives'. We then descended into the basement of the local fish and chip restaurant, commonly known as 'Hell's Kitchen'. Well nourished, we left the car at Achintee at 11.15 p.m. in bright moonlight. As we ascended the track it occurred to us that we might as well test the condition of the snow. We decided to continue to the summit of the Ben. Above the snow line all feelings of drowsiness left us and we thoroughly enjoyed the latter part of the ascent. Clouds came over the moon and a cold wind moaned across the plateau, which looked completely desolate and arctic in the half-light. We reached the summit at two a.m. and took shelter for a few minutes in the lee of the Observatory. Then we made for the top of No. 3 Gully where there was hardly any cornice, and proceeded to descend. The snow was in good condition and not too hard, so, after cutting a few steps we were able to stamp our way downwards in security towards Coire na Ciste. Conditions were too soft for glissading. The sky cleared again, and we saw the Great Tower, high above us, frost-spangled and gleaming in the moonlight. Surely the conditions were right at last for a successful assault. We were in the Hut by three a.m., trying to coax the warmth back into our feet after much wallowing in soft snow.

We made an early start, climbing the Douglas Boulder quickly by the direct route, there being little snow on the lower rocks. The first steep rocks beyond the Boulder Gap required a little clearing, but the first serious difficulty was again at the Little Tower. We attacked it direct, but all the rocks were heavily plastered and we were soon forced to traverse over steep slabs overlooking the Observatory Gully. The snow was new and dry, of the consistency of flour. It had not been thawed or re-frozen and it failed to adhere to the old film of ice on the rocks. Unfortunately, the latter was too thin to be chipped into satisfactory footholds. After about sixty feet of traversing, things improved and I secured a belay of a sort for the axe. I did not like the situation at all and felt obliged to warn Mac that I might not be able to stand the strain of holding him if he had the misfortune to slip. This is always a danger on a long traverse. If a second man comes off on the rope he executes a long pendulum swing before he can be checked. My caution was unnecessary. Mac proceeded with irreproachable precision.

We worked our way back to the crest of the ridge. The rocks were draped with massive icicles which, as we cut them down, bounced on the slabs with a merry, musical tinkle before plunging finally into the gully. It was such a day of gorgeous sunshine that we made light of our difficulties. We were both in splendid form and the Tower Ridge was giving us our money's worth. We, neither of us, wished for an easy passage.

Over an hour and a half was spent on the Little Tower. At length we were proceeding along the graceful, curving eaves of purest snow to the base of the Great Tower. For half an hour we fed and rested in the warm sunshine, gazing contentedly at the Alpine panorama to north and east of us. When we started on the Eastern Traverse the slope was already in shadow, not at all a bad thing for that dangerous-looking, steep band of snow which we must cross. I have known cases where parties have come so far and have been intimidated by that slope, so that they have either retreated or attempted one or other of the much more difficult western routes on the Tower. If one sees the place in summer the ledge-like structure of the lower rock explains why the winter accumulation of snow is generally perfectly stable, despite its steepness. It builds up gradually during the winter so that the successive layers have time to cohere by regelation. Beyond the traverse we gained the Tower crest by iced ledges, and that was the end of all serious difficulty. If only Frank Smythe and I had known what lay beyond the Tower Gap; even with our small pittance of available daylight, we should have been able to complete the ascent in 1925. On this occasion we cleared and crossed the Gap quite easily. Two ugly bulges of vertical snow above it turned out to be firm and good; a beautifully curved ridgeline of snow followed, corniced a little on one side. Then Mac cut a staircase up the final slope and we stepped on to the summit plateau after five and a half hours of actual climbing time.

The Tower Ridge is far from being the most difficult of the great ridges of Ben Nevis, but it is always interesting under snow. It is so delightfully varied, and the ice-boltered rocks at the Great Tower (to copy an expression used by Mr Winthrop Young in his Alpine classic, *On High Hills*) are so exceedingly impressive. The few hundred feet by which Ben Nevis overtops the other Scottish hills in the west makes an enormous difference to the difficulties of the upper parts of the climbs. The rest is due to the storage capacity of the plateau for snow and the strategic position of the Ben on the Atlantic Seaboard. W. T. Kilgour, in his book, *Twenty Years on Ben Nevis*, remarks that there seemed to be only two conditions of atmospheric humidity on the Ben—very dry or saturation. Under the latter and more common condition frost crystals would grow out into the wind at an enormous rate, up to several feet long on all sharp edges of rock, buildings or Observatory apparatus.

There have been several cases of benightment on the Tower Ridge. At Easter, 1937, after a very snowy winter, only one party succeeded in completing the ascent, Mr and Mrs S. H. Cross, of Cumberland. They actually cut steps across the face of the Great Tower, obliquely upwards in a westerly direction.

Surely that must have been more difficult than the Eastern Traverse, but it all depends on the previous weather history of the mountain. Their performance was a very fine one. On the same day two friends of my own proceeded too far and too late, with the result that they were compelled to spend a calm, frosty night on the rocks. They were none the worse, for I enjoyed an excellent climb with them two days later up Green Gully by the side of the Comb. There, we only succeeded in fighting our way up to the plateau by seven p.m.

Just before Christmas, 1939, with W. H. Murray and D. Laidlaw, I again climbed Tower Ridge. After a hard fight we reached the summit in bright moonlight. All around and beneath us was a sea of cloud silvered by moonbeams, from which only the high tops of the Mamores and the Glencoe peaks projected like black islands. Days such as these are indeed rare, but through them one lives life to the full. The worries of a modern civilised existence vanish into thin wraiths of unreality and we are back in the dawn of history among the gods, giants and mysterious animism of our remote forefathers, when sagas like Beowulf and the Norse Eddas were composed in a setting of great mountains and savage wildernesses of snow and ice.

On days when the Tower Ridge can be climbed fairly easily the Observatory Ridge may be quite impossible. This was so in early April 1939 on account of icing on the lower slabs. After many fruitless hours George Dwyer, Dicky Morsley and I abandoned the attempt and completed our day by a rapid ascent of Tower Ridge. At the end of April I was back again at the Clark Hut in a goodly company of climbers. Next day Bill Murray, W. M. Mackenzie and I started for Observatory Ridge. Several ledges required clearing of snow and there was some ice here and there, but I had little difficulty in leading up the lower, slabby nose of the ridge. The others were held in reserve for the snow and ice higher up.

A snow ridge followed, with rocky bosses at intervals. Soon we had to cut carefully up the Observatory Gully side of the ridge and back again to a broad snow stance on the crest, where we halted for lunch. There was now a choice between a difficult route along the crest or another traverse over apparently easier ground on our right into a steep gully. In February, 1938,

Murray, Mackenzie and MacAlpine had used the detour, but it had cost them much time and labour. On that occasion the party had encountered masses of dry powder snow which made the going exceedingly difficult, and even dangerous. This must have been the most severe ascent ever made of the Observatory Ridge. It cost the party fourteen hours and they reached the summit of the Ben at 11.30 p.m., having been forced to cut steps for several hours by the light of torches on the final slopes of Zero Gully.*

Mackenzie having led before lunch, it was now Murray's turn. We followed him up a wall to the crest of the ridge. In front was an ice-encrusted rocky tower. The snow covering became very thin as we approached its base, and Mackenzie anchored himself. The leader ran out ninety feet of rope, so we had to untie and include an extra sixty feet in our linkage, as we had been tied on a single 120-foot length. First came a delicate traverse to the left, then a direct ascent, partly on rock and partly on notches cut by Murray in the ice, and finally to the lower end of an ice-covered, rocky scoop. This gave the leader much trouble, as it was a nasty place. I fully understood when it came to my turn to follow. This fine lead brought us back into the sunshine. For all that, it was so cold that we continued to wear all our woollies and helmets. Things went much better now. The crest rose in front of us in a beautiful snowy curve, and Zero Gully on our left was no longer at an enormous distance below.

At four p.m. we cut steps across into the bed of Zero Gully. We could see our friends on the Tower Ridge, negotiating the Eastern Traverse. I was now on familiar ground, as Colin Allan and I had climbed the lower half of Slav Route on 4th April, 1936, and finished up Zero Gully, being forced to cut steps continuously for three hours and negotiating two ice pitches. I carried a clinometer on that occasion and found that the average inclination of the gully was fifty-six degrees for a very long way. This is a very steep gradient indeed for Scottish snow and usually indicates a hard surface of snow-ice. On this occasion,

* See *S.M.C.J.*, Vol. 21, p. 337, 'Fourteen hours on the Observatory Ridge' by W. M. Mackenzie, also *Mountaineering in Scotland* by W. H. Murray, Chapter XI (Dent, 1947).

however, the snow-ice was in excellent condition. By working without a halt and changing over the lead at intervals, we emerged on the summit at 5.30 p.m. Zero Gully is seldom corniced at the top. Our splendid climb had taken us just six and a half hours, a very different experience from the notable February ascent of the year before. As the strength of the parties involved on the two occasions must have been approximately the same, the difference in time taken can only be ascribed to the very troublesome condition of the snow in the month of February. This dry, powdery snow is common enough in the Alps and must be perpetual on the upper slopes of Himalayan peaks.

Next day Bill Murray and I climbed the North-East Buttress. That, too, was an ideal day. We attained the First Platform directly by Raeburn's Arête. In many places great care was required owing to ice on the ledges, but the rock was otherwise dry. Two hours saw us on the Platform. Higher up we encountered a good deal more snow, and it was a little difficult to regain the crest of the ridge from the snowy gully on the left, some way below the Second Platform. We knew the structure of the ridge and the beautifully incut holds available on this wall, when once the snow had been cleared away. To all other climbers who essay the route under snow conditions I should give the advice not to be daunted by the forbidding appearance of this wall. As soon as we regained the crest we had an alternation of snow and rock all the way to the top. The few difficult sections were short. Near the top the rocks were again heavy with frost crystals. Without halts, we gained the summit in two and three-quarter hours from the First Platform. We descended by the Ledge Route from Carn Dearg, normally a quick route of descent when the lower rocks are snow-free. Of course, the North East Buttress would present very formidable problems in winter or early spring after heavy snowfalls. It can always be expected to be much more difficult than Tower Ridge. It is interesting to recall that these two routes were, apart from gullies, the earliest climbing routes on the Ben. The Tower Ridge was first climbed by Norman Collie, G. A. Solly and J. Collier in April 1894 and described by them as 'a superb climb of about 2,000 feet of ice, snow and rock'.* The first

* *S.M.C. Journal*, Vol. 3, p. 158.

ascent of the North East Buttress, by the brothers Hopkinson in September 1892, was obviously not complicated by snow and ice.

In conclusion a word may be said about descending the Ben in winter by the Arête in the direction of Carn Mor Dearg. In severe conditions this may be extremely difficult. Parties have been compelled to cut steps all the way, and it has taken as long as two hours to reach the saddle at the head of Coire Leis. The best descent to the corrie is by a uniform slope of scree some way short of the saddle itself (where there are terraces of crag). Moreover, in mist or twilight, it is not always easy to hit off the correct route to the edge of the Arête. Parties have got into difficulties and accidents have happened when they have gone by mistake to the end of the North-East Buttress and attempted to descend its eastern face, which is craggy and may be badly iced.

Many other climbs on Ben Nevis will be done in winter conditions which have hitherto been regarded as purely rock climbs, as there is always progress in mountaineering technique, but sufficient has been written in this chapter to show what a grand field for adventure and unending variety is offered by the truly Alpine, wintry defences of Ben Nevis. They must never be lightly regarded; for a sunny April day with warm, dry rocks can, within a few hours, be transformed into a raging storm of hail, snow and tearing cloud, with a film of ice on the rocks and masses of whirling spindrift. There is yet another danger for the inexperienced. Winter days are short: even April days are followed by long nights. A party may be capable of climbing the lower two-thirds of a route like Tower Ridge, but be utterly outclassed by the icy defences of the last 500 feet. It is then that a weak party may panic and an accident happen to an exhausted member on ground which he could normally descend or climb in comparative safety. It is vital that the decision to retreat should be taken as soon as prudence and commonsense urge its advisability. It takes more than a few, brief visits at Easter time to confer a comprehensive practical experience of snow, ice and weather on a difficult mountain like Ben Nevis.

CHAPTER XII

SKYE AND THE CUILLINS

INTRODUCTION AND GEOLOGY

THE traveller who catches his first glimpse of the northern
end of the Cuillin range from Sligachan sees a fantastic
skyline of jagged, black pinnacles and cliffs, all the more
impressive by contrast with the bare, rounded hills and rolling
moorland which are the only visible part of the interior of the
island, as seen from the road between Kyle, Broadford and Loch
Ainort. Often he sees nothing but a mass of dark, drifting cloud,
followed by an intriguing vision of the sharp pyramid of Sgurr
nan Gillean, seen for an instant and again swallowed up in inky
blackness. No wonder that Sheriff Nicolson, most famous of the
early pioneers of climbing in the Cuillin and himself a native of
Skye, exclaimed that Sgurr nan Gillean ought by right to have
been at least 10,000 feet high from its appearance! If one has
already seen the skyline of the Cuillin from the sands of Morar
or from a mainland peak, as far away as Ben Nevis or even
beyond Glencoe, it is difficult to understand how such mountains
can remain so well concealed from the usual route of approach.
They are, of course, a small range, as regards area, tucked away
into a southern pocket of this big, sprawling island, between the
sea inlets of Loch Slapin and Loch Brittle, and much more conspicuous from the south and south-east than from the north.
Small as they are, they have drawn to themselves many artists
and lovers of mountains and amongst them not a few distinguished names.

Dr Samuel Johnson, on his journey to the Western Isles in
1773, was not impressed, unless by the bareness and primitive
desolation of the island. Sir Walter Scott was conducted to Loch
Coruisk in 1814 and was overcome by the rugged grandeur of
the place. He put his impressions on record and persuaded
many others to go and see for themselves.

The first well-known mountaineer to visit the Cuillin was
Principal J. D. Forbes. As Professor of Natural Philosophy at
Edinburgh, and later Principal of St Andrews, he was a famous

Alpine explorer and investigator of the flow of glaciers. At his first visit in 1836 he climbed Sgurr nan Gillean by what is now known as the Tourist Route, but which most modern tourists, and some climbers as well, have found sufficiently difficult. After several years of travel and Alpine exploration he returned to Skye in 1845, explored the Cuillins thoroughly and made a map of the range. Sheriff Alexander Nicolson did much more than Forbes, returning again and again, continuing his exploration and pouring forth his love and enthusiasm for the Cuillin both in verse and prose. He climbed Sgurr Alasdair in 1873, the highest point of the island, which was later named after him. From a bivouac by Loch Coruisk he climbed Sgurr Dubh, experiencing no small difficulties, especially during the rough descent through Coir'an Lochain in growing darkness. Nicolson absorbed the very spirit of these mountains when he wrote, 'There is an ever changing life in the play of the clouds that float serenely through the blue sky or hurry frantically across the riven peaks, or descend softly like darkness into the bosom of the hills'.

Perhaps the best-known of the long line of explorers of the Cuillin was Professor J. Norman Collie, a distinguished chemist, but equally notable as a mountaineer in the Alps, the Rockies and the Himalaya. Collie came to Sligachan to fish, but the fine weather drove him to climb the mountains. In later life, when he had given up climbing, but still returned again and again to Skye, he used to say that at one time he 'had got into a bad habit of climbing mountains and only in his old age had he become sane again!' We may well rejoice over the long years of Collie's insanity, for he made many great expeditions on the Cuillins, including the Bhasteir Tooth, the Thearlaich Dubh Gap, the first ascents of the great southern face of Sgurr a Ghreadaidh, the north-west ridge of Alasdair and the Cioch pinnacle. Many of these were made along with John Mackenzie of Sconser, a Highlander of the old school and almost the only Scottish professional mountain guide. Collie and Mackenzie grew old together and passed away within a year or two of each other during the recent war, for Collie returned to Sligachan in 1939 to live his last years within sight of his beloved hills.

For many summers Collie lived at Glen Brittle Lodge with

his friend Colin Phillip, the artist. He himself was no mean per-
former in water-colours, and this explains the intensity of charm
and the truth in his description of his favourite mountains.

'The individuality of the Cuillin is not seen in their summits,
which are often almost ugly, but in the colour of the rocks, the
atmospheric effects, the relative largeness and harmony of the
details compared with the actual size of the mountains, and
most of all the mountain mystery that wraps them round.'
Collie had climbed on the Alps, the Rockies and the Himalaya,
and he knew what he was talking about, so that he could sense
'the secret beauty born of the mists, the rain and the sunshine,
in a quiet and untroubled land'. Whoever has climbed on the
Cuillin and got to know and love them should not fail to read
the entire article from which the above is but a fragment.*

Many other distinguished mountaineers have climbed on the
Cuillin, including Charles Pilkington who first ascended the so-
called Inaccessible Pinnacle of Sgurr Dearg in 1880 and W. W.
Naismith, the founder of the Scottish Mountaineering Club. It
was A. P. Abraham, of Keswick, who first popularised the
Cuillin for climbers with the publication of his *Rock Climbing in
Skye*. The first *S.M.C. Guide to the Isle of Skye* appeared a little
earlier, in the year 1907. Subsequent years, with the exception
of the war years when Skye was a restricted area, have seen an
ever increasing flow of climbers to the Cuillin, both from England and Scotland.

It is worth asking why there is such superlatively excellent
climbing on the Cuillins, for nowhere else in Britain is the rock
so perfectly rough and sound. From one point of view a rock-
climbing novitiate spent in Skye is a doubtful advantage. One
is led to expect too much from other mountains. One gets into
bad habits, relying on the perfect soundness of small holds for
pulling up with the arms, without testing all holds with care,
preserving one's balance at all times, developing habits of neat
and accurate foot-work and not relying on the friction of abnor-
mally rough rock on rubbers and trouser knees. One should not
expect to be able to climb easily and safely on such steep rock
faces on other hills or mountains—certainly not on the Alps.

* Originally ' A'Chuilionn', *S.M.C. Journal*, Vol. 4, p. 259, but also in Collie's
Climbs on the Himalaya and other Mountain Ranges.

A few remarks on the geology of the Cuillins may not be out of place. Except for a few rocks near the coast, the great mass of Skye rock is igneous in origin and belongs to the Tertiary epoch, very recent when compared with the main rock masses of the Scottish Highlands. In early tertiary times vast floods of lava poured out of fissures and covered over two-thirds of the island. Similar rocks are still to be seen among the hills of the northern part of Skye, where the rock pinnacles of the Quiraing are worth visiting, but not for climbing purposes.

In later tertiary periods there were great intrusions of coarsely crystalline gabbro, which cooled under the pressure due to the great weight of overlying basalt (lava). There was also an intrusion of granite, partly cutting into the gabbro, chiefly on the eastern side. Since these remote times there has been an enormous amount of erosion. The earlier sheets of basaltic lava have been removed, and the tough, resistant gabbro now stands up as the peaks and ridges of the Cuillin. Here and there it is interrupted by more recent and minor intrusions of smooth, brittle basalt.

It is the hardness and the roughness of the coarsely crystalline gabbro that makes this rock unique in its excellence for the purpose of the mountaineer. Apart from the Cuillin it occurs only in lesser masses in the mountains of Rum and at one point of Ardnamurchan, but the grand climbing available on the peaks of the Lofoten Islands off the Norwegian Coast is also dependent on gabbro rock. The granite of the Red Hills near Sligachan is in striking contrast to the Black Cuillin, for it has weathered into long talus slopes of red scree which clothe the hillsides and protect the rounded hills from further erosion. The actual shape of the Cuillin peaks is frequently determined by the subsequent intrusions of basalt or trap rock, which cause planes of weakness, not entirely without their uses for the climber, as they may offer easy lines of attack and passes across the mountain chain. The highest summit, Sgurr Alasdair, is made of trap and also the Inaccessible Pinnacle of Sgurr Dearg, so that the above principles should not be taken as an infallible guide to the texture and resistance of the rocks.

Even after the main contours of the Cuillins were developed there have been noteworthy changes owing to the erosive action of rain, streams, frost and ice. Most spectacular are the huge boiler-plate slabs with glacial markings in the Coir' a' Ghrunnda and Coire Lagan and at Coruisk, which is a typical rock lake produced by glacial erosion. The gabbro of the Cuillin retains the impress of the last ice age better than the other Scottish mountains, owing to its hardness, but the ice ages affected most of Britain.*

EASY CLIMBING—THE HOLIDAY SPIRIT

My first experience of the Cuillin was very fortunate, so it may serve as an introduction for others. I attended a Meet of the S.M.C. at Sligachan in June 1923. We arrived on a stormy evening and heard reports of heavy snow on peaks and ridges, only the Tourist route being possible on Sgurr nan Gillean. There was a grand, climbing atmosphere about Sligachan. The Inn was a real home for mountaineers. Next morning we sallied forth along the track to the Bealach a' Mhaim, not expecting much of the weather, but determined to get to the top of Bruach na Frithe (3,143 ft.), the easiest peak of the range. The mist began to lift as we walked up the grassy Fionn Choire. What a magnificent view from the summit for my first experience of the Cuillin! Large, wool-pack, cumulus clouds were lifting off the western tops. There were the black, jagged peaks and ridges, unique and distinguished in form, and far beyond them lay the azure western sea. As the authors of the Skye Guide remark, 'Fine weather in Skye is worth waiting for'. It is an island of beautiful surprises.

Off we went, six of us, down the western ridge over Sgurr na Bhairnich and An Caisteal with that entrancing view still before us, until we became engrossed in the difficulties of the narrow ridge over the three tops of Bidein Druim nan Ramh (the peak of the ridge of oars). Not that this ridge is normally difficult for a competent party, but now the ledges were smothered in snow and it took us a long time to traverse the peaks. By this time the view had again changed, and we looked straight south over Loch Coruisk to the sea loch of Scavaig. It was hard to say which was the more entrancing shade of blue, for the depth and purity of these Skye colours must be seen in order to be believed.

* See *The Tertiary Igneous Rocks of Skye* by Alfred Harker (H.M.S.O. 1904).

It was late afternoon when we halted on the Bealach na Glaic Moire (2,510 ft.), the easy pass across the ridge connecting the Coruisk valley with Coire Tairneilear (The Thunderer), to the north. Then the mist enfolded us again as we picked our way carefully down the latter corrie, keeping close under the rocks of Sgurr an Fheadain, so as to avoid difficulties. One can never reckon on finding a Cuillin pass that is altogether easy to descend in mist. There is often only one easy way down, which ought to be properly memorised beforehand. We were hours late for dinner, but Mr Campbell, of Sligachan, was used to the ways of climbers.

On the first day we had expert guidance from the veterans of the Club, but, on the Monday, four of us, relatively inexperienced, were turned loose on Sgurr nan Gillean to fend for ourselves. A long walk over the moors, keeping to the left of the spectacular, deep gorge at the foot of Coire a' Bhasteir, led us to the base of our climb; I had selected the Pinnacle Ridge for the day's work. After lunch we found things quite easy until we reached the top of the Third Pinnacle. Now there was to be some real rock climbing, starting off with an awesome descent. Two of the party disliked the prospect, descended to the southeast, by-passed the difficulties and finally rejoined us at the last gap between the Fourth Pinnacle and the final slope of Sgurr nan Gillean.

The warm sun was fast clearing the snow off the ridge, with the result that we had little difficulty with the descent, for the holds are ample. Its bark is far worse than its bite, a common experience with the excellent rock of the Cuillin. In dry, summer conditions one can traverse round Knight's Peak (the fourth Pinnacle) without ascending it, but there was too much snow on the ledges of the north face. So we climbed it and had to spend a good deal of time over the following descent, the snow being now in a slithery condition. It also meant that our reunited party of four was slow on the long final ascent to the top of Sgurr nan Gillean (3,167 ft.).

The mists were eddying around the summit, but the repeated clearances displayed a succession of Brocken Spectres, as the sun and wind were just in the right positions. So far as I know, Sgurr nan Gillean is one of the best situated peaks for this phenomenon, as the west wind throws out a screen of cloud perfectly illuminated by the afternoon sun. In the evening our President referred to these appearances as being most gratifying to one's personal vanity, for if two of us stood fairly close together, each saw a huge composite shadow of both projected on the background of luminous cloud, but only his own head was surrounded by a brightly coloured halo.* Each could thus rest assured of his own peculiar odour of sanctity, and that the other man, of a certainty, must be filled with enmity and lying when he claimed the pre-eminence for himself. I have seen these spectres on many other Scottish hills and on Alpine peaks, but I still think that those on Sgurr nan Gillean were the finest. The last of the clouds went racing over the Red Hills to the east of us, climbing up like an unending procession of woolly sheep over Glamaig and pouring down the other side in the direction of Marsco. To the west the sea shimmered in the sun, and the Long Island, as they often call the Outer Hebrides, was a clear, pale blue from Barra Head in the south to the Butt of Lewis in the north. How fascinating were the pale brown moorlands, the hills of Trotternish and the long arms of the sea lochs of Skye in all directions!

Two of our party descended by the south ridge, or Tourist Route. Ronald Burn, who had accompanied me over the Pinnacles, was not an expert on rocks, but his ambition was to climb all the separate mountains and all the separate tops in Scotland (including the Isles), over 3,000 feet in height. At the other end of the arc of the Cuillin horseshoe was the Inaccessible Pinnacle of Sgurr Dearg. That had to be included, and Burn was gaining his qualification. So he readily agreed to proceed by the narrow, western ridge, from which we descended by the easy Nicolson Chimney. It was not entirely a scree gully, however, as Burn had expected; so he incautiously wagered me a bottle of beer that we had not descended the authentic Nicolson Chimney. After this had been paid I was, of course, in honour bound to take him up the Inaccessible.

Next day Ronald Burn succeeded in adding Am Basteir and the Bhasteir Tooth to his collection of Munros and tops. We were led by W. N. Ling, who used to partner Harold Raeburn

* This is very seldom seen.

in the earlier, difficult, guideless ascents in the Alps, and who also achieved with him two notable pioneering campaigns in the Caucasus prior to the 1914–18 war. There were also present Henry Alexander, author of the Cairngorms Guide and later Lord Provost of Aberdeen and Sheriff G. D. Valentine of Skye, whose knowledge of the Cuillin and its wild life, and especially of the golden eagle and its haunts, was unrivalled. It was a most enjoyable day. We went up the west side of the Bhasteir Gorge, paying a visit to the Caves, and traversed Am Basteir from the col between it and Sgurr nan Gillean, continuing by a short, difficult descent to the Tooth and then into Lota Corrie by the original route, returning over the Bealach nan Lice and the Fionn Choire. I should say that all three days' climbing, covering the Pinnacle route to Sgurr nan Gillean and continuing by the west ridge, Am Basteir, the Tooth, Sgurr a Fionn Choire, Bruach na Frithe and the Bidein peaks to the Bealach na Glaic Moire is eminently suitable, in good weather conditions, for novices who have had previous experience of rock climbing and the use of the rope. Most of the rock is of moderate standard, and no part is very difficult. It is more direct to descend the western face of the Tooth by Naismith's route, but this is precipitous and more difficult. Certainly the holds are sound and adequate, but they are easier to find by doing the route upwards to begin with.

We younger men, E. C. Thomson, C. Philip, Burn and I walked over to Glen Brittle next day and ascended Sgurr Dearg, after which I got them all up the Inaccessible Pinnacle by the short and difficult side. There is an excellent block for a belay on the small summit, the whole ascent being possible on an eighty-foot length of rope. By common conspiracy we persuaded Burn that he must stand upright on the small block on the summit, or he could not be credited with having climbed this important peak. The top of the Pinnacle is at least twenty feet higher than the summit cairn of Sgurr Dearg on the adjacent mountain top, so it is the Pinnacle and not the other which is the true summit of the mountain. Burn took no chances and fairly climbed the two tops.

On the descent to Coire Lagan we were in dense mist, which thinned out as we got down to the upper corrie above the lochan.

The Cioch, Sron na Ciche, Skye

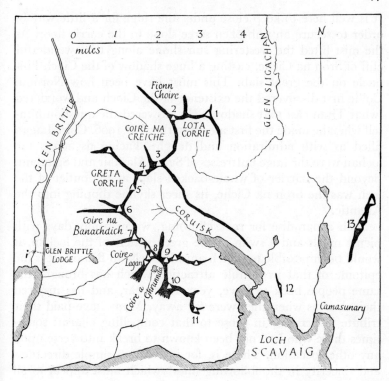

MAP B THE CUILLINS

PEAKS

		height in feet
1	Sgurr nan Gillean (peak of the young men)	3,167
2	Bruach na Frithe (brae of the forest)	3,143
3	Bidein Druim nan Ramh (peak of ridge of oars)	2,850
4	Sgurr a' Mhadaidh (foxes' peak)	3,010
5	Sgurr a' Ghreadaidh (peak of clear waters)	3,190
6	Sgurr na Banachdich (smallpox peak)	3,167
7	Sgurr Dearg (red peak). Inaccessible Pinnacle is close at hand	3,226
8	Sgurr Alasdair	3,251

3 peaks in line downwards are, in order, Thearlaich, Alasdair and Sgumain, the first named after Charles Pilkington, the highest after Sheriff Nicolson. Next to 8 going towards 7 is Sgurr Mhic-Coinnich, named after John McKenzie, the Skye guide.

9	(From this) Sgurr Dubh na Da Bheinn, the ridge of the Dubhs branches to the right (black peaks)	3,069
10	Sgurr nan Eag (notched peak)	3,037
11	Gars-bheinn (echoing mountain)	2,934
12	Sgurr na Stri	1,623
13	Blaven (hill of bloom) with Clach Glas to north	3,042

N

It is well here to keep close under the ridge for a little way in order to secure an unbroken scree slope to the corrie floor. As the mist lifted the westering sun shone along that wonderful cliff of Sron na Ciche, casting a huge shadow of the Cioch Pinnacle on the great slab. This must have been how Norman Collie first discovered the existence of the Cioch and wondered 'what Titan cast that shadow'. He answered the question himself when he made the first ascent in the year 1906. Coire Lagan filled us with admiration and delight. Facing us across the lochan were the huge buttresses of Sgurr Alasdair and Sgumain. Beyond the barrier of whale-backed slabs at the outlet of the loch was the Sron na Ciche, its sheer skyline dipping into the Atlantic.

Such a paradise for rock climbing, warm sunny days with picnic meals and a swim in the green waters of the lochan, it would be impossible to match anywhere else in Britain. It is the epitome of that irresistible attraction which has brought the same people back to Skye, year after year, and has inspired their dreams when they were far away. Many have paid their tribute in verse or in prose to that compelling charm; sometimes those who had not been known to break into verse upon any other occasion. There is, for instance, a simple directness and sincerity in the following lines* which must appeal to all who have felt the magnetism of the Cuillins:

> Oh, the spirit of the Cuillin, her tryst with you she keeps
> In the heart of Corrie Lagan, where the jade-green lochan sleeps,
> And you lose all sense of weariness as in its depths you lie,
> For there's magic in the lochans on the misty Isle of Skye.
>
> There are days when the Black Cuillin are afloat in silver mist
> And a fairy wand has turned them into isles of amethyst;
> You can perch on top of Dearg and watch the clouds roll by
> As they fill each lonely corrie on the misty Isle of Skye.

We stayed with Mary Campbell at Glen Brittle. Ravenous as we were with our day's exertions, we enjoyed an ample and excellent dinner. Then, as we were settling down to fill our pipes, the door opened again and Mary entered with a second meal of two boiled eggs per man, scones and tea. These were

---

* *Glenbrittle* by I. M. E. Bell, adopted as a song by the Ladies' Scottish Climbing Club.

the days when it was good to be young and carefree. We could not offend our good hostess, so we set to again and did our best. Towards midnight Philip and I strolled out on to the beach. The moon was up: a line of silver spangled and shimmered across Loch Brittle, with the faint outline of Canna beyond and one light winking across at intervals—as full of mystery and charm as any fairyland. The Alps and the Caucasus have shown me grander scenes by far on a bigger canvas, but Glen Brittle has never lost that more intimate appeal, a grandeur and peace of its own, perfect in its blending of mountain, moor, sea and sky.

Our last day was a simple ridge walk back to Sligachan by way of the tops. We were not a fast party and it was a hot day, perfectly suited to lingering on the tops. We traversed Sgurr Banachdich, Sgurr Ghreadaidh and the first top of Sgurr a' Mhadaidh, descending into Coire Tairneilear from the Thuilm ridge. We reached Sligachan at 11.30 p.m. and they gave us a full dinner! Most of us, too, had an early breakfast in order to catch the 7.30 a.m. boat from Broadford.

HARDER AND LONGER VENTURES

In July 1924 I was again in Skye, this time with Frank Smythe, whom I had met in 1921 at Wasdale, when he had given me my first taste of difficult rock climbing. After a day spent on the round of Sgurr nan Gillean, Am Basteir and the Tooth we moved to Mary Campbell's cottage at Glen Brittle. G. Barlow and E. W. Steeple, joint editors of the first edition of the S.M.C. *Guide to the Island of Skye*, were also staying there. We did not climb with them, but they were grand people to come back to in the evenings—those long summer evenings when we never troubled to descend from the ridges until after sunset, and when after-dinner talks went on until after midnight. Those evenings with gorgeous sunset colours and the long views across the Atlantic to the pale blue hills of Harris and South Uist were part of a life at the opposite pole from the industrialism, ambitions and alleged progress of a modern age. Which of them was the real world? We could not be sure, but we were content to live life to the full. It is, perhaps, this atmosphere of careless contentment, so typical of summer days in Skye, that explains why fewer new climbing routes have been made in the Cuillins than in any other principal climbing area of Britain during the last quarter of a century.

For the first few days we could not forget the rain which hardly ceased to shroud the hills. Barlow's theory was that fine weather might be expected when the barometer was at its lowest. He and Steeple went out every day, but not to climb. They prowled about in lower Coire Lagan, playing an entertaining game. They looked for surveyors' bench marks. Each scored a point when he found one. It was surprising how long the game lasted, but at length the bench marks failed them. Then they proposed to place competing rain gauges in the corrie. We approved of this idea, on the principle that rain, like other unpleasant things, must be guided by the law of perversity. So far we had done only minor climbs, but now, as if by magic, the weather improved. We at once planned to traverse all the main ridge of the Cuillin in one expedition. This great expedition, the longest of all British rock climbs, although of only moderate, average difficulty, was first carried out by A. C. McLaren and L. G. Shadbolt in the year 1911. Starting from Glen Brittle they traversed the thirty odd peaks and tops from Gars-bheinn in the south to Sgurr nan Gillean at the northern end of a seven and a half miles' long horseshoe of mountain ridge and descended to Sligachan in about seventeen hours. T. Howard Somervell, the Mount Everest climber, had done it in two hours less in 1920. Smythe and I were no record makers: we just wanted to do the main ridge. Barlow and Steeple chaffed us on our lack of originality, suggesting that we should rather cross all the passes, swim in all the lochans and avoid all the peaks, to which Smythe replied that we would stick to the ridge, but might, for a wager, carry with us a complete edition of the *Encyclopaedia Brittanica*!

I shall not describe our successful traverse of the Main Ridge in detail; I actually did it again eleven years later. Mary Campbell awakened us with tea and eggs at 1.30 a.m. on a dismal morning of drizzling rain, with mist within 200 feet of sea level. We ate the breakfast and went to sleep again. At a quarter to five Smythe roused me to a brighter prospect and we started within half an hour. At eight o'clock, on the summit of Gars-bheinn, sea and sky were a deep, pure blue. A yacht lay at anchor on Loch Scavaig. We imagined that we could have thrown a stone down her hatchways. Scavaig was a marvellous tracery of interlacing wavelets, sparkling in the morning sun. Eigg, Rum, Canna and the Outer Hebrides were all clear.

We used the rope on four occasions: for the descent of the short side of the Thearlaich-Dubh gap, for the ascent of King's Chimney on Sgurr Mhic Coinnich, for the descent by the short side of the Inaccessible and for the Naismith route up the Tooth. It was a grand day of sunshine and north-westerly wind. We carried no water with us, but used a rubber tube so that we could suck up small quantities from rock pools. Latterly, we had to descend for water at the Glaic Moire Bealach, and again before tackling the Bhasteir Tooth. Smythe did not descend on the latter occasion and was quite parched on Sgurr nan Gillean, as a result. He used rubbers throughout the expedition and they were worn out at the finish. We reached Sgurr nan Gillean at seven p.m., but took a long time for the leisurely descent to Sligachan where they gave us a grand dinner, after Smythe had borrowed a pair of trousers for use whilst his own were being mended. It was a great ambition fulfilled, which we did not neglect to celebrate before retiring somewhat unsteadily to bed up a narrow and steep staircase at the back of the hotel, the most difficult pitch of the day!

We had already made a new variation route on the west ridge of the Cioch. On our return to Glen Brittle we again set out for the Cioch and Smythe led it by the direct route from below. This is one of the best-known standard four (or severe) routes. After lunch it was my turn to tackle the Crack of Doom, an intriguing, narrow rift, first climbed by Pye and Shadbolt in 1918. They rated it as pretty severe but short. Every inch of height in that almost holdless crack was gained by strenuous contortion and wedging, with a hard pull over a chockstone to finish. We ended the climb by the direct route, made some time before by A. S. Pigott and John Wilding.

After the Cioch Direct and the Crack of Doom we had only one full day left for climbing. That same evening, just before sunset, we were looking at the skyline of Coire Lagan from Glen Brittle Post Office. On the face of Sgurr Sgumain we caught sight of a long, intriguing, vertical crack with a shorter parallel

crack at a lower level on the left. We knew of no routes on that
face. But for the long, revealing shadows of approaching sunset
we should not have spotted the cracks. The eye of faith grasped
the possibility of a new route. Next morning was fine and we put
the matter to the proof. It led to the most thrilling day's climb
of the holiday and a genuine, new, natural route, with a
character all its own.

We did not rush things on such a fine day, but bathed in the
cool, green waters of Lochan Coire Lagan and lunched at
leisure on the hot slabs. The approach was by the easy traverse
from the Lochan towards the Sgumain Stone Shoot, a route that
should be known to all Skye mountaineers. Soon we were at the
lowest rocks of the climb, but the sky was now becoming overcast with threatening clouds. Leading by turns, we started up
the steep rocks which soon approached the vertical on both
sides, a narrow chimney offering the only line of advance. This
was the immediate objective, approached by steep slabs and a
mantelshelf problem.

At this point the Trap Dyke, which is the main feature, or as
one might say in musical language, the recurring theme of the
whole climb, first appears high up on the left, cutting through
the gabbro wall like an overhanging piece of ornamental
masonry. We were now hemmed in on both sides by unclimbable walls, but a steepening groove continued straight ahead to
a thin, vertical chimney. This proved to be the crux of the climb,
and it almost defeated us at our first attempt. It was the knowledge that it was the only way which caused us to persevere and
find the key to the problem, in the form of a hold for the right
hand in the hidden narrows of the cleft. It was then possible to
raise the left foot high up on to a hold on the opposite wall. As
in many similar pitches one must never get too far inside the
cleft. The rest of the chimney was strenuous but feasible.

We were now fairly launched upon our venture, devoutly
hoping that the rest of the route would 'go'. Neither of us wished
to contemplate a return down that chimney. We left a small
cairn to mark the route. The next pitch went up a crack behind
a huge flake of rock, rather like a miniature Kern Knotts Crack.
It lent variety to the route and led us out on to an open, slabby
face. A few moves upward and to the left brought us into the

Sgurr Sgumain:
The Trap Staircase

line of our Trap Dyke, and a most interesting place it was, too. I have never seen such a perfectly preserved specimen of its kind, and a veritable staircase for tired mountaineers—or so we thought at the time. The Dyke was built of horizontally jointed, columnar basalt. For a height of nearly seventy feet it led straight up like a ladder at an angle between sixty and seventy degrees, entirely unsupported on the left side, with a gabbro wall on the right which offered occasional handholds, as every good hand-rail should, except that this one was fitted on the wrong side!

There were still pitches to be climbed, as our staircase had to accommodate itself to the contours of the edifice, which was built of gabbro with alternate terraces and intervening walls. After crossing the first terrace we had to ascend an exceedingly strenuous, ten-foot, vertical corner. Later on came another pitch where the stairway had become wildly contorted, loose and overhanging. The solution was by a steep, difficult climb up the gabbro wall on the left, but the gabbro slabs, though very steep, were also extremely rough and firm.

So it went on, until the angle eased off and we gained the crest of the West ridge of Sgumain, a narrow but easy ridge of shattered pinnacles which abutted against the foot of a vertical cliff, some 200 feet high. We did not see it all clearly, as there was now a blustering wind which was swirling the mist across the ridges. The hour was advancing, but we were sure that we could not be far beneath the summit of the mountain and we wished to finish our climb by as direct a route as we had pursued from the start.

After fifty feet of scrambling we were up against the sheer wall. Above us was a terrifying chimney, so much undercut that there seemed to be no way of even reaching its base. Again the gabbro was rough and excellent. Climbing straight over steep slabs to the left, there were just enough holds for pulling up into the niche below the chimney, and there was even a spike for a belay. I cannot say how I managed to lead the chimney itself. I remember pulling up with all my weight on a spike of gabbro which projected somewhat *downwards* towards me. This sounds ridiculous, of course, and was only possible by reason of the rough, sharp crystals which projected everywhere from the surface of the rock. Another spike protruded against my body, and I had to swing round past it to the right in order to raise myself sufficiently to secure a foothold on the right wall of the chimney. The next move had to follow at once, but when once the left foot was planted on the other side, I could rest for a moment.

The remainder was orthodox but very strenuous. Above the chimney and out to the left was a huge bollard for a belay. More welcome still was a small cairn of stones. It was as comforting as the patch of moss which Mungo Park found in the West African desert. Someone had been here before, and that was enough to put new heart into us. Still another chimney remained to be surmounted, strenuous and undercut at the bottom, but safe in spite of its steepness and narrowness. Then we turned round into a square, open corner, climbed an easy wall of trap and came out on the ridge, quite close to the summit of Sgumain. In blustering wind and rain we raced down the easy side of the mountain, stumbling over the unstable blocks of the Sgumain stone shoot and trudging across the sodden moor to Mary Campbell's cottage and a good supper.

Between the years 1935 and 1948 I was unable to visit Skye. The outline of the Cuillin reasserted its spell at once as we crossed over the moors from Carbost to Glen Brittle in the last light of a glorious evening in May 1948. We were hospitably entertained by Mrs MacRae at Glen Brittle, and the atmosphere was the same as when I made my early visits. When we started climbing next day on the Window Tower and the South Crack of the Inaccessible it seemed incredible that I had managed to forget the Cuillin for so many years. So I made up my mind to revisit the West Trap Route on Sgurr Sgumain. I was with my wife and my old friend Colin Allan. We had some difficulty in getting properly started on the climb, the initial part proving wet and strange. The crucial chimney was as impressive as before, and it was time to return to Glen Brittle for dinner when we reached the base of the North-West Tower below the final section. However, we returned to the attack next day after doing a new variation on the White Slab Route in Coir' a' Ghrunnda. Certainly I managed to lead the chimney, but, at the end

Sgurr Sgumain:
Terminal Tower

of the day, my wife was so impressed that she forbade me ever to do so again! I had conveniently forgotten the existence of the upper chimney, and that had been the last straw, a sort of insult added to injury after a hard day's climbing. This final tower was first climbed in 1920 by E. W. Steeple and G. Barlow. They do not waste more than a sentence or two on the description, saying that 'The climb is somewhat severe, on very rough but clean-cut rock with few holds.' We all agreed that it was somewhat severe.*

The best of the difficult rock climbing in Skye is certainly on the Sron na Ciche. On the whole, the guide book is fairly lucid, but routes are apt to become difficult to disentangle from each other on the Western Buttress. Colin Allan and I set out to find a route which had been only once climbed before. We had a most enjoyable day and some very good climbing, with one steep groove which nearly defeated us altogether. From the top of the Sron we ran down to upper Coir' a' Ghrunnda and enjoyed a perfect swim, diving from a huge boulder into more than eight feet of clear, cold water. The loch lies at a level of 2,300 feet. When we returned to Glen Brittle and puzzled over the diagram of Sron na Ciche we decided that we had been on three different routes linked up and completed by one new section which contained *our* very difficult groove. We could not be certain of finding it again.

On another day we visited lower Coir' a' Ghrunnda and climbed the White Slab route direct, a most enjoyable climb, but not so difficult as the guide book led us to expect. We then crossed over the Sron and descended the Sgumain stone shoot, proceeding over the Girdle Traverse of Sron na Ciche. This is altogether delightful in its variety of situations. Only on the Western Buttress is it not so well defined. We used the opportunity to make a loop on the climb by ascending the Crack of Doom and returning to the Girdle by the Kelly route on the Cioch upper buttress. I found the Crack much easier than when

---

* The 1948 edition of the *Skye Guide* with its revised classification of the climbs for difficulty puts only the 'Crack of Doom' in the highest or 'very severe' class, the final Tower of Sgumain being rated as 'severe'. There is an intermediate category 'hard severe'. The distinctions are too fine and must involve a considerable personal equation, but, having been up one route twice and the other three times, I have no doubt whatever that the Sgumain climb is much harder than the other.

I first did it eleven years before, most likely because I kept farther out, used my eyes better, finding one or two press-holds for the hands which I had failed to notice on the former occasion, a tribute to the gain in balance and experience during the intervening years. I think Colin expended more effort than I did, trusting to the strength of his more powerful arms. All these climbs are well worth a visit, especially the Mallory Slab and Groove route on the Sron. Coir' a' Ghrunnda is exceedingly impressive with its huge boiler plates of glaciated slabs.

Whoever has been on the Cuillin Main Ridge will wish to explore the crags and corries on the Coruisk side, and also the outlying group of Blaven and Clach Glas. I have enjoyed grand days in both places. Colin Allan and I started our 1934 holiday in a rather unorthodox way after motoring up from the south. It almost seemed as if we were wasting a fine summer evening in the Inn at Broadford, but we tore ourselves away in time and set up camp by the shore of Loch Slapin. Then the third member of the party, Dr Myles of Forfar, turned up. After supper we went for a stroll in ordinary walking shoes, up the hillside to the west. Myles turned back to camp, and we went on with the intention of climbing the nearest hill, just for the view! We had consulted no map, although we had a rough, general idea of the layout of the Blaven range. Our first peak had a sharp, serrated ridge-line with a delightful view to the east. The greater ridges beyond looked intriguing and impressive against the colours of sunset.

The night was ours to use as we pleased. Our energy and faculties were enlivened by the cool evening breeze and the after effects of a good supper. We decided to try an overnight traverse of Blaven and Clach Glas. After descending to the next col we were in doubt about a sharp-ridged peak on our right. We had never been here before and it might be Clach Glas. We made sure by climbing it and returning the same way. It was not Clach Glas after all. Proceeding along the other, or southward ridge, we began to run into difficulties near the top. It was never really dark on that glorious June night. At true midnight the northern horizon was a flaming band of orange and the Outer Hebrides were clear and black beyond the western ocean. In between were the dim, black, serrated ridges of the Cuillin.

There was hardly a breath of wind. The slabs of Clach Glas slowed us up, but were not really difficult. There was just enough difficulty to keep us from becoming drowsy. It was good, interesting climbing on perfect rock all the way to Blaven, the higher top of which we reached at half-past two. A contented somnolence half overcame us during the descent by a sheltered gorge and easy slopes of moorland, with the early morning songs of the birds and the growing light to remind us that a new day of our holiday had started and that we had made a good beginning. Without disturbing our friend we crept into our sleeping sacks at four a.m., sleeping on the dry turf without troubling about a tent. After a swim in the sea-water of Loch Slapin before breakfast we felt as fresh as ever. Myles wanted to climb Blaven that day, and only with our protests that it was Sunday, and therefore a day of rest, did he begin to suspect how we had passed the midnight hours. The map showed us that the bag for the night included Sgurr nan Each, Garbh-bheinn, Clach Glas and Blaven.

In June 1935 we had another unorthodox day. We were camping at Glen Brittle and rising rather late in the mornings. On this morning we heard that a motor boat was going round to Loch Scavaig at ten a.m. With a great rush we caught the boat and proceeded to eat our breakfast as we slipped down Loch Brittle and round the Rhu. Again it was one of those perfect summer days of blue sky and hot sun. When we landed at Scavaig we crossed over the little peninsula to a secluded bay under the cliffs of Sgurr na Stri. This is the most delightful swimming pool that I know. Great, black slabs of gabbro bend over and drop straight into deep, clear, pale green water with a sandy bottom. At one place there are caves. The year before, with Dr Myles, we had spent a Sunday on Sgurr na Stri, a delightful little hill, only 1,623 feet high, with perfect rock for a first day's climbing practice both on the Scavaig and the Camasunary sides, and the finest view possible of the main chain of the Cuillin from the summit. That day had included a perfect swim in the little bay of Scavaig, and we had marked it for a return visit.

The effects of luxury bathing early in the day are demoralising, however. We ate our lunch by the shore of Loch Coruisk and both went to sleep for the rest of the afternoon. At five o'clock we roused ourselves and set out for our intended rock climb on the steepest buttress of Sgurr Coir' an Lochan. There we ran into serious difficulties and were obliged to retreat from an impossible, steep groove which proved to be a *cul de sac*. Only by roping down twice did we reach *terra firma*. Clouds were pouring over the main ridge and darkness was not far away. Before everything became blotted out we laid down our course for the Bealach Coire Lagan, but we were soon swallowed up in drifting mist. At length we had a fresher breeze in our faces and a great blur of darkness on our left. We were on the main ridge, but it was too broad to be the pass at which we were aiming. We immediately began to descend on the other side, hoping for the best. There were steep rocks on our left which forced us more and more to the right, down a slabby face. After much difficulty we came out below the mist into a bare, rough corrie without any lochan. It was the Coire na Banachdich, and we had forgotten the guide-book injunction to keep well under the cliffs of Sgurr Dearg. As the book remarks, the Glen Brittle side of the pass is unsuitable for tourists. We got to our tent by midnight.

My most enjoyable day's climbing from Coruisk was in September 1933 with Sandy Harrison. We climbed slowly up the Banachdich corrie through a curtain of mist which began to disperse as we halted for lunch on the northern summit. Coruisk was still a seething cauldron of cloud. At intervals the stately ridge of Sgurr a' Ghreadaidh would emerge from the vaporous stew, and we could even catch a glimpse of the Bideins and of Sgurr nan Gillean. We had a long day ahead of us, so we quickly ran down to the Banachdich-Thormaid Saddle and then, ever downwards, by an easy scree gully to within 1,000 feet of the floor of Coruisk. It was a warm afternoon when we sought the start of our climb up the south face of Ghreadaidh near a little rowan tree. It was reputed to be the longest climb in the Cuillin, with a past history of at least one party which had been benighted before completing it.

Every Skye enthusiast should pay at least one visit to the upper glen of Coruisk. The southern peaks of the Cuillin are much more impressive than when seen from Glen Brittle. They seem to tower above one with their huge impending cliffs and long lines of savage boulders and scree. The impression was deepened for us by the fleeting battalions of cloud and streamers of sunshine which poured through the jagged rents. The notched skyline of the ridge seemed stupendous in its remoteness and height. As Norman Collie wrote, 'Fortunately the Cuillin are never inferior mountains. . . . It is the atmosphere that adds both dignity and charm to these Scottish hills, making them appear far bigger than they would be in the clearer air of the larger mountain ranges, and giving them the softened colour and perspective so necessary to emphasize the real beauty of true mountains.'

We started our climb, soon running up against a steep nose of slabby rock. After a short traverse to the right the way upwards became clear enough, by an eighty-foot chimney of trap rock which required very careful handling. The continuation was up long grooves, by which we attained the crest of the buttress. It is needless to attempt to describe the long, middle part of the route in detail, as we experienced little difficulty on the long backbone of the buttress until we reached the little saddle underneath the final, steep nose below the northern summit of Ghreadaidh. We had to be wary of loose rock on the left face of this 150-foot nose. The final ascent was on a steep ridge of excellent rock. The Long Climb had taken us little over two hours.

The climbing, on the average, is only moderately difficult, but the scenery of the Coruisk face makes it a grand route. Any difficulties are in route finding rather than in detailed technique. It makes a first-class mountain traverse, with a choice of routes for descent on the Glen Brittle side. Our return was by An Dorus and the Ghreadaidh corrie, with a delightful bathe in a pool below the great gorge in the lower corrie.* For climbers visiting Glen Brittle, who are fond of river pools for swimming, this one below Greta Gorge is almost perfection, besides being accessible in less than ten minutes from the main road. Just as good are the Fairy Pools in Coire na Creiche, not so very far upstream from the bridge on the main road to Glen Brittle.

This rambling chapter on the Cuillin seems at times to stray a good deal from the serious business of rock climbing. All this

* Ghreadaidh means clear water.

must be attributed to the charm and care-free atmosphere which seem to have much the same effect on all holiday makers who come under the spell of Skye. One infallible cure is the traverse of the Main Ridge. In 1935 Allan and I hoped to include Blaven and Clach Glas, as well as the outliers Sgurr Dubh Mor and Sgumain, in the expedition. This was my second traverse of the Ridge, but the additional items were cut out by a sudden change of weather, scudding rain and a sou'wester bursting upon us as we were traversing the Bidein peaks. We continued to Sgurr nan Gillean and then returned to our base at Glen Brittle. As we passed the Lodge gates Mr MacRae asked us where we had been. When we told him he shook his head and asked us why on earth we had done it.

We did not camp that night. Mary Campbell gave us a glorious supper of ham and eggs, and we slept in comfort. I awoke about six a.m., very thirsty. Outside it rained, but there is a convenient little burn at which I filled a jug. Colin still slept when I came back with the water. Without opening his eyes he held out a hand and raised himself a little on the pillow. I held the water to his lips and he drank nearly a pint before relapsing into sleep. Our next awakening was six hours later, when, despite the continued rain, we betook ourselves to Loch Brittle for a swim before breakfast. I hope to traverse the Ridge again, for the third time, whenever I get the opportunity.

The first complete traverse of the Ridge with the addition of Blaven was effected on 12th June 1939, by Ian G. Charleson and W. E. Forde, starting from a camp below Gars-bheinn and finishing at a camp in Harta Corrie. In September of the same year W. H. Murray and R. G. Donaldson repeated the expedition from Glen Brittle, again using a destination camp, already prepared in Glen Sligachan. Since then Mr S. Thompson has done the whole expedition alone, starting from and returning to Glen Brittle in a little over twenty hours, in August 1944. The most troublesome part was the return to Glen Brittle at nightfall from the head of Loch Scavaig round the base of the hills.*

So far, nothing has been said of the charm of the Cuillin, when coated with spring snow. The weather may be capricious

---

* Accounts of these expeditions are to be found in the *S.M.C. Journal*, Vol. 22, p. 127, and Vol. 23, p. 277.

in March or April, but the reward of a fine day of spring sunshine on these glorious, sparkling ridges, set high above azure
seas, must be superlative. I draw on the experiences of my friend
John Wilson who has visited the Cuillin several times in the
month of March. He finds three types of weather: (1) like poor
summer conditions with cold, wet rocks and occasional ice, but
with snow confined to the higher ridges, (2) mixed weather with
a north-west wind and snow below 2,500 feet, when one battles
along the ridges against blinding snow scurries. A section of
ridge, easy in summer, may become an inferno of driving snow
and ice-plastered rocks under these conditions, and (3) a north-
east wind may be followed by several perfect, sunny days of
pure delight. Even in perfect conditions the Banachdich section
of the ridge demanded a long afternoon of effort, with much step-
cutting and places where roping-down tactics were necessary to
ensure any progress at all. He concluded his account with a
climb on Bidein Druim nan Ramh; 'Coruisk lay at our feet.
All about us the peaks of the Cuillin danced to the blue of the
vault above. Heaven and the world were ours.'*

* See *S.M.C. Journal*, Vol. 23, p. 61.

THE PASS OF RYVOAN AND GREEN LOCH, CAIRNGORMS

LOCH AN EILEIN, CAIRNGORMS

CHAPTER XIII

THE CAIRNGORMS

THE Cairngorm mountains are the nearest thing we have in Britain to an isolated, self-contained range of an almost continental type, as regards climate, flora and fauna. They are far enough from the western sea to ensure a tolerably dry climate, and the mean height is sufficient to guarantee a hard winter with plenty of snow remaining on the heights until well into the Spring, thus rendering possible very good skiing on large areas of their higher slopes. There is an air of remoteness and vastness about them which inspires both respect and exhilaration, despite the fact that the contours of their summits are somewhat rounded and unimpressive in form.

There are many satisfying, distant prospects of the Cairngorms. The view from Craigellachie behind Aviemore is, perhaps, the most accessible, but if a hill road be taken northwards from the main road, just north of Loch Alvie, proceeding up the hill far enough to see things in their proper proportions, there is no finer view in Britain of a great mountain range. In the foreground are the woods around Loch Alvie, then the forest of Rothiemurchus stretching south-west beyond Loch an Eilein and eastward to Loch Morlich. Beyond are the massive outlines of the Cairngorm giants, blue in the distance and not too easily distinguished, the one from the other, until we get to know them well by walking and climbing amongst them. Cairngorm is on the left, Ben MacDhui merging with Braeriach, with its many western corries, in the centre, and, across the gap of Glen Einich, Sgoran Dubh on the right leading the eye across Glen Feshie to the lower hills beyond.

It is an impressive façade which, however, leaves us still puzzled without explaining the real charm of this range of hills. In his *Scenery of Scotland* Sir Archibald Geikie chooses this view to drive home his main conclusion about all the Scottish mountains, that they are remnants of a dissected plateau, worn down by ages of combined erosion by the action of sun, wind, rain, frost and ice. Only the resistant portions are left today and they, too, have been sculptured into rounded forms. But these forms are by no means ugly or ungainly when we get to know them. Professor Norman Collie once wrote of them as follows: 'To many people the Cairngorm Range is composed of shapeless, flat-topped mountains, devoid of character. They do not rise like the Matterhorn in savage grandeur, yet the sculptured sides of Braeriach, seen from Sgoran Dubh Mhor, are in reality far richer in beautiful, intricate mountain sculpture than the whole face of the Matterhorn as seen from the Riffel Alp'.*

This is praise, with a vengeance, but Collie was a painter as well as a mountaineer and scientist of distinction, and his people came from Deeside. He had no doubt that the ancient mountains of Scotland showed a wonderful strength and repose in their outlines, 'so that the bigger mountains seem to rise without effort from the moors and smaller hills that surround them'. The Cairngorms, like all lands of far distances, should be seen in fine weather with enough blue sky and cloud to bring out the aerial perspective and the play of shadows on their vast masses of rolling upland. It is then that one realises what Fiona Macleod, writing of the mountain charm in the month of June, called the 'blueness of blueness' of distant hills. Hence the origin of the name Cairngorm (the blue mountain), although the local name, from the colour of the granite cliffs, is Monadh Ruadh (the red mountains).

The appearance of these mountains is very similar from lower hills to the south of Deeside. There, too, we have difficulty in recognising the giants of the picture, obscured as they are by the lesser, rounded foothills. Surely the key to the charm of this belt of country is rather in the valleys than on the summits, for there are many beautiful and impressive glens; clear, rushing rivers and wild, secluded lochs, not only in the lower valleys but high up in the bare corries beneath the summit plateaus. Nowhere in Britain is there a more attractive country for high-level walking, for long days on the heights, going from one peak to another, and for that most genuine and delightful form of travel which starts from one valley, crosses a pass or a mountain top and descends by a different glen to some other place amid contrasted scenery in a different valley.

* See 'A'Chuilionn' by Norman Collie, *S.M.C.J.*, Vol. 4, p. 265.

Difficult climbing has not been much developed in the Cairn-gorms. Great distances must be covered from the available places of habitation in order to reach the most interesting corries where rock climbing is possible. Good roads do not pene-trate far into these mountain sanctuaries, although there is an abundance of good paths and rights of way. The same obstacles prevent a good deal of first-class winter climbing. Weather changes can be rapid on the mountains, especially in winter, so that the utmost precautions should be taken on an expedition to the high Cairngorms in mid-winter. There have been many tragedies and near-tragedies, nearly all caused by the lack of reasonable care and forethought as regards clothing, equip-ment, food and general fitness.

In my earliest climbing days the Cairngorms exercised a great fascination over me. My first venture was a cycle trip from my home in Fifeshire, with the object of catching a glimpse of the big peaks with the interesting names. Going north in the evening I spent an hour or two at the summit of the Cairnwell Pass on the way to Braemar and breakfasted by the Linn of Dee. The southern aspect of the Devil's Point and the higher hills behind made a deep impression and gave birth to a resolve to explore them fully. Then I carried on westwards across the watershed and down Glen Tilt to Blair Atholl. A year later I climbed Ben MacDhui from Derry Lodge by Loch Etchachan and enjoyed a grand view of the corries of Braeriach and Cairn Toul. Two years later came the opportunity to explore the former after a night spent at Alltdruie Bothy (now wholly in ruins), situated in a beautiful meadow surrounded by forest, dominated to the south by Carn Elrick and the Lurcher's Crag, the majestic northern outposts of the Larig Ghru Pass.

In mixed weather, with much wind and cloud, Mr R. P. Dansey and I crossed the Larig and climbed over slopes of huge granite boulders into the Garbh Choire Dhaidh where the infant Dee plunges over the edge of the plateau of Braeriach in a 600-foot cataract. About half a mile back from the edge are the Wells of Dee, the true source of the river, which we visited after climbing up fairly easy slopes beside the waterfall. The summit plateau of Braeriach is the geratest British mountain area around and over the 4,000-foot level. It is a thinly eroded expanse of red granite, consisting mostly of sand with a scanty covering of mosses and other lowly plants. The Wells are close under the 4,000-foot level, little mossy hollows in the plateau with several small streams flowing out of the ground and soon uniting together to form a vigorous young river of clear, cold water.

There is a strange charm about this vast, arid expanse, so close to the sky and the clouds, with far prospects on every side of the massive, everlasting hills. This roof of Scotland is not altogether desolate. It is the haunt of the snow bunting, the dotterel and the ptarmigan, which can often be surprised with a brood of yellow-brown chicks in early July. Overhead one may occasionally see the golden eagle sailing swiftly over the plateau with hardly a perceptible flicker of his wings, but seemingly intent to remark any small creature which may be moving amongst the stones, when he will swoop down suddenly upon the prey, even from a height of over 1,000 feet. Once, close to the summit of Carn o' Claise, on emerging from behind a huge boulder on the ridge, I surprised an eagle perched on the summit cairn. Photography was not possible. The bird stared at me for only a second or two before vanishing at a great speed.

The other great, high plateau of the Cairngorms lies between Ben MacDhui and Cairngorm. This we visited on our next expedition, ascending easily from the Larig track over the Lurcher's Crag to Ben MacDhui and taking a somewhat lower route on our way to Cairngorm, so as to enjoy the view from above of Loch Avon (2,377 ft.), one of the wildest scenes right in the heart of this mountain land. Cairngorm is the northern outpost of the range, with a long, easy ridge running down northwards to beautiful Loch Morlich, by which route it can be very easily ascended. All these mountains can be readily climbed from Speyside by a strong walking party, properly clad and shod for the hills.

The best route for Braeriach is either from the summit of the Larig Ghru track or from Glen Einich at the point near the site of the lower bothy (now destroyed), just beyond where the road crosses the main stream, by following the line of the Beanaidh Beag and striking up into Coire Ruadh for the summit. It is even better to make for Coire an Lochain which encloses the highest British loch at a level of 3,250 feet, a wild rocky hollow overhung by great crags, which are still more impressive in spring when huge ice-floes cover the loch and the gullies and ledges are all snow-covered.

For Cairn Toul it is best to proceed to the end of the Glen Einich road, just short of the Loch, where the Upper Bothy once stood before it was burnt down during the recent war. A good path strikes up to the left by Coire Dhondail. This takes one steeply up to the stony plateau between Braeriach and Cairn Toul, so steeply that the backward views across Loch Einich to Sgoran Dubh are exceedingly impressive, as the Einich wall of that mountain has five great rocky buttresses which give very good climbing.

For those who wish to enjoy some rock scrambling of an easy nature, the Fiacaill Ridge between Coire an Lochain and Coire an t-Sneachda, the two main, northern corries of Cairngorm, offers an interesting route to the summit of Cairn Lochan (3,983 ft.) and thence to Cairngorm. It is one of the few, narrow rock ridges in this group of mountains.

LONG HILL-WALKING EXPEDITIONS

The Cairngorm Mountains are ideal for very long expeditions, either passes between Deeside and Speyside or traverses of several peaks in one day. The hardest and longest of these is the traverse of the six highest Cairngorms, which was first effected in a single day by Messrs H. J. Butchart, L. J. Davidson, H. G. Drummond, H. Kellas and I. M. McLaren, all of Aberdeen, starting from Loch Builg at midnight on 21st June 1909. They crossed over Ben Avon, Beinn a' Bhuird, Cairn Gorm, Ben MacDhui, Cairn Toul and Braeriach to the lower bothy of Glen Einich, a distance of twenty-eight miles, involving 9,000 feet of climbing in nineteen hours. A similar traverse taking Cairn Toul last (after Braeriach) and finishing at Corrour Bothy in Glen Dee was effected in fourteen and three-quarter hours by R. P. Yunnie and a party of three in July 1932. No one appears to have started and returned to the same base, which would make the expedition a good deal longer.

The making of records is against the whole spirit and tradition of mountaineering, but a long hill traverse such as this is the

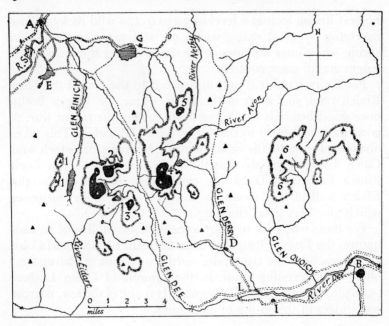

MAP C   THE CAIRNGORMS

MOUNTAINS

								height in feet
1	Sgoran Dubh Mor (two tops)	.	.	.	.		North top	3,635
							South top	3,658
2	Braeriach (several tops)	.	.	.	.	.		4,248
3	Cairn Toul	.	.	.	.	.	.	4,241
4	Ben Macdhui	.	.	.	.	.	.	4,296
5	Cairn Gorm	.	.	.	.	.	.	4,084
6	Beinn a' Bhuird (two tops)	.	.	.	.		North top	3,924
							South top	3,860
7	Ben Avon	.	.	.	.	.	.	3,843

A	Aviemore	G	Glenmore Lodge, on Loch Morlich
B	Braemar	I	Inverey Village
D	Derry Lodge	L	Linn of Dee
E	Loch an Eilein		

PASSES

From A southward to Glen Dee or Glen Derry is the **Larig Ghru**. From River Nethy southward to D is the **Larig an Laoigh**.

nearest thing we have in Britain to mountaineering or exploration on the greater mountain ranges of the world. It is in the
course of such an expedition that one really gets to know the
contours of the landscape and the changing aspects of the hills
from different points of view. As the day advances we acquire
an additional source of information, not always accurate but
strangely insistent, in our sense of muscular effort. Towards the
end of a long, hard day we become acutely sensitive to any
slight increase of gradient or roughness on our route. This sense
is ever with us in a minor degree, but enables the trained
mountaineer to progress always with a minimum of effort and a
fuller appreciation of the ground than an unskilled person. I
have always wished to effect the traverse of all six Cairngorms,
but the opportunity has, thus far, eluded me, so that I have
had to be content with two partial successes.

On the 8th of June 1946, John Wilson and I camped in our
car on the Derry Lodge road above Deeside. We had no
definite plans and it was a rainy evening, but John hankered
after an attempt on the big six Cairngorms, with a return to our
base, an almost impossible programme as we had to motor
south on the following evening. The project was made still more
unreasonable by the fact that I had only a pair of rubber-soled
walking shoes available. The weather cleared about three a.m.
and we started an hour later on a dank, cold, misty morning.
We struck eastward through the hills by a long, straight,
V-shaped cleft leading from Glen Derry to Glen Quoich, a
curious place which I learned was part of a great fault crossing
Scotland by Loch Lubnaig, Loch Tay and Glen Tilt. Deer
looked down from the edges of the defile, birds sang cheerfully
and the clouds parted in front of us, revealing the smooth,
elephantine bulk of the southern shoulder of Beinn a' Bhuird.

As we swung to the left, contouring over the moor before
descending to the upper part of Glen Quoich, the huge mountain continued to dominate the scene, overlooking a mysterious
sanctuary of old Scots pine trees, still partly concealed by
isolated masses and streamers of morning mist. We missed the
old bothy which is marked on the map but has now disappeared.
What a grand place for a bivouac and a camp fire, redolent of
peacefulness, freedom, great spaces and the kindlier aspects of

wild nature! Both John and I agreed that it was a valley to live in. The gently rounded contours of the mountains were more akin to the atmosphere of these wooded valleys than any of the more naked and abrupt hills of the west. Deer were numerous above the woodland, and we watched a small herd, the movements of which were impeded by a hind which was encouraging a young fawn.

It was very cold on the plateau when we reached the south top of Beinn a' Bhuird at seven a.m., but the distant view was exceedingly clear, with all the beauty of shimmering cloudlets above the south-eastern valleys. On the way to the northern or main summit, two miles to the north of us, across a stony, undulating table-land, we admired the huge cliffs of the eastern corries, especially those above the Dubh Lochan, which gleamed like a mirror in the morning sun. Great snow wreaths encircled the rim of the plateau, and we promised ourselves a return visit in order to explore the buttresses of rock and the steep gullies.

By now our ambitions were trimmed to a measure of equality and reasonableness. We decided to leave Ben Avon alone and to be content with Ben MacDhui. A strong, fresh, south-east wind kept us on the move. We did not mean to miss any intervening peaks, of which the first was Beinn a' Chaoruinn, three and a half miles away, with an intervening drop to 2,650 feet from our stance at 3,924 feet. That stretch was rough going though fairly easy, but the succeeding descent carried us into the deep V-shaped valley traversed by the Larig an Laoigh track from Glen Derry to Nethy Bridge. We crossed the track at an altitude of about 2,300 feet, followed by the steepest climb of the day to the summit of Beinn Mheadhoin (3,883 ft.), which we accomplished within the hour. The last of our scanty store of provisions was consumed at the outlet of Loch Etchachan (3,058 ft.). There was now a regular path to the top of Ben MacDhui (4,296 ft.) which we attained at 2.15 p.m. This is the highest of the Cairngorm mountains and, until the year 1810, was believed to be the highest Scottish mountain, although the issue was not decided in favour of Ben Nevis until the Ordnance Survey of 1847.

We met several parties on the summit and John Wilson considered that he had never before enjoyed a finer view as regards

distant visibility. To the south were the Lomond Hills of Fife
and the Ochils, to the west Bens Vorlich, Lawers, More and
Schiehallion, then Ben Alder, Creag Meaghaidh and Ben Nevis,
which was partly in cloud. The Five Sisters of Kintail and the
mass of Mam Sodhail were clear to the north-west, and Morven
in Caithness to the north. The Garbh Choire of Braeriach
carried a lot of snow. Our return route was over Cairngorm of
Derry and the long ridge to Derry Lodge in its surroundings of
scattered pine forest. We regained our car at 5.30 p.m., after
twenty-three miles of walking and 7,000 feet of ascent, a satisfying day, filled with variety and enjoyment.

Our other attempt on the 'big six' was no more likely to
succeed, but there was no harm in trying. Such a programme
can always be shortened if necessary, as soon as the inexorable
realities of space and time begin to overpower the ill-considered
ambitions of map-reading mountaineers. With us was Ian
Charleson, who had not climbed for several months. We were
staying at the hospitable cottage of Mrs Lorimer, beautifully
situated amidst the pines on the shore of Loch an Eilein, and
the date was early October 1947. The only thing in our favour
was a third quarter moon, so we decided to start at 3.30 a.m.

It would weary the reader to go over the expedition in detail.
There was plenty of time and much thoughtless hilarity at the
breakfast table, but we were only ten minutes behind schedule
on starting out. The first seven miles took us to the foot of Coire
Dhondail at the head of Glen Einich, so that the actual climbing
did not begin until about six a.m., and the moon had remained
persistently obscured all the way. The Dhondail track is really
excellent, a graded progress to a height of about 3,300 feet. The
clouds were ominous, with a fierce, cold, west wind, but the
cloud level kept above us as we rose. Losing a little time by
getting too far up on Braeriach, we reached Cairn Toul at
8.30 a.m., an exceedingly chilly spot for our second breakfast.
We visited the Wells of Dee on the way to Braeriach and enjoyed
our most comfortable siesta of the day by the Pools of Dee at the
top of the Larig Ghru Pass. By now it was obvious that the
Eastern Cairngorms were out of the programme. In June things
might have been different.

Rain and flying scud met us on the last lap before reaching

Ben MacDhui at 1.30 p.m. We had been warned, but the clerk of the weather was evidently satisfied with our submission, for he allowed us to finish the day peacefully by including Cairngorm, where we assembled at four p.m. Ian and I returned over Cairn Lochan, descending by the Fiacaill Ridge. He had gone very well indeed, although he needed a little coaxing to get him across the slopes of the Lurcher's Crag and on to the Larig track before dark. When we neared the Cairngorm Club Bridge over the Allt na Beinne, Ian appeared to savour the prospects of a good supper and fairly took the bit between his teeth, striding along the forest path at a pace which stretched me to the utmost. We had done the 'big four' if not the 'six' and we all enjoyed ourselves to the full. When I measured it out on the map I found that our day of sixteen hours had included 7,700 feet of ascent and thirty-one and a half miles, most of it fairly rough going. I hope there is still time for the longer expedition!

In mid-June 1938 I spent a long day, entirely by myself, on Braeriach and Cairn Toul, approaching from White Bridge in Deeside. It is on such occasions that the spirit of the mountains enters into one's very being, unhindered by even such distraction as the presence of a like-minded companion. There was no cause for haste and I spent some time in the Corrour Bothy, that famous haunt of mountain men and hikers, below the crags of the Devil's Point. The visitors' book of the Dundee University College Rucksack Club made good reading. One band of New Year enthusiasts had made themselves very comfortable, although the frost was keen. The entry in the book said, 'Tonight we have a fire, a magnificent fire. In its fiercest moments it has driven us into the back of the bothy. Shirts have been abandoned. The "old dogs" are suffering from burnt knees'. These were the stalwarts of the Ptarmigan and Creag Dhu Clubs of the Glasgow area.

I made my way onward and upward into the Coire Bhrochain of Braeriach. After a shower of hail the Black and Braeriach Pinnacles were clearly defined against a background of swirling mist. I progressed easily up the lower slabs of the former, and then up a narrow crack about forty feet long, where the holds were just sufficient and which kept a yard or two to the right of the true nose. The latter was too steep to climb with its roof-tile structure of smooth slabs. Easier rocks continued to the teeth on the Pinnacle crest. It is a good climb and not too difficult. This is also true of a flank attack on Braeriach Pinnacle which I climbed next, but not for the sharp, vertical edge at the end of its ridge. The highest summit of Braeriach is immediately above.

In bad weather, scudding cloud and repeated showers of sleet, I made my way round the rim of the plateau over Sgor an Lochan Uaine to Cairn Toul. Then the sun came through and showed up a brilliant Brocken Spectre as I rested by the cairn. Every step down the rocky ridge was sheer delight in that lovely evening, with all the distant hills intensely clear in their rain-washed colouring of blue and purple. I got back to the car after nearly twelve hours' absence.

I had still to make a promised call at Thistle Cottage, Inverey, the home of Maggie Gruer* and the best-known hostelry in the Cairngorms. Bill Mackenzie and I had stayed there the previous night and our hostess had given us a ham and egg breakfast at six a.m. Bill had been ticked off for attempting to sign the visitor's book in pencil, as the ink was solid in the bottle provided. This evening I had little time to spare, but the kettle was on the fire and a welcome brew of tea appeared in a few minutes. I took out a lump of gingerbread from my sack and my hostess gracefully accepted a slice, at the same time going to a cupboard and placing before me a plate of butter, which I spread on my own slice. I noticed that she herself took jam. In fact, she told me that she preferred jam, at the same time fixing me with a humorous twinkle in her eye. Then I took a bite and understood. It wasn't yesterday's butter! But I stared her out, even taking another slice and some more butter. Meanwhile, she chatted away about the great figures of the past who had come to Deeside, from Queen Victoria and Mr Gladstone to the latest mountaineers from Aberdeen. She was surely entitled to her little joke at my expense.

---

* Maggie Gruer was the friend of generations of walkers and climbers in the Cairngorms. She welcomed them at all hours of the day and night, and somehow there was always room for everyone. She died at her home in March 1939 at the age of seventy-seven.

CHAPTER XIV

CAIRNGORM GRANITE

FOR all-round mountaineers the Cairngorms, along with which, for the purpose of this chapter, is included the mountain mass of Lochnagar to the south of Deeside, offer great attractions, both in summer and winter. Good rock climbing is available, but one must be prepared to walk a long way in order to find it, or else pitch a tent or bivouac in some remote corrie. Lochnagar belongs to the same granite formation as the Cairngorms, the rock structure and scenery being very similar. The southern boundary of the granite lies beyond Creag an Dubh Loch and Broad Cairn, above the uppermost recesses of Glen Clova, near Bachnagairn. Lochnagar and Creag an Dubh Loch provide, in fact, the best rock climbing of the whole district, and the 700-foot crags of the north-eastern corrie of Lochnagar are outstanding in every way, both for summer and winter climbing. The other most attractive and accessible area is the long face of Sgoran Dubh above Glen Einich, with its five great buttresses of rock and numerous gullies.

Granite climbing is by no means easy, for the crags, at a first attempt, may appear to offer very little between easy scrambling and vertical walls of imitation masonry. There is much loose rock in many places, and the rounded edges offer few belays. None the less, the climbing can be both difficult and safe for those who have mastered the technique and faced the limitations of the material. Vegetation is often found on ledges and in chimneys and cracks, but this is avoidable and not at all troublesome. Difficult climbs should not be attempted in wet weather, as the granite is often coated with a thin green or greenish-black patina of lichen which becomes very slippery when wet. A similar caution should be extended to the use of any vegetable holds in wet conditions. Plants cannot root themselves deeply on granite. Only a few notes can be given on the location and character of several typical climbs, for the Cairngorms will always be a paradise for the hill walker rather than a popular area for rock climbing.

SGORAN DUBH

The Glen Einich road is closed to motors, but a bicycle can be very serviceable. From Aviemore to Loch Einich is about ten miles, but the nearest of the five buttresses (No. 1) is not quite so far. In May 1932 we held a week-end Meet of the Perth Section of the J.M.C.S.* and thoroughly enjoyed our six-mile walk beyond the locked gate up Glen Einich. Near the upper limit of the forest there is a sharp bend to the right which discloses the snowy dome of Sgoran Dubh, flanked by its buttresses of rock, one of the noblest vistas in the Scottish Highlands. We camped on piles of dry heather in the stable of the Upper Bothy, short of Loch Einich. Both bothies have now disappeared, casualties of the recent war when this region was used as a training ground for mountain warfare troops. After our evening meal we visited the Loch with its beautiful beach of granite sand. The moon was glancing down over the shoulder of Braeriach and there was a strong ripple on the waters. To the right was the black, serrated outline of the Pinnacle Buttress and, beyond the southern end of the loch, the faint, whitish streak of the waterfall descending from Loch nan Cnapan—as wild a scene as Loch Coruisk in the heart of the Cuillin hills of Skye.

Next morning, after an ample and leisurely breakfast, Colin Allan, Dr Myles and I crossed the stream at its outlet from the loch and toiled upwards to the foot of the rocks. It is quite easy to recognise the five buttresses, but by no means so simple to identify the known climbing routes. Between Nos. 2 and 3 buttresses is a prominent, deep gully which drains an upper corrie. Centrally placed in this corrie is a conspicuous mass of rock which, as seen from the direction of the Upper Bothy, is shaped rather like a diamond. Our objective for the day was to climb the Diamond Buttress situated in the Fan Corrie, for rock climbers are optimists and have no scruples about naming a climb whilst it is still no more than a hopeful figment of the imagination. Of course, we considered that we might have some success with the lower rocks as well before starting on the real business of the day. It would be time enough after that to traverse into the Fan Corrie, rather than to reach it by an easier but less interesting route.

* Junior Mountaineering Club of Scotland

I shall not recount our troubles on the lower rocks. We failed to find any of the established routes, although we did come upon a cairn which seemed to indicate the upper end of one of them. We encountered many difficulties on the slabs and ribs of that complicated buttress and were repeatedly compelled to execute difficult, horizontal traverses (several of them even in a downward direction) when we were utterly defeated by the smoothness and steepness of the face above us. It was very good sport and we thoroughly enjoyed our lunch above the lower rocks. We began to understand why most of the early routes on Sgoran Dubh, generally climbed at Easter time when the days are not long, did, in fact, avoid the greater difficulties which would appeal to the modern rock climber.

As we crossed over easy rocks into the Fan Corrie our buttress rose before us, looking more attractive than ever. It began with an *arête*, pleasingly interesting but fairly easy. We moved continuously, all together, to the foot of the steep face beyond. Then we roped up and put Colin on the lead. The wall rose with exceeding steepness for close on 100 feet, but the leader progressed steadily on small but sufficient holds to a secure stance with a belay at forty feet. Then came a fifteen-foot chimney. The climbing was difficult and interesting, and the whole of this face was airy and impressive. Above the steep part was an easy, upper ridge with one or two small gaps, leading to a short snow slope and an easy cornice of snow below the rim of the plateau. Less than 200 feet of walking took us to the cairn of Sgoran Dubh Mor (3,635 ft.).

Allan left us soon afterwards, but Myles and I continued over Sgor Gaoith (3,658 ft.) and descended to Loch Einich by the fifth or Pinnacle Buttress. The Pinnacle, which is conspicuous from the Glen Einich road, is easily climbed from its upper neck, but is even easier to avoid altogether. On another occasion I climbed it directly from below, which involves a very difficult, short pitch. The slabs below the Pinnacle are very awkward to descend, the best plan being to keep well to the south. For those who want a long, interesting climb of moderate difficulty the Pinnacle Buttress can be cordially recommended. It is best to choose a route on the lower slabs a little to the left of the Pinnacle and to cross the neck behind it before resuming the ascent.

As I have already stated, the Sgoran Dubh routes are, in general, not easy to identify, as there are so many ribs and ridges which look so much alike when seen from the Einich road.

There is, however, one such continuous rib, some little distance to the right of the gully between Nos. 2 and 3 Buttresses, which can be cordially recommended as giving a 500-foot climb, perfectly continuous, on sound rock of no more than difficult standard. The foot of the rib can be identified from the road near the site of the upper bothy, as it lies above a long, thin, sandy groove running down to the moor. The rib ends below and not far to the right of a little grassy saddle overlooking Fan Corrie. When my sister and I climbed it in September 1941 we crossed this saddle and finished our day by a lateral route which joined the original route on Diamond Buttress below its upper ridge. It is now established that this lower rib is the Rose Ridge which was originally climbed in April 1904.*

The only other route on Sgoran Dubh which I propose to describe here is quite easy to identify on No. 1 Buttress, and is typical of Cairngorm granite at its best and soundest. No. 1 Buttress is split by a long, deep gully, overhung by impossible-looking cliffs on the left, and by the clean-cut edge of Roberts Ridge on the right. The nomenclature of the cliffs of Sgoran Dubh would have been simpler if the two halves of No. 1 Buttress had been numbered separately, thus corresponding to Nos. 2 and 3 Buttresses which are also separated by a narrow gully.

Ernest Roberts, Denis Howe and I made the first ascent of this fine route on 24th April, 1938, a day of perfect weather and dry rocks. We named the climb in honour of our friend's sixty-fourth birthday. He had retired from his profession within the previous year, but not from mountaineering. On this climb he thoroughly enjoyed himself. The route, 450 feet in height, keeps as close as is practicable to the edge overlooking the gully and finishes in a short, steep ridge. We took two and a half hours to complete the climb.

The first objective is a small rowan tree growing out of the base of a chimney, about fifty feet up. The tree is not only useful

* There seems to have been some doubt about the matter, and the 1938 edition of the *Cairngorms Guide* took a different view.

as a belay, but assists the leader in reaching the niche behind it. The chimney is rather difficult and the rocks above it are somewhat exposed, without very satisfying holds. One must beware of anything loose on such a steep face. The route goes somewhat leftwards, with one very bad step to the right on to a slab with a belay. We are now above the steep, lower wall. The intermediate section, set at a more moderate angle, offers many good stances and leads directly to the upper wall, which is almost severe in standard at isolated places. It seems possible to avoid this by keeping more to the left. The main pitch exceeds sixty feet in height and involves the ascent of a long fissure, not deep but not far short of vertical, with a very awkward part below the middle but a sufficiency of good holds near the top. It is perfectly sound rock, with no vegetation.

There now remains a short, steep wall leading to the slabby roof of the end block of the ridge, but there is a surprise at the end, for the block is almost completely isolated from the main mass of the mountain. There is a vertical drop of about eight feet to a sharp, rock edge, leading over to steep and easy rocks which run up to the summit plateau. It is not a pleasant descent for the last man, for the knife-edge has a long, steep drop on both sides. The view through the notch, past the savage crags of the next buttress to Loch Einich, with the massive, rounded outline of the flank of Braeriach beyond, is one of the most impressive in the Cairngorm region. Our party went to the top of the mountain and returned along the ridge to its northern end which overlooks Loch an Eilein and the woodlands of Rothiemurchus, as fine a panorama of a very different type.

OTHER CLIMBS IN THE CAIRNGORMS

I have already mentioned the climbing in Coire Bhrochain of Braeriach. A good deal of exploration can still be done in this remote, savage corrie, as well as on the crags in the innermost recesses of the Garbh Choire. There is also an interesting ridge leading to the summit of Sgor an Lochan Uaine. On the northern ramparts of Cairngorm there is more accessible and splendid winter climbing below Cairn Lochan in the corries which flank the Fiacaill ridge (which is very easy), the rock climbing being mostly found above the huge slabs of Coire an Lochain.

BLACK SPOUT PINNACLE, LOCHNAGAR

RESTING MOUNTAINEERS, SGORAN DUBH
Left to right: C. M. Allan; Author; D. Myles

Visitors to the Shelter Stone at the head of Loch Avon will find opportunities on Shelter Stone Crag and also above Loch Etchachan, where the routes are, however, very short.

The Garbh Choire lying at the northern base of Beinn a' Bhuird is full of possibilities, the Mitre Ridge being the finest and best-known of these. It was first climbed by two parties, by separate routes in the lower section, in July 1933. The more direct route, by Messrs E. A. M. Wedderburn, P. D. Baird and E. J. A. Leslie, was particularly difficult on the lower slabs. I myself climbed it by the shorter, side route in May 1935 and was greatly impressed by the narrow, steep ridge on the upper part, where a delicate traverse and a thin crack on the precipitous western wall had to be negotiated in order to circumvent a tower. There are also fine crags above the Dubh Lochan on the eastern side of the South Top of Beinn a' Bhuird, in a corrie where I enjoyed a grand snow climb in early May 1948.

LOCHNAGAR

Lochnagar and its subordinate peaks are ideal country for hill walking, as well as for rock or snow ascents. The best way to get an idea of the country is to traverse the mountain, either way, between Glen Muick and Glen Callater. A good path ascends the north side from Allt na Giubhsaich (on the opposite side of Glen Muick from Spittal, which is the end of the driving road, about nine miles from Ballater in Deeside), mounting by an easy gradient to the summit. Those making for the rock climbs above the Lochan, at 2,575 feet above sea level, should leave the track at the commencement of the Ladder or zigzags beneath the Cuidhe Crom summit, and cross the neck between that peak and the Meikle Pap to the right of it. There is a wide summit plateau, the highest point (3,786 ft.), being beyond the main mass of the crags. The southern descent to Loch Callater is also by a good track, about six miles long, over wild moorland. At one point there is a glimpse down a valley to the east to the Dubh Loch, which is dominated on the south by the equally impressive line of 700-foot crags of Creag an Dubh Loch. The Dubh Loch is also accessible by path from the head of Loch Muick. Loch Callater is connected by a rather inferior road to the main Cairnwell road, about two miles south of Braemar.

P

The Glen Muick approach is much better, both for camping and climbing. The Lochnagar corries and gullies carry a great deal of snow in winter, but the gullies are not good for climbing in summer.

Most of the rock climbing is either fairly easy or very difficult. Considerable experience is necessary for the latter, and it is not a very good place for the training of novices, owing to the general lack of good belays and prevalence of rounded holds. The Eagle Ridge of Lochnagar, to which is devoted a separate chapter, is a good example of the very best climbing on granite, or on any other kind of rock for that matter. It is almost unique in Britain as a long, severe climb on a steep, narrow ridge. In the limited space available in this chapter it is only possible to direct the rock climber to a few other selected routes of varying grades of difficulty.

The gullies are not to be recommended, as they are loose and the rock is usually unsound. The most formidable is the Douglas Gully of Lochnagar. A strong party may be able to climb fairly easily to within 150 feet of the top, and yet be defeated by a short wall of smooth, loose, slabby rock. In August 1946 a climber had to remain there, unable to move up or down, for eight hours before being rescued. Mr C. Ludwig made the first ascent alone in September 1933, but he maintained that the top section was unjustifiable. The Black Spout is perfectly easy, but may offer difficulties in winter owing to a cornice at the top. Raeburn's Gully makes a good winter climb. There does not seem to be much sense in attempting Douglas Gully as a rock climb, when it is flanked on either side by such excellent face and ridge routes as Eagle Ridge and Shadow Buttress B. The latter is rather typical of many Lochnagar buttresses, having an exceedingly steep and difficult lower wall followed by an easy upper section.

It will be better to mention one or two buttress or face routes of moderate difficulty, so that a visitor may get an idea of the topography of the mountain and the feel of the rock underfoot. The classical route of this type is the Tough Brown Ridge, first climbed by Messrs Tough and Brown in August 1896. The route demonstrates the difficulties of climbing on Lochnagar granite; for the lower part of the ridge (which would be much more

The Cliffs of Lochnagar

1 Eagle Ridge
2 Parallel Buttress
3 Tough-Brown Ridge
4 Raeburn's Gully

5 Black Spout Pinnacle
6 Black Spout
7 Black Spout Buttress,
  (West Buttress on right)

accurately described as a buttress) was not climbed by the pioneers. They started up the rocks near the base of Eagle Ridge (which is a true ridge but was first named Eagle Buttress), traversed to the right along a gently sloping shelf beneath Parallel Gullies and Parallel Buttress, and gained the crest of their buttress by a very steep climb. The upper continuation was perfectly easy. In June 1939 W. H. Murray and I descended from this buttress into Raeburn's Gully by a steep, but not specially difficult route, but the direct route up the lower wall of the buttress was only climbed in July 1941 by Miss N. Forsyth and myself. It proved to be one of the hardest climbs I have ever done. Parallel Buttress, first climbed in 1939 by W. H. Murray and myself, showed different features, having a short severe section near the top. For those who hanker after the impossible there is always the challenge of the terrifying wall of Black Spout Pinnacle* above the foot of the Black Spout.

I fear that I have been diverted from moderate routes for moderate climbers. Shadow Buttress A or Black Spout Buttress are excellent climbs of this standard. There is some very good and variegated climbing on the West Buttress. The routes are often linked by ledge traverses and are difficult to describe, so that hard and easy ways are often close together. On the west side of Lochnagar the Stuic Buttress above the green loch is worth visiting.

Creag an Dubh Loch is much less explored than Lochnagar. The granite appears to be more closely jointed, tending towards a roof-tile, slabby formation with correspondingly increased difficulty. The Labyrinth, a long, fascinating climb of about 700 feet, goes up a curious, inner amphitheatre of the mountain on very sound rock, and finishes close to the summit. Miss Forsyth and I found it exceedingly difficult at our first ascent in 1941†, and it was pleasant and interesting to have our opinion confirmed a year later by Mr S. Thompson, a very good climber, who had not read the account of our ascent. His route was almost the same as ours.

A WINTER CLIMB ON LOCHNAGAR

Raeburn's Gully was first climbed in November 1898, when there was very little snow and the main difficulty was a great, vertical wall of rock across the gully at about middle height. Harold Raeburn's party used combined tactics, the leader being obliged to hook his ice-axe by the pick over the edge of a jammed block above him in order to overcome the pitch. There were lesser difficulties and a through route between large boulders above this point, but there was, of course, no cornice of snow at the top.

A mixed party of four of us set out from Allt na Giubhsaich for Lochnagar on April 23rd, 1939 with Raeburn's Gully as our objective. There had been a fresh snowfall during the night and it was a morning of dull skies and hard frost. A cold wind helped us to maintain a good pace to the saddle between the

* Climbed in August 1949 by W. D. Brooker and D. A. Sutherland. See *S.M.C.J.* (1950).
† See *S.M.C.J.*, Vol. 23, p. 32.

Cuidhe Crom and the Meikle Pap. Then the sun came out and revealed the great horseshoe of crags, all plastered with snow and ice, with gleaming white streaks where the sun shone through the upper notches of the gullies on to the buttresses. After a laborious traverse round the steep slopes below the rocks we gained the snowfield at the foot of our gully. We could only hope that an accumulation of old, consolidated snow had built up against Raeburn's rock wall, so as to allow us to cut steps most of the way to the top of the pitch, but we could not see so far from below on account of the narrow, curving line and the lofty rock walls of the lower gully.

The snow was in good condition, as the coating of new powder was comparatively thin. We made good progress by kicking steps until the gully narrowed and steepened, after which every step had to be slashed out with the axe. In the centre was a snow-filled trough or runnel, clearly a channel for occasional snow slides or minor avalanches. As it was almost certain to be lined with ice we kept well above it, on the right. The gully now curved to our left and revealed, high above us, a wall of ice extending right across, with a cave underneath it at the right-hand corner. This was obviously the crucial problem for the day, and its aspect was rather discouraging. However, we persevered and soon climbed into the cave, which proved a commodious shelter and a safe anchorage for the rest of the party while the unfortunate leader was attempting to climb the ice wall.

Some refreshment was obviously desirable before tackling the pitch, so we ate in comfort and listened to a series of humorous tales from Dr Myles. Long after I had left the comforts of the cave and was uneasily perched on the face of the icy cliff I could still hear the ladies laughing at some droll occurrence among the farm 'touns' of Angus, racily put across by a native of the same county. I could only hope that they were paying some attention to my rope as well, as I had little other sense of security.

I traversed along underneath the wall, armed with an ice axe and a small pick. The latter is an exceedingly useful tool when one must cut both hand and footholds at close quarters on a wall of ice. It was a slater's hammer with a short shaft, the hammer having been burned off short in an oxy-acetylene flame. My friend Dick Morsley presented it to me after our first ascent of Green Gully on Ben Nevis. At the far side of the gully were one or two rock holds which helped me to make a start on the ice. I doubt if the ice wall exceeds fifteen feet in

vertical height, but such ascents are better counted in inches when one considers their duration and severity, accentuated as they are by the cramped and tiring posture of the climber.

At one point I was able to insert a forearm through a hole into a cavity behind some massive icicles, but all the other holds had to be cut, and made both capacious and insloping, as it was no place for risking a fall. With a horizontal run-out of rope from the cave I should have fallen a long way before the rope tightened. At length I was able to reach over the top and feel for holds

The Ice Pitch; Raeburn's Gully, Lochnagar
I could only hope that they were paying some attention to my rope.

over a sloping granite slab, but it, too, was coated with a thin veneer of ice. This was the crucial movement, as the pick of my axe had but a slender grip above the slab and the short axe was badly placed. The frost rendered the holds perfectly secure, in spite of the fact that I was climbing a wall composed of a whole row of icicles cemented together. Somehow I managed to swarm over the slab and obtain a satisfactory anchorage in the snow-ice above it.

Having cut two huge steps and buried my axe to the hilt in the hard snow I summoned the next member of the party. Everyone came up safely, but the pitch had taken us an hour and a half to overcome. The next stretch was much better; steep, hard snow covering a chaos of huge boulders. There was no sign of any tunnel. Where the rocks were extra large they protruded from the snow and we pulled ourselves over the ledges, avoiding the ice in the crevices between the blocks. Then the gradient steepened again and the gully floor became one uniform slope of snow-ice. It meant hard and continuous step cutting for the leader and took a long time, but the upper end of the gully was now in sight and there were no intervening obstacles. Here and there a covering of powder snow had to be swept aside before cutting the steps, but conditions were surprisingly good on the whole.

A lad appeared on the cornice at the head of the gully, watching our labours with interest. He told me that he had come up the Black Spout by himself, finding it fairly easy. Then he disappeared again. The cornice was not particularly large. For most of the way round the top of the funnel it was overhanging, but, at the left corner, it was just vertical and not at all high. Our labours continued, only two persons moving at a time, the first and third or the second and fourth. We could not afford to take risks. Soon we came to a small, rocky neck, about fifty feet below the cornice, and our last good anchorage. The encouraging lad had re-appeared after being 'awa' for a danner round the taps'. He came to see the finish.

I cut steps to the left corner of the cornice, swarmed up on to a long hummock of icy stuff and crawled along it beneath the overhanging eave of snow. Very gently, for the snow was powdery, soft and dry, I wriggled upwards through the gap and over the wall to freedom and the mountain top. We were all on the plateau at 6.20 p.m. after a grand climb of six hours' duration. The weather had been perfect with little wind and continuing frost. Towards the south-east the horizon was bluish-black with promise of further snowfall.

NOTE.—A considerable rock-fall in Raeburn's Gully occurred previous to the summer of 1946, sweeping away the great pitch altogether. One or two pitches of a minor character have been created lower down.

CHAPTER XV

ARRAN GRANITE

THE granite peaks of the Isle of Arran, rather like those of the Cairngorms and Lochnagar, have acquired a bad name with some rock climbing purists, on account of unsound rock, lack of belays and vegetatious ledges. At the same time, mountaineers love the Arran hills for the excellence of the ridge walking, the attractive character of the summit views and the scenery of the glens.

Arran climbing started with Lugless Willie Lithgow who climbed Goatfell (Goatfield Hill) in 1628. He dilates on the marvellous view of Northern Ireland, the Isle of Man and the hills of Cumberland, 'Three Kingdoms at one sight'. Other pioneers speak of the delightful contrasts of such views from Arran peaks, embracing rocky hills, green Glen Rosa, the yellow sands of Brodick Bay, the sunlit slopes of Corriegills and the surrounding seas.

Serious rock climbing started about 1891 when W. W. Naismith and Gilbert Thomson, founders of the Scottish Mountaineering Club, began their explorations on the north-east face of Cir Mhor (the great comb), the central hub of the Arran peaks, and one of the most stately of Scottish mountains, though but 2,618 feet in altitude. By 1894 many climbers were engaged on the Arran cliffs, and in 1895 the best of the classic climbs, the BC Rib of Cir Mhor was climbed by Bell, Boyd, Green and Napier. They went up by a series of steep slabs and narrow ledges, but good belays were lacking for the rope. The best known climb of those days was the Oppenheimer Chimney of Beinn Nuis, led in 1901 by E. A. Baker. The party was all-English, consisting of Baker, Puttrell and Oppenheimer, and was almost defeated at one point. It does not seem to be clear whether the climb was ever repeated. The rock of Beinn Nuis is rather unstable and treacherous and it may well be the case that a rock-fall has, since then, altered the configuration of the place. Harry MacRobert was the leading spirit in the exploration of the southern gullies of the A'Chir Ridge between 1908 and 1911.

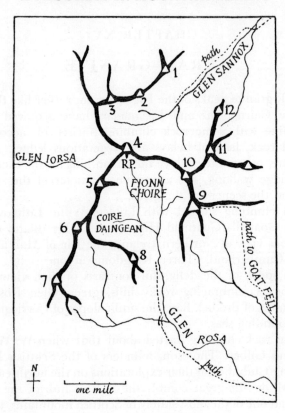

MAP D   ARRAN RIDGES

PEAKS

		height in feet
1	Suidhe Fhearghas	2,081
2	Ceum na Caillich (Witch's Step)	2,300
3	Caisteal Abhail (Castles)	2,817
4	Cir Mhor (Great Comb)	2,618
5	A'Chir	2,335
6	Beinn Tarsuinn	2,706
7	Beinn Nuis	2,597
8	Beinn a' Chliabhain	2,217
9	Goatfell (Hill of the Wind)	2,866
10	North Goatfell	
11	Mullach Buidhe	2,688
12	Cioch na h' Oighe (Maiden's Breast)	2,168
RP	Rosa Pinnacle	

For a long time nothing new was reported from Arran and, meanwhile, the favoured type of climbing had changed from gullies to faces. In 1939 A. S. Pigott and B. K. Barber made the first route on the east wall of Rosa Pinnacle, Cir Mhor, and in 1940 J. F. Hamilton and G. S. Roger, of the younger school of Glasgow mountaineers, climbed its South Ridge, the finest face of rock on the island. The main revival of Arran climbing was due, however, to a small group of naval engineers who were stationed at Largs for several years during the war. The leaders and recorders were G. H. Townend and G. C. Curtis.* They made many new and excellent discoveries and established Arran, once and for all, as a grand centre for climbing on sound, rough rock with routes of all degrees of length, interest and difficulty.

Arran has a remarkable variety of rock formations, both sedimentary and igneous. The great Highland Fault cuts right across it from Blackwaterfoot on the west coast, by the line of the String road to the east coast near Corrie. To the south are the lesser, rounded hills of the Old Red Sandstone. To the north is a great nucleus of granite, thrust up through beds of shale and sandstone, tilted at an angle, with the slate next the granite. Here and there are basalt dykes in the granite, forming chimneys at A'Chir and elsewhere. Sir Archibald Geikie points out that the two sets of joint planes in the granite are inclined at an angle in a somewhat irregular manner, so that the processes of weathering and erosion have broken up the rock into characteristic, rounded blocks, like huge piles of masonry with edges which are both rounded and etched. The structure varies a good deal, for the south faces of Cir Mhor and A'Chir are wonderfully sound and rough, with good belays (especially on Rosa Pinnacle) and very little vegetation. Beinn Nuis and Cioch na h'Oighe are not at all sound. There is a close resemblance to the cliffs of Lochnagar and the Cairngorms and also, curiously enough, to the ancient Torridon sandstone ridges of Ross and Sutherland.

Even for beginners there are many interesting expeditions, but Arran granite is not the best place for novices in rock climbing. Goatfell (2,866 ft.), the highest peak, is an easy excursion from Brodick or Corrie, and can be combined with a ridge

* See *S.M.C. Journal* for 1944, 1945, 1947.

walk over North Goatfell to Mullach Buidhe and Cioch na h'Oighe (2,168 ft.), the rocky peak overlooking lower Glen Sannox. As the latter has precipitous cliffs the walk had better be done in the reverse direction. Both Glen Sannox and Glen Rosa are beautiful valleys surrounded by mountains and traversed by clear, rushing streams. They meet beneath the Saddle (1,413 ft.), connecting Cir Mhor with North Goatfell, and both can be traversed in a grand walk between Brodick and Sannox. The main ridge of the Arran granite peaks bounds these glens on the side opposite from Goatfell, and the keen hill walker will wish to traverse it from end to end. It demands great care in mist, but all technical difficulties of a rock climbing nature are easily avoidable. This horse-shoe of mountains is a far shorter and easier proposition than the Cuillin Ridge of Skye, but it does make a good, hard day on the hills with any amount of variety and a succession of glorious views of mountain, glen and sea.

In May 1945, George Collie, Charlie Gorrie and I left Sannox shortly after ten a.m. An easy heathery climb, followed by an upper grassy shoulder, took us to the first summit, Suidhe Fheargas (the seat from which King Fergus the First surveyed his domains). Easy going continued to the top of Ceum na Caillich (the witch's step), from which there is a steep and moderately difficult descent to the next gap. An easier way is possible, lower down on the northern slopes, but no real climber should have much difficulty, and, presumably, the Caillich got over the place easily enough. A long, rocky ridge from Glen Sannox to the summit is now named Broomstick Ridge. A long ascent from the gap took us to the top of Caisteal Abhail (2,817 ft.), where we halted for lunch amongst the weird granite tors on the wide, flat summit. We were enveloped in dense mist, which deprived us of one of the finest views of the island, towards the grand, steep, northern face of Cir Mhor with its fluted cliffs.

We took a compass bearing before leaving, for The Castles, as the mountain is usually named, can be a very confusing place in mist, a meeting place of four ridges, with steep cliffs falling away to upper Glen Sannox. Running down an easy scree slope, we were soon out of the mist and enjoyed bright sunshine for the rest of the day. Cir Mhor (2,618 ft.) was the next halting place at 2.45 p.m. The way was now easy to a saddle before the rise to A'Chir. Here again, a traverse round the base of the cliffs on the western side, above Glen Iorsa, would avoid all difficulties, but we were determined to have some rock climbing in our day's expedition.

We thoroughly enjoyed ourselves on the A'Chir Ridge. The rock and the holds are good. The ridge is not at all difficult—least of all the apparently sensational bridging of the A'Chir Gap. The ridge is very narrow in places and the changing views, both near and far, are entirely delightful. There is one interesting traverse on the Rosa side before reaching the summit, but the rock holds are very good all the way. The actual summit block presents a little gymnastic problem for those who are purists in such matters. The hour and a half we spent on this ridge seemed to us far too short. Rather a dull, sweaty ascent followed to the top of Beinn Tarsuinn (2,706 ft.), and in little over half an hour we were on Beinn Nuis (2,597 ft.), our last summit for the day, at six p.m. We refreshed ourselves for the final three-mile walk to Brodick by a delightful swim in a long, deep pool of the Rosa burn, at the turn of the glen.

Next day George Collie and I returned to the base of the southern cliffs of Cir Mhor with more serious intentions. Hamish Hamilton had assured me that the South Ridge of Rosa Pinnacle was one of the few top-rank discoveries of the century in Scottish rock climbing—an incredibly steep climb of nearly 800 feet on grand, sound rock, narrowing at places to a veritable knife-edge! We had a perfect, sunny day with a gentle breeze, ideal conditions for a difficult climb. After lunch on the warm heather slopes beneath the crags we left our sacks and started off in rubbers for the climb, aiming at the foot of a prominent S-shaped crack, which is the main feature of the lower tier of cliff.

It is a formidable crack, soon approaching the vertical. The cross section is awkward, a central rib flanked by two narrower cracks. The positive holds were soon left behind, but the rough walls gave plenty of friction grip. Near the top I found a spike on which I was glad to belay the rope as I rested for a while, for the final upward move on to a slab on the right was very awkward and exposed. Immediately above the slab was a great

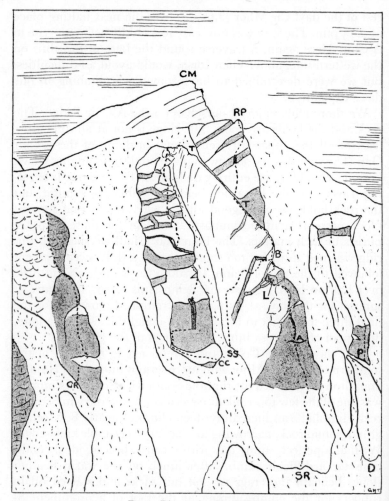

Rosa Pinnacle Cir Mhor

This diagram has been borrowed from the Scottish Mountaineering Club Journal (1945), Vol. 23, p. 242. Some of the lettering, therefore, is not relevant to descriptions in this chapter. The full key is, however, included, and interested readers may refer to the original source for routes not described here.

CM	Cir Mhor Summit	L	Lay-back Crack (not on route
RP	Rosa Pinnacle Summit		described)
SR	Start of South Ridge	B	Three Tier chimney
A	Severe Crack	TT	Easy Terrace
		SS	Sou'wester slabs

Not described: CR, Cubic Route; CC, Caliban's Creep; P, Prospero; D, Prospero's Prelude. Cubic and Caliban are just difficult, D is easy, but P is severe.

triangular flake of massive proportions with a comfortable niche behind it, a perfectly secure stance for bringing up George.

We were now about the centre of the steep, lower cliff, in a comfortable and agreeable situation, with a splendid view over the nearer hills across the Firth of Clyde, but with no answer whatever to the urgent question: where next? I failed to get very far to the left. To the right was a delicate corner with a flat triangular slab beyond. Just above George was a steep slab, split by a crack and ending under a slightly overhanging wall, about eight to ten feet high. The crack narrowed and split the wall, forking like a letter Y below the top. It was not a very high wall, but the crack was too narrow for anything but sideways wedging of the toes and there was no guarantee of positive holds above the Y. Neither Collie nor I knew where Hamish Hamilton's route went, so we chose to explore the traverse on the right rather than to risk falling off the overhang. The traverse turned out to be fairly simple, leading to steep flakes of rock which brought us out above the Y crack. From the easy slabs above George safeguarded me on the rope as I descended to explore the holds above the lower crack. They were clean-cut and perfect. Later in the week we met Curtis, who told us that Hamilton had led the Y crack directly, a very fine piece of climbing which was justifiable because Hamish had been up the other way on a former occasion and had, no doubt, assured himself of the good holds above that very severe crack.

We were now at the foot of the middle tier of cliff on Rosa Pinnacle. Townend had told us something of a good lay-back crack by which it could be ascended from the left. We found another overhanging crack straight above us, but could not identify the Townend pitch. So the middle tier was again solved by a traverse to the right and a very steep climb up the east wall, where the holds were extremely sketchy in places. The final tier of cliff to the crest of the Lower Pinnacle was delightful climbing by the Three Tier Chimney and a blunt knife-edge below the top.

There remained the conical wall of the Upper Pinnacle, approached by an easy ledge. Steep slabs led up to the right, but I was unable to force my way to the crest in that direction. A short traverse to the left admitted us to a slab, up which we climbed to the edge of the vertical eastern wall. The climb finished along a beautiful knife-edge on the upper crest. The Upper Pinnacle occupied us for fifty minutes out of a total climbing time of three hours and forty minutes. Hamilton was right, and the South Ridge of Rosa Pinnacle will take its place among the classics of British rock climbing.

Those who do not feel equal to trying conclusions with the S Crack may still taste the delights of an ascent of Rosa Pinnacle. At the end of our holiday week George had taken to photography and Charlie, who had a game leg as a result of his war experiences in North Africa, wanted to climb Rosa Pinnacle, but could not rely on his injured limb for anything too strenuous. Townend and Curtis, those indefatigable explorers, had designed the Sou'wester Slabs Route to meet such a case.

It starts from the scree higher up and farther to the left than the direct route and attacks the buttress on the flank. Curtis and two of his friends were also with us as a separate photographic party. The climb is nowhere above 'very difficult' in standard, the rock is perfect and the situations are delightful. We rejoined the direct route at the foot of Three Tier Chimney on the upper band of cliffs of the lower Pinnacle. I lost the way on the Upper Pinnacle and involved Charlie in a short, severe pitch after all, but he pulled up all right, and we finished by a huge, upper slab, exactly at the top of Rosa Pinnacle.

There are many other excellent rock climbs in Arran. I cannot speak of the north-east face of Cir Mhor, but believe that the BC Rib is excellent. George and I enjoyed a grand climb of over 500 feet on the face of A'Chir above Coire Daingean, near its head. Townend had recommended Pagoda Ridge to us and we found it excellent. It runs up between Nos. 4 and 5 gullies, and looks almost impossible, as seen from near the top of Beinn a' Chliabhain. George and I found that it had a sort of roof-tile slab structure, with any amount of incident and difficulty on steep, sound rock, taking us at least two and a half hours to climb. On another day we had good sport on long ribs of steep slab leading up from Glen Rosa to Goatfell. These climbs are all much better suited to rubbers than to nailed boots.

If Arran granite, like Skye gabbro, encourages the care-free holiday spirit in the rock climber, it may be as well to sound a note of warning. Charlie and I went off one morning to seek out one of two new routes by Townend and Curtis on Cioch na h'Oighe. Their names were Midnight Ridge and Twilight Slabs, presumably because both had been first climbed very late on a Saturday night, so as to lose nothing out of a short week-end. We could not identify either climb, but negotiated a severe and nearly vertical pitch of almost ninety feet on a loose rock wall above a little rowan tree. It was the worst, hardest and least secure piece of rock climbing during the entire holiday. Townend told us that the face of Beinn Nuis was of a similar character but worse.

On that day we travelled from Brodick to Sannox on a bus. Charlie carried the rope and excited the interest of another passenger who *knew* something about mountaineering. The conversation proceeded roughly as follows:

Mr X: 'You will be all right since you have boots and a rope. It won't matter at all if it rains'.

Charlie mentioned that we also carried rubbers, but this evoked a peculiar and dubious look from the stranger.

Mr X: 'The rock is very rotten all over Arran'.

Charlie: 'I am not sure about that, but isn't it as good as on the Cuillins in Skye?'

Mr X: 'Oh yes, for Skye rock is very rotten, too. Have you been on Rosa Pinnacle of Cir Mhor?'

Charlie: 'No'.

Mr X: 'That is the very worst rock in Arran'.

Charlie: 'Where can one find the best rock?'

Mr X: 'It is best on Beinn Nuis'.

We had seen Beinn Nuis. We haven't climbed on it. We do not intend to!

Q

CHAPTER XVI

THE NORTH-WEST

THIS chapter deals with the rugged, shapely mountains of north-west Scotland, beyond the line of the Dingwall–Skye railway. They are, for the most part, sharply distinguished from the main mass of the Scottish Highlands, and they also differ from such local regions of volcanic and eruptive action as the Cuillin of Skye, the granites of Galloway, Arran and the Cairngorms or the good climbing porphyrites of Glencoe and Ben Nevis. They are well worth a visit from all three points of view—scenic, climbing and geological.

They presented very difficult problems to the earlier geologists, and out of these arose more than one famous controversy. Hugh Miller, author of *The Old Red Sandstone* and other geological publications, who was a native of Cromarty, once thought that the striking scenery of Wester Ross and Sutherland was founded on a western extension of the Old Red Sandstone which plays such a large part on the east coast of Scotland from the Shetlands to the Borders. But the great mural precipices of Suilven and Liathach, most characteristic of this interesting region, proved to be a much older rock and much more resistant to denudation. In Sutherland it stands up in great, isolated peaks, mountains that so impressed Dr John Maculloch between the years 1811 and 1821 that he wrote of '. . . mountains which seem as if they had tumbled from the clouds, having nothing to do with the country or each other, in shape, material, position or character'.

Whoever obtains his first glimpse of Suilven, either from the sea to the west of Lochinver or from the moors between Oykell Bridge and Alltnagealgach, must agree, if the appreciation of mountain form is engrained in his nature and enthusiasms. The same can be said of the first sight of Liathach across Glen Torridon, of the view of the great corries of Ben Bhan of Applecross from the road between Lochs Carron and Kishorn or of the Teallachs from the gorge above Dundonnell. In the latter examples the mountains group themselves into larger ranges

A Winter View of Liathach from Loch Clair

rather than isolated peaks, but the tremendous frontage of wall-like precipices of horizontally terraced, dark red or purplish rock is the same in all cases.

My own introduction to the Torridon Red region was fortunate and made a great impression upon me. The Easter Meet of the Scottish Mountaineering Club in 1923 was arranged for Kinlochewe and Loch Maree, with the option of a start at Dundonnell and a cross-country journey to Loch Maree. Ernest Roberts was with me, but no one else went to Dundonnell. There was a breath of spring in the air as we reached Little Loch Broom, and plenty of snow on the higher tops as we started out for An Teallach on the following day.

Whilst Roberts was in the post-office my ice-axe caught the attention of a passing tramp. Hearing that the axe was used for cutting steps on the ice of the mountains he looked puzzled for a moment, but brightened up eventually and said, 'I see, you are fishmongers. You cut out big lumps of ice, carry them in your sack and sell them to the fish shops in the city'. We pushed on, but when I looked round I could see him still staring after us rather quizzically, as if not quite satisfied.

A good track through the woods led us up the hillside, with the spiky tops of An Teallach to the west. The range opens out towards the north-east, enclosing two magnificent corries, the northerly one below the highest summit, Bidein a' Ghlas Thuill (3,483 ft.) and the other, more impressive corrie ringed about with crags enclosing the waters of Toll an Lochain. This was our objective as we made our way up successive, slabby terraces of rock to the lip of the corrie. We lunched by the shore of the Lochan in warm sunshine. In its still waters were reflected the snow-terraced cliffs of Corrag Bhuidhe of An Teallach, one of the most fascinating visions of mountain architecture in all Scotland. The sandstone is of a dark purple hue and horizontal in its bedding. Many of the sheets of rock overlap the lower ones. A thousand feet of cliff were clearly delineated by the snow-covered ledges. It was a mountain face to be admired rather than climbed. Several of the terraces may be accessible to the mountaineer, but they often contract to the thinnest of ledges, hardly a break in that vertical sweep of precipice. Torridon sandstone has few positive holds; they are mostly rounded and there are few, if any, belays. No climbing route goes directly up Corrag Bhuidhe from the lochan.

Reluctantly, we turned our attention to a steep, snow-filled gully on the right. Here we made rapid progress to a fork where the left branch soared up to the skyline in a series of impossible-looking pitches. After some interesting climbing up the right fork we reached the summit ridge and attained the little rocky nose called Lord Berkeley's Seat. Pleasant and interesting scrambling followed over Corrag Bhuidhe (the yellow finger, 3,425 ft.), across a little saddle, and finally, on to Sail Liath (the grey heel, 3,100 ft.), the last top of the range. We had no time to include the highest top, which was far behind us. The ridge took a good deal of time, as the sandstone had weathered, in many places, into huge piles of biscuit-shaped slabs—unstable heaps where an incautious step might easily unbalance the whole edifice and bring it down about our ears.

The view from the summit was one of delightful contrasts—westward over a loch-studded moorland to Gruinard Bay and the islands, north-west to the intriguing, isolated peaks of Coigach and Assynt which I hoped to explore in the near future, and southward across a tortuous maze of mountain country where lay our next day's journey. One prominent feature concerned us most, the rocky cone of Beinn Dearg Mhor above the flat valley of Strath na Sheallag. At its base lay the cottage of Larachantivore where we hoped to pass the night. A rapid glissade down a snow slope helped us over the first stage. After a longish walk we reached the flats, crossed the stream and were groping our way at dusk across the half-mile of boggy ground towards the cottage.

We had a big programme for the next day, but we laid a good foundation with a breakfast of porridge, eggs, scones and butter. Before eight a.m. we started for Beinn Dearg Mhor, aiming for the crags on the side of the big, northern Coire nan Clach. Ice axes were hardly necessary, as we had chosen a fairly easy route on the right-hand rim, and we were basking on the summit in our shirt sleeves at eleven a.m. It was a calm day of clear sunshine. After a descent by the other bounding ridge of the corrie we returned to Larachantivore for lunch, shouldered our packs and bade our kind hosts good-bye.

The walk before us was about twelve miles to Letterewe on the north shore of Loch Maree, but the route lay over two passes of about 1,700-feet altitude with a drop between to 500 feet. For quality of scenery it was one of the finest walks that I have ever done. Approaching the first summit we wound up a narrow glen on a good track, crossed a ridge and a wide stretch of moorland with a lochan here and there and were intrigued by the appearance of new ranges of mountains opening up in the south-east. But the grandest prospect came later.

The way led down a narrow, steep glen. Rounding a corner we gazed down on the waters of the Fionn Loch, a wonderful pattern of interlacing wavelets of burnished gold in the early evening sunshine. The upper part of the Fionn Loch is separated by a narrow isthmus from an inner lochan almost surrounded by savage crags. This Dubh Loch is a true mountain tarn. Above and behind is the long rocky flank of Ben Lair (2,817 ft.), two and a half miles of cliff overlooking Gleann Tulacha, with the red sandstone crags of Slioch (3,260 ft), appearing over it on the left. Still more to the left was the dome of A'Mhaighdean (3,060 ft., the Maiden), another remote mountain with attractive possibilities for rock climbing. As we kept swinging downwards to our right we were impressed by the steep cliff of Torr na h'Iolaire (the eagle's cliff) just above us. The view opened out westward along the Fionn Loch and disclosed the bold, precipitous face of Beinn Airidh Charr (2,593 ft.), above the southern shore of the loch. A camp at the head of Fionn Loch would be a veritable paradise for the enthusiastic rock climber, for I do not know of any other corner in the Scottish Highlands with so much opportunity for exploration in grand and imposing surroundings.

It was not the climbing opportunities but the contrast, the grandeur and the beauty of the scene that held me spellbound. Such visions are, not infrequently, granted to the hill wanderer who penetrates into the secret places of nature at break or close of day. If he is in accord with his surroundings he is enabled to accept the revelation and, for a time, to sense something above and beyond it. Of the sum total of such fragmentary experiences something at least is integrated with the personality and never lost. Such moments may come on hard and difficult mountaineering exploits. Sometimes they serve to cheer and encourage when the chances of success, or even of survival, seem heavily loaded against one, but at other times, such as the one presently described, all is peace and transcendent beauty. An older friend, who did not climb but who fished the moorland lochs of the north-west once expressed it to me thus: 'The sense of beauty is so overpowering as to make one feel almost afraid'. Surely here is part, at least, of the answer to the question: 'Why do men climb mountains?' and the reply cannot be either made or understood unless the golden memories return on the instant, and, even so, the words are totally inadequate, whether written or spoken. All I can say is that I know of no region where such experiences are less uncommon than in the mountainous area around Loch Maree, especially at the season of spring when mountains, lochs, woodlands, sky and cloud have all renewed their youth.

Roberts and I crossed the causeway of stones between the Fionn and Dubh Lochs and slowly climbed the path for over a thousand feet to our last pass for the day. Darkness had fallen when we reached Letterewe on the northern shore of Loch Maree, but the keeper very kindly ferried us over to the hotel on the other side; the perfect ending to a strenuous day, as the boat threaded its way between the islets in the light of the full moon.

It is hard to decide which is the finest mountain in the district. The honours are evenly divided between Beinn Eighe and Liathach. The first is conspicuous as one approaches Kinlochewe from the east. The eastern end of the long range has peaks capped with greyish white quartzite, giving it a distinguished appearance, but offering long slopes of toilsome screes to the climber. The grandest feature of Beinn Eighe is the Coire Mhic Fhearchair which separates the two western summits, Ruadh Stac Mor (3,309 ft.), the highest top and Sail Mhor (3,217 ft.). This is one of the most impressive corries in Scotland with its lonely lochan backed by symmetrical masses of cliff. We approached it by a long path up Glen Grudie from Loch Maree. Where the path ends a short, rough climb leads to the lip of the corrie. A floor of Torridon sandstone slabs rims the loch. On the left are long scree slopes descending from Ruadh

Stac Mor, an easy way of gaining the main summit of Beinn Eighe. On the right are the great sandstone cliffs beneath the summit of Sail Mhor, with no feasible route of ascent, except a wide, straight gully opening out just below the rim of the upper corrie. This is Morrison's Gully, a good route for descending when filled with snow, but there is a small pitch near the bottom, so that careless glissaders should take warning.

Straight across, on the far side of the lochan from the line of approach, are three great buttresses of rock, sweeping up through 1,000 feet to the rounded summit of Coinneach Mhor. They have all been climbed, the left-hand one being the easiest. The lower rocks are of Torridon Red and very difficult, but the larger, upper portions are of Cambrian quartzite, a more amenable rock, very sound and offering good holds. The junction line between the two rises at a moderate angle from left to right.

Roberts and I went for the northern or left-hand buttress and we thoroughly enjoyed ourselves. We had quite enough on our hands, considering the amount of snow and ice covering the lower ledges, and I must confess that we did not climb the sandstone directly, but traversed along from the left into the gully between the northern and central buttresses. Some distance higher we traversed out of the gully on to our buttress, and the excellent jointing of the quartzite enabled us to climb almost straight to the summit. The rock was delightfully steep and exposed, interesting throughout but never very difficult.

The day finished with a joyful traverse of ridges and peaks, with a series of glissades and an easy descent to Kinlochewe. My last day of that holiday was a sort of continuation of my southward progress across the mountains, starting from Glen Torridon and crossing over Sgorr Ruadh (3,142 ft) and Fuar Tholl (2,968 ft.), with a steep descent to Coire Lair leading to Achnashellach railway station, in time for the evening train for Inverness. The upper moorland between these two mountains is the most rough and desolate country I have ever seen. It is the country of the great thrust-plane movements, when whole mountains were crumpled up and thrust bodily for several miles in an approximately north-westerly direction over the underlying strata. There is a little hill, Sgurr Dubh (2,566 ft.), to the

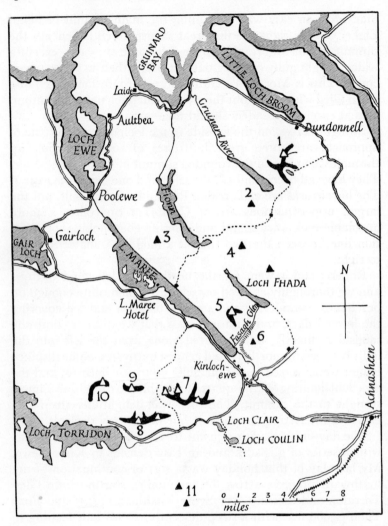

MAP E   WESTER ROSS
                          MOUNTAINS
                    height in feet   height in feet
  1 An Teallach   .   .   3,483   7 Beinn Eighe   .   .   3,309
  2 Beinn Dearg Mor   .   2,974   8 Liathach   .   .   .   3,456
  3 Beinn Airidh a' Charr . 2,593   9 Beinn Dearg   .   .   2,995
  4 A'Mhaighdean   .   .   3,060   10 Alligin   .   .   .   3,232
  5 Slioch   .   .   .   3,260   11 Sgorr Ruadh   .   .   3,142
  6 Beinn Mhuinidh   .   2,231

south of Glen Torridon, which I visited with my wife in 1946, and which shows a complexity that must surely derive from this distant epoch of great disturbance. Our route was fairly direct. We started on Torridon Red, climbed many terraced escarpments of quartzite, ascended a steep cliff of Torridon Red to the first summit, crossed a small dip and finished by a gradual rise of little over 100 feet of quartzite to the true summit.

My first experience of Liathach was again at Easter time. Four of us were in the northern Coire na Caime. L. St. C. Bartholomew and I were bent on doing a rock climb, and it promptly began to rain with some degree of persistence. I don't think we climbed anything of importance, but we enjoyed ourselves on the rough Torridon sandstone, until the slabs conducted trickles and streamlets of water down our sleeves and through other gaps in our defences. So we called it a day and climbed rapidly, by easy slopes, to the main ridge, where, by pure chance, we met our friends descending from Spidean a' Choire Leith, the highest summit. The problem was to effect a descent to Glen Torridon in the mist. At first everything went very well by a series of glissades, suspiciously well I should say. Then we got below the quartzite and were faced by tiers of Torridon Red crags. These took a long time to negotiate, but, fortunately, we had several hours in hand. We then understood why Liathach presents such an imposing appearance when seen from Loch Clair at the head of Glen Torridon. Bartholomew and I could liken ourselves to several of the early Alpine explorers in the classical period when it was considered meritorious to traverse a little-known pass across a high range of mountains, even although no summit was actually climbed!

At length, in June 1946, I revisited Liathach with my wife. Coire na Caime is very remote, but I wished to view its possibilities for rock climbing. So we penetrated to the farthest and most westerly arm of the corrie, and made for its right-hand bounding ridge. This is the well-known, northern Pinnacle Ridge of the mountain. We attacked the lower nose fairly directly and encountered at least one section where we were compelled to use the rope. This was really difficult, but the remainder of the ascent to the top of the nose was moderate scrambling and no more.

The ridge itself is wholly delightful and exceedingly like the granite ridges of Arran. I remember one gap, in particular, which resembles the famous one on A'Chir. After topping the last pinnacle, Meall Dearg, we crossed a little neck and the red rock gave place to grey quartzite on the last rise to the top of Mullach an Rathain (3,358 ft.), which we reached at 4.30 p.m. The view was glorious, with the Outer Isles clearly visible and a mass of black storm clouds brooding over the Cuillins of Skye. Everywhere else, from the Teallachs in the north to the hills of Monar and Affric in the east, all was clear and sunny.

We could not afford to cut our programme short on such a delightful afternoon, so we decided to traverse all the other tops of Liathach on the return journey. The first part is very easy until one comes to the narrow ridge over the Fasarinen pinnacles. That was the most enjoyable part. There are no serious difficulties, but plenty of good scrambling. At any rate, we did not require to use our rope. For those unskilled in any kind of rock climbing it is always possible to descend a little on the Torridon side and use a sheep track in order to avoid the difficulties.

Beyond the Fasarinen the Torridon sandstone finally gives place to angular blocks of quartzite, making the eastern half of the ridge much more toilsome. A longish ascent took us to Spidean a' Choire Leith (3,456 ft.), the main summit. At seven p.m. we were on the last, eastern top, Stuc a' Choire Dhuibh Bhig. The descent gave us no difficulty, as we had traced our course in the forenoon when we were ascending the track which runs up the Choire Dhuibh Mhoir from the Torridon road to the gap between Liathach and Beinn Eighe. This is the most useful line of approach, both for Liathach and for the cliffs of Coire Mhic Fhearchair on Beinn Eighe. The combination of the Northern Pinnacles with all the other tops of Liathach makes a long day, but it is a grand expedition, full of interest and variety.

Even if one does not wish to climb rocks this north-western region, with its fascinating variety of scenery, holds much more of interest for the hill walker if he learns the key to the architecture of its mountains. The geological structure, in rough outline, is not difficult to grasp. In only a few cases is it legibly engraved on the face of a mountain so that a single informed glance can take it in. The view of Suilven from the north, near Suileag, is perhaps the clearest of such pictures. The foundation of the mountain is a rough plateau of ancient Lewisian gneiss. Most of the rough desolation of the north-western moors owes its origin to the eroded and pitted surface of this hard rock, and the result is a marshy, ill-drained landscape studded with many lochans, where glacial action has carved them out or left moraines to dam them back.

Above the gneiss the main bulk of Suilven consists of wall-like crags of red Torridon sandstone, a hard rock which is often of conglomerate type. The bedding is nearly horizontal and never, at any rate, inclined steeply. It is difficult rock to climb with its vertical cliffs and horizontal terraces. There are many overhangs and the holds are usually rounded and not in-cut. It is the great precipices of Torridon Red that characterise the scenery of the north-west. They are everywhere spectacular, on Beinn Bhan of Applecross, Coire na Caime of Liathach, An Teallach, the Coigach hills, Suilven and Quinag.

On most of these hills there is a covering stratum of Cambrian quartzite. On Beinn Eighe and Liathach it weathers into sharp, angular blocks and scree, very toilsome for the hill walker. At many places, however, there are quartzite crags of perfectly sound rock which give very good climbing.

This succession of rocks is subject to many irregularities, owing to the violent earth movements which have subsequently contorted the strata and thrust huge masses bodily across the lower rocks for distances as great as ten miles. To the south-east are mountains more akin to the main masses of the central Highlands, built up from varieties of younger schists. There is occasionally some good climbing to be had on this rock, but there is apt to be hardly any middle way between the easy and the impossible. Schists seldom give rise to bold mountain forms, but occasionally produce impressive corries occupied by dark lochans and walled around by screes and crags. Only one other formation need be mentioned, the Durness limestone. A narrow strip of this separates the Torridon rocks from the schists and gives rise to underground streams and 'swallets' near Inchna-damph on Loch Assynt and to caves near Durness. The limestone crags near Inchnadamph are of no interest to rock climbers.

The coast-line of the region is both rugged and beautiful most of the way from Loch Carron to Cape Wrath. On a sunny day with a fresh westerly wind and quick-moving clouds I know of no more beautiful stretch of coast than Gruinard Bay, with its white, sandy beaches and rocky coves, a background of little hills and the blue Atlantic with an island foreground and the distant pale blue outline of Lewis and Harris. At almost all seasons the splendid variety of colouring has attracted artists— colouring of sea coast, of lochs studded with wooded islets, of mountain vistas seen through groves of ancient woodland, and everywhere the procession of shapely clouds drifting in from the Atlantic. The western end of Fionn Loch is rather bare and desolate, but Horatio Macculloch, who painted the scene, describes his first view as 'a splendid mirror set in a fretted frame of Alpine scenery'.

Many pictures have been made of Loch Maree and its islands. There we have a mental background of ancient history, folk-lore and the superstition which still abounds in the countryside. On the Isle Maree bull sacrifices continued until the year 1678 as a cure for insanity. The Isle had been, for many years, the dwelling place of Saint Maelrubha, a disciple of St Columba. A draught of Loch Maree water was deemed a cure for almost any disease.

Belief in witches and fairies was very common. When Hugh Miller visited Loch Maree in 1823 he was told of a woman who had spent a year with the fairies. As late as 1840 the pious inhabitants of Aultbea set out to suppress a 'water kelpie' which had been seen on a loch in the Greenstone peninsula. The loch is still called the Loch of the Beast. At North Erradale, near Gairloch, is a sea cave, Uamh an Oir (the cave of gold), where long ago, twelve men headed by a piper marched in to seek for gold, wandering for miles in the cavern, so that the music of the pipes could be heard at a village many miles away. Neither piper nor men were seen again: it was supposed that they had 'forgot to turn'. Many superstitions, such as the power of the evil eye, usually exerted nowadays on cows or sheep, are still believed despite the strict disciplinary influence of the church.

Indeed, I have heard it hinted that a certain cross-eyed old woman could turn herself into a hare when it suited her purpose, and resume her own form when she wished! The average tourist will hear very little of such matters. The people do not talk of such things to strangers.

CHAPTER XVII

ROCK CLIMBING IN THE NORTH-WEST

GNEISS

THE Lewisian Gneiss, as the oldest and undermost rock formation, seldom appears in the form of crags on the higher parts of the mountains, but, where it does, it offers very good climbing. In western Harris there are many great crags and headlands of gneiss, the most impressive being Strone Ulladale which has furnished a grand climb of over 800 feet. There are several gneiss crags near Dundonnell which I have not visited, but they are reported to give good climbing.

When spending one or two off-days at Gruinard Bay my wife and I enjoyed delightful climbing on two small crags of gneiss which can be cordially recommended for their technical interest. One is a little 500-foot hill called Carn na h'Aire close to the bridge over the Gruinard River. Several routes are possible, but the outstanding feature is a huge, steep slab. The hill makes a splendid view-point. The other is close above the road about one and a half miles north, overlooking the sea beyond Gruinard House. This offered three climbs of about 200 feet in height, one of which was almost severe. The rock is delightfully steep and sound with very small holds. More difficult routes are awaiting attention and there are also easy ones.

The most attractive area for climbing on gneiss is at the head of Fionn Loch and above Dubh Loch, just beyond. Not much has been attempted on the long cliff of Beinn Lair, and nothing so far on A'Mhaighdean or Craig an Dubh Loch. Most attractive of all is the north face of Beinn Airidh Charr (2,593 ft.), rising between Fionn Loch and Loch Maree. Two ex-Presidents of the Scottish Mountaineering Club, W. N. Ling and G. T. Glover, enjoyed some wonderful climbing on these cliffs in the years 1909 and 1910, but, since then, the place has been unjustifiably neglected.

A lofty pinnacle of rock juts out from the main mass and is

Slioch and Loch Maree

Gruinard Bay, Wester Ross

known locally as Martha's Peak. Martha was a shepherdess who chose to climb the rocks in order to seek some errant members of her flock. Accounts of her misfortune vary somewhat. Probably she was really in search of goats. In any case, she sat down to admire the view and improved the time by winding thread on to a distaff, which slipped out of her hands and fell down the cliff. In the attempt to recover the distaff she, too, fell over and was killed.

Jack Burt, Malcolm Matheson and I had a grand day on Beinn Airidh Charr, when staying at Kinlochewe during Easter week 1928. I don't think we knew of the legend, but the weather was perfect and there was 1,200 feet of interesting climbing for us on good, dry rock, as grand and steep as we could desire. On the lower part we spent a good deal of time on difficult slabs, but above them the rock was more broken up, so that we were soon on the top of the lower cliff, where a short level stretch led us to the foot of the next wall. As we rose the view downward and westward across Fionn Loch to Gruinard Bay was wide and beautiful.

The middle tier gave us continuous hard climbing, up steep rocks with good but small holds. Then again came an easy stretch to the foot of the last wall of rock beneath the summit. A scree-filled gully had to be crossed first of all before we grappled with a very steep, 200-foot rock rib which led directly to the summit. Just below the top a sensational traverse had to be made across the face to the right—a thrilling finish. A few yards beyond the top of the cliff was the summit cairn. We had taken a little over three hours for the climb.

I well remember the return by boat across Loch Maree from Letterewe. A choppy sea was running, owing to the fresh east wind sweeping along the full extent of the loch. All was forgotten in the glory of the sunset, which tinged the summit of Slioch a vivid pink. The combination of crimson snow, orange sky and blue water contrasted with the silver birches, green firs and the russet of the bracken, is one that cannot be excelled in any of the great mountain ranges of the world. Every season has its own colour contrasts, but Loch Maree is never dull, even in late summer when much Highland scenery becomes almost commonplace.

TORRIDON RED SANDSTONE

Now we come to the great, mural precipices of Torridon 'Red', the most characteristic and spectacular features of the mountain scenery of the north-west. These great cliffs offer the most un-compromising challenge to the rock climber, which it is hard for the expert to resist and usually harder still to meet with success. He has really no valid excuse for refusing to make the attempt. It is true that the crags resemble gigantic walls of masonry, but the walls are broken by ledges and clefts. The sandstone weathers to form rounded edges with few, if any, out-standing spikes for belays: but the rock is both firm and rough, splendidly rough in most places, with a conglomerate structure and numerous firmly embedded fragments of quartz and gneiss. It is very hard to solve a definite problem or to strike the golden mean between the easy and the impossible, but patient explora-tion has yielded and will continue to offer rewards.

Suilven has been already mentioned, with its main mass of Torridon 'Red' cliffs rising from a base of Lewisian gneiss. The western peak, Caisteal Liath, or the Grey Castle (2,400 ft.), presents its craggy front to Lochinver and the western sea. It is not easily accessible, but I think that Nancy Forsyth and I chose the most attractive line of approach on an isolated fine day in the poor weather of August 1942. Leaving our cycles at Inveruplan (between Loch Assynt and Lochinver) we walked over the hill to Canisp Lodge, crossed the river and a good deal of marshy ground, emerging finally upon the bare, undulating moorland with the huge dome of the Grey Castle about two miles ahead. As the long ridge of Suilven runs from east to west we were approaching the mountain end-on and, whenever we looked up, saw only the graceful, tapering dome of our peak with its 600-foot wall of cliff. We had plenty of leisure to examine the rocks and decide on our line of advance. The southern view was also delightful, over a loch-speckled moor-land to the sharp outlines of Cul Beag, Ben More Coigach and Stack Polly; the ridge of the latter as sharp and serrated as a cock's comb. West of these was a glimpse of Skye with the faint outline of the Cuillin over Gruinard Bay. Behind us were the distant hills of the Outer Hebrides.

In the early afternoon we were at the base of the lowest tier of rock, a pleasant hundred feet or so of slab climbing taking us to the main terrace which crosses the whole face below the middle, vertical wall of rock. We knew that the easy way was by a shallow gully at the southern corner of the terrace, a route which was grassy in its lower part and loose higher up. The central sweep of cliff was not only vertical but overhanging at many places. So we edged along towards the north-west corner, beyond which we should be on the flank of the Suilven ridge and less likely to discover any continuously interesting route.

An indentation in the cliff offered us a starting point for our climb, although it was neither gully nor chimney, but a steep scoop with a very steep rib of rock on the left. I started with difficulty in the groove and managed to transfer on to the rib. The holds were few and poor, but I was able to climb up to the right on to a ledge directly above the start. After some prospecting along a ledge I climbed another ten feet to a secure stance and brought my second up this sixty-foot pitch. We were now on a horizontal ledge which we traversed for about thirty feet to the right. The worst overhang was beneath us, but the face above was little short of vertical, with numerous, narrow, shelving ledges, no in-cut holds and no belays. It was typical climbing on Torridon Red sandstone. I remember a severe mantelshelf problem followed by thirty feet straight up to another ledge.

The climbing was of the most airy and exhilarating variety, with backward and downward glances over the loch-spangled moorland and the blue waters of the Minch. One feels especially favoured if progress is made at all, although there are usually a variety of possible starting places as one glides along the narrow, horizontal bands either to the left or to the right. The cliffs of the Grey Castle are more amenable than the 'Red' walls of the western buttress of Coire Mhic Fhearchair or those of the corries of Beinn Bhan of Applecross, where one may be unable to distinguish any ledges at all for many hundreds of feet.

As we progressed we were gradually forced obliquely upwards towards the centre of the cliff. We halted on a comfortable stance at the top of a wall. Here we prospected a ledge leading back to our left, but it petered out at a corner of the cliff. Nancy now took the lead, moving to the right, finding the key to the

R

final section. Steep, interesting rocks led us straight up for over 150 feet to the end of all our difficulties, with a hard ten-foot crack near the finish, as a parting gesture of goodwill. Then we unroped and climbed up easy boulders to the summit of the mountain. The serious climbing had occupied us for three hours.

We traversed the summit ridge to the eastern top, finding it easy and grassy for the most part. A dry stone dyke actually crosses the ridge about the middle. Only at the far end did we enjoy a little more rock climbing. The small, eastern top mentioned in the Guide Book is really a small tooth on the descending ridge from the most easterly of the main tops, which are quite distinct and of about the same height when the mountain is viewed from the direction of Suileag. The hill walker can easily gain the centre of the summit ridge by one or other of several grassy gullies, either from north or south. The gullies are easy enough, but great care should be exercised when descending, on account of loose stones. We ourselves descended a loose, northerly gully and soon gained a good track which led us to the little bothy of Suileag, from which a track continues to Little Assynt on the main road. It was a delightful evening and we turned round many times to contemplate the warm, friendly, colouring of our peak in the rays of the declining sun. Suilven is one of the grand, little mountains of Scotland.

I have not enjoyed any more climbing on Torridon Red in the Coigach and Assynt districts, but Stack Polly offers many delightful and interesting problems. Quinag has a historic and difficult route, the Barrel Buttress, and the Coigach peaks are but little explored. The Coire na Caime of Liathach has been mentioned elsewhere. It has many formidable buttresses of cliff, but it is not easy to pursue a well-defined route. At the end of June 1947 my wife and I enjoyed a very difficult climb on a steep buttress which terminates on the main ridge of Liathach on the next subsidiary top to the east of Mullach an Rathain. At one or two places we were forced to discard boots and proceed in stocking soles. The climb went in three sections, not just directly following each other, of 130, 200 and 210 feet respectively, the standard varying considerably from moderate to severe. Careful choice of route is essential if sporting difficulty and continuity are to be achieved, without landing in an *impasse*.

The southern limit of the Torridon Red is in the Applecross peninsula on the cliffs of Beinn Bhan and Sgurr na Caorach. One of the most delightful discoveries of Professor Norman Collie was the terminal pinnacle or eastern buttress of Sgurr na Caorach (2,539 ft.). It is quite easy to reach from the Applecross road, a mile or two beyond Kishorn Bridge. With careful route finding the climbing is not specially difficult, starting in the gully which separates A'Chioch (the pinnacle) from the upper ridge. Even after climbing the pinnacle there is much more to be done as one follows the ridge over several humps, with intervening deep depressions, to the top of the mountain. In June 1947 my wife and I had a grand, sporting climb on A'Chioch, in the course of which we straightened out the routes of our predecessors, the issue remaining in suspense for a considerable time. We learned enough to whet our appetite for another bout with these grand crags on some future occasion. They demand a technique peculiar to themselves, and exact such a measure of respect that I usually carry a *piton* with me, even although I have not yet been compelled to use it, either as a last hope of victory or a safeguard in defeat.

CAMBRIAN QUARTZITE

This uppermost member of the Torridon family of rocks is more often execrated than commended. It is generally encountered as an objectionable covering of grey, angular scree, of all sizes, above the red sandstone, making the passage of the ridges exceedingly toilsome and the ascent of steep slopes even worse in summer conditions. Those who have traversed the north-eastern tops of Liathach and Beinn Eighe will hardly believe that any good thing can ever come out of the Cambrian quartzite.

In Coire Mhic Fhearchair of Beinn Eighe the state of affairs is very different. Quartzite forms the main part of the three great buttresses and is exceedingly steep, sound rock. The ascent of the northern, or left-hand buttress has already been described. In August 1946 my wife and I tackled the southern one. It was raining and the lower tier of Torridon Red cliff, with no positive but all rounded holds, and running all over with trickles of water, was altogether too desperate and formidable an adventure for us. I knew that George Bower's party had climbed it in dry conditions, using rubbers, in July 1919. They had found the 'Red' part a severe climb. We compromised by working our way up the gully to the right and traversing on to the buttress by a ledge which enabled us to ease our consciences, to some extent, by climbing the uppermost 150 feet of the sandstone to a broad terrace at the foot of the quartzite cliff.

The rain now abated, having achieved its malign objective, and permitted us to enjoy ourselves. At first the climbing was easy, but, later on, the cliff became a good deal steeper as we neared the terminal tower. The rock was sound, with square-cut holds, and I remember a splendid 100-foot pitch which was very steep indeed. Then we gained an upper terrace below the vertical, final crag. The left wall was smooth and unclimbable, with a curious, square-sectioned, horizontal arm of rock protruding over the top of a vertical chimney, like a big gun from the battlements of a fortress. If we could reach the 'gun' we knew that there was little difficulty above it.

A traverse to the right was easy, but did not, at first sight, offer a key to the fortress, although we passed by and rejected one chimney, as it did not appear to go high enough. Farther round I ascended another for over forty feet, traversed out to the left on steep slabs and climbed up the remainder of the face so long as there were any holds at all. Only ten feet of smooth wall remained to be climbed. We had to retreat. Another attempt, in the line of the original chimney, was no more successful. It almost appeared as if we should be beaten after all. I may say that I had not read Bower's account of his ascent, although I knew that the buttress had been climbed.

Something drastic had to be done. We retreated along the terrace until we reached the foot of the chimney which we had rejected. The outcome was both surprising and a trifle disappointing. The chimney was easy. It was unnecessary to pursue its upper continuation, which was steep, narrow, holdless and nearly vertical. I traversed out to the left on to good, steep slabs. There I discovered two things: the gun was just below the terrace on which I stood and another convenient chimney split the face, leading to the top of the buttress. That was the dramatic solution to the problem. From Bower's account

The Buttresses of Coire Mhic Fhearchair, Beinn Eighe

I conclude that he found it at once, and was also somewhat dissatisfied that the finish was tamer than it had any right to be.

For the rock climber who uses Kinlochewe as his base there is a whole range of quartzite cliffs along the south-western and western faces of Beinn Mhuinidh (2,217 ft.), the hill on the northern side of the main valley extending between the glen leading to the Heights of Kinlochewe and the Fasagh glen* which separates it from Slioch to the north-west. The earliest climb on this face goes up to the left of a conspicuous waterfall, visible for miles from the main road west of Kinlochewe. The others are on a band of cliff more to the north-west and starting from a conspicuous terrace which girdles the steep face of the hill. This part of Beinn Mhuinidh is called the Bonaidh Don. Our most enjoyable route went straight up the cliff from the terrace, where it has just turned the corner northwards above the Fasagh glen. This gave an exceedingly steep and continuous climb of 400 feet on sound rock, with a standard which is almost severe on the final eighty-foot wall.

There are many more problems on this excellent wall of cliff. We ourselves found another good route near Fasagh Corner, and two more near the waterfall. It is a grand place for spending an easy day, or even a pleasant afternoon and evening. I have not found space to mention the Torridon Red buttresses of Ben Hope (3,040 ft.), the most northerly Munro of Scotland, the schistose crags above Lochan Coire Ghrannda on Beinn Dearg of Ross, where we enjoyed a delightful slab climb of 500 feet with a severe finish, or many another little-known rocky peak in this fascinating region, but the reader may rest assured that there is still a great opportunity and reward for the single-minded mountain lover.

* Often named Glen Bannisdail or Bianasdail.

CHAPTER XVIII

THE CHASM OF BUACHAILLE
ETIVE MOR

ON the south-east side of Stob Dearg of Buachaille Etive
Mor broken rocks and scree descend for about 500 feet
beneath the summit in a sort of wide funnel, below
which the mountain face is cleft by a great, vertical rift between
precipitous cliffs for about 1,500 feet or more, ending on the
gently sloping moorland not very far above the road in Glen
Etive, about a mile and a half below its junction with the main
road west of Kingshouse.

The early age of British rock climbing specialised in the
ascent of gullies, and its most exciting problems were encountered where the gullies were bridged by huge boulders with
caves underneath them. Such difficulties were usually accentuated by a stream of water coming over the chockstone and
clothing the rocky walls with spongy, green moss, circumstances
in which the older pioneers appeared to put forth their best
efforts and find keen enjoyment. The Chasm of the Buachaille
was bound to attract attention in the early days of Scottish rock
climbing, and its history is, in fact, a long one.

In July 1898 J. H. Bell (a past president of the S.M.C., but
not related to the author) and J. Maclay were forced to retreat
after a hard struggle, from below a 100-foot waterfall pouring
down over a seemingly impregnable, vertical cliff. This point
is now recognised to be less than half-way up the Chasm. In
June 1903 the ablest Scottish climber of his time, Harold Raeburn, accompanied by Dr and Mrs Inglis Clark, entered the
Chasm above this difficulty. They found a good deal of old
snow and, at one place, traversed about fifty feet through a
snow tunnel. Time was against them, for Raeburn had to catch
an evening train at Tyndrum. They escaped on to the south
wall at a point where two severe pitches still remained to be
tackled, above which was the culminating difficulty, now known
as the Devil's Cauldron. Their climb ended on the Lady's Pinnacle, about 200 feet high, situated on the south wall. Dr Clark

considered that this was the most prolonged piece of difficult climbing in his British experience.

Raeburn, however, returned to the assault in April 1906, accompanied by W. N. Ling. Although it should have been obvious that the Chasm would be most likely to yield its last secrets as a pure rock climb, uncomplicated by snow or water, and preferably after a long, dry period, the pioneers of those days were in the habit of doing their Scottish climbing in the early part of the year and spending their summer vacations in the Alps. Climbing the Chasm was thus rendered much more difficult by the presence of masses of old snow which had partly melted away from the side walls of the gully, the rocks of which were often exceedingly smooth and water-worn. If the weather was fine and the sun was hot, copious streams of descending water added to the difficulties.

Raeburn and Ling put up a very good show. At certain places stocking-sole technique was necessary. At others the snow was of some assistance, as it piled up against the walls and lessened the effective height of the pitches. Raeburn reported that this applied to most of the pitches which were climbed in 1903. Finally, they too were driven out on to the south wall at a point where the last pitch, 'a black, slimy slit of smooth rock, down which gurgled enough water in gallons per minute, to furnish an ample supply to a fair sized town', loomed high above them.

The next attempt resulted in a successful ascent of all but the direct route up the back of the Devil's Cauldron. A reconnaissance on the previous day solved the problem of the 100-foot pitch which had frustrated the party of 1898, and a fixed rope was left hanging down the pitch. The ascent was started at 6.15 a.m. (from the foot of the first pitch) on 13th April 1920 by R. F. Stobart and Mr and Mrs N. E. Odell. There was plenty of snow and running water. The mist closed down on the party after second breakfast at half-past ten. Combined tactics were necessary at a pitch where smooth, waterworn, vertical walls converged at middle height and permitted the necessary bridging tactics. At the back of the Devil's Cauldron the waterfall hung suspended as a 100-foot curtain of great icicles, but the party were able, by a second use of combined tactics, to climb

a vertical chimney on the south wall. So ended the Chasm and
its difficulties at 5.20 p.m.

The first direct ascent of the back of the Devil's Cauldron was
effected on 30th August 1931 by J. G. Robinson and I. G. Jack.
They took four hours to reach its floor and another three to
climb the pitch. This triumph was the climax to a number of
attempts by a small band of enthusiasts.

Colin Allan and I had no part in the exploration of the
Chasm. Our first visit, entirely unplanned, was in May 1932.
It was not a complete success, as we were defeated by a considerable flow of water at the middle section of the Cauldron,
but we returned to the Chasm, year after year, as a sort of
standard climb which never failed to yield a grand day of
strenuous rock work in magnificent surroundings. If we could
climb Buachaille by the Chasm, run down to the Etive and
enjoy a swim in its long pool and feel no fatigue, we concluded
that we were in reasonably good training.

We spent a pleasant evening at Kingshouse, but left our
friends after eleven p.m. in order to pass the night in our own
way. About midnight we were seated on the pier at Lochetive-
head, watching the full moon rise over the shoulder of Ben
Starav. We sat for so long, absorbing the peace and beauty of
that perfect night, that a half-formed impulse to climb the
mountain died away of itself. About four miles back on the way
to Dalness we found a little wood where we spread our sleeping
sacks on a carpet of pine needles and went to sleep. There is
nothing more delightful than such a bivouac in a cool, spring
night. A few midges awoke us between four and five a.m., but
they were only a handful of skirmishers, and not the hordes of
summer-time. Our day commenced with a swim in a cold, deep
pool of the river Etive. Then came plenty of breakfast—kippers
toasted over a wood fire, boiled eggs, pork pies, bread, cheese,
marmalade and tea. We paid tribute to dietetics and vitamins
with a final course of oranges. Nowadays, even were it possible,
I should doubt the value of such a preparation for a day's
climbing. Then, the procedure was normal, and most enjoyable
too.

A few introductory pitches loosened our muscles before the
walls of the gully closed in about us. A triple pitch loomed

ahead, with three huge chockstones in succession, each surmounting a cave. The ascent was effected on the right wall.
This is almost the only vegetatious pitch in the Chasm, but even
here there are good rock holds where required. We made one
pitch of it and traversed back on to the floor of the gully above
the waterfall. The next long pitch was up a slabby wall of red
rock, on the left, with an awkward traverse to the right at the
top of the difficulty, where the holds were not in-cut. The
leader should have adequate length of rope for this pitch. In
wet conditions it can be very wet at the bottom.

Little need be said of the successive difficulties which we
encountered below the 100-foot waterfall pitch which had
defeated the earliest explorers. They are all interesting and
varied, but Colin Allan and I, in successive visits, became so
familiar with them that we did not use the rope at all on this
lower section. This is a confession rather than an example to be
followed. Some of the pitches are exposed and difficult. If we
took guests with us we always roped them up. The reputed
sixth pitch is a test of the dryness of the Chasm. It is a straightforward staircase with the usual waterfall pouring down. In wet
weather it means a certain drenching on the stair on the left.
We discovered an alternative through-route by a cave on the
right, but this is mossy, slimy and difficult and unlikely to be
drier. If the sixth pitch is dry one has a reasonable expectation
of being able to climb the rest of the Chasm. The last pitch
below the cross-roads is a delightful, airy problem on a nearly
vertical rib on the left, followed by a lofty traverse back to the
bed of the gully above a waterfall.

Now we arrived at the Cross Roads, where a transverse,
eroded dyke forms two gullies, to left and right. It was a good
place for lunch. Any party that has had enough difficulty or
enough climbing for the day can escape here on either side, the
more interesting being the right or north side, with a pleasant
descent from the crest of the north wall, involving some good
practice scrambling. Allan and I contemplated the waterfall.
The only possible route was obvious enough, by a near-vertical,
shallow cleft on the right-hand buttress of the fall. The first
thirty feet to a little pinnacle, with stance and belay, were easy.
Then the holds became small and more widely spaced. At a

return visit in 1945 I found some loose rock in this upper section, but there are still sufficient sound holds. It is an exposed pitch with small but adequate holds, technically excellent if one goes about it with care and deliberation. At the top there is a perfect stance and belay. Although it is possible to continue up this wall, the better way is to make a short, difficult traverse into the gully bed, cross this and go up the other wall for a few feet to a narrow ledge which goes almost as far as the lip of the next waterfall. The handholds are few and wide apart. The ledge peters out towards the finish and the rock is very smooth and rounded. Delicate balance and a long arm span are necessary if one is to be successful in negotiating the Piano Pitch, as it has been named. Careful selection of holds and study of the direction of stresses are essential to make each movement safe, especially for a short man. Brute force and rush tactics may land one in the pool beneath the waterfall. I have seen two seconds who have slipped in at the last move. It is only eight or ten feet down to the water. Those who slipped were, of course, lowered into the pool!

After some inclined, water-worn slabs which are not too easy, we came to a narrow rift with smooth walls, about sixty feet high. About twenty feet up on the left was a rounded bulge projecting from the wall, and just above this point the walls converged to their narrowest aperture, about three feet or so. The stream came down in a fall at the innermost part of the rift. This pitch may, unfortunately, be avoided by climbing out of the gully on the left. The back of the rift is somewhat undercut, which would make it altogether impossible to climb up there by orthodox chimney tactics. I have never tried, as it must be a very wet proceeding. It is not a cave pitch, and the neat solution of the problem makes use of the bulge of rock on the wall. Combined tactics were used by the Stobart-Odell party in 1920. I think that Colin Allan was the first man to climb the pitch unaided by the direct method. He climbed it in boots, which makes the performance all the more creditable on smooth, rounded, waterworn rock, taking into consideration the corresponding qualities of Allan's boots, which seldom had many nails at all!

I led up to the bulge by bridging movements with feet on one

The Converging Walls Pitch:
The Chasm

wall and hands on the other. There is a good stance at the bulge, hardly enough room for two people, but no belay. Colin pushed up past me, wedged between the walls, reached across to a handhold on the opposite (north) wall and pulled himself over and up with both arms. He was strong enough to do it in that way and I respected his performance. Somehow, I failed to get the knack, so that I had to accept a good pull on the rope. This failure made me think on ways and means of making up for my relative lack of stature and arm strength.

The solution is applicable to many other, difficult, cross-stepping traverses on severe rock climbs. The guiding rule is to spare no effort in order to get high enough, and somewhat above the holds which one is aiming for. One should also study the holds for one or two moves ahead. Accurate co-ordination of eye and limb replaces brute force and hard pulling. In 1933, when climbing the Chasm with G. C. Williams, I led the Converging Walls Pitch and found that I had a good reserve of energy. The landing on the north wall is still on rounded rock ledges, but is perfectly secure. If you lead the pitch and have doubts of the ability of your second it is a good idea to make him take off his boots and proceed in stocking-soles. There is a belay on the north wall some distance above. On one occasion Colin was taking up a lady climber to the first bulge, when the latter had the misfortune to slip. Colin was obviously enjoying himself as the lady executed a few pendulum swings below him on the rope. Then he simply took in the rope, pulling her up as if he were landing a fish. He was a good man to climb with.

As in first-class drama, there is now a breathing space. The Chasm is walled in on both sides to a height of over 100 feet. Numerous pitches succeed one another, all in the line of the watercourse where there should now be only a trickle of water. At one point there is an easy exit on to the south wall. A somewhat difficult, short cave pitch lies below the great hall of the Devil's Cauldron. There is an undercut handhold near the top on the right wall of the cave and a good hold above.

The Devil's Cauldron is a savage and magnificent place, the north wall of 200 feet being vertical and unclimbable. The impressive wall on the south side is cleft by a narrow vertical chimney. At first sight the wet repulsive slit at the back of this narrow enclosure appears to be utterly unclimbable, so that it is small wonder that the earlier parties never attempted to do so. Unless after dry weather in summer, and preferably no earlier than June, as there is often snow in the Chasm till well on into May, one should not attempt the direct route up the back of the Cauldron.

The weather had deteriorated when Allan and I got thus far. I was deputed to lead the first fifty or sixty feet to a small platform underneath a narrow undercut chimney which was the crux of the climb. Although reasonably dry at the start, the last ten feet below the platform sprayed me fairly effectively. Colin joined me on the stance and I belayed him for his attempt on the crucial chimney. Conditions were altogether against him. Like all strong men he delighted in forcing himself up and pulling with both hands, keeping far too close inside the chimney and so becoming the butt for a vigorous stream of water from above, which poured over his head, down his neck and down his sleeves. He failed to gain a foothold on the north wall, but was wise enough to retreat in good order. I was so overawed by the sight of my friend in the guise of a mermaid that I called out for a complete withdrawal while we were still not too chilled to grasp the rocks. On the floor of the Cauldron I took off all my clothes, wrung them out and put them on again. It was worth doing. We traversed out of the Chasm by the south wall, but we had enjoyed a good day's climbing.

The next time I visited the Chasm was in the company of G. C. Williams on 9th July 1933. There was only a trickle of water at the back of the Cauldron. I had a hard struggle with the crucial chimney, and retained a wholesome respect for the place. Above it I found a little rock arch where Williams belayed me for the final, straight section of the pitch. From below, this appears to be far worse than what goes before. The side walls are vertical and the water comes trickling down over mossy slabs which seem to be almost as steep. The reality is much more comforting. The technique is orthodox backing-up, such as is used for most chimneys, and the exposure, with a sensational drop to the rocky floor of the Cauldron, need not worry any confident expert. With feet pressed against the wall in front and palms of the hands at my hips pressed against the wall behind,

I progressed upwards, a few inches at a time, with very little effort and almost as much comfort as if I had been seated in an armchair with my feet against the sides of the fireplace. At intervals I could rest across the gap and take a bird's-eye-view of the countenance of my second. Fortunately, the holds improve below the upper over-hanging chockstone, which is the last difficulty.

In the first edition of the *Central Highlands Guide* the exit pitch from the Cauldron is given as 175 feet high. The earlier explorers thought it must be 200 feet at least. Debunking is a sordid occupation, but I have measured the height with a reliable surveying aneroid with a four-inch dial, and the result was between 105 and 110 feet. Climbers are but human: they would not indulge in such an irrational sport without a lively imagination, singularly sensitive to the impress of diffi-culty and the self-satisfaction of victory. Even the crux is not so difficult and strenuous as I have suggested. In August 1945 I led an English climbing friend up the Chasm. The Converging Walls Pitch pleased him, but it was only at the Cauldron that he

The Devil's Cauldron

became visibly impressed. Then it dawned upon me that, after a lapse of twelve years, which had taken my own age very close to the half-century, I might not be able to lead the crux at all. I discounted the effect of those years in better co-ordinated movements and economy of effort. By keeping as far out of the chimney as possible and resting frequently I was able to gain the critical foothold on the north wall without any undue effort. It is true that the other wall shrinks away to nothing at a certain height and that the position feels and appears to be highly precarious, but exposure is not the same thing as danger. August 1945 was, however, a dry month in the West Highlands.

It is seldom that conditions are good enough for a comfortably dry ascent of the back of the Cauldron. On all other occasions but the two already mentioned Allan and I were obliged to climb out of the Cauldron by the chimney on the south wall. In 1920 the Stobart-Odell party used combined tactics for climbing this severe chimney. About 1938 or so, E. R. Zenthon climbed it alone, and W. H. Murray has also climbed it recently. Our problem was to find a safe way up the south wall for more ordinary climbers in conditions when the back of the Cauldron was too wet. We found the best solution at our second attempt, only using the chimney for the first twenty feet or so. The second can then safeguard the leader over a severe traverse out of the chimney, by an exposed corner and along a smooth, narrow ledge on the south wall. The movement is as difficult as anything on the direct route, but it is safe and dry. The leader can then climb straight up to an excellent stance and belay, from which he can safeguard his second. The final ascent to the top of the wall is by a moderate, upper chimney. The climb finishes on the top of the Lady's Pinnacle, which was first reached by Harold Raeburn, Dr and Mrs Inglis Clark in 1903. So history tends to repeat itself, but there is no easy ascent of the Devil's Cauldron and the Chasm keeps its best pitches for the end.

CHAPTER XIX

THE EAGLE RIDGE OF LOCHNAGAR

In the *S.M.C. Guide Book to the Cairngorms* (1938 Edition) this is named
Eagle Buttress. Climbing experience has shown that its true character
is that of a very steep ridge with an exceedingly sharp crest at many
points. The name has, therefore, been altered to Eagle Ridge.

ALTHOUGH it is still possible to make new and difficult
routes on Scottish crags they are generally somewhat
artificial and seldom follow a conspicuous natural line or
architectural feature. A climbing friend once commented on the
year's discoveries, saying that it appeared to him to be much
more meritorious to discover and climb a natural route of
moderate difficulty than a severe, gymnastic problem of an
artificial nature. He was right, of course, but could not suggest
where such an ideal discovery might be made. Surely not in the
overworked regions of Glencoe, Ben Nevis or the Cuillin Hills
of Skye.

Perhaps something might be hoped for on Aberdeenshire
granite which has a bad reputation amongst rock-climbers for
cliffs that look attractive and imposing at the first view, but, on
closer inspection, offer nothing whatever between impossibly
vertical faces without any holds at all and easy ways interspersed with heather, grass and loose blocks, offering little of
interest to the serious climber. Without any definite plan of
campaign, but in the hope that something good had been over-
looked by former visitors, three of us went to Deeside in early
June 1936 with designs on the cliffs of Lochnagar.

Along with my old friend, Dr Myles of Forfar, was Mr W. G.
McClymont, an enthusiastic mountaineer from New Zealand.
After hearing his tales of pioneering in the New Zealand Alps
we had to do our best to put up a good show with the mountains
of the old country. The weather played up to perfection as we
camped in a pleasant pine wood close to the road in Glen Muick.
On a lovely, sunny morning we breakfasted in a copious,
leisurely manner until we were approached by two gamekeepers
with a polite but urgent request to pack our tent and remove all
evidence of our sojourn as soon as possible. We realised the

fairness of the request, and hoped that the estate Factor would not come upon us and get the keepers into trouble.

In any case, Lochnagar is a good two and a half hours distant from Allt na Giubhsaich, and the earlier we moved off the more time would be left for the rock climbing. There was a delightful, fresh breeze as we moved up the well-worn track towards the mountain. We were not the only ones on the hill on such a glorious morning, but we soon left the route below the Ladder and crossed the Saddle between the Cuidhe Crom and the Meikle Pap, entering the great corrie beneath the horse-shoe of granite crags.

This is one of the finest mountain sanctuaries in Scotland. Beneath the great arc of cliff lie slopes of huge boulders, scree and heather ending at the shores of a dark lochan, 2,575 feet above sea level. Small wonder that the the youthful mind of the poet Byron, who spent long periods of vacation in the district, was deeply impressed by 'the crags that are wild and majestic, the steep, frowning glories of dark Lochnagar'.

A great buttress of rock with grand, sweeping lines caught the rays of the sun. It rose just beyond the steep rift known as the Douglas Gully. We did not carry the new edition of the *S.M.C. Guide Book*, but I felt pretty certain that such a magnificent buttress could not have been climbed without the Scottish climbing fraternity (including myself) hearing something about it. There was no need to look anywhere else. We decided to attempt it, although the time was a little past one o'clock. A few yards above the lowest rocks I led off from a patch of snow in the gully, soon landing on steep slabs with very little in the way of holds. That was all to the good, for the climbing became interesting at once. We climbed a steep, little chimney, then a steep crack and the going became easier to the crest of the buttress, about ninety feet up.

Traversing above Douglas Gully was impossible, and the edge of the buttress rose above us in an almost vertical, smooth wall. The remedy was to climb a little gully on the other side, and another chimney. The wall above us on the left was now steep and holdless, but the route continued across the western face of the buttress. Of course we wanted to climb back to the crest, and I ultimately succeeded in doing so by another succession

s

of chimneys, reaching the crest at a narrow notch with a precipitous view into the recesses of the Douglas Gully. Twenty feet
higher the crest of the ridge became steep, exposed and holdless.
We had to consider our chances, and especially the time factor.
There was definitely no possibility of avoiding the vertical section by a traverse above the Douglas Gully. Prospects of continuing our upward traverse on the western face were much
better, and included a rib by which we might hope to climb to
the top of the buttress. Not a very enterprising or direct attack,
it may be said, but we felt that we had no time to be fastidious.
There were even protests from the rear of the party against any
more holdless walls and smooth chimneys. It was useless for me
to assure Myles that he was really a much better climber than
he thought he was. We wanted to climb the buttress by any
possible route and we could not tell when we might still be
forced to retreat.

The upward traverse worked well enough. Far ahead was a
corner above some exceedingly steep rocks which seemed to
hang over a deep gully on our right (now called Parallel Gully
A). As there were no more possible openings on the slabby
cliff to our left we were inevitably confronted by these rocks. If
we could not climb them the buttress must be abandoned. With
the closing of any avenues for indecision the morale of the party
improved wonderfully and, within the next 200 feet or so, we
enjoyed the best climbing of the day.

An awkward corner led to a secure stance beside a huge
pyramidal block of granite which was delicately poised and
could just be rocked very slightly. It proved to be the key to a
very difficult situation, and I used it safely as a take-off for
swarming up to a scoop and a difficult crack somewhat higher
on the face. Another difficult crack led to a secure stance and a
perfect belay for the rope. This time there was no protest from
the rear, and my friend came up as if he were really enjoying
himself. The ensuing rocks were very steep, but provided with
small and satisfying holds. The last steep crack resolved all our
doubts, the end being both speedy and dramatic. We stood
together on the broad summit of the buttress at 5.45 p.m. A later
inspection of the Guide Book proved it to be an entirely new
route.

Of course the Eagle Ridge could not be left without some attempt being made to improve the route, straighten it out and climb it, as nearly as possible, on the crest of the ridge. We had climbed it by a sort of flank attack on the side of the buttress. Although we had enjoyed an excellent, difficult climb, we had not savoured its true character.

In the autumn of 1940 I was surprised and delighted to receive a letter, to the effect that Messrs W. S. Scroggie and J. G. Ferguson, of Dundee, had enjoyed a hard tussle with it in rather poor weather conditions in August of that year. Their climb was exceedingly meritorious under the prevailing conditions of rain and wet rocks, and they had made the route a good deal straighter. The new section was reported to be severe in standard, as rock climbers rate their difficulties. There were few belays, but the rock was sound. They had secured their advance by the use of four *pitons*, and they had climbed in stocking soles. As I expected, they had climbed back to the crest very soon after crossing it on the line of our route. There they had met severe difficulties which had ultimately forced them to abandon the crest, traversing again along the west face over steep rock and grass. They regained the crest by climbing a crack, and then mounted easy slabs to the summit.

It appeared, therefore, that the route up the Eagle Ridge was not yet entirely direct. But I respected the Ridge, and also the achievement of the men of the Corrie Club of Dundee, so I had little hope of doing better. Opportunities were few during the war, but on 24th July 1941, I had an excellent partner in Miss Nancy Forsyth. We had done one or two other climbs on Lochnagar, and weather conditions were perfect.

The first part of the climb—slabs, chimney, crest and subsequent chimney—was exactly as before. The smooth, steep wall on our left, decorated with a few hair-like cracks, had not been climbed by the Corrie Club men. It looks impossible. We soon found a *piton* lying loose on a ledge, doubtless dislodged by frost and sun from the cliff above. This we collected for a later emergency. Then we ascended steep, discontinuous ribs on our left. The climb to the crest was difficult, but not more than that. We soon reached the little cairn which had been left by the former party at the point where they reached the crest.

The Eagle Ridge now began to display its mettlesome quality. Almost at once the crest rose up before us in a steepening, narrow wall, easy at first, with big flakes of rock offering grand holds on their cross-cut edges. Then came a sudden steepening to the vertical where it was necessary to pull up over a sort of mantelshelf into a steep, smooth, holdless groove. Here we found another *piton*, securely fixed in a crack of the rock. I was unable to move it. In the prevailing conditions, with dry rocks, I was able to climb the pitch without touching the *piton*. The former party, of course, had vile conditions of rain and wet rocks, and the *piton* was well placed for securing the leader's rope over the next forty feet of severe climbing.

I soon realised this when I was compelled to traverse a yard or two to the right on very small holds. A return traverse, even more delicate, was made to the left at a higher level, with a final, severe pull up to a large, enclosed niche which provided perfect anchorage for man and rope. This severe section required fifty to sixty feet of rope. My second enjoyed it thoroughly.

Now the ridge thinned down to what is generally known amongst climbers as a knife-edge. There were occasional cracks and roughnesses on the flanks, making progress airy but not very difficult. The crest then rose in another smooth wall, leaving us with a ledge for a passage along its right base. This could not go on indefinitely; the gangway ended at a corner in front of a smooth, vertical wall.

Further progress was only feasible by a steep, difficult crack which split the wall on our left. It did not look at all hopeful, but I climbed the crack and surveyed our diminishing prospects from the sharp crest of the ridge. On my left was a sheer drop, slightly undercut, into the depths of Douglas Gully. The knife-edge crest on which I was sitting astride was neatly fitted to the middle of a triangle of blank, vertical cliff in front.

Here, if anywhere, our predecessors would undoubtedly have made use of another *piton*, but, although there was a suitable crack for the insertion of such an implement, there was no sign of its having been used. They must, therefore, have already traversed along the right face before they reached this point.

We were at the crux of the climb, but the wall in front was only about ten feet high. The rock was smooth, for the most part. Beside the crack where a *piton* could be used, but more to the left, was a small excrescence which might, perhaps, hold a boot nail. At the top of the wall, and somewhat to the left, was a sloping scoop with a raised edge on its left side. If that edge would provide a sharp, in-cut handhold it could be used for pulling up. There appeared to be a slight overhang about the wall, so that one secure foothold at the correct height on the left, as well as a steadying hold on the right, were absolutely essential before making the crucial pull. There would be only one critical movement; once the body was in the scoop the angle eased off, and I felt confident that safety lay within reach.

British rock climbing, as practised by its best exponents, has rightly set its face against the use of artificial safeguards, steeple-jacking methods and the use of ironmongery on the crags. So far we had used none. The Eagle promised to become one of the finest of all British ridges as a difficult rock climb, yet this diffi-culty was inescapably a part of the route. It was on the right of way. Almost before I knew what I was doing I had removed my boots and lowered them to my partner in a rucksack. Balance would be a critical consideration. I found a handy lump of granite, stood up against the wall and hammered in our one *piton*. Slipping a snap link into the ring and my rope through the link I felt a good deal safer. If the top handhold proved unsound I should have a clean drop on the side of Douglas Gully, but the rope held by my second through the snap link, would soon check my fall.

My right foot had a good hold, but not a high one. The hold for the left foot sloped badly. By raising my right hand to a higher crack on the face it was possible to get my left foot up to a small toe-crack. Here the balance was extremely delicate, as I reached up with the left hand and grabbed the edge of the coping above the scoop. It was a perfect hold. My right foot used the *piton* as a steady while I heaved myself up, pulling now with both hands side by side on the coping and hunching up my knees on to the scoop. There is no pausing in such a situation, for the scoop had only press and friction holds. Persistent effort, friction and wriggling put me within reach of another perfect handhold and I was safe. About fifteen feet farther along, the narrow crest gave me a good stance and a belay for the rope.

Eagle Ridge, Lochnagar:
The Crux

Then I hauled up the rucksacks and boots on the rope, which ran directly down the scoop and so afforded a complete safe-guard for my partner. Nancy came up perfectly, as I expected she would, but she did more than that. She knocked the *piton* loose with another lump of granite and took it out before climb-ing straight up on the thinnest of holds. All I did was to main-tain a taut rope to steady her balance. It was a wonderful per-formance. Thanks to Nancy we had not defaced a perfect climb by leaving any signs of mechanisation upon it.

Her performance made me wonder if I could lead up the crux without an artificial aid, with the knowledge that the upper handhold was reliable. In April 1948 I was again at Glen Muick and took my wife up Eagle Ridge. The climb impressed me as much as on the former occasion. Again I inserted a *piton*, but I used the correct holds at once, never touching the *piton* at all, the rope being slack all the time. When it came to my wife's turn to join me she reported two things. The *piton* was rather loose in the crack, and the end block of the coping, the crucial handhold, seemed to move very, very slightly as she pulled up on it. One cannot be too careful about pulling holds, especially on granite.

The difficulties continued, one after another. The next vertical step meant a move to the right and a stiff pull up another mantelshelf. Then came a minor replica of the crux, where I again took off boots. A coping slab protruded above the wall, and I managed to pull up, using the far edge of an inclined slab beyond. This led back to the crest and a succession of smooth slabs shelving steeply downwards to the Douglas Gully. Stocking soles are a great comfort on such places. I rested for a few minutes from the strain of the contorted posture needed for crawling up these slabs. When Nancy joined me we both commented on the grand, downward view along the narrow, serpentine ribbon of the ridge and the precipitous drop over the abyss of the Douglas Gully. We were near the end now. Steep but easy slabs landed us on the broad top of the ridge, level with the summit plateau of Lochnagar.

We had enjoyed three and a half hours of the very best of rock climbing, without any halt, for about 700 feet of ascent. We felt a luxurious and contented fatigue settle down upon us. The strain of the climbing, unheeded at the time, had left its mark. We had not come upon any further traces of the passage of the Dundee men, so we could not tell where they had left or regained the crest of the ridge, but we felt certain that everything above and including the crucial pitch was virgin ground.

My enthusiasm for the Eagle Ridge of Lochnagar has the same character of complete satisfaction as the experience of a great work of art. I remember a professor of mathematics who became almost lyrical over the beauty of some new, convergent, infinite series, by means of which he had solved an intractable problem. I think he was right in applying the concept of beauty to his solution. The achievement of a direct ascent of the Eagle Ridge, which indeed I shared with all who had climbed on it, was not the main factor in this enthusiasm. The ridge itself, unique amongst long, precipitous mountain ridges in Britain, was the object. The Eagle Ridge is very steep and narrow, with a symmetrical curving crest. There is a joyful variety about its climbing problems, a magnificent exposure and a persistent suspense about the outcome which is maintained almost to the very last moves. The surrounding rock scenery is grand on all sides and the distant prospect wide and satisfying. If the general character of the rock had not been sound and reliable the climb would not have been justifiable.

Of course this climb would have one drawback in the opinion of the friend whose views I quoted in the first paragraph. Although a natural route up the mountain, the standard of difficulty was more than moderate!

CHAPTER XX

THE ORION ROUTES ON BEN NEVIS

ONE has a natural tendency to look to Ben Nevis for the longest rock climbs in Britain. The Tower Ridge, including the direct ascent of the Douglas Boulder, must provide about 2,000 feet of vertical ascent, but, in summer conditions, much of it is very easy climbing. There is only one place to search for such a route, if we wish to preserve the height and raise the general angle and the standard of difficulty throughout. As long ago as 1925, when Frank Smythe and I were beaten on the Tower Ridge in difficult conditions of snow and ice, and again in early June 1932 when we had bad weather, we came to the conclusion that this exciting, new rock climb must start from near the foot of a formidable gully which separates the Observatory Ridge from the slabby face of the North-East Buttress. The gully had never been climbed at that date, nor has a complete ascent of it been made up to the present, but, on 5th April 1936, Colin Allan and I climbed it with the exception of the lower part, which was then a mass of prodigious icicles. Continuing the Guide Book nomenclature of the Nevis gullies, without a spark of imagination, we named it Zero Gully, and the name has been, more or less, accepted.

Above the foot of Zero Gully, rather less than half-way up the precipice, there is a large, gently inclined depression in the face of the cliff, which, in spring and early summer, generally retains a small snow-bed when all the other rocks are bare. We focused our attention on this prominent landmark in June 1932 and decided that an ascent to the snow-field, which we called the Basin, was within the bounds of possibility. We could do nothing at the time on account of the weather and the quantity of water which was streaming over the slabs above. If we could reach the Basin we considered that the upper rocks might offer several feasible ways to the crest of the North-East Buttress.

Two years went by without any opportunity of making the attempt. In September 1934 Sandy Wedderburn was entertaining two first-class Jugo-Slav mountaineers at the C.I.C.

Hut. I happened to be there with a guest of my own, and Sandy asked my advice, for he wished to take his guests on a really hard climb, something out of the ordinary. I passed on the new idea, and the result was that excellent discovery, now known as the Slav Route. The start was at the foot of Zero Gully and the lower 300 feet were exceedingly difficult. In the prevailing bad weather, with very wet rocks and a heavy storm whilst they were on the most difficult part, two *pitons* were fixed and used for security. The continuation of the climb, instead of going directly upwards to the Basin, was parallel to Zero Gully and much easier than the lower part. It occupied about the same time that my own party of two, moving fairly continuously, required for climbing the standard route on Observatory Ridge.

The Slav Route, while it did not solve my problem, appeared to decide two questions at least. Wedderburn did not consider that it would be possible to climb straight up to the Basin from Slav Route, and it was clear that good weather and dry rocks would be essential for reaching the Basin from below by any route whatever. My next opportunity was in July 1935 when I was accompanied by Miss Violet Roy of the Grampian Club. She was an excellent rock climber, well balanced and light. We had perfect weather conditions and plenty of time. The structure of the rock determined our general line, for this whole face, as seen from the C.I.C. Hut, is sculptured into huge ribs, running back leftwards from the vertical at an angle of about twenty degrees. One of these ribs passes upwards to the left of the Basin, and we attempted to follow it.

The point of view is very important in estimating the angle of a mountain face. From the foot of Observatory Gully this wall appears to be so nearly vertical that one instinctively regards it as an impossible climb; from the crest of Observatory Ridge, just above the lower nose, it looks quite vertical with some places which appear to overhang the base. From the middle slopes of Carn Mor Dearg, however, the impression is altogether different, and the angle of the face, seen partly in profile, is not nearly so intimidating. It is not exactly inviting, for the eye begins to appreciate the smoothness of the great, steep slabs, and the mind to doubt if they could be climbed, even if set at a moderate angle. The same type of problem faced Edward

The Orion Routes: Ben Nevis (*N.E. Buttress, N.W. face*)

L	Long Climb	SL	Straight Left Route	B	The Basin
E	Easy Traverse	Z	Zero Gully	M	The Mantrap
SR	Slav Route	OR	Observatory Ridge		

The summit of Ben Nevis is above OR. The left skyline is the crest of the North-East Buttress. The figures are standing on a snow-bed which, in most summers, does not entirely melt away. The figures are about 1,600–1,700 feet below the summit of Ben Nevis.

Whymper during his attempts on the Matterhorn, causing him to persist too long in attacking the Italian ridge above Breuil. Only later was he convinced that the general angle of the Hörnli ridge above Zermatt was little more than thirty degrees, although it had appeared to be impregnable, as seen from the Riffel Alp. The result was a successful ascent at the first serious attempt in 1865.

Our problem was a minor replica of his. The most revealing views of the face could only be obtained under two conditions. Either very early or late in the day, in mid-summer, the glancing rays of the sun show up its irregularities. As there is often very little sunshine on the Ben one may also see the rock structure occasionally when mist or cloud is dispersing and re-forming over the crags in isolated blobs and wisps which play hide and seek amongst the ribs, pinnacles and hollows. Such conditions are frequent, both on Ben Nevis and the Cuillins. I have often learned a good deal on such a day, and it has guided my movements on a future climb.

We started slightly lower than for Slav Route and about fifteen or twenty yards to the left. About 150 feet of moderately easy slabs brought us to the first serious difficulty, where our rib swept upwards in a steep, smooth wall. I climbed up to the right of this on slabs with the minimum of holds and succeeded in pulling myself up on to the crest of the rib about fifteen feet higher up. My second did not enjoy this pitch, as she was not yet converted to stocking-sole technique. The easier way, as I have since discovered, is to traverse leftwards round a difficult exposed corner.

The main rib now rose at a uniform angle for a considerable distance without any belays whatever. The rocks were dry and my stockings gave me a measure of confidence. New, soft rubbers would probably have done equally well, but mine were age-hardened and useless on such smooth rock. After running out nearly 100 feet of rope I reached a grassy recess with a huge bollard of rock for a belay. Here we considered our next moves. For the guidance of other climbers I should say that by

THE LONG CLIMB, BEN NEVIS
Mrs Bell and the Author on the great slab

traversing a good deal farther to the left the ascent to the recess becomes a good deal easier, but no climber worth his salt would take such an unsporting course. In August 1947, when climbing this route with my wife, I was able to maintain a perfectly straight line from the start up to the grass recess, but the lower section was severe and very lacking in positive holds. Pat became a little impatient at the slowness of my movements, but appreciated the reason when she followed in her turn.

Slightly to our right an impressive rib of rock swept upwards at a uniform angle, obviously not far short of vertical. The rock was rough, corrugated and inviting, if only we could make a start on it from the slightly overhanging nose at the base. The alternative would have been to climb a cracked slab straight above us and to attempt to get on to the rib about a hundred feet higher, but that would have been less direct and attractive. I went along to prospect and found that the lower front of the rib had just enough small holds and cracks to permit of a lodgment for toes and fingers. It reminded me of the direct route up Eagle's Nest Ridge on Great Gable, but was rather longer and more difficult. The cracks continued and lured me upwards. Airy and exposed to a degree, the slabby rib provided a sufficiency of small but good holds. After running out about ninety feet of rope I came to a perfect stance. Somewhat higher was a belay.

The Great Slab Rib, as we afterwards named the pitch, is clearly visible from the C.I.C. Hut in the corrie, especially when it stands out in the evening sunshine. Seen from a stance of equal height on the Observatory Ridge, it appears to be altogether vertical and impossible. My second came up neatly and easily, but we were both climbing in stockings. I have come up on another occasion in boots, with no sense of security on such small holds, when I was second on the rope.

Above this the climbing became easier, as we trended obliquely upwards to the right towards the Basin. The latter place, where we lunched, is a wonderful eyrie with grand views of the Nevis crags and distant views across the Great Glen to the mountains of the north-west. It was pleasant to eat and rest in the warm sunshine, thinking that the most difficult part was over and that we were sure to be able to find a way to the crest of the North-East Buttress.

We resolved to continue on the line of our rib if that should be possible. It formed the northern rampart of the Basin and proved easy enough until it swept upwards in an overhanging nose, where there did not appear to be any way round on the left. I traversed to the right on very small holds, and then back to the left until I could see an opening directly upwards. This was a difficult piece of climbing, and I took my second much more directly upwards, so as to be able to hold her more securely on the rope. I am afraid that she found this the hardest problem of the day. At one place she came on to the rope altogether, presumably having no holds at all. However, our problem was solved, for the rocks ahead were now splintered into huge blocks, offering free passage to the easier ground above.

It was our last difficulty. As we proceeded, the character of the rock became lichen-coated and weathered like that on the crest of the North-East Buttress which we soon gained. We were very high, above the lower summit cairn on Carn Mor Dearg, but not quite so high as its main top (4,012 ft.). In less than half an hour we were on the summit of Ben Nevis, proud of our new discovery and contented after a splendid day's climbing.

That first climb on the north-west face of the North-East Buttress left many unsolved problems, the two most interesting being those of straightening the route up our rib from the northern rampart of the Basin and of finding a direct route from the Basin to the summit of the North-East Buttress. As a result of a good many later expeditions these problems were both solved and several other linking routes were climbed. Rock climbers are, as a rule, neither imaginative nor artistic when it comes to naming new climbs. They have, nowadays, by common consent, agreed to discourage eponymous nomenclature. Since the authors of new routes are no longer allowed to perpetuate their achievements in their own names, many of them have taken a peevish revenge by falling into the alphabetical, numerical or topographical systems which, as that distinguished editor of the *Rucksack Club Journal*, the late J. H. Doughty, once wrote, 'are the offspring of the same unhappy union—a marriage of impoverished imagination with the scientific spirit'. Is it possible to avoid the dilemma when there are a whole group of unnamed new routes, linked together like a network? I do not know, but I made the attempt by foisting a little astronomy on to the tolerance of the climbing community, and lumping all the routes together as the Orion climbs, from a certain resemblance between the principal lines and junctions of the network and the arrangement of the stars in that oldest of our constellations.*

The direct continuation of the rib was climbed by George Dwyer and myself in August 1940. It involved some delicate progress along a tenuous groove, just below the crest on the north side, and culminated in a short, severe pitch on minute holds, by which we climbed up into a smooth scoop which gave direct access to the upper rocks. The solution of the other problem, which was required in order to complete the upper half of the most interesting and direct route from the foot of Zero Gully to the top of the Ben, was effected by John Wilson and myself in June 1940. We thought that we were justified in calling it the Long Climb, and its description is the natural sequel to that of the earlier route to the Basin, in 1935.

John Wilson and I enjoyed perfect weather and we carried a surveying aneroid for the purpose of determining the altitudes at various points. We reached the Basin in about two and a half hours from the foot of Zero Gully, climbing mostly in rubbers but occasionally in stocking-soles. Having eaten our lunch in the Basin we considered the upper face of the mountain. Again there was a natural line for our guidance, the objective being a prominent tower-like projection to the left of the apparent summit of the North-East Buttress. An easy, rocky buttress would lead us to a long, steep, slabby rib which we might use as a sort of staircase for overcoming a vertical step in the cliff, after which things might be expected to be somewhat easier. This plan was good enough for us to be going on with, at any rate.

All went easily to the base of the steep rib, but this did not prove to be a staircase. It was overhung on the right by a vertical wall and had a similarly steep edge on the left. Directly above the rib was another short, steep wall which promised a few niches for holds. The slab rib was about ninety feet high.

* See *S.M.C.J.*, Vol. 22, p. 367, 'A Ben Nevis Constellation of Climbs'.

Climbing was easy at first until I gained the upper edge of the rib, but this soon swept upwards in a vertical line. Vainly, I felt about with outstretched fingers for any positive hold that might help me to pull up beyond the short, vertical section. There seemed to be nothing there but a smooth, unbroken surface. I was compelled to work my way horizontally to the left on very small ledges, leaning outward over vacancy until I was able to swarm up into a smooth hollow in the rock. Soon I regained the crest of the rib and found a secure belay.

The next problem was to climb the wall above the rib. This proved to be a very difficult piece of balance climbing on smooth inclined ledges, with the meagre assistance of palm friction on similar ledges higher up. There were no positive, in-cut holds at all. No doubt, the friction of stocking-soles and of the palms of the hands was more than adequate to counteract a slight leaning outward from the wall, but one never felt altogether sure about it when moving a foot, particularly when stepping up. Progress was by zig-zags, but we got up eventually. On a subsequent ascent I discovered that a direct upward route, though it looked more difficult, was really better, as the holds were more satisfying, despite the steeper angle.

We were now on much easier ground, and our next objective was a still larger and more conspicuous slab, far above us on the left. From a grassy ledge, upon which reposed a mammoth boulder, we edged our way upwards with alternate traverses and ascents. There was only one exposed move, across the top of an open, vertical corner. We were unable to climb the upper slab, but found a feasible way up its right-hand side, leading finally to a niche near the top. Here there was another severe move for the leader, a short, horizontal traverse with no hand-holds at all. But it led to a perfect stance and belay. Our aneroid showed that this upper slab was about 200 feet high. Both of these great slabs on this upper route can be readily distinguished from the C.I.C. Hut on a sunny summer evening, and also, of course, from the crest of the Observatory Ridge.

We were now approaching the tower-like projection or bulge near the top of the North-East Buttress, and had soon climbed to a position directly beneath it. The final steep pitch was a difficult, vertical wall, where some projecting nodules of quartz, strongly reminiscent of the Cobbler climbs, helped us considerably. Then the climbing degenerated into moderate scrambling, and we cast off the rope at 5.30 p.m. at a height of 720 feet above the Basin. In a few minutes we gained the crest of the North-East Buttress, well above the Mantrap,* and raced to the top of the Ben. It was five minutes to six.

We had completed the longest face climb on the Ben, a climb of 1,480 feet to the cairn on the top of the North-East Buttress, of which only 400 feet, partly at the top and partly at the bottom, had been easy scrambling, and practically all the rest had been continuously difficult, with several pitches of undoubted severity. The actual climbing time was six and a quarter hours, under favourable conditions, for a party of two. For a glorious hour we relaxed on the summit, fanned by a gentle breeze from the Atlantic, and then began to descend by the Observatory Ridge, so that John might take a few photographs of our route. The whole face was illuminated by the glancing rays of the evening sun. At 8.40 p.m. we recovered our boots from where we had left them at the foot of Zero Gully, and strolled down to the Hut for a leisurely supper.

Towards midnight we came outside again before turning in. The great face, on which we had striven for so many hours, stood high above us, dark grey in its impassive aloofness and mystery. We felt at one with Shelley as he contemplated Mont Blanc from the Vale of Chamonix:

> 'Power dwells apart in its tranquillity,
> Remote, serene and inaccessible:
> And *this*, the naked countenance of earth,
> On which I gaze, even these primæval mountains
> Teach the adverting mind. . . .
> . . . The secret Strength of things
> Which governs thought, and to the infinite dome
> Of heaven is as a law, inhabits thee!'

In August 1947 I was able to arrange for a photographic party on the Observatory Ridge while my wife and I repeated the Long Climb. The start was the same as before, but we were able to work out a new, very difficult and entirely direct ascent to the foot of the Great Slab Rib below the Basin. It was a

---

* The short, difficult pitch near the top of the standard route on N.E.B.

T

windless day with dry rocks, but a fluctuating bank of mist made photography difficult at the critical positions and times. Despite these handicaps, J. Earl MacEwen secured an excellent photograph of us on the upper part of the Slab Rib, using a Contax camera with a long focus lens. The mist prevented any successful photography above the Basin, and we should have preferred the rib photograph to have shown Pat on the more difficult, lower section of the rib.

On the first rib above the Basin I led the pitch, using the same traverse to the left as on the first occasion, but Pat, who is an excellent and fearless climber, came straight up the edge without traversing at all. She suggested that I could easily have done so myself, if I had only been confident enough to place reliance on a certain minute fingerhold. In 1944 the climb was led by B. P. Kellett, who was a better climber than myself, with Miss N. Ridyard as a second. She was the first to climb this edge directly, secured by the leader who, although, like myself, he had been up the climb before, did not care to do it directly without a rope. It is not a particularly dangerous place; there is one very delicate movement and no more.

Our 1947 climb finished in dense mist, rather higher on the N.E.B. than the 1940 finish, and with more difficulty at the end. We never saw the upper slab, though we must have passed very close to it on our left.

CHAPTER XXI

GLOVER'S CHIMNEY ON BEN NEVIS

THE Sunday after Easter 1947 was not a promising day for climbing. Four of us—John Wilson, the skier; Bill Thomson, the photographer; my wife, Pat and I were slowly plodding up the Coire na Ciste below the north-east face of Ben Nevis. We had breakfasted well in the Clark Hut, and it was only half-past ten by double summer time. The summit crest of the Ben was swathed in cloud, swirling along in front of a fierce west wind. We had thought of attempting the Observatory Ridge, but the prospect of meeting that wind high up on the narrow ridge, just where we might expect progress to be very slow owing to iced and snow-covered rocks, made us think again and seek a more sheltered, if not an easier route, on the upper cliffs of Coire na Ciste. On our right was a gentle, snowy depression covering the frozen lochan, just as it was twenty-five years before when I did my first winter climb up No. 2 Gully of Ben Nevis under the tutelage of my friend, Ernest Roberts. Then we had lunched in a hollow above its surface. The gully made a grand climb, and I was now hoping for just such another good day's sport. On my last climbing visit to the Ben, in August 1944, the weather had been so hot that we had completed our day with the refreshing shock of a dive into the clear waters of Lochan Coire na Ciste. Quite a short swim in the icy waters was sufficient, for they lie at a height of 3,000 feet above sea level and are never warm, even in the hottest summer.

Above us were snow slopes leading up to the beetling crags of the Comb, with its overhanging nose of black cliff. To the left of the Comb the slope steepened to the narrow, twisting rift of No. 2 Gully. John was ahead, attentively studying the icy face on our left, which rose up sheer for 1,000 feet, to the crest of the Tower Ridge. He was looking at the Tower Gap, from which a vertical groove, snow and ice-filled, fell away straight down towards us. This was the difficult Tower Gap West Chimney, far better known as Glover's Chimney, and named after Colonel George Glover who led the first ascent on 27th June 1902. Even in summer conditions, with dry rocks, the climb is by no means easy. There are awkward rocks at the bottom, and the final chimney is both steep and narrow.

Glover's Chimney was connected with one of the most exciting adventures in the early annals of the Scottish Mountaineering Club. On 28th December 1907, Messrs T. E. Goodeve, Charles Inglis Clark and J. H. A. M'Intyre, were climbing the Tower Ridge under snow conditions. When they got to the base of the Great Tower, they did not care to face the difficulties of the usual winter route round the south-eastern side of the cliff. So they worked their way across some ledges on the Coire na Ciste side, being gradually forced downwards into the upper part of Glover's Chimney, although they do not appear to have been aware of the difficulty of their position. The original account has it that, 'Stretching far below, there seemed to be a splendid snow gully to descend, which we could follow with our eyes about halfway down to Coire na Ciste.'

It was already approaching nightfall. They hopefully and carefully descended the steep gully until, at length, the leader could descend no farther. The icy rocks bent over in a convex curve, becoming sheer, vertical cliff. They now realised their position and danger. It was a starry night of keen frost. There was nothing for it but to retrace their steps, climb up the gully and attempt another way of escape to the summit plateau. So long as they could keep moving they would keep warm. They had neither lantern nor torch, but found that the stars gave sufficient light on the snow. At the place where they had entered the gully they turned off to the right and discovered that the system of ledges continued gently upwards in that direction. After incredible difficulties and much step-cutting they succeeded in extricating themselves shortly after midnight. But their troubles were by no means over. The summit plateau of Ben Nevis is a confusing place in the dark. They descended southwards instead of westwards, landing in a steep and difficult gully where M'Intyre slipped and Goodeve sustained several cuts and bruises. However, they continued the descent and reached easy ground above Glen Nevis by daylight.

Throughout the night a number of parties of the Club were searching the likeliest places on the Ben for the missing men.

The first party to find any traces included Dr W. Inglis Clark, the father of one of them, and a well-known pioneer of Scottish mountaineering. About four a.m. one of their lanterns showed up a line of fresh footprints in the snow of the summit plateau. Closer examination proved that three men had made the tracks, and a further search traced the footprints back to a cornice of snow at the edge of the cliff. When a lantern was lowered over the side it did not seem possible that anyone could have climbed up that ice-encrusted cliff. But the missing men were safe. They were out on the Ben for a stretch of thirty hours, and the cross route from the foot of the Great Tower to the plateau is still known as Goodeve's Route.

I had never climbed Glover's Chimney in its entirety under icy conditions. The first complete winter ascent was made by Dr Graham Macphee's party on 17th March 1935. They took eight hours to climb the gully from bottom to top, and experienced great difficulties. At Easter, 1938, I led a party up the lower severe section, but it was late in the afternoon. We had no time to finish, so we beat a prudent retreat. Next day the climb was completed by another party using our ice steps for the lower section. It cost them many hours, for they experienced severe difficulty in the upper chimney. In fact, the leader, as the hour was very late, was glad to accept a steadying rope from a member of another party who were crossing the Tower Gap, on the normal route up the Tower Ridge. He was a good climber, and, in my opinion, would have succeeded without any assistance, for he was already within ten feet of the Gap. I don't think that John was acquainted with all this history. I kept the knowledge to myself, in the full expectation of a very good day's sport.

Underneath the foot of the Chimney is an easy snow slope, leading downwards to the top of a cliff which sticks far out into the corrie like a black island in the snow. The early explorers, men acquainted with the Alps, called this the Garadh na Ciste, from its resemblance to similar isolated rocky islands on Alpine glaciers, which are locally known as *Jardins* (both words meaning garden). On the Alpine *Jardins* there are beautiful flowers in summer, but I have never yet found much sign of plant life on the Garadh na Ciste. We gradually kicked our way up the steep snow slope until we reached the base of the rocks. A gentle snowy curve descended to the summit rocks of the Garadh. John had already started to cut a ladder of steps in the green bulge of ice. Bill was entrenched in a shallow fissure between rocks and snow slope, and was securing John with the rope, the end of which was passed over an ice-axe driven deeply into the snow. It was necessary for safety that John should have enough rope to get past the icy part, so that he could drive his axe well down into hard snow, as a safe belay for securing Bill when it came to his turn to move. We decided that Pat and I should follow quite independently on our own rope.

John was in good form and did his work well. Our position was not too pleasant, as the chips of ice loosened by John from above, as well as a hail of smaller particles, kept showering down upon us. Such is always the lot of the followers during an ice climb. We accepted it stoically, but when I looked up and saw a fair-sized stone coming spinning and rebounding down the gully, far above John's head, I was not so happy about our chances. I looked carefully at the ice and found a trickle of water underneath. The west wind was having some effect. Even at this height there was a slight thaw. If it became pronounced, and if the wind rose to gale force, we should find ourselves in no enviable situation, progressing slowly for hours up that difficult gully and exposed to whatever missiles might be liberated above by wind and thaw. Gullies can be death-traps under such conditions. I had never believed that the danger could be really formidable on Ben Nevis. John was so engrossed with his labour that he had not noticed the falling stone which did not come near him. He was still on the ice-covered rocks, well to the right of the true gully. I watched anxiously for a long time. Not another stone fell. In fact, we found everything securely frozen as we got higher.

After a long wait, Bill followed on, joining his leader. When it came to my turn, I knew that John was well up to the day's work. Both he and Bill were taller than either Pat or myself, so the steps were rather wide apart for us. An extra intermediate step, here and there, was required for our greater security and comfort. We used one hundred feet of line. After two stretches of this we ascended an icy groove between two large, rocky masses. Then an awkward and icy stretch to the left took us into the long, middle section of the gully. There, Pat took over the lead. The bed of the gully was firm, hard snow, over which we made good progress. There were two short, icy bits, but nothing to cause much trouble. The gully cut deeper into the surrounding cliffs, which were all draped heavily with snow and ice. We were completely sheltered from the wind, but became gradually enveloped in thin mist or cloud, into which our forerunners had vanished. At length an opening appeared in the cliff on our left, and another, just opposite on the right. This was the historic Goodeve Ledge Route of 1907, which cuts right across Glover's Chimney from the base of the Great Tower. A good name would be the Goodeve cross-roads. The others were just ahead of us now, still on good, hard snow, but just underneath the upper Chimney which rose like a narrow, vertical shaft to a small, white nick on the skyline.

We called a halt for lunch, as we were still in shelter and required some sustenance, so as to enable us to face the formidable task ahead. If I had doubts about the outcome I kept them to myself. I had been up the Chimney before, but never in such icy conditions. Everyone was very cheerful, and there was the usual lighthearted banter. It was about half-past one when the advance guard prepared to start, this time with Bill in the lead. I rather suspected that the Chimney would take a long time. We were standing on a very steep slope, and the upper part appeared to lie back at a deceptively easy angle. It was, in reality, badly foreshortened, an illusion of perspective that concealed the truth that it was not far short of vertical.

At first there was a vertical step of about eight feet in height. After much hacking at the ice with the pick of his axe Bill got up, but there was little enough to hold on to. In summer one would have jammed and wriggled upwards by friction against the narrow, enclosing walls. These were now heavily coated with dense, polished ice. Some distance higher there was some snow-ice in the bed of the Chimney. The ice-axe could secure a grip on that. John was brought up to the same position, just behind the leader. I asked if the axe was firm. Bill was not entirely reassuring, but John could at least gain some additional security by wedging tactics.

Something like fifteen feet remained to be climbed. The walls were closer together, but still heavily coated with ice. There was no snow-ice now. The back of the Chimney was a flat slab of rock set at an angle of about seventy degrees, coated with about an inch of solid ice. I learned that there was a crack at the lower left-hand corner of the slab, but it did not extend very far. For what seemed like an age of waiting we watched Bill chipping away at the ice on the slab, using the pick in order to fashion a double staircase of thin, icy notches to serve him as handholds, and later as footholds. With incredible slowness his head approached the level of the white notch. We paid no attention to the hail of ice chips that continued to fall upon us, although my face received quite an array of small cuts here and there. At last the pick gripped the icy notch of the skyline. Then Bill's shoulders rose to the same level, and with a final heave he was sitting astride of the crest. Victory was assured us, but it had been a hard fight and a magnificent lead.

Then John crawled upwards, reached the gap and disappeared. He was going on to lead the last section of the Tower Ridge. It was now my turn for going into action on the first vertical step. Again, I knew what it meant to follow a leader who was taller than myself. I used the axe to clear away an additional hold on the rock walls in two places. There was little comfort to be had from any of these slippery push-holds. After the long wait below I was feeling rather chilled, especially my hands which were protected by thin leather gloves, already saturated with water. The vertical step was a severe proposition, but at last I reached the snow-ice below the slab. Well secured, I took in the rope from below and held Pat while she climbed up beside me, very rapidly, too. I suppose that the gentle tension of the rope was some slight encouragement.

The last man does not get the best out of a ladder of ice steps. They get worn and rounded. I was very careful about the next six or seven feet. I could only get my knee on to a little rocky ledge on the left, and using one's knees is always bad for the balance of the body. Besides, my gloved hands could find little purchase on Bill's ice notches. I was able to fashion a new one of the correct size in the rocky crack on my left, but I was still about six inches too short for that first step. Pat wedged herself

in and offered me her left knee as a stand. I accepted the offer
unashamed, to my great benefit. The step was much easier, and
I was soon perched on the ice notches, each of which I enlarged
and sharpened as I ascended. When I reached the gap I was
more than ever impressed with the excellence of Bill's lead.
Again Pat came up cheerfully and rapidly, with the rope no
more than safely taut. Astride of the gap, I could have held the
heaviest of men on the rope if he had come unstuck in that
Chimney.

There was now only the final part of the Tower Ridge to be
climbed. The steps led round the corner on the left, and then
steeply back to the crest of the ridge. The snow was of doubtful
consistency on the steep part, but the axe could be driven in
deeply. The crest of the ridge was easy until it abutted against
the last icy wall. There Pat took over the lead and proceeded
round a corner and up a steep, narrow groove of snow-ice to the
edge of the plateau, where we all met and shared our satisfaction
in the successful issue to a hard climb. We took off the ropes and
coiled them up. There was a strong west wind on the summit,
with drifting cloud and hardly any view.

John and Bill had gone on ahead. When we reached the old
Observatory we found no sign of them, but on the leeward side
of the snow-covered ruins was a boisterous party of four girls
and a man enjoying the Nevis weather. Two wore slacks, but
the other two girls only ankle-socks and skirts, while the man
wore shorts. They were grouped for a photograph. In answer to
our inquiries after our friends came a broad Yorkshire response:
'Ay, they're in there', with a wave of the hand pointing to a
small aperture in the ice-encrusted walls of the Observatory.
Soon a pair of purple legs issued backwards from the opening,
and a fifth girl came out, full of admiration at the interior of the
cave. They were knowledgeable people, as well as tough, for the
young man, after surveying us briefly, asked if we had come up
by the Tower Ridge, and then informed the others that we
were the *real* mountaineers. I don't know so much about that,
for neither Pat nor I would have cared to climb the Ben in
their rig-out.

When they had all gone we crept into the cave, which, from
being a cheerless, broken-down relic of one of the rooms of the

old Observatory, had been transformed into a fairy grotto of crystal walls and stalactites of ice. There sat John and Bill, eating sandwiches, and looking like two trolls of the Jotunheim or, if you like, two 'abominable snow men' of the Himalaya. When we were all refreshed we emerged and plunged downhill towards Achintee over some of the most execrable, breakable snow-crust that I have ever encountered. Now the crust held our weight, but with the next step it cracked and submerged us to the knees. The easiest way was a curious dancing or tripping kind of progress. When we came to the steeper slopes down the corrie of the Red Burn it was just possible to glissade down the soft snow on our seats, which, of course, became thoroughly soaked. But we had our day and enjoyed it all.

CHAPTER XXII

ROCK CLIMBING IN ENGLAND
AND WALES

SCOTLAND occupies only a small place in the history of rock climbing technique. If the rock climbing illustrations in this book have been chosen, for the most part, from Scotland the reasons are the greater extent and variety of Scottish rock, the more recent discovery of the harder climbs and the fact that they are far less known south of the border than they deserve to be. It is only within the last fifteen to twenty years that Scottish standards of difficulty have approached the level of the harder climbs of England and Wales. There, the available masses of rock have been much less extensive and their cultivation by so much the more intensive. Rock climbing has, therefore, emerged as a separate and highly skilled sport in its own right, almost apart from mountaineering. It has maintained an exceedingly high reputation for skill and endurance, and has avoided the bane of some European schools who indulge in the free use of *pitons* and snaplinks, long descents on the doubled rope and similar mechanised methods.

With a multiplicity of routes of all grades of difficulty in a very limited area of rock a correspondingly greater exactitude of description and classification has been necessary. The new series of rock climbing guide books—for the Lake District by the *Fell and Rock Climbing Club* and for Wales by the *Climbers Club*—are unsurpassed in lucidity and accuracy. The field of possible climbs is by no means worked out, but the new routes which continue to emerge tend to become increasingly difficult, up to the limit of human possibility, and also less easy to follow without a minute description.

No British mountaineer can be considered to have completed his education without some practical experience of what has been done in Cumberland and North Wales. He need not do so as an essential part of his training for subsequent Alpine experience, nor should he confine his rock climbing experience to England and Wales or he will miss much that can only be learned in Scotland—greater variety of rock, long traverses, unsound and shattered rock which has not been 'gardened' by previous climbers, and so on. He will miss the problems of route finding which abound on the larger, more complicated and less-charted Scottish mountains. No Scot or Scottish-trained rock climber should conclude, from the chapters of this book which have aimed at exhibiting the boundless scope of the Scottish Bens in providing new adventure in rock climbing, that the ascent of established climbs with the aid of a guide book is mere repetition work and, in no sense, an adventure in itself. The Scottish trained climber may have much to learn from the more advanced technique of the English, and the process of learning can be both an education and a delight.

Standards of difficulty have not yet been thoroughly established and crystallised in Scottish rock climbing. The author is well aware of this and, consequently, not without great benefit to his education and experience, and not nearly so often as he would have wished, has visited Cumberland and North Wales so as to gain some practical experience of the relative standards of difficulty and exposure of Scottish and English rock climbing routes. For a rock climber it is really a kind of pilgrimage to go to Wasdale and disport himself on the Napes Ridges, Pillar and Scafell. To one who neglects the historical and traditional aspects of the sport it is enough to recommend the perusal of *A Short History of Lakeland Climbing* by H. M. Kelly and J. H. Doughty.*

This brings me to a curious confession. I started my rock climbing alone in North Wales as a consequence of reading *British Mountain Climbs* by George D. Abraham. I cycled to Bettws-y-Coed during an August Bank Holiday when I was working near Birmingham. On the first day I climbed the two Carnedds and made an obscure and terrifying ascent of the Black Ladders. Had I even then, as several of my friends now allege, an affection for green vegetatious rocks? Then I made the round of the Snowdon Horseshoe in thick mist, which finally cleared and showed me a wonderful profile of the cliffs of Lliwedd. On my last day I climbed Tryfaen by the North Gully, with great enjoyment, especially on the rugged, firm rock

* Reprinted from Journal of Fell and Rock Climbing Club, 1936–7.

The Long Climb
Ben Nevis
The lower slabs

Tophet Wall
Great Gable
'Safety Second'

near the summit. A traverse of the Glyders with a fascinating glance into the depths of the Devil's Kitchen completed the holiday. At Christmas I was back again on Tryfaen with a friend, reaching the summit at sunset by the north ridge and regaining the road in darkness. I learned the real meaning of the Milestone Buttress as, owing to the breakdown of my friend's motor cycle, I had to walk the ten miles to Bangor in little over two hours in order to catch the evening train for Crewe.

I was invited for Whitsuntide 1921 to join a party at Wasdale Head. It was there I first met Frank Smythe, the others being Mr A. B. Roberts and Dr Keen. Smythe had already done a good deal of rock climbing and knew the whereabouts of all the routes that he wanted to climb. It was a fascinating week for me, with my natural Scottish canniness rudely shaken by the high lights of the programme. It started with the Arrowhead Ridge of the Napes, taken direct, followed by Needle Ridge for the descent and Kern Knotts Chimney after lunch. As there was a high wind Eagle's Nest Ridge and Needle were left for the next visit. Next day we went to Pillar and did the North Climb. Roberts was lowered into Savage Gully, but Smythe, too impatient to await the safeguard of the rope, led straight over the Nose. I was greatly impressed. Having little technique and no long reach, I managed to struggle up somehow or other. The other, shorter climbs on Pillar, did not leave the same impression.

It rained overnight but, Tuesday being fine, we all went to Scafell. Deep Ghyll was the forecast, but Smythe had other plans and deflected us to the left on to the oozy rocks of the traverse on O. G. Jones' route up Scafell Pinnacle. I felt very much of a passenger on the steep rocks below the *Arête*, and that climb was the high light of the holiday. By contrast, the descent by Slingsby's Chimney and the Crevasse was interesting but safe, if not all easy. Roberts left us that evening. I was gradually getting used to the technique with its airy situations and tenuous holds. The fourth day's performance comprised Napes Needle (very difficult and abominably smooth), the Eagle's Nest Direct (rough, firm and perfectly delightful in its exposure) and the Doctor's Chimney on Ennerdale face. Then

Keen went home and Smythe proposed a visit to the C Gully on the Screes. Anyone who has read Abraham's account of this revolting place with its wet and unsound rock will understand how my sub-conscious self (at least) prayed for bad weather. The relevant recollection from Abraham which kept running in my head was something like this, 'Promise me that you will avoid the C Gully on the Screes. It's a deadly place!' After a restless night I awoke to the dull monotony of heavy rain beating on the roof of Burnthwaite Farm. I turned over and slept peacefully for several hours. After Frank Smythe left I had one more climbing day in the company of Mrs Kelly, that most graceful and finished rock climber who founded the Pinnacle Club, for women only, as a protest and a vindication of the self-sufficiency of her sex on the crags and mountains. On that day we hardly used the rope and I learnt a measure of poise and self-confidence which has developed and grown with the years.

In October 1929 I was a guest of T. C. Findlay and John Wilding at Tal y Braich, the delightful hut belonging to the Rucksack Club, above Ogwen in North Wales. They took me up the best route on Milestone Buttress of Tryfaen, followed by the Grooved *Arête* with its delightful slab and corner near the top. Findlay and I were left alone during one or two days of bad weather when I did no more than Amphitheatre Buttress on Craig yr Ysfa, and a tour round Aberglaslyn, Port Madoc and Harlech Castle. Conditions improved later when we were joined by Mr Chisman, who put me through my trials above Idwal. Hope route on the Slabs was followed by Holly Tree Wall, which I enjoyed immensely, especially the awkward step at the crux. A good route, or series of linked routes, took us almost to the top of Glyder Fawr before we packed up and descended by an easy way in heavy rain. It was good of Chisman to ask me to lead throughout, as it gave me an excellent idea of Welsh standards of classification.

Next day we went to Lliwedd, where I had the privilege of leading Route 2 on the East Peak, a first-class climb, well engineered and delightful throughout. The holds are small but adequate and the great, vertical sweep of cliff is exceedingly inspiring. Our return over Snowdon and Crib Goch was enlivened by a series of storms, with some wonderful intervals when the lighting and cloud effects over the western outliers of Snowdonia were both weird and impressive. To my great regret I have never been able to re-visit this beautiful and compact group of mountains. Shall I ever try conclusions with one or two of the more recent routes on Clogwyn dur Arrdhu? My friend, George Dwyer, acclaims them as the longest and hardest routes in all British rock climbing.

On Christmas Day 1931 H. M. Kelly showed me the very high standard of Lakeland climbing. After a night of rain the familiar and graceful outlines of the Langdale Pikes flirted capriciously with the scud of ragged cloud racing across their summits before a strong westerly wind. I expected that we should have a day of fell walking, but I was mistaken. Although we were following the well-worn track towards Esk Hause, I noticed that the eyes of the leader were often fixed on a crag high up on our left, the most prominent buttress of Bowfell. We left the track and approached the foot of the rocks. To any conventional climber, if such there be, the prospect of those black, slabby rocks, with small trickles of water dripping from the overhangs, would not be exactly inviting. Kelly was engaged in earnest converse with Holliday, our third man, younger than either of us but chosen as leader for the day's expedition. During the previous summer Kelly had led a new and more direct route up the face of Bowfell Buttress, and he wished to verify the details of the pitches. In summer the route had been climbed in rubbers; we should have to stick to nailed boots and chance the numbing effects of wet rocks and a cold wind. We had plenty of rope—100 feet for the leader and eighty feet between second and third. It was decided to go on with the climb.

The first forty-five feet were on the line of the original route and easy enough. A forty-foot chimney was rather narrow, with a difficult exit above a chockstone half-way up. Apart from some discomfort the chimney was, of course, no more difficult than in summer conditions. Then the trouble started, where our route diverged from the ordinary way by a difficult traverse to the left. I felt the balance rather trying and my reach insufficient. We were now on an eighty-foot stretch of slabs in an exposed situation. It was too difficult to wear gloves and the sun had disappeared behind a leaden sky, with a cold wind blowing across the face. Holliday was crawling slowly over the smooth wall like a fly. Then Kelly moved quickly and neatly to join him at the next stance. A traverse to the right followed, aided by a doubtful looking flake of rock, which, however, proved secure enough.

Soon we were at the foot of the Garden Wall, a sixty-five-foot pitch and the crux of the climb. I was by now inured to anything and proceeded, from a safe and comfortable stance, to light my pipe and await developments. Kelly was safeguarding the leader. For me the world seemed curiously detached: I became a spectator and nothing more. Holliday was proceeding with methodical caution and steadiness, but I somehow became aware that the situation was tense. High up, the leader was spreadeagled on the cliff, hardly moving at all. Kelly seemed anxious, knowing that the solution of the difficulty was well to the left of Holliday's position; and the intervening stretch of rock appeared to me to be altogether devoid of holds. Could the leader hold out long enough in order to reach security? His movements were now exceedingly slow and tentative, and his fingers must have been absolutely numb with cold. Inch by inch he seemed to glide across the wall, supported by minute cracks and bulges which were quite invisible to us. At length Kelly broke the silence with, 'Now you have reached the awkward step; you have only to make one upward movement and you are in safety'. It was one of the finest displays of climbing I have seen, under terribly trying conditions.

Kelly followed on, and I passed his rope carefully up from below. All too soon I myself was leaving the friendly ledge and committed to the passage. Consciousness was focused exclusively on the here and now, so exclusively that no detailed recollection remained to me afterwards except the relief with which I drew my leg over the top of the Garden Wall. The buttress still loomed high above our heads; as for the bottom, we could hardly be expected to see that after passing so many bulges of rock. Another exercise in faith succeeded the Garden Wall, round another overhanging corner into the undercut base of a narrow, mossy chimney. The movements of the leader could no longer be seen, and Kelly soon vanished after him. Then there floated downwards some fragments of a careless and indifferent conversation followed by a tugging at my rope. They did not even trouble to keep it taut as I ascended.

We were at the end of the difficulties and the rest was easy scrambling. We had taken nearly three and a half hours for the odd 250 feet of the climb, but we had hardly noticed the passage of time. I asked Kelly about the standard of difficulty. 'Well', he said, 'Last May I thought there were one or two places which justified its being classified as a "severe", and today the conditions are not of the best'. At the summit of Bowfell it was blowing a fresh, westerly gale. To the west were Scafell and Scafell Pike, limned in dark purple against a stormy sky. To the south was the Old Man of Coniston, whom we were to visit next day, after disporting ourselves under even worse conditions on the bastions of Dow Crags. A fragment of Windermere gleamed to the left, and towards the sea was the glow of a stormy sunset. Then we raced down the ridge and the even slopes of the Band to the upper end of Great Langdale. We had earned our Christmas dinner.

At the Jubilee of King George V in May 1935, H. M. Kelly was again my guide under vastly different conditions—glorious hot weather and sun-warmed rocks. Four of us had two delightful days on Dow Crags and Gimmer. The latter appealed to me very much indeed on account of the excellence of the rock and its airy exposure, a paradise for climbing in rubbers.

My most recent visit was in September 1940, when five of us camped for three days at 'Down in the Dale' barn near Wasdale Head. These were George Dwyer (now a guide in Wales), Dick Morsley, Jack Henson, Percy Small and myself. We slept in our sleeping sacks on a huge pile of dry bracken, warm, snug and untroubled by insects. George and Dick were self-appointed cooks, so we others lay comfortable until breakfast was ready. The first night it rained, but Sunday morning was fair and overcast with a coldish wind. I feared a breakdown of the weather and used all my persuasive efforts to get George to lead us up Central Buttress on Scafell. That may have been unwise and presumptuous for a first day, but two days of rain would have washed out my chances, and with British weather it pays to be bold. Scottie Dwyer is a man of few words, but entirely reliable. Once before he had refused to lead a very severe Glencoe route with which he was not personally acquainted because he did not feel in good form. This time he was against my proposal, but not outright. He eventually consented, with reluctance, to take Dick Morsley and myself. I have never regretted that day. There was a chill wind, and in many places the rocks were wet, but C.B. gave me all the thrill I wanted. Two days later, after good training and in warm sunshine, it would still have been one of my finest climbs, but a deeply graven and unforgettable experience would have been lacking.

In the 1936 edition of the *Scafell Guide* Central Buttress is the second last of the 'very severes'. It was first climbed in April 1913 by S. W. Herford, G. S. Sansom and C. F. Holland. These are great names in the history of English rock climbing: the partnership of the first two has not been excelled in the intervening years. The *Guide* goes on to say, '470 feet, very severe and exposed. Rubbers. Combined tactics and rope engineering almost essential on the Flake Crack. Leader needs 100 feet of rope'. Hence Scottie Dwyer's caution.

The climb started up a steep slab with two rather difficult movements. At the top of the first pitch we were hailed by Syd. Cross, Mrs Cross and A. T. Hargreaves from below, bestowing a few words of advice, caution and encouragement. Cross had led C.B. in boots without any combined tactics at the Flake Crack. Several wet mantelshelves brought us to the Oval, the comfortable ledge below the Crack. George was leading in stocking soles on the wet rock, as he thinks they grip better than when the rock is dry. Certainly I found them excellent, but the rubbers were useful to keep the feet warm where there was a long halt at a critical place. As visiting guest I chose the last place on the rope and remained for a long time on the Oval.

Dick followed George to the foot of the Crack. Then the latter worked up its lower half to a large rock spike, secured his rope over the belay and also a shorter length with two slings for his legs. Dick then climbed up to him but failed to insinuate himself between George's legs, being forced to retire for a rest and try again. This time he passed upwards through the human archway and gained an upper hold. After resting for a minute he worked himself up until one foot rested on George's head. With a great effort he grabbed the top of the Flake with his left hand. With a still greater heave his right hand followed suit and he pulled up to the level coping of the wall. Meanwhile, Jack Henson took a photograph from the right-hand corner of the Oval. Various spectators were dotted about below and on the lower slopes of Pike's Crag. We were in the limelight or the pillory, whichever way we were disposed to regard the matter.

It was now my turn—easy enough to the foot of the Crack and a foot or two beyond. Measured in terms of height the Crack is only twenty-five feet to the critical spike and fifteen feet more to the top of the Flake. On such places one realises that heights are divisible without limit. The Crack affords no definite holds; the slab on the right is smooth and little short of vertical. Progress is by inches, nor is there anything much to prevent one slipping back faster than one advances. My right foot was on the last hold. It became a continued struggle, wedging the left arm and foot, pressing and slipping with the right ones. George's legs came gradually nearer, but I knew that the tension of the rope offered just a little material as well as moral support. The next difficulty was to maintain a straight position whilst threading my way upwards between the sling ropes. At last I was through and could rest again.

Then I got my right foot on the spike and grabbed the last hold in the Crack. So I climbed on to George's shoulder and finally on to his head with the left foot, my right serving as a mere steadying hold on the smooth face. With my right forearm in the Crack I pushed up, struggled and grabbed the crest with my left hand. Another push, a grab with the right hand, a short struggle and I lay on top of the Flake. At last I was warm again with my efforts. By the time I rejoined Dick at the belay my expression had already returned to its smug composure, as much as to say that pitches like the Flake Crack were everyday incidents of Scottish rock climbs! Needless to say, George came up quickly and quietly on a slack rope. He had utilised a hold inside the upper Crack, unnoticed by either Dick or myself, and was sure that he would lead the Crack in one run-out on his next visit.

We proceeded easily along the top of the Flake, past a little tower to a sheltered, grassy ledge that was out of the wind. The route now ascended and traversed back to the right at a higher

level. The easy interlude ended with the thinnest and most
exposed traverse of the climb. George led with his usual lithe
grace and agility, but something out of the way did happen. A
holdless, vertical corner succeeded the traverse, and for a bare
instant both of the leader's feet slipped. One hand was well
placed and recovery was so rapid that the incident was barely
noticeable. I doubted if I had seen aright and only mentioned
it to him after the climb was over. A nod and a quiet smile were
the response.

Dick and I were thoroughly chilled. Secured from both ends
he started off along the traverse, down on to a sloping foothold
with a dripping wall of rock above on the left. The worst step
was still downward to the right, into the right-angled corner
below George. Dick hesitated and his left leg wobbled slightly.
Then George took in his rope and he climbed the corner. When
I started off the wind began to puff along the face in little gusts.
On the descending step I found a steady for a finger of my left
hand and got both feet together. Then I got a wrinkle on which
I could press my right hand. Down I stepped to the corner with
my right foot, the left hand glided to the other hold, and both
feet to the corner. I was never actually out of balance after I
had found the necessary handholds. These small pressholds for
a finger or two make such places justifiable. It was easy enough
to climb the corner, first inside and then outside, but not so
easy for the leader.

We now moved to the right to a commodious, grassy ledge.
George climbed up a corner, traversed again to the right and
then climbed to a higher anchorage. This traverse was also
somewhat delicate, but nothing to the one already described.
The final part of the climb was up a wettish gully and a little
buttress. After four hours of steady, concentrated climbing we
emerged on top of Scafell at 5.40 p.m. Was it all an enjoyable
experience, with its background of uncertainty, wet and cold?
I got a tremendous kick out of it. Enjoyment, present and continued, is not the yardstick by which we measure a great rock
climb.

Any more descriptions of English rock climbs would partake
of the nature of an anti-climax. After C.B. I shall content myself
with little more than a list of what we did. On our visit to Pillar,

I was deputed to lead Jack and Percy up the North West Climb. This is a most enjoyable climb of classical type, dating back to 1906. I must have come quickly into good form, as it went surprisingly easily for the first (or easiest) of the very severes. It is 400 feet long and pleasantly exposed near the top. After a reunion for lunch I was sent to lead the South West, which Dick and George had already done.

It is a very severe slab climb, but they are slabs with a difference, gloriously rough and prehensile. The final pitch must be very near the vertical for a slab climb. I then left the others, crossed Jordan gap and went over Pisgah to Pillar Fell in order to enjoy the wonderful evening lights.

We had another day on Scafell, as George had designs on the last 'very severe'—Great Eastern by the Yellow Slab. When we passed Mickledore the rocks were dripping with rain and the cliffs shrouded in mist. So I was made to learn my classical history and lead George up Moss Ghyll, a delightful climb. We descended by the ordinary way from Scafell Pinnacle. After lunch the mists were chased away by the sun, so that George, Dick and I enjoyed a grand afternoon on Moss Ghyll Grooves, a delicate severe of 265 feet and one of the finest discoveries of H. M. Kelly, who led it in 1926. For pure, continuous enjoyment I should esteem this route as highly as any that I have climbed. It is essentially very steep and exposed climbing on slabs and fine grooves. The upper part overlooks the Flake on C.B. George engineered an unorthodox finish where vegetation was brought into the service.

My final half-day was spent on the Napes with Jack and Percy. Tophet Wall was climbed in 1923 by Kelly and Pritchard, and the former had recommended it to me on more than one occasion. It gave us a grand, continuously difficult route of 250 feet on small holds. A high wind made the final pitches somewhat harder. For curiosity we again climbed the Napes Needle, and I could detect little sign of wear since I was last there in 1935.

If I were asked my considered opinion about the relative standards of difficulty of English and Scottish rock climbing I should be inclined to say that the main problem is the lack of any uniform Scottish standard. Scottish climbing districts are many and widely separated. Only at Ben Nevis, Glencoe or in Skye is there much rock climbing by many climbers, and each resort tends to have its own *clientèle*. The problems of English and Welsh classification were tackled many years ago and have been continuously under review. The tendency will be for Scottish rock climbing guide books to follow the English classification. This may still leave one or two 'very severes' north of the Border!

There are many lesser climbing grounds in England. Some of the Pennine gritstone is excellent, and I have been indebted to Kelly, Wilding and other friends for taking me on Laddow, Castle Nase and Kinder Scout. Southern England also has its crags. Charlie Gorrie gave me a strenuous evening on Harrison Rocks near Tunbridge Wells. Its value as sport is undoubted, but the style of climbing on these vertical outcrops of sandstone puts a premium on arm-pulling and allows too little credit for balanced footwork. I write with diffidence and a scanty acquaintance. The long traverses on Harrison Rocks must leave one limp. Charlie has promised to take me on Beachy Head when I next visit him. By comparison, good carboniferous dolerite will appear to be perfectly sound! I was brought up on that.

PART IV

ALPINE MOUNTAINEERING
TECHNIQUE

CHAPTER XXIII

ALPINE VENTURE

NOWADAYS there are very few, if any, young British mountaineers who are in a position to spend months of leisure in the Alps, learning the craft from scratch under the supervision of Swiss guides. It is, moreover, very unlikely that this will be feasible in the near future. Even during the inter-war years it was only possible for the few, and the unfortunate result was that these people, in general, failed to realise the full scope of British mountaineering, particularly as regards Scottish winter climbing. Even now it is not fully appreciated that an all-round British experience can train a man, so that he can go to the Alps with confidence, in the company of others as well trained as himself, and tackle a moderate programme of Alpine climbing without the services of professional guides.

It is the purpose of this and the following chapters to show how this should be done, what additional technique and equipment are necessary, to make suggestions as to the best districts and expeditions to start off with and, in general, how to arrange party and programme so as to gain the maximum of new and valuable experience.

To those who are going to the Alps for the first time I would offer four pieces of advice, if they are to make the best use of their time and money when abroad.

(1) Be an all-round British mountaineer, cultivating particularly the technique of difficult winter climbing, preferably in Scotland. Go out in all weathers on long hill traverses in complicated country. Undertake long rock-climbing expeditions where route finding is also necessary.

(2) Be in good physical training before going to the Alps. This is essential, for the Alps will test your stamina. It is perfectly true that one cannot acclimatise oneself to Alpine altitudes by climbing on British hills. Nevertheless, a great deal which is attributed to want of acclimatisation at great heights is often caused by defective training and poor physique, after many

months of city life without adequate walking exercise in the open air. Acclimatisation comes more easily and quickly to those who are fit at the start of the holiday.

(3) Choose a moderate programme for a first visit to the Alps. Don't rush out in a Matterhorn-or-nothing frame of mind. Aim at climbing a few lesser peaks with comfort and safety under your own power and guidance until you learn how Alpine peaks and glaciers differ from British mountains. Never land yourself in the foolhardy and dangerous situation of being overmastered by your surroundings at a critical turn of the day's work. Alpine weather can be fickle and changeable like all mountain weather. The Alps are not like British mountains. They have no guaranteed, easy ways down for an emergency.

(4) Be properly equipped. Little more is required than suffices for difficult Scottish winter ascents. Knowledge and experience are required, however, and can only be gained by practice. This chapter will give an outline of what is necessary, but cannot be a substitute for adequate practice, which should be obtained, in the first instance, on the easier peaks. It is foolish to visit the Alps with the intention of going for difficult rock climbs alone, where the glacier sections are either very short or so popular that they are well tracked in advance by other parties.

The main differences between Alpine and British mountaineering fall under three interconnected heads.

(1) The scale of the expedition is much greater, both as regards space and time. The time factor, if retreat should be necessary, is much more important than in Britain.

(2) Alpine peaks, even in summer, carry enormous masses of snow and ice. The mountains are, geologically considered, a younger range, and are much more rugged and precipitous than British hills, sometimes by any and every avenue of approach. Range of altitude implies range of temperature, so that Alpine snow can change much more quickly from a safe to a dangerous condition.

(3) The altitude factor affects the human frame, especially during the first few days of a holiday. Most people, particularly younger persons, acclimatise themselves to the rarefaction of

the atmosphere on high peaks fairly quickly, but this varies a great deal with the individual, and cannot be predicted before-hand. Even after a week's hard climbing some people are still weakened at the higher altitudes. This may be dangerous in bad weather or at a difficult crisis. The healthy climber, in good training, is unlikely to be affected by mountain lassitude after the first few days.

Above the snow line the ultra-violet fraction of sunlight is very active, as it is not absorbed by the denser atmosphere and water vapour which screen the valleys from its influence. Even when the sun is hidden behind clouds it is advisable to protect the face, and especially the eyes. The heat rays are also intense and the radiation comes, not only from above but, by reflection, from the snowfields. Dark glasses are not essential, but light-coloured Crookes glass, which is impervious to ultra-violet rays, is best. The rest of the face, particularly the more delicate parts, must also be protected by some form of glacier cream or paste. This keeps the skin soft, as well as protecting it from radiation. Again, it is a mistake to imagine that there is no danger on the glaciers on a dull day. The principal danger is during the first few days of a holiday. The skin gradually acquires a tan and develops, to some extent, a protective pigmentation, but this varies very much with the individual, and may not develop at all in some persons.

The most difficult situation is when the leader is traversing a featureless snowfield on a fine day with a light, translucent mist. The eyes are badly strained, having nothing on which they can focus. Glasses must not be removed, or an extremely painful attack of snow blindness may follow. Greasing the skin around the eyes and over the eyelids is often a partial help, but is no substitute for direct protection by well-fitting glasses with good ventilated frames which prevent the entry of light at the sides.

EXTRA ALPINE EQUIPMENT

Crampons are not essential for the easier Alpine expeditions, nor even on certain difficult ones. It is a good thing to learn to traverse Alpine glaciers and to thread an icefall with nailed boots and an ice-axe. I spent three summer holidays in the Alps and did some very good expeditions before I owned a pair of crampons. On some of these, I am prepared to admit, crampons would have been very useful at several places and would have saved a lot of time. That is their true function, as time savers on long snow and ice expeditions.

They also provide a sense of false security, or even a source of real danger, if carelessly used. One is tempted, when ascending a slope of hard snow-ice, to delay too long before cutting adequate steps. Crampons demand larger steps than boots for full security. The chief danger is during the descent, when the snow has become softened under the influence of the sun. It is then that the snow balls up dangerously within the framework of the crampon spikes. A bad slip is a real possibility and, as such slopes are often badly crevassed, there is serious risk of calamity overtaking a party. A remedy, not too easy to apply with regularity, is to knock off the balled snow with an ice-axe; but it is both safer and better to discard the crampons and rely on nailed boots and the ice-axe. Some forms of heavy tricouni nailing are also a source of danger, although not so dangerous as crampons in heavy, balling snow.

Crampons must be accurately bent and fitted to the boots. Ten spikes are needed, with the front pair just underneath the points of the toes. Don't use them on rocks, which will soon blunt the spikes. Learn how to use them easily and properly, so that the spikes do not wound the other leg or foot. On a steep slope the spikes should bite at right angles to the slope.

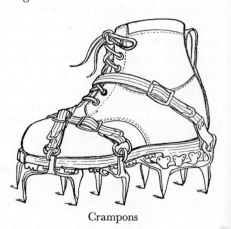

Crampons

This means flexing joints and sinews in an unaccustomed and tiring manner, and should be practised at first on easy expeditions. Straps must be kept reasonably tight, but must, on no account, restrict the circulation in the foot, as this may give rise to frost-bite in severe conditions of weather or exposure. Before starting a campaign the spikes should be sharpened. Only ill-advised use on rocks can blunt them quickly.

Snow Glasses have already been mentioned. They should fit easily and without strain and have ventilated frames. Actual protection against ultra-violet rays is necessary. Tinted celluloid is not usually satisfactory.

Glacier Cream generally contains an opaque pigment, such as barium sulphate, besides the greasy element. It is conveniently put up in tubes. If you have not a sensitive skin an unpigmented grease may do well enough. The most sensitive parts are the lips, nostrils and eyelids. Washing the face is inadvisable, even if it were easily possible, above the snow line. The back of the neck should be protected. A wide-brimmed hat is very useful.

Clothing. The main requirement is protection against cold, wind and extremes of temperature. This means a light, windproof jacket and plenty of light woollies. The possibilities of benightment and provision for an enforced bivouac are dealt with elsewhere.

Orientation. Finding the way in the Alps under difficult conditions depends on the same principles and practice as on homeland mountains. Alpine maps are very good and detailed. So are Alpine guide-books. Routes to the huts are well marked where this is practicable, but this cannot apply to huts which are approached over glaciers. In addition to map and compass it is extremely helpful to carry a pocket aneroid or altimeter. This may, if properly used, give valuable and essential information, for Swiss maps are well-contoured and give the heights of many subordinate points. Torches should always be carried. They have largely replaced the folding, candle lantern, but the latter is very light and can be exceedingly useful, as there is much less wind on the Alps than on our own mountains.

Ironmongery. Easy ways of descent are not common on Alpine peaks. If one loses the way there may be a short section of difficult rock which must be descended. It is therefore essential to master the simple technique of roping down, as previously described. In fact, roping down is a not-uncommon feature of many standard routes on rock peaks, especially in the Chamonix district. The party should carry a spare length of Alpine line for the purpose, as well as one or two short rope slings, *pitons* and *karabiners*. Their use is obvious and has already been mentioned, although discouraged, for British climbing.

Accidents. A comprehensive rescue service is maintained in most Alpine centres. It is manned by professional guides and can be brought into action very speedily whenever an accident has been notified. As it is run by the local authorities the rescued can be forced to pay the cost incurred, which may be fairly heavy in particular cases. A rescue party may set out early the next morning if it is known that a party has been in difficulty and has failed to reach its destination. There is no difference in procedure, in the event of an accident taking place, from what would be necessary, for instance, on a winter expedition in Scotland, but the effects of exposure on a high, Alpine peak may, of course, be much more severe.

CHAPTER XXIV

ALPINE TECHNIQUE

(1) ROCK CLIMBING

LITTLE need be added to what has already been written on British rock climbing. It is essential that British experience should cover long expeditions on rock of medium difficulty where some degree of route selection is necessary and a roped party moves all together with the maximum degree of speed consistent with safety. This means, in effect, that experience of Scottish mountains is essential in all seasons and weathers, but particularly when the mountain is partly covered with snow and ice.

Verglas, a thin coating of ice on rocks, is quite common on our Scottish mountains in winter and early spring. In variable weather it is also common in the Alps. In summer it may often occur, at great heights and on north faces, in fine weather in the early morning, although it generally disappears as the day advances. It is far otherwise when a thunderstorm deposits hail or snow on the rocks where it melts and then freezes to a film of ice. This condition is extremely dangerous, demanding unremitting care, and is often made more intolerable by a cold wind. It is one of the hazards of Alpine weather. As there is often no easy route of descent the hazard is formidable.

Difficult snow and occasional stretches of ice on high, rocky ridges are common in the Alps, even in good weather. A rapid change of weather for the worse, during a long Alpine expedition can transform an easy rock ridge into something both severe and dangerous. Rock-falls are seldom a real danger in Britain: in the Alps they must always be guarded against.

When storm signs appear a party must be able to move together, continuously and rapidly, over rock faces and ridges. There is no time for elaborate safety measures or tie-on belays. Safety consists in the ability to effect a speedy descent before conditions become still more difficult. That is where the advantage and speed of a guided party is most obvious. There is no reason why a team of amateurs, properly trained to work together on long rock expeditions at home, cannot achieve a similar result. Do not avoid all unsound and shattered rock at home. Alpine summits and ridges are generally riven by frost and are often both shattered and rotten. Practise roping down on the homeland crags, so that it becomes a familiar technique. It saves a lot of time.

(2) GLACIERS

The lower reaches of Alpine glaciers are excellent for practice, both for step-cutting and for the use of *crampons*. Start with easy ones where there are no sudden falls. Get to know the lie of the *crevasses*, and how this is altered where a glacier makes a sharp bend, or where a tributary glacier comes in from one side or the other. It is not always easy to predict the trend of the crevasses in such cases, as much depends on gradients and the shape of the rock bed underneath. You will thus get to know the easiest routes. Sometimes one should stick to a moraine at the edge or a medial moraine, but not always by any means. In mid-glacier the crevasses are usually transverse, but at the margin they are often longitudinal. Careful selection will show the best route on to and off the ice. Moraines may be unstable and dangerous, with loose blocks poised on the ice, which is often coated with a poorly adherent layer of sand and gritty stones.

Where a glacier is not snow-covered it is known as 'dry glacier', a complete misnomer in warm, moist weather when the surface can be a pestilential morass of soggy snow and water. It is not generally necessary to rope up on dry glacier, as the crevasses are open and avoidable. Suitable glaciers for practice can be found at most centres. The lower flattish basins of large glaciers, such as the Gorner and Zmutt near Zermatt, the Aletsch behind Bel Alp and below the Konkordia, the Mer de Glace at Montenvers, the Ober Aletsch, the Fee above the Lange Fluh, the Arolla glacier and many small ones are perfectly suitable. But everything depends on the season and the weather. A snowy season with very little sun makes glaciers easier, but a hot, dry season opens the crevasses, especially on the higher glaciers, and makes them much more difficult.

After a reasonable amount of practice the most useful and interesting sequel is to try to negotiate an icefall. Here the problems are more difficult. There is a maze of crevasses, with many unstable-looking slices and towers of ice (*séracs*), which look as if they were ready to topple over at any time. In the natural course of events they must do so, sooner or later. A good route will avoid traversing beneath them, but that is not always possible. In the early morning they are usually fairly safe. The first heat of the sun is the loosening agent. The best route through an ice-fall may vary from year to year. An unknown ice-fall may necessitate a careful reconnaissance expedition in order to save time next morning, when all speed is needful for the ascent of the selected peak. One of the most important things is to memorise the main features of the passage and so be able to retreat by the same way, without confusion, if an *impasse* is reached. I have known a competent mountaineer who was caught napping on the Mer de Glace at nightfall, was unable to find a way off and was compelled to pass a chilly night on the ice.

No general rule can be given for route selection through an ice-fall. The centre line often leads to much avoidable trouble. The concave side of the bend of a glacier, with its smaller radius, is likely to be easier than the convex side. The side of the glacier which is better shaded from the sun is usually less crevassed, such crevasses as exist being better closed. Only on straight glaciers can the best line be expected along the centre.

It is a good plan to trace out a feasible route from a commanding view-point at a distance, to memorise it and then try it out. This is the explorer's method and must, of course, be superseded by knowledge gained from maps, guide-books and the evidence of the passage of other parties, especially of guided parties. It is, however, only by some experimental exploration that one can acquire both experience and self-confidence in the Alps. The important thing is to gain that experience where there is no undue risk. When ascending a mountain, if one is likely to be returning by the same route, it is of the utmost importance to observe carefully and remember the salient features of such things as a route through an ice-fall.

(3) SNOW-COVERED GLACIER

This term applies to most snowfields above the 'dry glacier'.

w

Threading an Icefall

Crevasses, open or snow-covered, may be encountered all the way up a big peak, even not far from the summit, unless it is a steep, rock mountain which does not carry much snow. Such *terrain* is safest in the early morning after a night's frost. At such a time the surface snow is well frozen and the danger of falling into a crevasse is a minimum. It is not, however, entirely absent. Put on the rope, therefore, and keep it reasonably taut between the members of the party. A moderate interval of twenty to thirty feet between members is best. Under the influence of a hot sun the snow-covered glacier will be much more trouble-some during the descent, especially on a hot afternoon. There is here an additional danger in the physical and mental fatigue arising from hard work accomplished and the stifling glare and heat from sun and snow. At such a time it is vital that every member of the party should be on the alert.

The leader probes the snow with his axe for crevasses as he advances. The second is prepared to check him at once if he inadvertently slips into one. A good leader will, from surface undulations, guess the lie of a concealed crevasse pretty accurately, but this is the fruit of long experience. Crevasses generally occur in systems, and the line of advance should never be parallel to the prevailing direction of the crevasses, or the whole party may be strung out along the insecure, snowy cover of one long crevasse at the same time. Cautious zig-zagging can avoid this.

If there is a trough along the centre of a glacier it may be an indication that the crevasses are compressed and less open. Surface water usually means the absence of crevasses. Narrow crevasses may have a considerable, lateral overhang, built up by partially consolidated snow. They are not, therefore, as safe as they appear.

The strength of bridges across crevasses varies enormously. A bridge only six inches thick may be safe in summer after a night's frost. In winter a bridge may not be safe although its thickness is over six feet. The leader must, in doubtful cases, have enough rope to cross to a position of complete safety, and he must be belayed by his second from a perfectly safe stance. If due vigilance is observed no one should ever slip more than half-way into any crevasse, so that he can help to extricate himself. When a foot goes through the surface it is unwise to struggle in order to free it, but better to fall gently forward at full stretch and try to hook the pick of the axe into firm snow in front. The same applies to doubtful snow-bridges. The body weight is thus more evenly distributed over a fragile surface.

It is now obvious why it is better to avoid parties of only two climbers on a snow-covered glacier, especially if there has been a recent snowfall, and more particularly for parties with little experience of such work. However, a party of two is often good for other reasons.

When leaving the upper glacier or snowfield and taking to the rocks, there is generally a long, wide, marginal crevasse which must be crossed. This is the *bergschrund* or *rimaye*. It may be a formidable problem. It is not always right up against the rock, for some ice adheres to the latter. One must look out for some place where the *schrund* has been filled up with ice, rock debris or hard, old snow; or there may often be a snow bridge. Otherwise the gap may either be impassable or a severe problem, for the farther, rocky side of the *schrund* is always higher and it may be overhanging. The only way may be to lower a man into the chasm where it is partly filled, so that he may cut steps in the ice of the opposite wall. This may be the major obstacle in the day's work. When one is descending a peak by an unknown route the *bergschrund* may be troublesome. If there is no bridge, but the lower landing is good, the gap can often be jumped and each moving member safeguarded by the others during the process.

(4) RESCUE FROM A CREVASSE

We must now briefly consider means for extricating a climber who has been so unfortunate as to fall right into a crevasse. The immediate thing to do is to fix the rope leading to the victim by anchoring it to a well-secured ice-axe. The other man is now free to take action, but must first establish communication, which should not be difficult if the linking rope is short. Crevasses often widen below the surface, and the victim is unlikely to be able to climb up by his own, unaided efforts. Even if he is uninjured he is almost certain to be badly incommoded by his waist loop sliding up and pressing against his ribs. A second rope is almost essential. There ought to be enough spare rope available for the second to cast a free end with a loop on it, in such a way as to reach the victim. Admittedly, this may not be at all easy to do, where, as in the case we are considering, there are only two climbers in the party. With three or more climbers the rescue is a simpler problem.

The victim can now tie on to the second rope as well, or, better still, thread it through his waist loop and use it as a stirrup rope for one foot. The second rope is now drawn up tight and secured, with the victim's foot raised as much as possible. The latter then stands up in the stirrup while the second takes in and fixes the original rope. This process can be

CREVASSE AND SNOW BRIDGE

Mont Blanc region

repeated as often as may be necessary. At the rim of the crevasse there may be some difficulty, for the ropes tend to bite into the edge and are difficult to extricate. There is also the danger of fraying the ropes against the ice, but this is much less than one might expect for, by this method, the rope being hauled up is not under strain.

Certainly, Alpine line is weaker and cuts more deeply into the ice. I had one personal experience of this as victim, having slipped about ten feet into a crevasse without injury. The rescue rope was a part of the same length of 120 feet of Alpine line. I admit that I felt very apprehensive as I dangled inside the cold, blue depths before the friendly rescue line came down to me. While feeling truly grateful for the security and strength of Beale's Alpine line, I considered that it would have been safer and less painful to have used a heavier rope. Many Alpine climbers have never had this experience at all. A long time ago A. F. Mummery gave good advice on this subject, coupled with some witty sarcasm pointed at climbers with such misguided tastes as to forsake the sunshine and joys of the brilliant Alpine scene in order to wallow in the cold, dismal chasms of the interior of the glaciers!

He advised a party of two to keep a doubled rope between them when crossing fissured, snow-covered glacier. I have found it good advice. The rope runs, as usual, between the waist loops of both climbers. The second carries a small loop near his waist loop, suitable for the insertion of the ice-axe when belaying. From this loop the rope returns to the leader with another loop near his end, but with a length of loop about three feet longer than the other. The free end is then secured loosely to the leader's waist loop. If the leader should fall into a crevasse he can easily provide himself with a foot-loop for extricating himself. The same procedure can be used to safeguard the other if necessary, or if the lead be changed.

There are several ways of improving this method of rescue. When the victim can stand up in the foot-loop on the second rope the other can slacken the original rope sufficiently for his friend to slip the loose part down through his waist loop, tie a knot in it and so fashion a loop for his other foot. He may then climb up more easily, using his feet alternately and leaving his ribs free, as well as his arms. This is most useful if he is far down in the crevasse. The principal danger is, however, that there may be a very long period of delay before the second succeeds

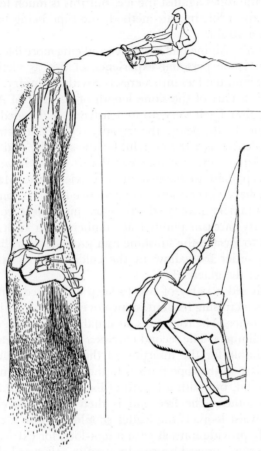

Rescue from Crevasse

in getting the rescue rope to the victim, who is meanwhile half strangled, cramped and losing strength. A foot-loop on the free end of the rope, hanging from the knot of the waist loop, will help greatly, or the same result can be achieved by carrying a spare loop of line with a short, spliced ring at each end and a snap-link.

These methods are, of course, equally applicable to certain critical situations in rock climbing, and they can easily be practised at home, on trees or convenient small crags. Unless they have been practised and are thoroughly familiar it will not be easy to apply them successfully in a crisis where there may be additional complications, exhaustion or injury. The simplest method is usually the best in a crisis, and simplicity implies familiarity.

Can the uninjured climber, swinging at the end of a rope inside a crevasse, help himself if his second is only able to anchor the rope and nothing more? If the climbing rope were a chain of separate links and the victim were provided with two detached foot loops, each with a hook at the other end, so that he could hook himself on to the chain wherever he liked, the problem would be solved. He could bend and straighten his legs by turns, at the same time moving the hooks alternately up the chain. This will explain the Prusik knot technique for self-rescue from a crevasse. This knot is a device for fixing a looped rope securely to a hanging rope in such a way that the knot tightens when strain is put upon it from underneath, but so that, when the strain is released, the knot can be slid up the hanging rope to a new position. The knot itself, according to Mr P. J. H. Unna, is an old nautical device called the 'bale sling'. Dr Prusik, a continental mountaineer, adapted it for rescue work in climbing.

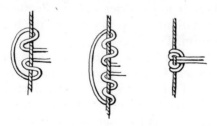

PRUSIK KNOT

The climber carries three loops of Alpine line of respective circumferential lengths as follows—the stature of the climber, three-quarters of this and a small one between three and four feet. The middle loop is first attached to the hanging rope;

the shortest is used as a shoulder support; the longest is used when the climber stands on the first loop to be fixed. Upward progress is made on either foot alternately as the loops are slid up the fixed rope. The diagram shows the way of making the knot.

It is not possible to make an efficient, non-slipping knot of this type unless the loop is made of a lighter rope than the main rope. Loops of line on a main three-quarter rope are all right, but not loops of three-quarter rope; loops of line are even better on a full-weight main rope.

(5) UPPER SNOW-SLOPES AND COULOIRS

Here, the experience required is not very different in quality, but is really a considerable extension of what has already been gained on the higher Scottish hills in winter and spring. That pregnant phrase, 'the condition of the snow', has much new significance on the big Alpine peaks. On Scottish winter snow the heat of the sun is never very powerful. It does not, therefore, soften quickly. In the Alps, during summer, rapid softening takes place every day in fine weather, but there is also a spectacular change under the influence of a warm, moist wind from the south. When the *foehn* wind blows, snow peaks get into bad condition and difficult routes may become dangerous as well.

Alpine snow generally falls in dry flakes on the upper slopes. The atmosphere is much drier than in Scotland where moist winds from the Atlantic help to compact the top layer of snow to the sub-stratum. This does not always occur in the Alps, and never so quickly as at home. When climbing the Gross Silberhorn in the Bernese Oberland with Frank Smythe we encountered conditions of this nature on the steep portion of the narrow eastern ridge. Smythe at once proceeded to cut steps in the underlying ice. This made progress safe, but very slow. If there is any doubt about the condition of the snow the extra time and labour must be expended, for avalanches can be started very easily, and even more so in a steep gully or *couloir*. In a *couloir* there is the additional danger of stonefall from the flanking crags, also due to the thaw conditions.

An equal degree of caution is advisable on very steep, open

snow slopes. If they are bordered or broken up by rocky out-crops it is safer to link the route up with these or keep close to them. If it is necessary to cross such an open slope it is better to do so as high up as possible. Sometimes the slope is intersected by a narrow, semi-concealed crevasse. This often gives rise to an icy band covered by new snow which may not be well compacted to the under-layer. At a broad, snow saddle on a ridge crevasses are common, just where the slope eases off.

If soft snow is suspicious but must be ascended the danger of a snow slide (or the less violent type of avalanche) is always less for a direct ascent than for a traverse. The axe can be driven in deeply in front; one may even use the arms in a sort of upward swimming advance which distributes the weight and compacts the snow.

In many places there are signs of former avalanches, in the form of masses of balled snow at the foot of the slope, but often there is little evidence of possible danger. It is quite true that the avalanche danger is less if one ascends at the foot of a wall of rocks, but one may thereby be incurring the greater peril of stonefalls from the cliffs, or of the fall of masses of ice if there is a snowfield above. If such slopes must be descended it should be done as early in the day as possible when the upper slope is still in shadow.

If crampons are worn they must be kept clean and not balled up with compacted snow. A slip on balled-up crampons is fatal, as one is perfectly helpless, It is better to take off the crampons betimes and proceed in boots, securing every step with the driven-in ice-axe.

(6) ICE SLOPES

Routes up Alpine peaks involving steep ice are best avoided during a first visit. Short, icy sections are often found, however, on many upper snow slopes and ridges. They are much more common when a relatively snow-less winter is followed by a hot summer. Then they may occur on normally easy snow ways up a mountain. They should present no difficulty to any moun-taineer who is well versed in the technique of ascending Scottish ice. This practice should have included the cutting of steps single-handed on the descent.

I had to do this when descending the upper, northern slopes of the Aletschhorn. There was a very narrow crevasse across the slope and a considerable band of ice below it. It was a troublesome job in the teeth of a strong, cold, north wind. Careful belaying is essential on an ice slope. Crampons are very useful, but the spikes may not bite on very hard, steep ice; and it must be remembered that larger steps are required for crampons than for nailed boots. The latter are sometimes more useful. Continental climbers tend to rely overmuch on crampons.

There is no unique style for cutting steps in ice. Good balance and economy of effort are the essentials, and much practice is necessary. All steps are cut with the pick, unless on easy crust. The leader can often proceed by finishing only the alternate steps, leaving the intermediates for the attention of his second. In zig-zag progress cut larger steps at the turns. For traverses on a steep slope a continuous ledge may sometimes be required. For a steep descent one may have to face inwards and use notches for handholds as well, or it may even be expedient to lower a man on the rope and let him cut a staircase upwards for the descent of the others. Roping down from an ice *piton* is the last resort.

On a long Alpine expedition the problem is to save time without sacrificing security. A good stance is absolutely essential for security on steep ice. The pick of the axe may be of very little use as a belay on really hard ice. A *piton* may be required to secure the descent of the last man. There is no doubt that a slip on ice on the part of a lower member of the party can easily be checked by the leader. Where the party is perched on a ladder of notches in very hard ice it is very doubtful if a slip on the part of the leader could be checked. The inference is that the party should be competent and the advance of the leader between two good stances ought to be short. On a long ice slope the whole party may, of necessity, be on the ice at the same time. Ice *pitons*, as described earlier in this book, are worth carrying on such an expedition, and can usually be recovered by the last man.

(7) CORNICES ON RIDGES

These are much more common and insidious in the Alps than

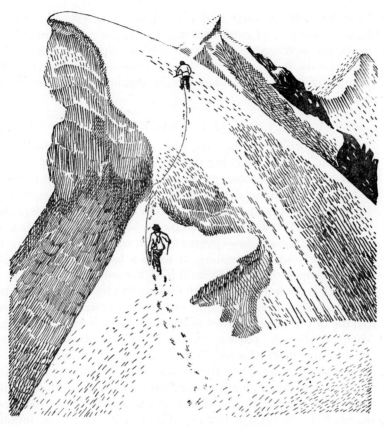

Cornice on an Alpine Ridge

in Scotland. The suspected edge of the ridge should be given a wide berth. The line of possible fracture may lie considerably back from the edge, and there may be an incipient fracture, bridged over with new snow and almost entirely concealed. Gentle slopes to windward and steep ones to leeward of the prevailing wind favour the growth of cornices. Variable snow-laden winds may give rise to double cornices on certain mountains with sharp ridges. Very careful leadership is necessary on such mountains as the Lyskamm of Monte Rosa.

Alpine cornices can break away in any sort of weather. When a ridge is narrow and obstructed by towers or *gendarmes* one may be driven off the crest and compelled to traverse along the flanking slopes and even underneath a cornice. The snow beneath the overhang is usually in bad condition, but the only thing to do is to cross the danger zone at high speed, and unroped if necessary. No one should remain stationary in such a position.

(8) THE DESCENT

In general, there are no easy ways down on Alpine peaks. If bad weather is approaching the first thing to do is to get off the rocks before they become plastered with snow. The next thing is to know the main details of the easiest way down over the upper snow slopes and glaciers, so as to be able to avoid icefalls and mazes of crevasses. This involves a good practical experience of route finding on snow-covered glacier, combined with correct orientation and map reading. It needs a lot of practice. Good habits, formed on the homeland hills, are invaluable.

There is the habit of frequent observation from diverse points of view, of mentally working out and memorising the main details of the possible ways of descent and, wherever possible, checking them by reference to map and guide book. This is a fascinating exercise for an off-day or an idle hour on the mountain side when returning from some other expedition, and it is worth the trouble. Another plan, less easy to arrange but even more useful, is to prospect the lower part of the descent beforehand. It is always a better expedition to traverse a mountain than to return by the same route, but it may be wiser for a guideless party to return the same way if they have not been able to prospect the descending route beforehand.

Much can also be learnt from good photographs which give a very good idea of an unknown mountain face, when studied in conjunction with map and guide-book. Most Alpine guide books have excellent line drawings with the routes clearly marked.

Never wait until the clouds and mist gather before making the necessary observations. A still better rule is to call a halt when time is seen to be running short or bad weather threatens, consider the position fairly and act at once if a balanced judgment favours retreat. Remember that it is quite easy to lose the way, either before getting off the glacier or amongst the faint tracks, cliff terraces and woods below the glacier, after the onset of darkness. Little more need be said about the technique of descent. A tired party is apt to take a much longer time than is expected. Fatigue begets carelessness. Many an accident happens on relatively easy ground during the descent.

The technique of glissading will have been acquired on Scottish mountains, but much more caution is necessary in the Alps, both on account of the liability of snow slopes to peel off or avalanche and of the prevalence of crevasses where they are least expected. Only slopes with a gentle, uncrevassed run-out are suitable. Even then, glissading must often be carried out by a roped party. Sitting glissades are seldom advisable at all.

(9) ALPINE WEATHER AND SNOW CONDITIONS

Alpine weather in summer is generally much better than British west coast, hill weather. But all mountain weather is variable and liable to sudden changes. The weather signs can only be learned by experience. Weather in the western Alps, especially the district of Mont Blanc, is not so good as in the eastern Alps. It is often possible, before starting out from the valley, to obtain by telephone from the Swiss Meteorological Bureau a competent and reliable weather forecast. Guides are often very good forecasters, especially in their own valleys.

North and north-east winds are usually good, but very cold on the heights. Small plumes of cloud on peaks and ridges are really composed of particles of snow, swept away by a strong, cold wind. South and south-west winds mean unsettled weather, if not worse. The Alps are not nearly so windy as the Scottish hills, but the wind on a high peak menaces the climber on account of its low temperature and the threat of frost-bite. In exceptional cases and during storms it would be unwise to tempt the fury of an Alpine blizzard on a high ridge or peak. The storm may be short-lived but sufficiently violent, even in summer.

The following are usually signs of good weather: red sky at night; wind blowing up a valley in the day-time and down again at night; clouds dissolving in wisps and reforming higher up, as a sign of improving weather. One must always allow for the deflection of the wind by the surface contours, unless one is on an isolated peak. The best rule is to follow the drift of the upper clouds.

In good weather glaciers, névé and snowfields freeze up properly during the night. This is always a good sign.

The following may be taken as signs of approaching bad weather. At sunrise a good deal can be learned. The pink glow which rapidly changes to golden with a sky which is free of all but high, light clouds is good, but a yellow sunrise is not good and a brilliant green is very bad indeed. Readers of Mr F. S. Smythe's earliest book, *Climbs and Ski-Runs*, will recollect the aftermath of such a sunrise when the party was fortunate in surviving a series of terrific thunderstorms on the south-west ridge of the Schreckhorn. In general, it is no good sign when the sun rises above a dense bank of cloud. Similarly, a crimson sunset with a flaming display of brilliant bars of cloud portends bad weather. Low morning cloud is not uncommon in the Alps. It is more important to decide whether the cloud is tending to rise and disperse or to spread and thicken.

Thunderstorms are not uncommon during a fine weather spell in summer, especially during the afternoon. They are local phenomena, but their effects can be disastrous during a difficult expedition. If one is on a high ridge it is better to leave it and put away all metallic gear such as axes, or at least keep them at ground level. Whoever has traversed high Alpine rock ridges may have seen the evidence of lightning strokes, here and there. There is nearly always a preliminary warning, when the ice-axes begin to hum and sizzle and one's hair stands on end. The voltage gradient can be exceedingly great on a narrow, exposed ridge, and the danger of a lightning stroke is considerable. However, the very existence of the steady discharge must minimise the actual risk to some extent. Sometimes an unusual warmth precedes the storm. Afterwards, the precipitation of snow and hail brings cold, with the added danger of an ice film on the rocks.

Any storm is likely to be followed by icy rocks, snowed-up ledges and a general blurring of landmarks. In addition to cold and fatigue the party will have to face all such additional technical difficulties during the descent. It is surprising how rapidly the bad weather which accompanies the southern *foehn* wind can alter the condition of the snow by softening it and making it liable to avalanche.

After a spell of bad weather a big peak may require several days to get into good condition for climbing. Authorities differ a great deal in their estimate, but, even in July or August, a period of two days is about the minimum for a big peak with steep slopes. In winter it will take much longer, of course. South slopes will get into condition more quickly by shedding their load of new snow in the form of avalanches. New fallen snow is composed of bulky, feathery, interlocking crystals. This soon changes, mainly under the influence of the sun, but more slowly otherwise, into more compact granular particles which are less adherent to the sub-stratum. More heat will melt some of the snow and form a wet film which slides easily, especially if it lies on slabby rocks or on ice. This must occur, particularly on any surface which exceeds forty degrees in gradient, for Alpine snow on an open slope seldom lies at a steeper angle.

This brief outline will give the climber some idea as to where to suspect avalanche conditions in summer. It is obvious that northern slopes will be dangerous for a longer period after bad weather than southern ones. Small rock peaks and easy passes get into condition very quickly. Avalanches are more likely on convex than on concave slopes. This chapter does not profess to concern itself with conditions in winter or spring when the avalanche danger is far greater. In summer there is hardly any danger from avalanches of dry, powder snow, or from wind slab, the latter being an exceedingly dangerous type. Dry powder is occasionally encountered, even in summer, but never in any quantity or depth. The only remedy is to cut steps in the underlying surface if the latter is icy.

A party of two coming down from a remote, high hut after a spell of bad weather and new snow, would do well to employ Mummery's double-rope technique as a precaution against snow-covered crevasses. These are much more difficult to detect under a covering of brilliant new snow. Home-trained mountaineers should be especially careful on any steep snow.

(10) RECONNAISSANCE, ROUTE SELECTION

It is always desirable to have a general idea of the topography of the district. This may be got from map and guide book, but should always be supplemented by a few easier expeditions. Here, again, the preliminary study of good photographs, usually plentiful in Switzerland, will help considerably. They should have for their objective the viewpoints commanding the general plan of the glaciers to be traversed on the approach to the peak which is to be climbed. Map and guide book will help to interpret the view. Try to estimate heights and distances accurately. If this has been done at home the scale and perspective will have to be readjusted for the larger features and clearer atmosphere prevailing in the Alps.

The next thing is to observe the ridge or face of the mountain when it is lighted in an oblique manner so as to throw long, glancing shadows. The location of new or old snow can be studied. It is quite possible to distinguish snow from ice on a distant slope. There is a sort of metallic gleam about the latter, something different from the uniform whiteness of snow.

Route selection must allow for the average amount of snow on the mountains as compared with other years. A snowless summer means a lot of ice high up, especially on southern faces. Much snow means easy, well closed glaciers, but difficult rock or rock and snow ridges. Ridges are preferable to faces. It is, however, very difficult to judge the true inclination of a face. Faces have a habit of being either extremely loose or extremely difficult. Ridges, unless serrated with many rock towers, are the natural highways to a summit. If a ridge has a precipitous step in it, try to find a snow way in order to gain the ridge above the difficulty. The classical generation of Alpine pioneers and guides used the glaciers, both dry and high, as the avenues to the summits. There was sound sense in their attitude, even although they evinced an unfounded prejudice against rock climbing.

When starting in darkness for a long expedition it is a great help to know the first part of the way. This should have been prospected on the foregoing evening and any steps should have been cut, wherever required. It is worth while to be able to save energy, time and worry by achieving fairly easy progress in the hours before dawn.

Assuming then that a practicable ridge has been chosen as

the main feature of the way to the summit, let us sum up the more important points in route selection.

(1) A way must be found for threading or avoiding any considerable icefall on the approach glacier. To avoid it by climbing along the rocks on either side may land one into unforeseen difficulties beyond. The guide book will usually describe the best way, but it may be difficult to find without a preliminary reconnaissance.

(2) The way through and beyond the icefall must avoid any danger from casual falls of rock or ice from lateral cliffs.

(3) The approach to the ridge must avoid snow slopes which are excessively steep near the top. They may merge into ice and involve crevasses and bergschrunds.

(4) Shattered or pinnacled rock ridges may be excessively difficult and time consuming. This cannot be estimated from a distance. What appears to be a short, vertical step on a ridge may be almost impossible, or may involve a dangerous traverse on insecure snow and shattered rock as an avoiding action.

(5) It is always more interesting to traverse a peak than to return by the same route. The easier way must be chosen for the descent and is better prospected beforehand.

(6) Keep plenty of time in hand for unforeseen difficulties, or an adverse change in the weather. It is the worst kind of folly to persevere in an expedition against your better judgment, in the face of worsening weather.

(7) Avoid descending steep snow *couloirs* unless the snow is well frozen. Avoid descending steep snow slopes which have been exposed for many hours to a hot sun—or treat them with the utmost caution.

(8) Do not look for difficulties, as on homeland mountains. The Alps are difficult enough already. Select the easiest way, once you have decided on the aspect of the mountain to be climbed.

CHAPTER XXV

ALPINE PLANNING

(1) THE LEADER

ALPINE expeditions require more planning and direction than those on British hills. The leader should be selected rather for his general capacity and experience than for any particularly brilliant climbing qualities. In the old days, when nearly all Alpine expeditions were guided, including new ascents and exploration, the capable and experienced amateur was often the genuine as well as the titular leader of the party. The leading guide was more competent in the practical details of rock, snow and ice. He had an excellent sense of weather and an unsurpassed knowledge of the mountains around his own and neighbouring valleys. But a well-travelled amateur with much experience, a trained mind and some scientific attainments was the undoubted leader on a new and unknown expedition.

That is why it is best to have a leader with previous Alpine experience, especially for the first guideless venture of a British party. It is best of all if the leader has profited from former expeditions with good guides. It is not the function of the guide to teach his client. A prospective amateur leader must have the ability to learn from a good guide, and later on from his own experience. The good guide will greatly hasten the process of learning, but he is not indispensable. An Alpine leader can be made on British mountains, only part finished if you like, if he has made use of all his opportunities and learnt all that the homeland, and especially the Scottish hills can teach him, with their diversity of rock, snow, ice or blizzard.

Even then he has a great deal to learn when he comes up against such big mountains as the Alps. With a leader of this type the first year's programme will have to be trimmed to modest dimensions in order to keep within the bounds of safety. Much more will be learned from a moderate programme, if it is well devised so as to include peaks and expeditions which are most typical of Alpine as opposed to British mountaineering, and so as to avoid all peaks of great and recognised difficulty.

If the programme centres on the big, popular peaks by the standard routes it is often possible to follow the tracks of guided parties. This takes the novelty and initiative out of the climb. Better a small guideless adventure on a lesser-known peak, involving plenty of glacier and snow work, than an unpaid-for but, in a way, professionally assisted ascent of a mountain such as the Jungfrau, the Matterhorn or Mont Blanc. There are many excellent, severe rock climbs in the Alps, but it would seem to be a pity to go there in order to concentrate on the same sort of experience as one can enjoy at home. This is not a plea for avoiding either of these types of expedition. It is simply a question of gaining as much new and valuable experience as possible during a first visit to the Alps. The ultimate result may be less spectacular when afterwards recounted to an uncritical but admiring circle of friends, but much more will be gained in the long run.

Maps and guide books will assist the leader, but they require interpretation. Glaciers and icefalls have a habit of belying their description. Maps must be interpreted in the light of past experience of the upper Alpine world of snow and ice. The first expeditions should be on easy glaciers and passes. Reconnaissance will be repaid a hundred-fold before going for a difficult peak. General principles are very similar to those applicable to winter mountaineering in Scotland, but one is not seeking difficulties, of which there are already enough.

A good leader will always use his party to the best advantage, allocating to each his spell of temporary leadership where he is most competent, never at any time rushing the pace for the weakest member, but keeping a reserve of strength in the party for unforeseen contingencies. The start should be early enough to leave a considerable margin of time for unexpected delays and difficulties. It is the duty of the leader to consider beforehand the timing of the programme, so as to pass places of possible objective danger (falling stones or ice) before the sun renders them really dangerous, and to provide against such dangers during the descent. This involves careful route selection.

It may be necessary to start at an hour which seems ridiculously early in order to be able to descend by an exposed *couloir* when it is still frozen and unsunned. If this is neglected the party may have to wait for several hours and descend it very late indeed, after the period of maximum danger is past. The same rule may hold for steep snow slopes where there is avalanche danger. Finally, the leader should have a good eye for changes in the weather. Excess of caution, in this respect, is often out of place when going to an Alpine hut, and may result in the loss of a perfect day for a big ascent. Caution is, however, essential during a difficult climb. It is not the glaciers which are dangerous but the upper slopes and ridges. An amateur party must often retreat where a strong, guided party would complete the climb.

(2) HUTS AND ACCOMMODATION, FOOD

Accommodation depends on the means, tastes and toughness of the party. Swiss hotels are well run at moderate prices, if one avoids the non-climbing, luxury establishments at popular centres. In most small, high-level hotels the wants of climbers are well understood and supplied. Breakfast for a long expedition can be arranged for almost any hour, however early, although there may be a small, extra charge before six a.m. Certain things are different in Swiss hotels. Breakfast is a light meal of rolls, butter, jam and coffee. This is certainly a better plan at early hours. Food packets are usually ample and varied and can be ordered to suit requirements. It is well to examine the contents before leaving. I was once let down very badly, and the effect of a breadless packet with extra tough meat of a peculiar type and much unripe fruit was weakening on the upper rocks of the Grépon. It is worth while to be able to start directly from the hotel, after a comfortable night's rest, if at all practicable. This is only feasible with hotels close to the mountains and at least 6,000 feet above sea level.

Alpine huts vary a good deal. Very few supply meals* and offer preferential and dearer sleeping accommodation in small, individual bedrooms. Generally, all the climbers sleep on a

* In pre-war days huts in the Austrian Alps supplied food and privileged accommodation and also some French and Italian huts. In Swiss huts, except for certain privately owned hotels at high levels, sometimes situated close to the S.A.C. hut, there are only common sleeping accommodation and cooking facilities.

common wooden shelf, parallel to each other, and often very crowded. Each has a palliasse and one or two blankets. The sexes may be segregated or not, according to the size of the hut and the population. Most large huts have a caretaker during the summer season. He supplies boiling water and does simple cooking with the food provided by the climber. Wood, carried up by porters for use in the stove, is necessarily expensive, and the stove is only lit during limited periods of time—usually in the early morning and evening. If the hut is popular there is a waiting queue, and it therefore pays to arrive early.

In Switzerland the huts belong to the Swiss Alpine Club, but, in practice, they serve all travellers. The same holds good in France and other Alpine regions. If one climbs regularly in the Alps one ought to join the Club. It is a huge organisation with a very moderate annual subscription and practically no entrance qualification, especially for foreign members. Before 1939 the subscription was between £1 and £1 10s. for different sections.* Membership confers many privileges, such as reduced accommodation charges (but not for wood or service), a better guarantee of accommodation for late arrivals at the hut, corresponding privileges in the huts of other Alpine clubs (such as the French), reduced fares on several Swiss mountain railways (but not main-line railways), an insurance cover for personal accidents in the Alps, a copy of the excellent, illustrated monthly, *Die Alpen*, the right to participate in sectional Meets of the Club which offer opportunity for valuable experience and contacts and, finally, an added self-respect in making use of the huts.

The huts have transformed Alpine mountaineering. They bring long and difficult expeditions within the compass of a day's work, even for an amateur party of moderate powers of endurance. They may be crowded and uncomfortable at times, but they are a very present help in bad weather. Sometimes, expecially in some districts of the Eastern Alps, they shorten the expedition overmuch. This enables the guides to earn a living more easily from untrained, inexperienced amateurs. It is a good idea to plan an Alpine holiday so as to avoid the popular huts—those which serve the very popular peaks or lie on the routes of much frequented passes, and, in fact, those huts which

* In 1948 the S.A.C. subscription worked out at about £2 per annum.

can be too easily reached from the valleys. Many huts are attained by wonderfully engineered paths up rock faces; some involve difficult glacier ascents and the negotiation of icefalls. These are less likely to be crowded. All are clearly indicated on the excellent Swiss maps.

Free spirits and tough bodies may prefer a high camp or a bivouac. This can be very delightful in the Alps, but it means a heavy porterage and a limitation on the mobility of the party. It is not advisable to camp above the tree line if the camp is to be occupied for more than a night or two. The tree line in the Alps may run to 6,000 feet and over in certain valleys. For a long and difficult expedition a bivouac would require to be a great deal higher, probably on the cheerless and stony moraine of a glacier.

Such an experience is worth having. The solemn grandeur of the night on the upper glaciers or on a rocky platform on a mountain ridge leaves an imperishable memory. The cold and stiffness of the windy dawn are soon forgotten. One becomes a real explorer, independent of huts and their nondescript human associations.

High camping is simpler in the Alps than in Scotland. The chance of rain is very much less, although the cold may be considerably more. There is less wind on the Alps than on our own mountains, but lower night temperatures make protection against wind a primary requirement for a good bivouac. If no tent is carried, light-weight, wind-proof sacks are extremely useful, as well as portable. A sack to hold two people is often a good idea. It may not ensure complete comfort during a night passed on an exposed ledge high up on a mountain, but it is a life preserver and usually much more than that. I can testify to its value on more than one occasion; never during bad weather but only under normal conditions of night frost with a light breeze blowing. When two are in a sack, each warms the other. Boots must be removed and the feet encased in layers of socks and stuffed into the rucksack. Boots should not be allowed to freeze, or it may be very difficult to put them on in the morning.

Hot drinks, even in small quantity, can be extremely comforting. An aluminium kettle and a Meta burner are light to carry and worth their weight in gold. The exploits of Messrs

Hope and Kirkpatrick* in the Alps are of great interest as an instance of what can be done by detailed planning and experience, but individuals must plan for themselves.

They specialised in weight reduction for equipment, were twenty times benighted in fourteen seasons of Alpine climbing and arranged the most elaborate meals in exposed situations using the minimum of equipment. For a night in an Alpine hut each man carried nine pounds; for a twelve-hours' expedition from a hut only six and a half pounds. This included cooking and first-aid equipment, lantern, rucksack, crampons and other kit carried in the sack, but not ice-axe or rope. Those who are interested in mountain bivouacs should certainly read their experiences, and also those of Julius Kugy,† another Alpine veteran who lived and enjoyed the unfettered life of the mountains to the full.

It would be quite useless to give detailed advice about food and provisioning. Alpine mountaineering involves longer and harder effort, taken as a whole, than most British mountaineering. The fatigue is correspondingly greater, but a fit man recovers from it with remarkable rapidity. A good rule is to eat very little when exhausted. Diet for actual climbing should be based on bread, for hard climbing means a large output of energy and additional intake of calories. The rest of the diet has, as its main function, to contribute variety, to prevent the eliminating organs from clogging up and to enable one to take in the extra carbohydrate with comfort. Deficiencies of other foods can be made good in the valleys. Dried fruit is excellent. Less fit individuals may feel that they require more sugar in place of the starchy food which they are unable to metabolize. Guides often eat surprisingly little during an expedition.

The hard work of climbing, combined with the heat of the sun and the reflected heat from the snows, causes much perspiration with a consequent desiccation of the body. If one has not contracted the habit of continually indulging a thirst one is less likely to be troubled by it in such circumstances. It is a waste of energy to carry watery foods on long and severe expeditions where load must be reduced in the interests of speed and

---

* *Alpine Days and Nights*, W. T. Kirkpatrick (Allen & Unwin).
† *Alpine Pilgrimage*, Julius Kugy (John Murray, 1934).

endurance. Sucking snow is not a good practice. Thirst is best controlled by avoiding foods which encourage it, moving at such a pace as will allow of breathing through the nose and not talking too much during the ascent.

(3) CLIMBING PROGRAMME

An Alpine holiday can be planned on two different lines. The first is to work from a good centre which is used as a permanent base for ascending the neighbouring peaks, never remaining away from the base for more than one or two nights at a time. This is a good plan and will usually give the best experience-value for a first visit to the Alps by a guideless party. They will have a chance to become really familiar with certain peaks and glaciers. Thus, a great deal more can be learned of the structure of these mountains and glaciers, and failures can be turned into successes by repeated attempts and reconnaissance. The centre should be fairly high, over 5,000 feet at least, and not too popular. One or two neighbouring huts are an advantage. If possible, there should be a choice of both snow and rock peaks of varying degrees of height and difficulty. Many such centres are available.

The other plan is to travel light, arranging to make a descent into a valley every four or five days for re-provisioning and an off-day. Between the descents the plan is to cross high-level passes, living at huts and collecting peaks between the huts. Thus, one can get a fair acquaintance with the topography of a whole range. This method is suited for a party which has already gained a reasonable degree of experience during pre-vious holidays when working from a centre. Of course, by restricting the climbing to easy passes, an untried party can tour the Alps in this way with enormous pleasure and satisfaction, but they are unlikely to gain so much technical experience.

Of course, the two methods can be combined. The best thing to do is to read some of the Alpine classics, relating to the days when the old pioneers had plenty of leisure to wander from one valley to another, especially Sir W. Martin Conway's *The Alps from End to End*, a delightful book which would entice any genuine mountaineer to follow the author's example. Among the best districts for this sort of pilgrimage, best supplied with

huts and passes, are the Bernese Oberland and the Central
Pennine Alps between Zermatt and Chamonix. Less well-known,
but equally interesting, are the more easterly groups between
the Oberland and the Bernina.

One of the charms and advantages of foreign mountain travel
is the opportunity of making contacts and friendships with other
climbers. Many of them speak English, but it is most useful to
know some German or French or both. When there are only a
few people in a hut they quickly become friendly. Guides, too,
can be most friendly to a competent amateur party, and many
guides do not speak English. The amateurs should try to bridge
the gap. Remember that the guide is in his own country and
you are the foreigner. It is but common courtesy to try and
understand them in their own tongue. Friendly conversation
with Swiss climbers and guides has often furnished me with
valuable hints and information about routes and mountains, but
there is a way of doing these things whilst preserving courtesy
and mutual respect.

(4) SUBSIDIARY INTERESTS

Many of the great Alpine explorers were scientists whose writ-
ings reflected many more observations and thoughtful comments
than were concerned with the actual business of climbing and
route finding. The true mountaineer should not neglect the
many interesting features of Alpine pastures, forests and valleys,
their flora and fauna and the pastoral life of the people.
Climbing can be much more interesting if one has some knowledge of topography, geology and the history of valleys and
passes. This study is closely related to the character of Alpine
scenery both below and above the snow line. As in other
mountain lands one may profitably forsake the high peaks upon
occasion, in order to visit the grand scenic features, deep gorges,
lakes and rivers of the valleys.

The botanist and lover of flowers will spend many, happy
off-days on the Alpine meadows, especially in early summer
when the variety and brilliance of the flowers are more striking
than in the later months. Even amongst the rocks and on the
glacier moraines the eye is delighted by small, brilliant-hued
flowers. Their season is very short, but the sun is so powerful

that they make up for the brevity of life by a supreme burst of gaiety and beauty. After many hours, or even days, above the snow line, in the white glare of the sun reflected back from the upper snowfields, it is a great joy to get off the glacier, remove one's snow glasses and catch sight of a cluster of deep blue gentians between the boulders on the moraine.

Alpine birds and animals are also of great interest. It is a revelation to see a small herd of *chamois* scampering up the steep rocks above a glacier. I have seen a female, followed by a kid, making an apparently effortless ascent of the steep cliff of the Évêque above the Arolla glacier, a face which is generally reckoned to be unclimbable. They have very small feet and are much more sure-footed than the Scottish red deer who seldom venture on to such difficult ground. On the borders of the glacier are these delightful small animals, the marmots, with their whistling cries. They are often heard but seldom seen. Even on the highest summits the lunch-hour of the climber is often shared by the choughs, although it is hard to imagine that they can subsist on the leavings of the mountaineer.

Most mountaineers nowadays are photographers. It is far easier to take good pictures in the Alps than on our British hills with their variable weather, with little sunshine, or in the anticyclonic summer weather with persistent heat haze. The sharp and rugged outlines of the Alps lend themselves to making striking pictures. In good weather the exposure varies very little from one day to another. One must, of course, have an eye for the composition of a picture. A few guiding principles should be kept in mind.

Avoid flat lighting and aim for shadows on the peaks. Choose a view-point about middle height between peak and valley, wherever possible. Select a good foreground. This may be difficult, and one may have to devote an off-day for this purpose alone. There are good foregrounds for most peaks, as is shown by the excellence of Swiss photography. Good shadows are particularly necessary for all photographs above the snow line. In such circumstances the intensity of the light is so great that photo-electric exposure meters are not a reliable guide, but meter readings for exposure ought to be reduced twice or four times. Owing to the good lighting and clear atmosphere one may achieve excellent definition in distant views, even with a miniature camera. It is seldom necessary to use an aperture much larger than f/6·3. Panoramas from a mountain summit are more difficult. They must be taken very early in the morning. Good weather haze develops quickly after sunrise.

The subject of exposure meters and colour filters is too complex and technical to discuss in this place. To get good results above the snow line it is certainly advisable to use a filter to screen out the excess of ultra-violet radiation. Colour filters help to record cloud effects. Colour film presents fewer advantages over monochrome in the upper world of the everlasting snows than it does in the valleys. The great thing is to capture the wonderful sheen and the delicate half shadows on the snow and ice in the foreground. This demands a careful study of lighting conditions and the lens must often be shaded.

PART V

ALPINE EXPEDITIONS

NOTE

It is hardly possible to arrange the chapters on Alpine Expeditions in exact order of increasing difficulty or magnitude whilst, at the same time, grouping them according to districts. More detailed accounts of the ascent of several greater mountains have, therefore, been relegated to separate chapters (4, 30, 31, 32). The easier expeditions are mostly described in Chapters 26-28, but it must not be imagined that only these districts are suited to a first season's work by British-trained mountaineers. In general, this is not true for Zermatt, although it is largely so for Bel Alp, Saas Fee and Arolla. It is not true for the Chamonix area, in general.

There are many other districts admirably suited to this purpose. The author started in the Hohe Tauern group in Tyrol, but the Swiss Alps are nearer and, on the whole, offer more variety. Among such districts may be mentioned the Lötschenthal, the peaks above the Maderanerthal culminating in the Tödi, the region between Steingletscher and the Furka and the easier peaks of the Bernina.

From personal experience in the summer of 1949 the author was particularly impressed by the region between Stein and the Furka, with a centre at Göschener Alp, reached by track in 3 hours from Göschenen on the St. Gotthard railway. The Dammagletscher hotel, at 5,700 feet is excellent. Both snow and rock peaks are accessible from radiating valleys, with several convenient huts for the longer expeditions, none of the peaks exceeding 12,000 feet in height. The district is not well-known, but there are climbs of all degrees of difficulty. Although the glaciers are not very extensive, some are exceedingly steep and riven. Practicable passes on all sides can be used as avenues to the peaks or to the neighbouring valleys.

Most interesting rock climbs are those of the Salbitschyn (some exceedingly long and difficult routes on excellent rock), the Hinter Feldschyn, the Blauberg group and the south ridge of the Gletschhorn (from the Furka side). The Sustenhorn is an attractive but not difficult snow mountain. The main peak of the district, the Dammastock, is a more serious expedition by its east face, and more easily climbed from the Rhonefirn on the western, or opposite side from Göschener Alp. There are many peaks on the chain of the Dammastock, which is part of the main water-shed of Europe, separating its eastern glaciers which feed the Reuss (and ultimately the Rhine) from those to the west which are the ultimate source of the Rhone. Somewhat to the south, in the same line, is the graceful Galenstock, a shapely peak of snow and rock.

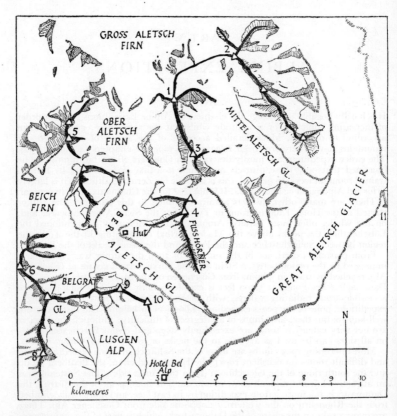

MAP F   BEL ALP AND ALETSCHHORN

height in feet

1	Aletschhorn	13,720
2	Dreieckhorn	12,540
3	Geisshorn	12,290
4	Gross Fusshorn	11,900
5	Schienhorn	12,490
6	Nesthorn	12,530
7	Unterbächhorn	11,730
8	Gisighorn	10,440
9	Hohstock	10,420
10	Sparrhorn	9,930
11	Eggishorn	9,630

CHAPTER XXVI

EXPEDITIONS FROM BEL ALP

Location and Access. Paris–Simplon express to Brig, the last station in Switzerland before the Simplon tunnel to Italy. Take the auto-bus from the station yard to Blatten (terminus), which is about 4,500 feet above sea level (Brig is only about 2,200 feet). Bel Alp hotel is high above Blatten, at over 7,000 feet, but the path is good and the ascent should take only two hours or so. Luggage can be taken up on the post mule.

NEXT to the Arolla district I should select Bel Alp as an excellent place for a first season in the Alps. It is always a grand place to spend the first few days of an Alpine holiday, with a good selection of easier mountains for training purposes. Acclimatisation proceeds very satisfactorily at such an altitude.

Bel Alp occupies an excellent strategic position. To the south one has an unobstructed view of all the major peaks of the Pennine Alps from Monte Leone above the Simplon Pass westward to the Fletschhorn above Saas Fee, the giants of the Mischabelhörner, the Matterhorn, Weisshorn and Dent Blanche. From the northern windows of the hotel one looks straight up the Gross Aletsch glacier, the longest in the Alps, on the left side of which are the Fusshörner, a range of rocky pinnacles which afford very good climbing. Still more to the left, sweeping right round to the west, is a horseshoe ridge of lesser peaks, the Belgrat, walling in the grassy pastures of the Bel Alp between north-east and west. Most of the giants of the Bernese Oberland are too far away, but the Nesthorn and the Aletschhorn are accessible if one spends a night at the Ober Aletsch Hut, less than three hours away. There is, therefore, a good variety of both rock and snow peaks, with a preponderance of rock climbing for those who prefer it.

If, at a later stage of the holiday, more snow climbing is wanted on big peaks there are several alternatives. One may follow the Aletsch glacier to the Konkordia Hut and use this as a base for such bigger game as the Jungfrau, Mönch, Gross Grünhorn or Finsteraarhorn. Alternatively, one may follow the Ober Aletsch to the Beich Pass and enjoy some good climbing from the Lötschenthal, which has good peaks on both sides. Finally, it is very easy to descend to Brig and take train for Zermatt or train and bus to Saas Fée. This is usually a better plan than to start off on the big peaks of Zermatt or the Oberland right away. The Bel Alp district is perfectly suited for an initiation to guideless climbing. The snowfields beneath the Belgrat are small, and the Ober Aletsch glacier is easy. The great Aletsch glacier is about 1,000 feet below the hotel, but it does afford excellent practice in negotiating the lower part of a huge Alpine glacier.

Easier peaks for training expeditions are available on the Belgrat horse-shoe, of which the nearest to the hotel, the Sparrhorn (9,930 ft.), involves no rock climbing and can be done inside three hours, up and down. From this a narrow, but not difficult rock ridge runs northward to the Hohstock* (10,417 ft.). This is good, pleasant climbing and the subsequent descent to the next col is a little awkward. If there is still time one may continue over one or two more high points on the ridge and descend by means of a southern spur and a small snowfield.

At the other end of the horseshoe is the Gisighorn (10,440 ft.), which Professor Turnbull and I selected for our first expedition in 1936. We left Bel Alp at 9.40 a.m., ascending by the Tyndall monument, a most useful landmark for the descent from any of these small peaks and 600 feet above the hotel. We then contoured in a great arc to the col just west of the Gisighorn. This gave us a wonderful view across the wild recesses of the Gredetsch valley to a range of rocky pinnacles which separate it from the Baltschieder valley, at the head of which stands the Bietschhorn, one of the most shapely rock peaks of the Alps. We then enjoyed an entertaining ridge climb, with one short, difficult descent, where roping down may be necessary for a few feet at one place, and reached the summit in less than three hours. The view was grand, especially of the Bietschhorn to the west and the Nesthorn to the north. The descent by the easy east ridge, got us back to Bel Alp inside two hours.

* This is point 3175M, named Hohstock on the old map and in *Ball's Alpine Guide*. In the *S.A.C. Guide* the name is applied to point 3228M on the new map, a good deal farther along the ridge to the west. This involves a good deal of rock work of varying difficulty and several traverses.

On another occasion I visited this peak after three days of new snow, when we were fully occupied for several hours in making the easiest ascent by this same ridge. Those who move very fast on rock can tackle the much more difficult and narrow northern ridge from the Gisig Pass. This pass is normally used as an easy way to the head of the Gredetsch valley which lies beneath the precipitous southern face of the Nesthorn.

Turnbull and I started on a depressing morning of cloud and rain for the Unterbächhorn (11,730 ft.), the highest peak and hub of the Belgrat, from which a difficult, long and narrow ridge runs north-westward to the Nesthorn. Owing to the mist we could not be sure of our location until we reached the main ridge. Looking across it we saw, during a clearing, the crevassed little glacier which descends from the Unterbächhorn to the Ober Aletsch glacier. Turning leftwards along the ridge we were soon progressing up a beautifully corniced section to a subsidiary summit. We also found that we could have reached the ridge much more easily and much nearer our objective by using a straightforward snow route up the easy Unterbächhorn glacier, but that was always available for the descent.

It was good fun, however, to traverse the narrow, splintered ridge until we were faced by a tower of red rock. After this we had to traverse on the north-east side and regain the crest by a loose snow gully and a small, shaly chimney. The summit ridge of the peak is engagingly narrow and shattered, but the fragmentary views of the surrounding peaks, seen through the surges of cloud and backed by openings of blue sky and sunshine, were truly magnificent. On the descent one hour's exertions saw us off the rocks and on the upper glacier. This snow-covered glacier is not always to be taken for granted as being free from crevasses; I found quite a network of them during a subsequent visit. On the former occasion, however, there was no trouble and we enjoyed a 2,500-foot glissade, almost all the way to the upper meadows. In misty weather one should remember that the head of this glacier is rather confusing, as there are several rocky spurs in the neighbourhood, all of which are not practicable ways to the Unterbächhorn, which is close to a meeting place of several narrow, steep ridges. In good weather the expedition is not difficult.

Y

THE FUSSHÖRNER

Within easy reach of Bel Alp there is yet another fine range of rock peaks, the Fusshörner. Looking north from the hotel, and at a distance of about two miles, a subsidiary glacier, the Ober Aletsch, pours into the main Aletsch glacier from the left. The Fusshörner lie in the angle of the fork of the two glaciers. The range consists of thirteen rocky peaks in a line, several of them mere needles of rock, with the highest and easiest summit at the far end and the most attractive ones about the middle. As seen from the Unterbächhorn, No. 11 stands up like a thin finger of vertical rock. It is, however, not very difficult, as it has considerable length in the line of sight. We spent a fairly easy day on it in 1939.

Professor Turnbull and I, during our 1936 visit, had only the 1931 edition of the Swiss Alpine Club guide book for perusal, and we discovered that Fusshorn No. 8 had not yet been climbed, although the gaps on either side had both been reached. Here was our chance! We left about eight a.m., taking no ice axes but only 150 feet of Alpine line. More than an hour along the path brought us to the verge of the Ober Aletsch glacier, which we crossed without much trouble. By ascending the grassy alp towards the base of the rocks leading to the twelfth peak (near the southern end) we gained an excellent series of terraces, which were indicated to us by the movements of a chamois above us.

The terraces curved upwards along the slope, leading us into the great amphitheatre at the top of which were the peaks numbered from 7 to 11. There was one difficulty to men without axes, the crossing of two steep snow gullies, but after this we lunched comfortably in the warm sun, within reach of a stream of ice-cold water. A series of rock ribs offered rapid progress and led us to the base of a black, inverted triangle of cliff, just below the gap between numbers 8 and 9. There we roped up for the final climb.

The first pitch was a difficult chimney of eighty feet, followed by a delicate traverse to a wide ledge on the left. Easy rocks enabled us to reach a chimney below the gap in the main ridge. This steep chimney led to the notch, which was a hollow filled with huge boulders. From a little pinnacle on the south side the way seemed to be fairly easy to the top of No. 9 Fusshorn. Our problem was more difficult and involved two short, consecutive hand-traverses with only the merest foot-scrapes on the smooth rock wall. Neither was much more than ten feet long. The rest of the job was fairly easy and we were seated on the summit of No. 8 at 3.15 p.m. In the bright sunshine the shadows of the rock peaks lay clean-cut on the eastern snowfield, so that, by counting from the thin, needle-like shadow of No. 11, we had ocular demonstration that we were really perched on top of No. 8.

Our triumph had been too easily won. There must be something wrong somewhere. It seemed incredible that we were the first, even although it was only a minor rock peak. Also, there were one or two stones lying against each other at a curiously artificial angle. In the direction of No. 7 peak no descent appeared to be feasible. So we settled down to enjoy the warm sun and to take stock of our surroundings. To the east were the shapely summits of the Schreckhorn and the Finsteraarhorn, to the west the Nesthorn which we intended to climb and, of course, the complete panorama of the great peaks of the Pennines to the south. Then we descended as we had come. Except for the upper section, which exacted great care, the descent was both rapid and easy.

When we got back to Bel Alp we were received with respect as proved and considerable mountaineers. A Swiss lady, with whom we had become friendly, had discovered us with the telescope when we were sitting on the summit, and our descent was observed with great interest by many others, particularly at the stage when the Professor appeared to be hanging by his hands without any footholds at all! So we were only doing what was expected of us when we departed next day with the intention of climbing the big peak of the district, the Aletschhorn. No one expected that we should require the services of guides, even for such an expedition!*

I did not solve the mystery of No. 8 Fusshorn until I returned to Scotland. A recent number of *Die Alpen*, the periodical of the Swiss Alpine Club, recorded the ascent of No. 8, the last of the Fusshörner to be climbed, but it also described how the entire

---

* Described in the Introductory section of this book, as a typical Alpine ascent.

range of thirteen peaks had been traversed within twenty-four hours, a challenge put forward by Bel Alp to all British climbers who make exceptionally rapid traverses of the main Cuillin Ridge of Skye.

THE NESTHORN

I shall conclude this chapter with a brief account of the last ascent made by Professor Turnbull and myself in 1936. After an interval of bad weather we had only one day available before our return, and we went to the Ober Aletsch Hut, with the intention of climbing the Nesthorn (12,530 ft.) and catching the westbound train out of Brig on the same evening. We rose early and got away at 2.30 a.m. Our progress along the Beich glacier was fairly rapid although it was not very well frozen. It was a mild, calm night with a last quarter moon sailing along through a dappled sky of cirro-cumulus cloud. There was no difficulty at all until we reached the foot of the slopes running steeply upwards to the Gredetschjoch at the foot of the west ridge of our mountain. This first part is the same route as that which continues westwards across the Beich pass to the Lötschental.

We now put on our crampons and climbed the steep slope to the left of the left-hand rock island, close under the wall of our peak. This was a straightforward piece of dogged and unspectacular climbing, as it was perfectly easy to avoid the crevasses by keeping to long lanes of unbroken snow. At 6.30 a.m. we were on the Joch (11,560 ft.). After a short halt for food we moved on over a subsidiary hump of snow and up the west ridge. Crampons were very useful at the steep part where the surface was extremely hard, but the ascent could be made quite easily in nailed boots, although a certain amount of step-cutting would be necessary. At no point did we encounter genuine, brittle ice. We reached the main summit, without any other halt, at 7.45 a.m.

I had never before been on an Alpine summit at such an early hour, although it must be a common enough experience for guided parties, as the guides have no time to waste and have other clients to consider when they return to the valley. To the east was a sea of cloud with isolated peaks protruding from it and fading away into the far distance, but bad weather was

spreading over the chain of Mont Blanc in the west. At our feet lay the Rhone valley. We looked down through 10,000 feet to the little town of Brig and the entrance to the Simplon tunnel. I should have wished to have made an interesting traverse over the Nesthorn, returning by the south-east ridge to the Unterbächhorn and Bel Alp, but it is a long and difficult ridge, involving the passage of many difficult rocky towers, and vividly described by Mr G. W. Young in his book, *On High Hills*. That may still be possible, but would be better done in the ascending direction.

We had far to go before evening, so we cut our stay short and proceeded to descend as we had come. The ridge was in good condition but the slopes below the *joch* were already abominably soft wherever the sun had reached them, and the snow kept on balling on our crampons. The Beich glacier was suffused with a sultry heat and covered with long stretches of slush; but we plodded onwards with a semi-conscious rhythm, knowing that the best of the day and the whole of the holiday were now over, but that nothing had been wasted at the finish. We were speeding down the Rhone valley that evening.

NOTE.—The Ober Aletsch Hut is a good centre for many climbs, e.g. the Gross Fusshorn (11,900 ft. but, no glacier work, to the east, above the hut), Aletschhorn (described in introductory section), Schienhorn (12,490 ft. from the glacier south of the peak), and the Loetschenthaler Breithorn (12,410 ft.) (using the route for the Nesthorn to the upper snowfield with an easy continuation over snowfields to the foot of the peak).

CHAPTER XXVII

EXPEDITIONS FROM AROLLA

Location and Access. Arolla is situated in the heart of the Pennine Alps of the Canton of Valais. One goes by Paris–Simplon express to Sion, in the Rhone valley, the principal town of the Canton, and then by auto-bus up the tributary Val d'Hérens to Evolena or Haudères. Here the valley forks and only a mule path is available for the last five miles and 1,500 feet of ascent to Arolla which, with several excellent hotels, lies at 6,400 feet above sea level.

AROLLA is both an excellent and a delightful place for guideless climbing on snow and rock peaks. There is plenty of accommodation yet not enough to make of it a fashionable resort like Zermatt, Grindelwald or Chamonix. It is not above the tree line, so that very pleasant off-days can be spent in the woods, by the Lac Bleu de Lucel or on the flowery meadows above the forest. The Arolla glacier is not far away and is very easy for practice, and there are other steeper glaciers within easy range. There are easy rock peaks for training purposes and a selection of more difficult ones involving both rock and snow, yet not so high or remote as to necessitate spending a night at a high hut. This is an enormous advantage, as one can start direct from the hotel whenever the conditions are favourable. Moreover, the standard of climbing can be raised as the holiday proceeds so as to finish with one or two big peaks in the neighbouring valleys; either by crossing a pass to the west to the Val de Bagnes and the Grand Combin, or to the east for the Dent Blanche and to Zermatt with its galaxy of high and difficult peaks. What more can a mountaineer wish for? I have visited Arolla twice and could choose no better place for resuming Alpine mountaineering after the lapse of the war years.

For the local expeditions there is no better guide than a little book, now alas! out of print, by Walter Larden, entitled *Walks and Climbs at Arolla.* Here it will suffice to describe one or two typical expeditions of diverse types.

In 1926 we were a party of five, and our first day was spent on the Petite Dent de Veisivi (10,470 ft.), a delightful rock peak at the northern end of the range which bounds the east side of the Arolla valley. We started at five a.m.; descending the valley to the hamlet of Satarma we crossed the river and mounted the opposite slopes by a beautiful path through thickets of young trees, Alpine roses, junipers and other shrubs and flowers. Soon we were ascending the open slopes of the grassy alp, a longish ascent before we reached the western foot of our ridge. The rock was excellent throughout. We were somewhat delayed by two descending parties, for the latter are accorded priority when there is only room for one-way traffic. Just after noon we reached the summit where a wonderful view opened out to the east, across the deep valley of Ferpècle to the tremendous western face of the Dent Blanche.

We now commenced the traverse of the narrow ridge to the south-east towards the Col de Zarmine. It is possible and very sporting to traverse all the pinnacles, but the most difficult can be circumvented by a narrow tunnel on the eastern side. It is not a long rock climb, but very delightful. The descent from the col is easy, but may involve a short snow slope. When we got back to the valley the river was milky white and swollen into a foaming torrent. This always happens in the Alps, owing to the rapid melting of the glaciers in hot weather. There are other peaks on this eastern rim of the Arolla valley, all higher than the Petite Dent but not at all difficult. The Grande Dent is easy and the Dent Perroc somewhat harder but on good rock. High above Arolla is the fascinating rock pinnacle, L'Aiguille de la Tsa (12,050 ft.), standing at the head of its own small glacier. The easy route of ascent is from the Bertol Hut, by the snow-fields on the eastern side, but the best way is straight up the steep rocks of the Arolla face. Not much loose rock will be met if the correct route is taken, but it is not an easy climb.

The best and longest of the Arolla rock climbs is the complete traverse of the Aiguilles Rouges, a high ridge of three peaks and many pinnacles on the west side of the valley. Sometimes the north peak is left out, but it is a good place to gain the ridge and might as well be included. The start from Arolla should be no later than three a.m. as the southern peak is a regular hedgehog of a ridge, bristling with *gendarmes*. In 1926 a sudden onset of bad weather drove us back when we had only reached the lower Glacier des Ignes, but in 1928 three of us at least succeeded in

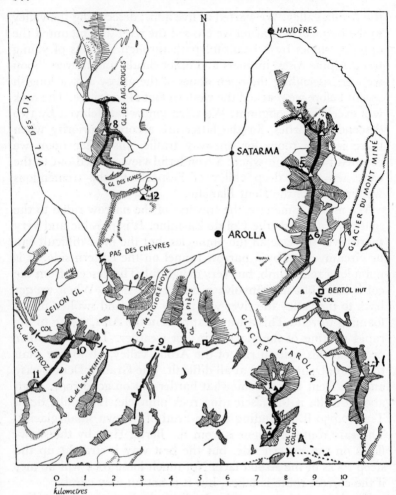

kilometres

MAP G   AROLLA DISTRICT

PEAKS   height in feet

1	Mont Collon	11,960
2	Évêque	12,270
3	Petite Dent de Veisivi	10,470
4	Grande Dent de Veisivi	11,250
5	Dent Perroc	12,070
6	Aiguille de la Tsa	12,050
7	Dents des Bouquetins	12,620
8	Aiguilles Rouges	11,980
9	Pigne d'Arolla	12,470
10	Mont Blanc de Seilon	12,700
11	Ruinette	12,730
12	La Roussette	10,710

climbing the northern and central or main peak (11,980 ft.) before we were compelled to retreat during a violent thunderstorm. A lofty rock ridge is not the best place to occupy when there is thunder about, the ice-axes sizzling with the electric discharge and one's hair standing on end.

The way is not difficult to find. A good path leads upwards by the Praz Gras Chalets, ascending to the lower end of the Glacier des Ignes. Keep to the right of this for the north peak. The ridge is easily accessible by the col to the north of this point. The ascent of the centre peak is steep and straightforward. It is the pinnacled crest of the South Peak that takes up most of the time and furnishes the best sport. Accidents have occurred more than once to parties who have endeavoured to descend directly from the South Peak by the steep *couloirs* to the Glacier des Ignes. The rocks are loose and dangerous. By continuing southward along the ridge a safe descent can be effected. It is better to verify this route beforehand.

In 1926 we enjoyed one excellent rock climb which involved a good deal of work on snow and ice as well. This was the south ridge of the Évêque (12,270 ft.), the higher peak which lies behind the Mont Collon. At first we had a long walk up the Arolla glacier to its head at the Col de Collon. There we dumped some of our surplus kit on the moraine of the glacier, as we intended to return that way and later proceed over a pass to a hut on the Italian side of the Dent d'Hérens. One of our party remained behind to guard the baggage.

1926 was a snowy year and the face of the Évêque, as seen from the level pass to the south, had a good deal of snow and ice on it. Walter Roberts, our leader, with much previous Alpine experience, considered that it was quite practicable and detailed me to lead. The lower section gave me a good deal of work with the axe, but there was no difficulty in selecting a route, to any one who had experience on Ben Nevis in snowy conditions. At first we trended leftwards across the face and then worked upwards to the right until we struck the south ridge. This gave us an interesting and difficult rock climb, over a narrowing ridge straight up to the summit. On some places the rock was loose and demanded a good deal of care. The summit view was magnificent, from the Grand Combin to the Dent Blanche and the Matterhorn, with a peep across the shoulder of Mont Collon to Arolla and its pine woods.

The return was more troublesome for a party of four and took a great deal of time, but gave rise to no incidents. Six hours after our departure we rejoined our friend on the moraine. He had spent a pleasant off-day in the sunshine. No one had molested him, but he had noticed a party at a considerable distance below on the Arolla glacier, who had loitered about and then retraced their steps rather hurriedly. Later, we heard the explanation. A clerical gentleman from our hotel at Arolla had taken two ladies for an excursion on the glacier. They had returned with the report that a band of smugglers was encamped on the moraine underneath the Évêque. They had heard loud voices and even seen one of the smugglers. It was safer to retreat!

The two imposing snow mountains to the south of Arolla are the Mont Collon (11,960 ft.), above the Arolla glacier, and the Pigne d'Arolla (12,470 ft.) on its right. The latter is a very easy climb from the col at the upper end of the Pièce glacier, from the left side. It is a longish day if taken direct from Arolla, but quite straightforward. In 1928 we were a lazy party at the beginning of our holiday. We ascended the moraine and the Pièce glacier in the afternoon to the little Jenkins Hut at the col. This hut is grandly situated and is also useful as a base for the easy western ascent to the Mont Collon, which can be followed by a southward descent, where there is reported to be a good deal of loose rock, in the direction of the Arolla glacier. Three of our party effected this a few days later, but I was not with them on that occasion.

We had a delightful evening at the Jenkins Hut, where we met Mr Stewart Jenkins himself with his guide. Before all other Alpine districts Mr Jenkins had a particular love of the Italian face of Mont Blanc for its sublimity, and of the Arolla district for the more pleasant and friendly aspects of the mountains. Several days later we again encountered him at the Cabane de Bertol whither he had gone to solve some new problem on the Dents des Bouquetins.

Next morning we left at five a.m. for the Pigne. We lost a little time by striking the lower icefall at the wrong place, but the ascent is fairly easy if one does not attempt a misguided short-cut. Through the thinning fog we saw the sun rise and climb the north ridge of the Dent Blanche. The upper snowfield was easy, the only crevasses being quite close to the summit, which we reached at eight a.m. After a long halt for a meal and the enjoyment of the glorious view we descended westwards to the Col de la Serpentine, for Charlie Parry and I wished to add the Mont Blanc de Seilon (12,700 ft.) to our day's bag, but Donald Mackay and Malcolm Matheson preferred to await our return.

The year 1928 was a snowless one with much ice on the ridges which were normally snow-covered. The first part of the east ridge of our peak caused us a lot of trouble with very soft snow unconsolidated to the hard ice underneath. We cut steps round the rim of a huge crevasse, the most beautiful I had ever seen, with a profusion of long, feathery ice crystals and hanging columns. Beyond was a narrow, steep slope of ice thinly veneered with slushy snow. We had promised the others to rejoin them in about two hours. In the prevailing conditions we could hardly hope to do so in four. We called it a day and retired, perhaps with less regret as we should really have preferred to make a complete traverse of this grand mountain rather than return by the same way.

The descent from the Serpentine to the Seilon glacier in the stifling heat of the early afternoon was damnable. The snow was very soft and crevasses were abundant. With four people on one rope and plenty of care there was no real danger, but, as first one and then another slipped half-way into a hole, the annoyance was uninterrupted and tempers were on edge. Such a purgatory of sweat and suspense is no uncommon feature of an Alpine expedition in hot, windless days. It makes one feel a longing for the small, cool hills of Skye with their pleasant corries and delectable bathing pools, conveniently forgetting the number of days when it rains persistently on that island!

At length we reached the level, dry glacier and had soon gained the little rocky neck of the Pas de Chèvres (9,350 ft.), by which we crossed over to the upper pastures above the Arolla valley. There we made a long halt and enjoyed a picnic tea and a bathe in a small tarn surrounded by meadows which were covered with beautiful flowers. Clad in no more than our shirts we forgot the fatigue and glare of the snowfields and whiled away two delightful hours of idleness in the warm sunshine.

During the remainder of that pleasant week at Arolla, Parry and I achieved two more difficult expeditions. The ascent of the Dent Blanche, the biggest peak of the district, is described in another chapter. We also returned to the Mont Blanc de Seilon, climbing it by a difficult rock route directly from the Seilon glacier. There is now a good hut in the Val des Dix, on the far bank of the Seilon glacier, from which the ascent of that peak can be made fairly easily by the Col de Seilon, at the head of the glacier. It is rather a long day, if taken direct from Arolla.

THE HIGH-LEVEL WAY TO ZERMATT

Many people with an extended holiday will wish to go to the bigger peaks around Zermatt. It is easy to post luggage in Switzerland, and it would be a great pity to go from Arolla to Zermatt by the circuitous and wearying descent and reascent, to and from the Rhone valley. Besides, the high-level route affords good experience of the upper glaciers and snowfields. A night is usually passed at the Cabane de Bertol (11,160 ft.), close to the *col* of that name over the ridge to the east of the Arolla glacier. In good weather the route is not difficult, although the crevasses will be much more troublesome towards the end of a hot season after a comparatively snowless winter. The way to the Bertol Hut is fairly well defined and need not be described. It should not take more than four hours to reach, only the final part being up a steep little snowfield. I was there both in 1926 and 1928, on the latter occasion before climbing the Dent Blanche.*

Our party of 1926 crossed to Zermatt with little difficulty in poor weather conditions. It was a snowy year, and bad weather had driven us back from an attempt on the Dents des Bouquetins. It was early in the day and we decided to pack up at 1.30 p.m. and cross the Col d'Hérens (11,420 ft.), in order to reach Zermatt the same evening.

Under the skilled leadership of Walter Roberts, steering by compass in a mist all the way until we reached the track along-

* See Map I, p. 380.

SOUTH RIDGE
OF THE ÉVÊQUE

AROLLA AND
MONT COLLON

side the Zmutt glacier, we saw very little of the surroundings, but kept surprisingly close to the correct route. It is a frequented route, but, owing to a continuous, gentle snowfall, only a few signs of tracks were visible at widely spaced intervals. The snow became softer and softer as we proceeded. After a long time we must have topped a gentle rise and began to descend almost imperceptibly. Soon we rose again. Then something dark loomed ahead in the mist. It was a party bound in the opposite direction, but soon we lost even their fresh tracks. After another longish interval the wind freshened up to a strong, cold breeze and we found ourselves on the Col d'Hérens.

We now descended for about 200 feet over rocks, half smothered in snow. The wind whirled the snow about us in all directions, but below the rocks we were sheltered. Then we came to the *bergschrund*, found a wide and convenient snow bridge and descended rapidly for a long way, soon halting on the slopes of the Stockje, the rocky outcrop dividing the upper end of the huge glacier of Zmutt.

There we had a meal, as we considered that the main difficulties were all behind us, although we had still far to go. Another snowstorm set about us, so that we strayed too far to the left. After the weather had partially cleared we found ourselves on easy slopes leading to the level glacier, with the descending track from the Schönbühl Hut dimly visible on the hillside above us to our left. Some distance lower we crossed the glacier in order to avoid an icefall. This was easily passed, and after about half a mile we climbed the moraine and gained the path.

It was rather tantalizing to be passing through this magnificent valley and seeing so little of our surroundings. Somewhere, high above us on the right, was the huge Tiefenmatten face of the Matterhorn, but black clouds, mist and rain enveloped us all the way. At 7.30 p.m. we consoled ourselves with a welcome supper at the Staffelalp Hotel. Then followed a two hours' tramp down to Zermatt, with much stumbling about on the narrow tracks in the darkening forest. At 10.30 p.m., thoroughly soaked, but still in good heart, we entered the cobbled street of Zermatt. The pilgrimage to the Mecca of mountaineers was accomplished.

CHAPTER XXVIII

ZERMATT AND SAAS FEE

SOONER or later every Alpine mountaineer gravitates towards Zermatt, and the older ones always return in order to view the scene of their former triumphs from such excellent and easily attained vantage points as the Riffel Alp, the Trift, the Staffel Alp or the Fluhalp. No book which ranges over Alpine climbing would be complete if it failed to include a description of the Matterhorn and some other expeditions from Zermatt. Nevertheless, Zermatt is not a good place from which to learn Alpine technique if one proposes to do without guides on the strength of previous British experience.

There are some grounds for this opinion. The Matterhorn dominates Zermatt. It is hard to resist when one knows perfectly well that the ascent by the ordinary route involves no glacier problems, that the rock climbing, although prolonged, is not very difficult and that the mountain is so popular that one can hardly lose the way—if the weather holds. The root of the matter is in these last words. The Matterhorn, perched on the main watershed of the Alps between Switzerland and Italy, seems to make its own weather, and it captures the very worst of the weather far more suddenly than any other mountain. Then it becomes transformed into a raging castle of the winds, its comparatively easy rocks sheeted with ice and snow, so that an unwary, guideless party may be hard put to it in order to escape with no worse punishment than a few frost-bitten fingers and toes.

The peaks around Zermatt which are most worth climbing are very high, and many are rather difficult and unsuited to the capabilities of a guideless party with little previous Alpine experience, especially if the party includes novices. Several of these peaks can, of course, be climbed in good conditions with a measure of safety by a party of British mountaineers in good training. The district is so popular in summer time that there will be plenty of guided parties about on the normal routes up the principal peaks, and there will often be useful tracks where route finding might otherwise be difficult. It is also true that the glaciers, though large, are not nearly so contorted and difficult as those in the region of Mont Blanc. It is comforting, sometimes, to see other parties on your mountain, but it robs a guideless party of half the experience they might gain from making an ascent which is really guideless!

No one can be expected to remain immune to the magnetism of Zermatt. The best one can do is to resist for a year or two. I started my own Alpine career with Frank Smythe in the Tyrol and still have a vivid recollection of our ascent of the Gross Venediger (12,000 ft.), on a day of frequent snowfall, cloud and wind. We did not go by the ordinary route but chose the more difficult north-west ridge. We were the only people to reach the summit on that day. On the way down by the ordinary route of ascent we came to a crevassed section of the glacier where a large, guided party from the Kursinger Hut had turned back. When we re-entered the hut no one believed that we had reached the summit. Of course, that is a special case. The Venediger was an easy, popular peak where one or two guides would conduct a party of what we should describe as hill walkers, though equipped for traversing glaciers and steep snow slopes. Even in those days, as long ago as 1922, Smythe had acquired a remarkable flair for route finding in the Alps. I myself was only deputed to take the lead for a short distance on the ridge where there were difficult rocks. So I played my part and we both shared the sense of achievement.

MONTE ROSA

My first Alpine expedition with full responsibility for a party was the traverse of the Mittaghorn and Egginer, a delightful rock ridge above Saas Fee, in 1926. A few days later two friends, J. F. A. Burt and Miss Burt, were sufficiently trusting to join me in an expedition over Monte Rosa, from Zermatt. Monte Rosa, in good conditions, is not at all difficult, despite its huge glaciers. The great scientific explorer, Professor Tyndall, once ascended it alone from the Riffelberg, with only a few sandwiches in his pocket. He was, at that time, studying the glacier systems in the neighbourhood, with which he was thoroughly familiar. Nowadays, one uses the Gornergrat railway to the second last station

Monte Rosa (from the Gornergrat)
Highest peaks separated by snow saddle are Nordend on left and Dufourspitze on right. Bétemps Hut is on rocks above glacier, at lower right corner.

at Rotenboden, high above the Gorner glacier and opposite the shapely little Riffelhorn. The way is quite easy down to the glacier and across it to the Bétemps Hut (9,190 ft.), which is perched on an island of rocks below the Monte Rosa glacier.

We made our height pretty easily on the first day by ascending the whole length of the Grenz glacier until close under the Sesia Joch on the Italian frontier. An easy snow ascent on the left brought us to the principal southern summit of Monte Rosa, the Signalkuppe (14,965 ft.), on which the Italians had built the Capanna Margherita, the highest hut in Europe. Such an expedition is worth making in good weather, if only for the magnificence of the view, especially at sunrise or sunset. There is generally a hut-keeper in summer and the place serves as a meteorological observatory. Accommodation is restricted, but few climbers remain overnight. In the evening we were quite a small party and all very good friends.

All good mountaineers go out of a hut to look at the weather before turning in. It was just before sunset, and a sea of clouds

hubel

Täschhorn
THE MISCHABEL PEAKS FROM THE EGGINERGRAT

THE OBERGABELHORN, NORTH FACE
Left to right: John Wilson and Arnot Russell

stretched below us to the east and south-east over the Italian valleys. Upon it lay a vast grey shadow. As we regarded it, the shadow of our peak continuously elongated and extended itself, clothing the valleys in darkness; although we were still in sunshine and able to admire the wonderfully pure orange to crimson hues on a bank of fleecy cloud which kept pouring, like a vast waterfall, over the snowy ridge of the Lyskamm. Far over the ridge, Mont Blanc, with its terrific Italian precipices, was still glowing in the sunlight. We appeared to be perched on a polar plateau on the roof of the world, and even the apex of the dark pyramid of the Matterhorn lay beneath us. Slowly, the sun approached the south ridge of the Dent Blanche like an immense fiery ball, rolled up the incline and gradually vanished as it came near the summit, leaving but a momentary gleam of farewell. Then the Lyskamm, Breithorn, Matterhorn and the others became purple for an instant and finally very pale and spectral.

> 'And the pale lords of sovereign height
> Watch the cold armies of the night
> Mustering their first assault'
>
> G. W. YOUNG, *On the Mountain.*

It is impossible for me to do justice to such a scene. A more spectacular sunset there might be in unsettled weather, but none more expressive of the aloof grandeur of great mountains and the relentless march of the universe.

One does not sleep well at such a great altitude. Even the hut-keeper admitted that he only stuck it for a week or two before being relieved by another man from the valley of Gressoney. I missed the sunrise, but we got away after breakfast, about 7.30 a.m. There was little if any wind, and our way lay over the lofty snowfields across the Gnifetti Col to the Zumsteinspitze, and then over another col from which we climbed by moderate snow slopes and rocks to the Grenzgipfel. From this point a short but interesting branch ridge projects westward to the Dufourspitze (15,220 ft.), the highest point of the Monte Rosa group and of Switzerland. On a subsequent occasion I gained this summit directly by the usual route from the Bétemps Hut up the Monte Rosa glacier and by the west ridge. The route is not at all difficult, although, on the latter occasion we encountered a little ice on the upper part of the ridge.

z

Our programme, however, was not yet complete. We returned to the Grenzgipfel and descended some rocks to the northward. This took a little time, as we traversed the steep, eastern face until we could regain the easier snow from underneath some projecting rocks. The route was now quite easy to the Silbersattel, the depression on the ridge leading to the Nordend which we reached in little over half an hour, although many a party has spent as long as three hours on this final stage under icy conditions.

Unfortunately, a mist was swirling about and boiling up from the Macugnaga valley, and, although still in sunshine ourselves, we could not look down the 6,000 foot eastern face of the Nordend; next to the Italian face of Mont Blanc, one of the grandest in the Alps. Many years later I spent an hour on the crest of the Monte Moro Pass, looking straight up the Macugnaga glacier at this great wall of snow, ice and rock. It seemed incredible that men should even attempt to climb it. It was the aftermath of a two days' storm and the racing clouds were playing hide and seek with the Monte Rosa summits, letting through streaks of sunlight and shadow, revealing this and concealing that, so that the effect on the beholder was much more awe-inspiring than it would have been had everything been manifest at once.

Our descent from the Nordend was uneventful. The snow was rather soft, but the Monte Rosa glacier was perfectly straightforward, even allowing us an occasional glissade. We got back to the Bétemps at 4.30 p.m. The knowledgable reader cannot fail to surmise that we must have had the benefit of existing tracks on such a long snow expedition on a popular mountain. This was so on the main glaciers, but not on the Nordend nor on the main part of the descent until we rejoined the standard route to Monte Rosa. The merit of the expedition for guideless parties is that there are no special difficulties, and that only a general experience of glaciers and mountain sense are necessary.

There are many fine mountains at Zermatt. The Breithorn is not at all difficult, nor are several mountains attainable from the Trift valley. The Findelen valley gives access to the Rimpfischhorn and the Strahlhorn, but the ascent of the former from the Saas valley will be described later.

THE ALPHUBEL PASS

One of the best ways of learning about the upper glaciers is to cross high passes from one valley to another. The passage from Arolla to Zermatt by the Col de Bertol and the Col d'Hérens has already been described. Our party of 1926, after an off-day at Zermatt, decided to make for Saas Fee by way of the Alphubeljoch, a pass at a level of about 12,500 feet over the chain of the Mischabelhörner, which bounds the Zermatt valley to the east.

We spent the night at the inn on the Obere Täschalp at about 7,270 feet and started before five a.m. next day. It was a dull, drizzly morning with the peaks swathed in a heavy layer of cloud. The first part of our route lay up a valley which looked very like a Scottish Highland glen under similar weather conditions. After an hour or two the clouds lifted as we approached the glacier, which offered hardly any difficulty, either in the matter of route finding or technique. We avoided the only icefall by keeping on the rocks above it on our left. As we approached the summit of the pass we encountered a good deal of fresh, soft snow, but we reached the top seven hours after we left the inn.

We were comparatively early, and the weather, though still overcast and misty, was no worse than that. After a halt and a consultation we decided to dump our heavy sacks and go for the summit of the Alphubel, which lay to the north of us along a snow ridge. There was only about 1,300 feet of height to be made, and the snow ridge was easy enough to begin with. Near the top, however, was a steep, icy section which demanded a lot of step-cutting, as we had no crampons. At the top we were in dense cloud, no wind and gently falling snow. The return to the pass and our rucksacks was uneventful, but the double journey took us about three hours.

One major problem remained, to find the way down the Fee glacier to the Lange Fluh, a long rocky peninsula which projects into the glacier above Saas Fee. This was by no means easy in a mist, for the upper end of the glacier was a complicated field of crevasses and *séracs*. We had to steer by compass and keep a fairly good line all the way, for our course lay down an oblique band of snow-covered glacier with a rocky escarpment on our left and a lower, crevassed section on our right.

After one false start among the upper *séracs*, from which we had to retreat and try again somewhat more to the north side, we never turned back. Now and again a thinning of the mist helped us by a glimpse of the rocks on our left, but most of the credit belongs to Walter Roberts, our leader. As we descended the glacier the mist gradually thinned out and revealed the upper end of the black rocks of the Lange Fluh, exactly what we had been steering for. The final, short descent over steep, broken ice was thus made fairly simple.

Nowadays, there is an S.A.C.* hut on the Lange Fluh, but in 1926 we had still a longish, but perfectly easy descent to make, on which we were helped by a good glissade of several hundred feet. In growing darkness we found the woodland path and were soon at the fleshpots of Saas Fee.

CLIMBING NEAR SAAS FEE

Saas Fee is a delightful Alpine centre, easily reached from Stalden on the Zermatt railway by motor bus to Saas Grund and a short ascent on foot. It lies on an extensive alp at a height of 5,900 feet, at the base of a horseshoe of high mountains. There are pleasant woodlands in the neighbourhood, and a good variety of peaks of all grades of difficulty, quite a number of which are suitable for British-trained, guideless parties at an early stage of their Alpine experience.

The easiest expedition is the traverse of the Egginergrat. This is a rock ridge, involving no glacier work, although some steep snow may be encountered below the Egginer. In 1926 I led a party over it, starting with the easy ascent from the Plattje (on the track to the Britannia Hut) to the northern summit of the Mittaghorn (10,330 ft.). From there to the Egginer (11,080 ft.), the climbing is continuously interesting, affording grand views of the precipitous walls and steep glaciers below the summits of the Dom and Täschhorn. We were thoroughly impressed with our previous day's route from the Alphubeljoch to the Lange Fluh. There was only one difficult piece of rock climbing, on the steep cliff beneath the summit of the Egginer. On the descent the object is to reach the track from the Britannia Hut with the least difficulty and enlightened commonsense. On the way back

* Swiss Alpine Club.

to Saas we were filled with admiration at the excellent construction and engineering of the track along the steep mountain face.

It is worth recalling that, on a subsequent visit in the year 1937, Percy Small and I ascended the steep, rocky wall of the Egginer, facing the Britannia Hut, and enjoyed a very hard rock climb. There is scope for some very good climbing on this face.

On the east side of the Saas valley are several excellent peaks. We opened our 1937 campaign with the Portjengrat (12,010 ft.), which involves little glacier difficulty but provides very good rock climbing. We spent a pleasant night at the inn on the Almageler alp, leaving about five a.m. next day and proceeding by a good path for most of the way to the Portje, the depression to the south of our mountain. Still more to the south is another good peak, the Sonnighorn, which can give good climbing. From the Portje we had a delightful view down the Italian valley of Antrona to the east, as the ridge is, here, part of the frontier line.

After a meal we took to the rocks and followed the ridge to the summit. The interest was sustained, but there were no passages of great difficulty. The Portjengrat was a popular peak on that fine day, and we had a number of parties in front of us. The usual way of descent follows the ridge somewhat farther in a north-westerly direction and has several difficulties, with one very steep slab in particular. I cannot speak about this, for Dr Burnett and I avoided the queue by going straight down a steep, rock rib towards the glacier. This more direct route involved us in some difficulties near the bottom, but we enjoyed our new finish, reaching the inn a little later than the others.

For the other peaks on this eastern range we used the Weissmies Hut, approached by a long, steep path from Saas Grund. Our first day took us to the Fletschhorn, which has two summits separated by a depression of about 1,100 feet. The northern summit (13,130 ft.) is named the Fletschhorn and the southern top (13,140 ft.) the Laquinhorn. Either peak is attained without much difficulty from the hut, but the traverse of both peaks makes a very good expedition.

We were rather a large party and started in doubtful weather about 6.30 a.m. The way lay across moraine and easy glacier slopes towards a point beneath the north-west ridge of the Fletschhorn. We did not cross over to this ridge but proceeded along an interesting little rock ridge which merges itself into the upper snowfield. Below this we ate our second breakfast, before splitting up into two parties. The rocks were very pleasant and Percy Small led across the upper névé and gained the ridge of our peak, not very far below the summit, which we reached at 11.45 a.m. There was a bitterly cold wind, but we sheltered in warm sunshine on some rocks on the east side and awaited the others (my sister's party led by Joseph Georges *le skieur*). They soon arrived and I consulted Joseph about our prospects for the Laquinhorn, as this was the first good day after three days of bad weather, and the sharp ridge of the next peak was encumbered by a good deal of new snow. Joseph was extremely helpful, telling us that the rocks of the Laquinhorn were not normally difficult, although the upper section might well be so, on account of ice.

His word was good enough for us, so Miss Hutson, Percy Small and I decided to tackle the ridge, leaving the others at 1.15 p.m., as they intended to return by the way they had come. The descent was easy to the Fletschjoch, involving one small but sporting bergschrund which we all jumped down in succession, after which we glissaded (roped) to the joch. The following 1,100 feet of ridge climbing were delightful and interesting. It reminded me very much of climbing the Tower Ridge of Ben Nevis in Easter conditions. On the upper section I found some difficulty with ice, here and there, but this was not continuous and the rock was very good wherever it protruded. We reached the summit of the Laquinhorn at 4.12 p.m. Our halt was a brief one, as we were in cloud and snow was falling. The continuation of the ridge to the Laquinjoch looked difficult and attractive. From other accounts I can recommend it as a very good climb, but we were now late and thought it advisable to descend by the ordinary way. Turning off down the west ridge where there were some tracks, we found everything quite easy over broken rocks and short sections of snow where we had one or two minor glissades. About two-thirds of the way down we left the ridge, descending over broken rocks and a final snow slope in very good condition for another roped glissade. After some easy glacier we regained the hut at 6.12 p.m. Miss Hutson was a very good rock climber and appreciated the variegated rock–snow–ice of the day's work. We all passed a very pleasant evening together.

Next day only Percy and I stayed on, and enjoyed two other good expeditions which cannot be detailed here. We ascended the Weissmies (13,230 ft.) by its long and narrow, north ridge. The glacier by which this ridge is gained at the Laquinjoch is quite easy, but the ridge is long, steep, difficult and narrow, the lower part being entirely on rock and the upper a narrow snow ridge, which is usually corniced on the east side. The difficult problems are, therefore, such as can be mastered on Scottish ridges in winter. The ordinary way up the Weissmies, by which we descended, has glacier difficulties only in the lower section, but none at all after the broad, upper shoulder of the mountain has been gained.

THE RIMPFISCHHORN

To conclude this brief account of climbing at Saas Fee an alternative route will be described for a return to Zermatt, again coupled with the ascent of one of the Mischabel peaks. We passed the intervening night at the Britannia Hut, easily reached by the excellent path along the flanks of the Egginer ridge. The hut was so named because the British members of the Swiss Alpine Club raised the funds for its construction. It has a commanding situation on a rocky spur at the lower end of the snowfields, at an altitude of 9,950 feet.

From the Britannia Hut there are two available passes, both leading across the range, one at each end of the Rimpfischhorn, and each leading to Zermatt by a different way. The Adler Pass lies to the south and is the higher and more difficult. The first part of the westerly descent is difficult but the remainder to the Fluhalp is straightforward. The Allalin Pass to the north is the oldest known route over the Mischabel range and is perfectly easy on the west side, joining the Alphubel Pass route lower down. One must always bear in mind that the Mischabel peaks have large glaciers and upper snowfields. In good weather the Allalin Pass is a reasonably safe expedition for a British-trained party. In bad weather the risk is much greater, but map and

The Rimpfischhorn from the west
Notched north ridge on left towards Allalin Pass   Adler Pass on the right

compass can work wonders. One must, however, be accustomed to use them, not only on British hills but also on typical large glaciers and huge fields of *névé*.

A group of us crossed the Allalin Pass (11,710 ft.) in August 1937. We left the Britannia Hut at 4.15 a.m. The way was almost entirely over snow-covered glacier which was very well-frozen. After plodding on steadily until 7.30 a.m. we halted for our second breakfast a few yards below the top of the Pass. For the latter part of our way we were on the right-hand side of the Allalin glacier,* underneath the rocks of the Allalinhorn, but not too close in. From the Pass we had the choice of two peaks, the easier Allalinhorn on our right and the much more interesting Rimpfischhorn (13,800 ft.) on the left. We chose the latter and traversed its southern snow slopes until our way converged on the usual route from Zermatt by the Findelen glacier and the Fluhalp. The final, steep rise to the summit involved some

* The approach to the Adler Pass follows this same glacier, but more to the left.

interesting climbing over rock and snow-ice, but it was not very difficult, as the conditions were good. We were on the summit before eleven a.m. There, our party broke up, several continuing their way to Zermatt by the Fluhalp while Percy Small, Hamish Hamilton and I contemplated another mode of return over the bepinnacled northern crest of the mountain.

While we were sunning ourselves in pleasant idleness a girl and a young guide, who had been on the summit before we arrived, passed us, making for the north ridge, as if they meant to shame us into action. With great skill and celerity they passed one tower after another and soon disappeared from view. We roused ourselves and followed.

The Nordgrat of the Rimpfischhorn justified its reputation, affording us a long, interesting climb on excellent rock. Only at a few places were we obliged to move singly. The weather, meanwhile, deteriorated rapidly. Before we reached the largest tower, snow was falling. On three occasions my ice-axe sizzled and hummed with the electric tension. We passed the tower by an easy traverse, low down on the east side. This involved us in a short, dangerous passage under a cornice, where we raced across unroped.

At last, surrounded by swirling mist, we came to the end of the rocks and descended easily to the Allalin Pass, from which we ploughed our way laboriously through the softened snow to the Britannia Hut, discovering many more crevasses on our return than we had ever suspected in the early morning.

CHAPTER XXIX

THE ROCK NEEDLES OF CHAMONIX

APART from its distinction as the most convenient base for the ascent of Mont Blanc (15,780 ft.), the highest mountain of the Alps and of Europe (if Caucasian peaks are excepted, as being located in Asia Minor), the Chamonix district is a paradise for the rock climber. Most of the rock peaks, however, involve some snow and ice work as well. They are approached by glaciers which, though often small in volume, are exceedingly steep, riven and contorted. In some cases the snow and ice difficulties constitute the major obstacles and dangers. The Chamonix district cannot, therefore, be recommended to newcomers to the Alps, however much British experience they may have behind them. They should first learn about the ways of glaciers, icefalls, ice-slopes and couloirs in less difficult and complex surroundings.

The usual way up Mont Blanc, by the Grands Mulets is entirely a snow route, very long and fatiguing but not normally difficult, if conditions are good and the weather fine. There are many other ways to the top of this noble mountain, the longest and hardest being by the precipitous Italian face to the south, above the Val Veni and Courmayeur. This is the grandest mountain face in all the Alps, with terrific ridges and precipices and with steep and riven glaciers.

To the east of Mont Blanc is the great basin of the Mer de Glace, surrounded by the Chamonix Aiguilles, fantastic pinnacles of rock, several of which are very considerable mountains in their own right. For instance, the eastern range of peaks above the Mer de Glace, separating it from the glacier of Argentière, is dominated by the Aiguille Verte (13,550 ft.), which was originally climbed from the Mer de Glace by a long and difficult route, entirely over snow and ice. An alternative ridge route does involve rock climbing, but the main problems are still centred on snow and ice. From the eastern, or Argentière direction, the ascent of the Verte is an incredibly long and formidable expedition, entirely over snow and ice. Beyond the

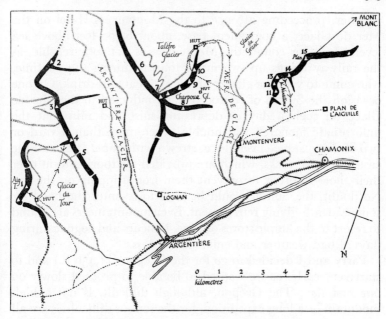

MAP H   THE AIGUILLES OF CHAMONIX

	PEAKS							height in feet
1	Aiguille du Tour .	.	.	.	.	.	.	11,620
2	Tour Noir .	.	.	.	.	.	.	12,590
3	Aiguille d'Argentière	.	.	.	.	.	.	12,820
4	Aiguille du Chardonnet	.	.	.	.	.	.	12,540
5	Aiguille Adams-Reilly (with col, north of it)	.	.	.	.			—
6	Les Droites .	.	.	.	.	.	.	13,220
7	Aiguille Verte	.	.	.	.	.	.	13,550
8	Aiguille du Dru	.	.	.	.	.	.	12,320
9	La Nonne .	.	.	.	.	.	.	10,960
10	Aiguille du Moine	.	.	.	.	.	.	11,200
11	Petits Charmoz .	.	.	.	.	.	.	9,410
12	Grands Charmoz	.	.	.	.	.	.	11,290
13	Le Grépon .	.	.	.	.	.	.	11,450
14	Aiguille de Blaitière	.	.	.	.	.	.	11,550
15	Aiguille du Plan .	.	.	.	.	.	.	12,050

Argentière glacier are many more rock peaks, gradually diminishing in height across the Swiss frontier towards the Pass of the Great St. Bernard.

THE GRÉPON

In the summer of 1929 I was able to spend only five days in the Alps. C. W. Parry and I arrived at Chamonix in doubtful weather, proceeding at once to the Montenvers Hotel on the Mer de Glace, a convenient base, about 6,300 feet above sea level. On other counts the Montenvers is not so agreeable, as the railway brings up swarms of tourists during the daytime, who come to visit the glacier and also to eat and drink. On one occasion the Sultan of Morocco was conducted to the Mer de Glace on such a day of depressing mist and rain that the unfortunate monarch was unable to see more than a yard or two of dirty, stone-covered ice, strewn with paper, tins and the cast-off cotton socks, which are provided for tourists to fit over their shoes in order to prevent them from slipping on the ice. No doubt, the Sultan would be glad to re-enter the hotel for some warmth-giving refreshment. Even mountaineers are bound to resort to the ample stores of wine, liqueurs and cognac during days of bad weather and enforced idleness.

Parry and I decided to go for the Grépon (11,450 ft.) and to start very early, as we wanted to be able to proceed slowly on our first day. The Grépon, although difficult, is not a high mountain or a long expedition, for the serious difficulties are all comprised within the last thousand feet of climbing.* We ordered our breakfast and our luncheon packets with the intention of setting out shortly after three a.m.

It was a calm, moonlit night as we made our way along the narrow path leading towards the foot of the Glacier des Nantillons, with a steep hillside on our left and an uninterrupted view down the other side to the valley of Chamonix, with a small group of twinkling lights 3,000 feet below and the dark ridge of the Brévent beyond. As night gave place to dawn we were toiling up endless, stony moraines, in the direction of the glacier. Our first aim was a small shelter on the Rognon, a rock which protrudes above an icefall in the middle of the glacier. The way was not difficult, but there is some danger at one point where the line of march is threatened by a group of very unstable *séracs*. At such an early hour there was little danger, but there is always some.

At the Rognon we sat down to a well-earned second breakfast, but made a most disconcerting discovery. I knew that the Montenvers was under new management since my last visit,

* The severe ones in the last 300 feet.

Climbing the Mummery Crack on the Grépon

but was entirely unprepared for such a display of malignance or ineptitude. There was neither bread, butter nor jam; there were none of those sweet and palatable delicacies so necessary to energise the jaded mountaineer in his first expedition of the season; the complete contents of these two, miserable packets were tough, inedible meat, slabs of cheese which were strong (or high) enough to climb the Grépon under their own power and lots of hard, unripe plums and peaches! Charlie sadly remarked, 'A mountaineer, like an army, marches on his stomach'. Let this be a warning to all who frequent Alpine hotels. We had almost lost the day before coming to grips with the mountain. Not only enjoyment but mere existence and survival were at stake!

We decided to rush the mountain on the meals of yesterday, and, at first, we did very well, indeed. Rapid progress across the glacier and over moderate rocks soon brought us to a point below the *col* between the Grépon and the Grands Charmoz. Here the serious business of the day commenced with the formidable Mummery Crack, which it fell to my portion to lead. The lower section was smooth and somewhat devoid of holds, but the rocks were dry and I thoroughly enjoyed myself, although I probably expended more energy than was really necessary. Parry entered the Crack by a delicate traverse from my left where he had been belaying my rope, a route which was perfectly sound for the second man, as he was secured from above.

Easier rocks now took us to the 'Trou du Canon', a rocky window from which we emerged to the sunny side of the mountain overlooking the Mer de Glace. More steep climbing, involving an awkward, vertical mantelshelf, led us back to a higher notch on the ridge, which we again crossed to a high platform on the Nantillons face, after which Parry took over the lead.

This is a terrific face of smooth, ribbed cliff which plunges straight down to the glacier. After a short, moderate passage came the 'Râteau de Chèvre', an ugly upward-sloping shelf with very few holds at all, where the rock is fairly smooth and the guide book recommends an upright posture. I disgraced myself by using my knees, and found the problem very difficult. An exit led to the northern summit of the Grépon, where we encountered a guided party of Americans who were taking movie pictures. They wanted us out of the way and were courteous enough to invite us to descend from the next point, the Grand Gendarme, on their doubled rope.

The descent into this next gap, even on the doubled rope,

needs a little care; for one must keep to a correct line so as not to miss the narrow landing at the bottom. The rest of the way to the foot of the principal or southern summit is absurdly easy, compared with the former section. Part of it is along a broad, horizontal ledge called the 'Route à Bicyclettes'. Below the final chimney we paused for a rest, already martyrs to the pangs of hunger, which were only accentuated without being at all relieved by nibbling at the indigestible contents of our rucksacks.

Only thirty feet of cliff separated us from our goal, but the weakness of malnutrition was upon us. The chimney was difficult, in fact overhanging for about ten feet, but our performance was pitiful. I made two futile attempts, and in the interval Parry fared no better. We were deeply humiliated, and it was only the approach of the Americans that stung Parry into a third, determined attempt which was ultimately successful. Charlie admitted to me afterwards that he was practically 'all out' at two places, for the first time in his life. I don't think we enjoyed our brief rest on the warm summit rocks. I have no recollection whatever of the view. We only wished to get down as soon as possible, before hunger had reduced us to complete impotence.

Meanwhile, Alfred Couttet, the leading guide of the Americans came up. He also wanted us out of the way; so he fixed a rope ring round the base of the small, metal image of the Virgin which adorns the summit of the Grépon, inserted his doubled rope in the loop and invited us to descend over the sheer, vertical cliff on the Mer de Glace side to an unseen ledge about sixty feet below. With a clean drop of about 2,000 feet one cannot entirely suppress a slight feeling of anxiety about the security of the rope, but the calm demeanour of Couttet was most reassuring and all went well. One after the other we descended, spun round in free air and landed on a solid flake of rock, along which we proceeded to the next notch in the south ridge, the Brêche Balfour.

For some reason we both appeared to have recovered our stamina. We continued over very steep, sound rocks on the Nantillons face to a small *piton* which facilitated our descent on the doubled rope for another sixty feet. We could have descended safely without using the *piton* at all. One major difficulty remained. An awkward corner led us to two jammed blocks forming the C.P. passage. Originally these initials, now vanished, were painted on the rock at this place by two early explorers, probably the guides Charlet and Payot. This passage was airy, exposed and awkward, leading to a little mantelshelf and a big slab beyond which we encountered no further difficulties. At the Col des Nantillons we rested and actually succeeded in consuming a very little of the least obnoxious remains of our food.

Care was necessary in descending the slushy glacier to the spot where we had left Parry's ice-axe, which we had not taken with us on the rocks. The glacier proved easy enough, but our progress downwards over the interminable moraines was very leisurely in a warm, muggy evening. It was nine p.m. before we regained the hotel.

LA NONNE

Three days of the worst kind of weather followed, during which we lived in idleness, paying an occasional visit to the Pâtisserie des Alpes at Chamonix to relieve the tedium and afford us a little exercise. Then the weather cleared, leaving me with one remaining day available for climbing, and all the rock peaks gleaming with new snow. We decided to go for La Nonne, the second peak of the long ridge which ascends from the Mer de Glace to the summit of the Aiguille Verte. After about three and a half hours' steady going we halted for second breakfast before seven a.m., high up on the Charpoua glacier. Our peak was straight above us on the ridge between the Charpoua and Talèfre glaciers, an ecclesiastical hierarchy of a ridge, comprising consecutively the Monk, Nun, Bishop and Cardinal. With some luck we hoped to ascend both the Nun and the Bishop.

Above us a great *couloir* swept up between rocky walls to the notch separating the Monk and the Nun. The early morning views of Mont Blanc and the intervening Aiguilles were superb. At first the condition of the snow was good and compact, and we made height rapidly. Then a traverse to the left on to the rocks was necessary in order to avoid a pitch in the gully. The rocks were not very difficult and enabled us to return to the *couloir* higher up, where the snow was still in a firm state. We felt sure that conditions were too good to last.

VIEW FROM THE CHARDONNET
Across the Argentière glacier

The *couloir* steepened considerably and we had to take the greatest care with the unconsolidated snow of the last few days. There was no other danger, for the rocks were still entirely in shadow. There was little likelihood, for the moment, of either avalanche or stonefall, with no visible sign of anything which had fallen. The evil snow continued, with the attendant difficulty of acquiring secure anchorages, until we were at last compelled to leave the snow altogether and take to the rocks.

Only about 300 feet remained to be climbed up to the neck on the ridge, but all our Scottish winter experience stood us in good stead, for the rocks were packed with snow, and in many places iced up. Thus, we took a great deal of time over what would, in good conditions, have been fairly easy work. The sunshine was gradually creeping down the mountain towards us, and we forced the pace accordingly. Another reason was the rising sea of mist which was filling the whole basin of the Charpoua glacier. The effects were exceedingly beautiful as the clouds surged up and down in great billowy forms, with entrancing views of the fantastic, rocky spires of the two Aiguilles du Dru. At 10.45 a.m. we gained the ridge a little way above the col.

The ridge of the Nonne gave us pleasant and interesting climbing. We passed a prominent tower, made a traverse on the Talèfre side, ascended some steep chimneys and regained the crest close to the main summit at 12.50 p.m. (about 11,000 feet). It was far too late for continuing to the Évêque. Under the prevailing conditions we were well satisfied with what we had achieved, for our time was almost identical with that given for the ascent in the Kurz *Guide to Mont Blanc*. Besides, we wished to enjoy a comfortable meal and a siesta on the warm sunny rocks. Climbing mountains must never degenerate into an ascetic discipline!

The shortest way down was by the Talèfre glacier, and we wished to locate the exact rocky *couloir* by which the descent had to be made. When we had found the top of it we ate our meal on the ridge just above it, and followed this up by a contemplative pipe. During this peaceful interlude there was a sudden roar from below and a cannonade of blocks swept down the *couloir* beneath us. This face, in its turn, was now in shadow, but we deemed it wise to give the mountain artillery at least another half hour to quieten down. There were no further alarms, and we commenced the descent at 2.45 p.m.

Even so, we were not too comfortable. An ominous quiet pervaded the mountain, which we were only too anxious to preserve. In a hushed and decorous manner we crawled down that loose and evil gully like a pair of cat burglars making a get-away after the telephone bell had rung in the house. We started nervously whenever a stone slipped out of its place. In such a situation I always feel thankful for my early training and experience on the small, unsound dolerite crags of the Lomonds and Dumyat in central Scotland. Unpleasant as the place was, there was no denying that there was something homely about it.

Nothing whatever happened. We crossed the *bergschrund* at our leisure and soon joined a well-marked track on the Talèfre glacier, passing the Couvercle Hut about five p.m. and continuing down the track to the Mer de Glace and the Montenvers without another halt.

This was a very different sort of expedition from the traverse of the Grépon, for we had the mountain entirely to ourselves and were compelled to rely on our own experience, mostly Scottish, for helping us to deal with steep rocks encased in new snow, steep snow gullies and a difficult descent over rotten rocks. This is no uncommon experience in the Alps if a guideless party is to make the best use of its opportunities in difficult conditions. Good judgment is required, and no undue risks can be taken on the first day or two after a spell of bad weather and fresh snowfall. Much experience is necessary for the longer and more difficult expeditions. Alpine snow is not so compact as Scottish snow and the sun is much more powerful. None the less, I have found that such days have frequently provided climbs of unusual interest and have proved to be an invaluable source of new experience.

TWO EASTERN AIGUILLES

It is a great mistake to suppose that the peaks above the Mer de Glace are the only ones worth climbing in the Chamonix district. Several other valleys, much less frequented, provide magnificent climbing. The educative value for British guideless parties is all the greater if they have the mountain all to themselves. One such district, which I have not visited, is the Trélatête *massif*, to the west of Mont Blanc. It is an excellent region for snow peaks. The Argentière and Tour glaciers, to the east of the Mer de Glace, give access to a grand variety of both rock and snow peaks, those between the Tour glacier and the Trient to the east of it offering some climbs of moderate difficulty, but most of the ascents from the Argentière being exceptionally long and difficult.

In 1938 Frank Stangle and I were chased down from the Réquin Hut on the Mer de Glace by foul weather. After two days in the valley, when bad weather drove us to the fleshpots and even the pictures at Chamonix, the barometer started to rise, encouraging us to toil upwards, in dismal rain and mist, to the Albert Hut on the Glacier du Tour. Our faith in the weather was not misplaced, for we enjoyed a first-class climb on the Aiguille du Tour (11,620 ft.) on the very next day. The normal route proceeds up the Tour glacier and crosses the easy Col du Tour, thereafter continuing along the high *névé* on the east side until it becomes easy to ascend either of the two summits, north or south, which are of approximately equal height. But Stangle and I were fascinated by the shining draperies of new snow on the cliffs and ridges overhanging the glacier above the hut, and we were told that this face had been climbed several times, proving both interesting and difficult.

Leaving the hut at five a.m. we moved rapidly up the Tour glacier until we found an inviting snow slope between the west ridge and a south-western spur. Ascending on very good snow until the slope steepened we then used rock and snow alternately. Having gained the west ridge at a level section our difficulties became more numerous, but they were of a type very familiar to those who habitually climb on Ben Nevis ridges in snowy conditions. We were soon forced to traverse to the right and abandon the ridge. One very difficult passage on to a subsidiary buttress ultimately led us back to the crest of our ridge. Here and there were slabs coated thinly with ice, but, in general, the sun and wind had cleared the rocks of snow and the holds were good.

Seldom have I been on a mountain where the top seemed so

near, but the intervening gaps and obstacles were so trouble-some. One *gendarme* had to be passed with considerable difficulty on the icy, north side to a deep-cut notch beyond. There was a short passage of difficult rocks, then a traverse on the south side and finally an oblique traversing ascent, again on the north, to the summit ridge. A little trouble ensued with steep snow and ice, but it was the last difficulty. After six and a quarter hours of continuous, hard going, without halts, we reached the summit and sat down to enjoy our lunch.

All around but beneath us was a lovely sunlit ocean of cloud, hiding all the valleys and even the lesser peaks. So pleasant was our comfortable perch that we sat for over an hour and a half, lazily following the undulations of the clouds as they swallowed up one peak after another and eddied to and fro about the satellites of Mont Blanc. All the great peaks were brilliantly clear from the Bernese Oberland and the Pennines to the Paradiso in the south. It is from such smaller mountains as the Aiguille du Tour that one may best appreciate the true form and grouping of a great range like the chain of Mont Blanc. Facing us, at the other side of the Tour glacier was a massive snowy dome with steep, rocky escarpments. We had designs on this peak, the Aiguille du Chardonnet (12,540 ft.), the most difficult of those which surround the Glacier du Tour. After such a day of brilliant sunshine it might be expected to be in good enough condition for our next expedition. We decided to have a try, starting very early on the morrow and going by the normal route, which lay entirely over snow and ice.

We started at four a.m., in bright moonlight. The glacier was fairly easy, only a few detours being required in order to avoid a field of crevasses. Our objective was a lofty saddle on the skyline to the north of our mountain, the Col Supérieur Adams-Reilly. Leaving the Tour glacier we moved up the lateral tributary Glacier de l'Épaule, keeping to the right-hand side of a small, rocky islet, and so avoiding an icefall. Then we crossed over towards the cliffs of the Chardonnet, as that line of approach to the col appeared to offer an easier way over the bergschrund. We were both wearing crampons, which were of great assistance to us on the steep wall above the bergschrund. On the Épaule there was another narrow *schrund*, surmounted

The Aiguille du Chardonnet
Dotted lines and arrows show route described, as seen from the Tour glacier

by a belt of ice. A traverse to the right and a steep, direct climb
solved the problem.

We reached this point after two hours of steady going from the
hut, without any halt. The route had worked out very well, but
on glaciers there are often alternatives. The upper col was
divided by a rock tower which we had passed on the Chardonnet
side. In the early evening, when we were back at the hut, we
saw a descending party coming down the other side of the
tower, apparently very quickly. One must just select a route in
the light of one's own observations, using common prudence.
Guide book directions cannot take account of the variations of
an upper glacier from one season to the next.

After a steep ascent and a traverse to the right we entered the
foot of a great, snow-filled gully, leading upwards for a long
way in the direction of the summit. It was bounded on the left
by a rocky ridge, but, as the snow was in excellent order, we
followed the gully nearly all the way, only avoiding such places
where the snow coating was far too thin on the underlying rock.
It would not have been a comfortable funnel if there had been a
party above us later in the day, for it was bound to serve as the

track of minor avalanches, snow slides or stonefalls when the sun had time to soften the slopes above. Only on the steeper parts were we obliged to move with great care, but, in general, our crampon spikes took a firm hold. We were in shadow and worked with a will in order to keep warm. Then, at long last, the slope eased off. We emerged into sunshine, and a short ridge led us directly to the main summit.

Two men were seated by the cairn. They had left the Albert Hut half an hour before us and had ascended by the more difficult route which finishes along the Arête Forbes, the rocky, eastern ridge of the peak. Forbes, who was Principal of St Andrews University, was a prominent scientist and Alpine explorer of the early nineteenth century. He travelled much amid the glaciers of this region, but was neither on the Aiguille du Chardonnet nor on the Aiguille Forbes to the south of it, which was named in his honour. The Chardonnet was first climbed in 1865 by Robert Fowler, with the guides Michel Ducroz and Michel Balmat, by the same route as we had followed from the col, which was reached from the Argentière glacier.

It was only eight o'clock and we had made very good time. Unlike most of my Alpine expeditions, this one had run exactly to schedule. We had actually improved on the time allotted to the ascent in the guide book. This was rather surprising on a snow route, as the quoted times refer to guided parties under good conditions. Well-trained British rock climbers can often improve on the official time schedule for an expedition which is mainly over rock, but these remarks should not be taken to mean that any expedition should ever be undertaken with the object of breaking a record, a practice which is entirely against the true spirit of mountaineering. It is good to be able to move fast at times, as it provides a time reserve for unforeseen contingencies, and allows one to enjoy some leisure in the high places.

We conversed with the others on the summit and learned from the guide that he considered that it would be feasible for us to make the descent by the more difficult Arête Forbes. The main difficulty was a convex bulge of ice on the descent from the ridge to an upper glacier. The guide thought that we could descend it before the heat of the sun had made the surface dangerously soft. We should scarcely have ventured on such a course without his assurance. He was, however, emphatic in saying that the Arête was difficult and would occupy us for at least an hour and a half before we could even reach the *mauvais pas*.

Meanwhile, we enjoyed our first meal and luxuriated in the sun and the marvellous panorama. The Argentière glacier lay, like a deep trench, at our feet. Beyond it, but seeming very close at hand in the clear atmosphere of the morning, were the formidable cliffs and hanging glaciers of the Aiguille Verte and Les Droites. A savage wall of precipitous peaks encircled the head of the glacier to the Mont Dolent, the point at which the frontiers of Switzerland, Italy and France come together.

There can be few more abrupt and savage prospects than the one which was spread out before us. The summit views from the snow peaks of the Oberland possess a beauty of rounded outline, spaciousness and purity. Those from rock peaks amongst rock peaks betoken savagery, but withal an opportunity for the skill and power of the rock climber. It is the blending of the savagery of sharp rocky spires with the cold austerity and deathly patience of ice slopes and hanging glaciers that suggests something inhuman, relentless and terrible, even when the morning sun floods the peaks and snowfields with unparalleled splendour.

At 8.45 a.m. we parted company from our friends. The passage of the Arête Forbes was difficult but delightful. There were *gendarmes* which had to be traversed or by-passed, and the descents were not always easy, on account of numerous icy pockets, for we could not make use of crampons on such a mixed ridge. Then we halted until eleven a.m., adjusting crampons and snow glasses and smearing ourselves with glacier cream, for the sun was now overhead and glaring down upon the upper snowfield.

After crossing a small bergschrund we worked our way downwards across a snowfield which bent over insensibly in a convex bulge to the top of the 'bosse de glace', mentioned in the guide book as being no higher than fifty metres. Far below us, seemingly at an immense depth, was a beautiful edge of corniced snow connecting the foot of the bulge with an almost level snow

Descending the Arête Forbes
Aiguille du Chardonnet

ridge running out to a rocky promontory. Thereafter, if we got so far in safety, the way continued downwards to the right through a maze of crevasses at a comparatively moderate angle.

Stangle went over the bulge and soon reported that the spike of his axe would not bite into the ice. His crampons were still holding, however. I descended and joined him. We were still on the curve and not quite at the steepest part. I lowered him on the rope to another stance, where he secured himself by hacking out a couple of large steps. My crampon spikes still held, as the ice was covered by a film of frozen snow, but the posture, with ankles painfully flexed, was very tiring, so that I relieved myself by cutting out a step every few yards, and derived additional security from the pick of the axe driven in above me.

I could well understand that such a place would be a good deal easier to climb than to descend. I had often climbed such slopes in Scotland under winter conditions, but had neglected to practise the accurate reversal of movements and positions required for the descent. The surface was still in shadow, owing to its steepness, and we were grateful for the film of frozen snow which relieved us of the necessity of cutting every step, a labour which would have taken a very long time. Crampons make all the difference, for, without them, steps would have been essential. There is no fixed rule in such circumstances. We entertained no doubts of each other's reliability, and proceeded by turns on a very short rope.

At length we came to hard snow and the slope eased off. We dropped down from the little ridge on to the *névé* and threaded our way between the crevasses, wallowing in sun-softened snow down the side glacier to the Glacier du Tour. It was a hot and tiring afternoon, but we had enjoyed the best part of our day in the bracing atmosphere of the upper ridges. The Chardonnet had fulfilled all our expectations, all the better perhaps on account of the order in which we had taken the traverse.

CHAPTER XXX

THE DENT BLANCHE

IT was a hot afternoon in July 1928. Four Scottish mountaineers, including myself, were sitting at ease after lunch, in
front of the hotel at Evolena in the Valaisian Alps. Outlined
against the blue sky, far above us and to the south, was a great,
jagged tooth of rock and ice. It was the Dent Blanche (14,318
ft.), the biggest peak of the district. We were proceeding to
Arolla, at the head of the neighbouring fork of the Val d'Hérens,
for ten days' climbing, and our final objective stood before us,
clear and challenging. The heat and dust of the Rhone Valley
lay behind, and we knew that Arolla could provide us with a
week of guideless climbing on lesser mountains, both rock and
snow, in preparation for the giant which now flaunted its
splendour before our eyes.

Six days later Charlie Parry and I started from Arolla for the
Bertol Hut, which is perched on a high ridge, at 11,000 ft.,
midway between the Arolla Valley and the base of our peak.
Our two friends, Matheson and Mackay, were to join us the
following evening, our intention being to climb a more remote
peak, the Dent d'Hérens, on the first day. But there was a
doubt, for the latter peak was on the Swiss-Italian frontier, and
these were the days when Mussolini's frontier guards occasionally fired at sight on climbers who descended from the mountain
frontier by unauthorised ways. At the hut we talked with the
guide of another party who was strongly against our project.
He said that the way was long and difficult. We might climb
our peak, but we should probably be so late on the job and
fatigued, that we might be driven to seek shelter at the Cabane
d'Aoste on the Italian slopes. We might easily end by cooling
our heels in an Italian gaol for a few days—if nothing worse
happened.

I could see that Parry was paying scant attention to these
gloomy forebodings. His eyes were fixed on the Dent Blanche,
looking like a huge lion in repose, unclouded and glowing with
the hues of sunset. Far to the right, projecting above the nearer

snowfields, was the upper cone of the Matterhorn, but Parry had no eyes for the Matterhorn.

If I was feeling uneasy about starting for the Dent d'Hérens I need not have disquieted myself. Parry was already convinced that the Dent Blanche was the most noble mountain he had ever seen, and equally determined to climb it next morning, in case the weather should turn against us. Nothing else mattered. There was the south ridge by which we must go, and I was supposed to know how to approach it, as I had crossed these great snowfields two years before when taking the high level route from Arolla to Zermatt by the Col d'Hérens, directly at the foot of the Wandfluh, or south ridge of our peak.

Many things conspired against our night's rest. The hut was filled with a guided party of lady climbers belonging to the Vevey Section of the Swiss Alpine Club. They held a sing-song until ten p.m. Then the guides stamped about and chattered, and a late party arrived. In spite of the close atmosphere, occasional rustlings and snores I suppose we secured a little sleep, but we were not sorry to rouse ourselves at two a.m. for breakfast.

In less than an hour we stepped out into a beautiful, starry night, with occasional flashes of distant lightning to the east. The glacier was very different from what it had been two years before. The year 1928 had very little snowfall and a hot summer, with the result that the upper glaciers were largely denuded of their snowy covering, moulded into hummocks and cones of ice and split by wide crevasses. We ran into a field of these within the first half hour. Of course, where there was a snow cover it was old, hard and safe, so that there was little danger. But it caused delay, mutual abuse and recrimination as we stumbled about in a jerky manner, linked as we were by the rope for reasons of safety. Soon the glacier improved and we could steer directly for our first objective. Halfway to the Dent Blanche there is a sort of dividing ridge on the upper glacier. To the right it rises to the Tête Blanche, a minor rounded summit, well-known as a view point; to the left is the rocky ridge of Mont Miné, running northwards towards Ferpècle, the head of the main Val d'Hérens. Between the two is one easy, descending passage on to the Ferpècle glacier, of which we had to cross the uppermost bay.

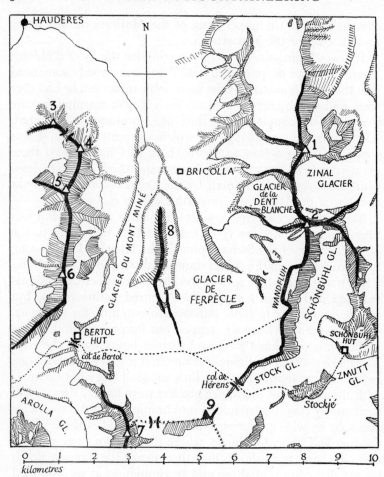

MAP I   THE DENT BLANCHE
                    (and environs)
                      PEAKS

				height in feet
1	Grand Cornier	. . . .	.	13,020
2	Dent Blanche	. . . .	.	14,320
3	Petite Dent de Veisivi	. . . .	.	10,470
4	Grande Dent de Veisivi	. . . . . .	.	11,250
5	Dent Perroc	. . . .	.	12,070
6	Aiguille de la Tsa	. . . .	.	12,050
7	Dents des Bouquetins	. . . . . .	.	12,620
8	Mont Miné	. . . .	.	10,580
9	Tête Blanche	. . . .	.	12,300

The Dent Blanche
Wandfluh ridge descends to the right; as seen from the Petite Dent de Veisivi

Our direction was not quite accurate. We struck the line a little too far to the north and lost some time in making the necessary correction. In 1926 I had been with a good leader with map and compass, for there was mist and a desultory snowfall when we crossed to the Col d'Hérens. Now I could see that a line too far north lands one on steep rocks, and one too far south on splintered cliffs of ice with a multitude of crevasses. As later events of the day proved, our observations were of some value. The Col d'Hérens is on an Alpine highway, crossed by many parties in the climbing season, but evident tracks were not to be found in the snowless summer of 1928. By 5 a.m. we had reached the base of our mountain.

We sought the easiest line of approach to the crest of the Wandfluh. On a big peak in the Alps, as contrasted with British hills, one is not looking for difficulties. A steep slope of hard snow-ice, with just a suspicion of bare ice here and there, faced us. In order to avoid step-cutting we put on our crampons.

Above this was a small cornice, through which we made our way to an easy rock ridge leading all the way to the crest of the Wandfluh. We gained the ridge just south of a prominent cairn which marks the approach from the Schönbühl Hut on the Zermatt side. Nowadays things are made much easier for the many who wish to climb the Dent Blanche by this 'ordinary' way; for the Swiss Alpine Club have erected a hut near this very spot which Parry and I selected for our first halt and a second breakfast.

For about three-quarters of an hour we sat there in warm sunshine, enjoying a comfortable, lazy sense of freedom. Only too often this necessary meal must be hurried through on some cheerless, exposed ridge in a freezing wind. We were confident of success. If a snowless summer was worse for glaciers and crevasses it ought to be correspondingly better for high ridges and rocks. The upper ridge of the Dent Blanche has a bad reputation for bulges and cornices of snow and for traverses over iced rocks, but on this perfect day, for as high as we could see there was no menace. With us it was almost a dead calm, but near the top we could see small clouds of whirling snow. Could it really be one of the major Alpine peaks? From where we sat the upper ridge looked no more difficult and not at all unlike one of the Cuillin peaks in spring.

We dumped our rucksacks in order to travel light, and because we should, in any case, have to return by the same way. We started off on snow and easy rock to a sort of saddle where there was a corniced snow ridge, but it gave us very little trouble. Then the angle steepened, and we made height quickly on sound rock with hardly any snow at all. Ahead of us was the great tower of red rock which is the main obstacle when the mountain is heavily coated with snow and ice. We traversed it by a system of easy ledges on the Ferpècle side, without encountering any ice. The steep climb back to the crest of the ridge would have been very troublesome otherwise. Above the Red Tower were several more *gendarmes* or obstacles, but we either climbed them directly or succeeded in turning them on one side or another. There was some snow and ice here and there, but nothing to worry anyone who had been trained on the ridges of Ben Nevis in winter. I have never known more rapid progress

on the summit ridge of a great mountain. We accepted our good
fortune thankfully in the main, but also with some regret that
the mountain was letting us off too easily. Above the steep part
there was a gentle ridge of hard snow which led us to the
summit at 10.40 a.m.—about two and a half hours from our
last halt.

At our feet lay the little village of Haudères, so steeply
beneath us that we got the impression that we could fling a
stone on to the little houses, 8,000 feet below. The view was by
no means perfect, for bad weather was approaching. Loud
rumblings of thunder came across the upper basin of the Zmutt
glacier from the cloud-capped Matterhorn. Meanwhile, we lay
basking in the sunshine on the warm rocks of the summit. All
around was a world of peaks, glaciers and snowfields. The
Matterhorn disappeared almost entirely in a pall of inky cloud,
and a sudden whiff of cold air recalled us to reality. Filled with
prudence and virtue we abridged our siesta and started off
downwards shortly after eleven o'clock.

We were feeling a bit above ourselves with success and, no
doubt, a trifle careless. I was coming down last at the beginning
of the steep part of the ridge when Parry gave a sudden shout.
I looked down, and there was his valuable ice-axe taking
a series of huge jumps in the air, until it finally vanished over a
lower cliff on its way to the Ferpècle glacier. It was obviously a
good axe since it was still intact when we saw it disappear. The
loss did not particularly affect us on the rocks, but it would be
a serious matter when we came to the ice. On an Alpine peak
and on the glacier an ice-axe is both a third leg and a sixth
sense to a mountaineer.

We sobered up at once; on the corniced part of the ridge we
took every precaution. At length we recovered our sacks and
crampons and had some lunch. Certainly, Parry would be safer
with crampons. The sky was now completely overcast, and a
mist was creeping over the snowfields. It was an easy descent to
the little snow cornice, but the utmost care was necessary on the
steep, icy slope above the glacier. Fortunately, the snow was
still hard and in fair condition, without much balling under our
feet. Before the mist closed in about us we took accurate compass
bearings on the Dents des Bouquetins and the Col de Bertol, so

that we should not miss the one critical passage on the glacier to the south of the Mont Miné rocks.

The return journey across the glacier was a nightmare. Since Parry had no axe he wore his crampons and marched in front. I was sorry for him, as the soft snow was continually balling up between the spikes of his crampons and had to be knocked off every few minutes. Somehow everything seemed to be wrong. We were often going downhill when I felt sure we should be on the up-grade. Parry kept diverging to the left. The heat was damnable. It was a quiet monotony of suffocation, without any sign of progress or hope. Still, we persevered, with frequent halts to adjust our compass bearings. After what seemed ages of listless plodding there came a sudden clearance. There we were, just at the spot which we had been aiming for, with the crevasses and ice pinnacles on our left and the broken cliffs on our right. Then came the thunderstorm with a smart shower of hail, a fresh cool wind and a clearing of the air. Behind us was the Dent Blanche, swathed in gloomy, black clouds from which the thunder continued to reverberate.

We crossed the ridge and steered well to the left of the Col de Bertol, so as to avoid the worst of the crevasses. For some time we made excellent progress, but at length we became involved in a host of half-bridged crevasses. I think that another 200 yards would have seen us clear of them, and not far from the hut. Parry had just crossed a crevasse and was about thirty feet in front of me. Although I was taking care to keep him on a tight rope when he was crossing the gap, the fatigue of the day had the effect of making me rather careless about my own technique. Very stupidly, I held a coil of about ten to twelve feet of line in my left hand. Altogether there was about forty feet between us, and Parry was carrying the remaining sixty feet, beyond his waist loop, in a coil over his shoulder. I was following exactly in his footsteps, when, quite suddenly, I went down through the surface at the edge of the crevasse.

The line bit rapidly into the ice wall so that, after the first drop, I fell no farther but commenced to swing like a pendulum between two walls of pale blue ice, about ten feet below the surface. It was rather a wonderful position. Underneath me, the blue depths continued for 100 feet or more, floored by jagged edges of ice with intervening black holes leading to even lower depths. I was in the narrowest part of the fissure. It was just possible to press my toes against the wall in front. My crampons were attached, spikes outward, to my rucksack, and the spikes bit into the wall behind. I still had my ice-axe, but could do nothing with it. We were climbing on Alpine line, strong enough for ordinary purposes, but rather thin and light. Had the line been badly frayed by friction with the ice? I could not be sure that it might not break at any moment. Even if I had the strength, constricted as I was with the rope pressing on my ribs, I could not hope to climb up the line. I thought bitterly of A. F. Mummery's flippant remarks in his classical chapter on the 'Pleasures and Penalties of Mountaineering', where he makes light of the danger from crevasses to a competent party of two on a glacier, and asks 'Why anyone should wish to dangle on the rope, in a dark and chilly chasm', proclaiming this to be 'one of those profound and inscrutable mysteries which may be regarded as past all finding out'.

Then Parry gave a shout from the upper world, and I remembered that he had a spare coil of line. He told me afterwards that my fall had pulled him down to a sitting position on the glacier, facing the crevasse, with his crampons firmly anchored against two of the conical hummocks on the ice. For the first few moments he was filled with anger and maledictions, but, as I was nowhere to be seen, he had time to reflect. I shouted back to him, asking him to make a loop on the end of the spare line and try and cast it down to me. With amazing luck the first cast was accurate, and the loop came right down above my head. I slipped on the waist loop and began to consider ways and means of climbing up. If I could only rise about two feet I should be in a still narrower part of the crevasse, with a good, icy ledge for a foothold.

The procedure was very simple. I hauled myself upwards a few inches on one line while Parry tightened up the other. So it went on, turn about, until I gained my foothold and proceeded to cut other steps with the axe. Thus I climbed up all the way to the top, where the last trouble was due to the original line being deeply embedded in the ice. Parry managed to pull it through after I had untied.

BB

The whole episode was over inside half an hour, but I felt that I had passed through an age of experience within that short space of time. It was only later, when I came to reflect on the details, that I realised how fortunate we had been. The line was not cut through by the ice; Parry was not dragged along the glacier when the shock came on him; we could communicate with each other, and he succeeded in finding me with the second line. Taken separately, the circumstances might not be too improbable: taken together the coincidence was remarkably fortunate.

We had learned our lesson and followed another piece of Mummery's advice during the remainder of the way to the hut. We kept a double length of line between us and exercised a double dose of caution. If there had been something uncanny about the ease with which we had climbed the upper ridge of the Dent Blanche it all went to prove that an Alpine expedition is not safely completed until one is off the glacier.

Matheson and Mackay were awaiting us at the hut. We did not move from the tea table until bed time. Nothing could keep us awake that night.

Engelhörner from the Wetterhorn, Bernese Oberland

CHAPTER XXXI

A TRAVERSE OF THE JUNGFRAU

IN the summer of 1925 I was climbing with Frank Smythe in the Bernese Oberland. It was my second visit to the Alps and my first introduction to really difficult climbs on the great peaks. I was therefore exceedingly fortunate in my companion, who had already done much since I was with him in the Tyrol in 1922. His programme was ambitious—very much so, when my comparative inexperience had to be taken into account. Even at that early stage of his mountaineering career he had an amazing capacity for route finding, especially in the classical tradition of snow and ice routes, which is the only sure foundation for the success of an explorer on the greater mountain ranges of the world. I think he regarded me as a safe man, not entirely devoid of the spirit of mountain adventure when the pros and cons had been weighed up in a philosophic manner, fairly competent on rocks if without much experience of glaciers, but always prepared to do my share of fighting our way out of a tight corner without any waste of words.

We slept one night at Wengen, so as to let the vision of the incomparable northern face of the Jungfrau sink into my impressionable mind; and then my friend announced his project after breakfast as a matter-of-fact preliminary to going off to fill our rucksacks with the necessary provisions. I was gently persuaded that the first day's excursion was a training walk to the Guggi Hut, and that we could use the railway as far as the Eigergletscher station on the Jungfrau Bahn, not leaving so very much height to be made to the hut. Thereafter, the expedition seemed, to my innocent mind, to be a series of straightforward steps over several successive basins of gleaming snow, a sort of majestic, spiral staircase ending at the beautifully moulded summit dome of our peak. From the Guggi Hut there was only about 4,450 feet of ascent to the summit, very little more than the height of Ben Nevis above Fort William. With a bit of luck the snow would be in good, hard condition, crevasses and *séracs* and ice would only be occasional difficulties, and our

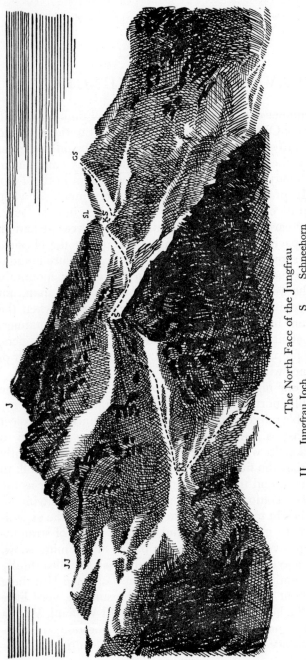

The North Face of the Jungfrau

JJ   Jungfrau Joch   S   Schneehorn
J   Jungfrau Summit   KS   Klein Silberhorn
SL   Silberlücke   GS   Gross Silberhorn
KI   Kühlauenen Icefall

prospects of success were excellent. Of course I am only out-lining my own inexperienced reflections at the time. I had accepted the adventure. Nor do I insinuate for a moment that my companion was not fully aware of what we were attempting and against what difficulties. He had a wide and deep knowledge of Alpine literature, as well as experience of climbing big peaks in the Oberland. I had a well-founded confidence in him, and there was little sense in asking a lot of questions which the course of events themselves would soon answer.

So it came about that we left Eigergletscher station with plenty of provisions for three days and a new rope, on the after-noon of Sunday, 19th July, en route for the Guggi Hut and the classical snow and ice route which traverses the north-west face of the Jungfrau. This ascent was first made by Rev H. B. George and Sir George Young with Christian Almer, Hans Baumann and Ulrich Almer on 29th August, 1865.* Like many of the classical snow and ice routes it has succeeded in maintaining its standard of interest and difficulty ever since. The classical pioneers and the great guides thoroughly understood ice technique and their standard of performance and endurance has not been superseded in modern times. The unexpected is always lurking round the corner on such expeditions and there are years, when the snowfall is at a minimum and the summer is hot, when this route on the Jungfrau may prove to be impos-sible owing to steep ice slopes and impassable icefalls. In 1925 there was enough snow and our prospects seemed good.

Little need be said of our toilsome ascent to the hut under a hot sun, except that I rather disgraced myself by slipping on dirt-covered ice and sprawling down for a matter of twenty feet before stopping myself. This was in full view of the telescopes on the terrace of the Eigergletscher Hotel. We were on dry glacier

* As in the case of most inventions and discoveries the eventual victors cannot take all the credit for this new ascent. The first part of the way by the Guggi glacier and the Kühlauenen icefall was traversed during the first ascent from the Wengern Alp to the Jungfraujoch in 1862 by Sir Leslie Stephen's party. This route was again used in 1863 by E. von Fellenberg and Karl Bädeker for the ascent of the Silberhorn. Both parties were well guided. Hans Baumann had been with Fellenberg and Christian Almer with Leslie Stephen. The 1862 party failed in their first attempt on the icefall but, next time, they carried a twenty-five-foot ladder and used it to bridge a crevasse. It was carried right over the Jungfraujoch and taken down by the other side of the mountain to Grindelwald. There were giants in those days!

and, of course, unroped. No doubt someone among the tourists would enjoy the spectacle. When we reached the hut it was untenanted. It is quite small, nobly situated on the crest of a long buttress which sweeps down from the Mönch, and high above the Guggi glacier. After fetching water in a can strapped on my back, which involved a descent and reascent of some rocks, I rested while Smythe prepared a meal. We thoroughly enjoyed a warm, comfortable and lazy afternoon.

Later in the evening two others arrived, a young Swiss doctor and his guide Hans Kaufmann. We knew the latter by reputation as one of the finest icemen of the Oberland. He told us that he was forty-five years old. It soon appeared that we were all bound for the same route. We decided to breakfast together and get away by 3 a.m. Kaufmann told us that, in certain years, the first great difficulty, the Kühlauenen icefall could not be ascended at all. We had examined it at a distance during the afternoon and Smythe considered that we could probably work our passage to the base of a long projection of ice which was joined to the unbroken *firn* above. About half-past nine we strolled out and saw the distant lights of Mürren and Wengen, far beneath us under a clear starry sky. More distant and nearer our own level, a solitary bright light shone across the black depths, the summit hotel on the Niesen (at 7,760 ft.), one of the finest viewpoints for the whole range of the Oberland. Then we retired to our blankets, but I slept fitfully and very little, as I still do when a very early start and a big expedition are in prospect.

We left the hut a little before the others, at about three a.m., on a clear, starry night. Beneath us were a few lights in the Eigergletscher Hotel. Quite a considerable distance above, a couple of lanterns twinkled now and then, belonging to a very early party on the usual route up the Eiger. We made an awkward little descent to the Guggi glacier, with much traversing across and lowering down slabs of rock, the chief nuisance being our candle lantern, troublesome alike to the bearer and more indirectly to the follower, on account of the flickering shadows. After about an hour we were on the smooth surface of the glacier, making for the foot of the Kühlauenen icefall. As we approached this formidable obstacle the stars faded out and the

Threading the Kühlauenen Icefall

dawn glowed pink and crimson on the lofty snows of the Jungfrau. Directly above us on our left was the steep, icy wall below
the Jungfraujoch, an extremely difficult climb from this side.

When it came to threading the mazes of the icefall the other
party was slightly ahead of us, and we adopted our own route
on the general line which we had planned on the previous
afternoon. We went over numerous chasms, narrow icy ridges,
and beneath many great *séracs*, but we were always able to
maintain a devious but steady approach towards the huge *sérac*
which we had marked out as the bridge to the plateau above the
icefall. The work was both engrossing and difficult, but we had
no reason to complain of the condition of the ice or of any snow
bridges. Neither of us would have relished the prospect of being
forced to return by the same route later in the day, after the
rays of the sun had loosened the stabilising influence of the

night's frost on these mammoth towers of ice, grouped around us in crazy confusion and at all angles of tottering decrepitude.

At length we converged on the other party at the base of the final obstacle. They had just retired from an abortive attempt by a steep, curving ridge of ice. It would have taken too long to finish. One other way presented itself and this led us all to the top of the promontory, with a certain amount of step-cutting in which we were permitted to take our share. As we foresaw, the long *sérac* continued without a break to a smooth sheet of *firn* rising at a gentle angle in the direction of a second great icefall between a spur of the Jungfrau on the left and the Schneehorn cliffs on the right. It was not necessary to tackle the ice. We climbed steeply upwards to the right on good, hard snow, cutting an occasional step as required. The rocks, when we reached them, were broken and entirely free of ice. It was easy and pleasant to climb on the firm rough surface of the gneiss.

As soon as we got to a comfortable perch we halted and proceeded to enjoy our second breakfast about 8 a.m. in the warm sunshine. It seemed almost incredible that we had been going for close on five hours without a halt; so engrossing had been our labours on the icefall that we had hardly noted the passage of time. The day was now growing very warm, and Kaufmann remarked that, owing to soft snow, it would take at least another six hours to reach the summit. Suiting actions to words, he and the doctor put on their sacks and moved off at once. In a few minutes we also moved on.

The remaining rocks to the top of the Schneehorn (11,200 ft.) were easy; for the cornice was not formidable and had shrunk away altogether at one point. Another great basin of level snow, the Giessenmulde, lay in front. At the far end was another icefall, obviously much easier than what lay behind us, with the modest little ridge of the Klein Silberhorn on the right. There was not a breath of wind. The sun rode high above the ice cliffs of the Jungfrau and concentrated his beams on the enclosed basin of snow, which reflected them back to us like a concave mirror. We began to appreciate the meaning of 'glacier lassitude' and that it had more connection with the hot room of a Turkish bath than with the rarified atmosphere of great altitudes.

The next icefall gave us little trouble, with only a short, steep slope where steps had to be cut, but it was followed by an area of deeply crevassed *firn*. Owing to the heat-softened snow we were obliged to move with the utmost deliberation as we pursued a zig-zag course between the chasms. It was my first experience of a really difficult field of snow-covered glacier. The crevasses were stupendous, and I have never again been so impressed with the scale of these apparently bottomless fissures, many of which were half concealed under a smooth, snowy covering with only a gentle but suggestive concavity on the surface. It was so still about us that it would not have been at all surprising, nor out of keeping with the uncanny atmosphere of the place, if either or both of us had slipped noiselessly through the skin of snow into the void beneath.

At length we passed beyond the danger zone and came to the third great basin of *firn*, the Silbermulde, the last and highest of the three snowfields which girdle the north-west face of the Jungfrau. At the far end was the Silberlücke, the lowest point on the ridge by which we must continue our ascent. This enclosed basin, so majestic and beautiful in its unruffled, snowy surface, was bounded on the right by the lovely, sharp, curved ridge leading to the Silberhorn.

It was our aim to ascend straight to this saddle. Ahead of us Kaufmann was already starting to cut his way directly towards it. The vertical height was not very great, but the condition of the ice was a more serious problem. He gave it up, saying as he came down again, "*Das geht nicht. Es dauert zu lange*". The wall was made of rotten snow overlying the ice. We thought that an approach was feasible some distance higher on the left, where the ridge threw down a long wall of rocks to the Silbermulde, the lower edge being separated from the *firn* by several *bergschrunds*. Our efforts were entirely in vain, so that we assuaged our disappointment by sitting down to refresh the inner man, meanwhile observing the exceedingly slow progress of the other party where Kaufmann was now cutting a ladder of steps with great care and deliberation, aiming to reach the crest of the ridge about midway between the summit of the Silberhorn and the saddle.

Our siesta was eminently satisfactory in its results. Smythe decided to take the longer but more assured route up the right-hand ridge of the Silberhorn, the route used by Fellenberg, Bädeker and their guides in 1863. After an easy detour we gained the ridge without any trouble. At first the snow was good on the crest, but, as the gradient became steeper, Smythe found that the snow could no longer be trusted for kicking secure steps. It became thin and soft, with little adhesion to the ice underneath. There was no choice left to us but to clear away the slush and cut steps in the ice. It is wrong to use the *we*, for the hard work fell to be done by the leader, my humble part being to enlarge the steps and provide him with reasonable security in the rear against any possible mischance. It took us a very long time, but our progress was safe and, at length we gained the summit of the Silberhorn (12,170 ft.).

Meanwhile, Kaufmann and the doctor had also reached the crest, after sending down some considerable masses of snow. The summit of the Silberhorn is a level, narrow, corniced ridge of snow. It continues down to the Silberlücke by a narrow, snow-covered rock ridge which is not at all easy to traverse. I had trouble with a pair of new boots which cramped my circulation so much that both feet were without sensation. I took off each boot in turn, succeeding after a time in restoring sensation and warmth by rubbing my feet, the odd boot meanwhile being precariously perched on the edge of the abyss. Very truly, my friend pointed out that if the boot took the plunge I had a very good chance of losing a foot by frostbite, if nothing worse befell. The warning was heeded, but it was one of those occasions when fatigue had given rise to an unpardonable degree of apathy and carelessness.

As soon as we got going again we were overtaken by one of those rapidly moving thunderstorms which are not uncommon in the high Alps in very hot weather. The air became quite dark around us and thunder boomed in the distance. There did not appear to be any definite cloud. The surroundings gradually darkened and faded from view. Our ice-axes began to hum and sizzle with the electric discharge. Our hair stood on end and there was a tingling sensation all over us whenever we raised ourselves more than a foot or two above the ridge crest. On an isolated ridge, during an electric storm, the potential gradient is known to be very abrupt. We could do no more than remain in our crouching position on the narrow ridge and hope for the best, and that the discharge would continue to behave in a mild and gentlemanly manner. It was obviously impossible to descend on either side. Discussing it afterwards, we both remembered one or two mild shocks, probably caused by raising our heads too high; but the most curious effect, so far as I was concerned, was a sudden, almost exhilarating brightening of the faculties. My apathy vanished completely, and I appeared to observe everything with concentrated zest and interest, without any trace of fear or anxiety.

As nothing more happened we began to move again, and I positively enjoyed that airy traverse with all its difficulties. Soon we passed the narrow section and reached the Silberlücke. The storm passed over and the sky lightened as we tackled the rock ridge leading to the final peak of the Jungfrau. This was interesting climbing without any great difficulty. Above the rocks the going became easier and the ridge broadened out, finally merging into the wider, open slopes of the Hochfirn, the snow-covered glacier underneath the summit cap.

When the difficulties abated my spurt of energy fell away with them. I have a vague recollection of that struggle up the Hochfirn as of something like an unpleasant dream. I had to rest for a few moments after every forty or fifty steps. At length I forced myself into a rhythm of deep breathing and found that I got on much better. Of course I was suffering from the combined effects of lack of acclimatisation to the altitude and some lack of training at the commencement of the holiday. Even with deep and rhythmic breathing the pace was slow enough. We could see the other party on the summit. They remained there a while, watching our progress, and then disappeared.

On the last rise there were a few crevasses and we had to walk circumspectly again, but that was the only difficulty, and we finally set foot on the summit of the Jungfrau (13,670 ft.) at 5 p.m. We rested for a few minutes to eat some food and take a sip of cognac from a small flask; but I have little recollection of the view except the utter isolation of the place, the wild and hostile grandeur of the sea of mountains and the enormous extent of glaciers on every side except the hazy depths of the valleys running north to the Lake of Thun which, itself, was quite invisible. The watery sun was rapidly disappearing into a dark belt of thunderclouds to the west of us, and there was little time to lose if we wished to avoid another storm on the heights.

It was a relief to start off downhill at last. It seems rather ridiculous and premature, but we already felt that we were back within the folds of civilisation, and had only to walk down the broad highway of the tourist route up our mountain! A long, straight, steep slope led downwards to the Rottal Sattel, hewn into a great staircase by the passage of countless guided parties. But it was not so easy as all that, for the slope was mostly ice and the whole staircase had suffered from the gruelling effects of the sun. We moved together and continuously, but with every precaution. Even so, we quickly reached the saddle, some distance below which we were glad to make use of a fixed ladder for crossing the *bergschrund* on to the gentle slopes of the Jungfraufirn. There was no further difficulty.

The weather gradually worsened and the Jungfrau retired into her mantle of cloud. Before the mist and sleet settled down we caught a fleeting glimpse of the summit dome of the Aletschhorn and the hills beyond the Aletsch glacier. It was almost the last straw when we found that we had to cross two subsidiary humps of snow before sighting that weird but welcome phenomenon, the Jungfraujoch Hotel, with its rows of little lights staring out of the face of a snow-sheathed precipice. Perhaps it was out of place in such austere and lofty surroundings, but it held out a very real welcome to a couple of tired mountaineers after seventeen hours of storm and stress on one of the greatest snow and ice routes of the Alps.

It may be that we were rash and optimistic in choosing such a climb for the start of an Alpine holiday. It taught me one lesson anyway, to treat the great Alpine peaks with profound respect; and I always look back on this climb with a mingling of pride and awe, as the most beautiful and impressive snow climb that I have ever done. It was one of the gifts that I owe to Frank Smythe, with his unrivalled flair for finding the way on the great peaks and his unbounded enthusiasm and energy in following it to the end.

CHAPTER XXXII

A TRAVERSE OF THE MATTERHORN

EDWARD Whymper's *Scrambles Amongst the Alps* does not seek to capture the imagination by picturesque turns of phrase or anything which might be considered dramatic in the style of writing. Most of the chapters are written in a prosaic, matter-of-fact manner, and we must go to the original drawings in order to get underneath the dour and rugged exterior of the famous mountaineer.

Like many another enthusiastic climber, I was drawn to the mountains by an early perusal of Whymper's *Scrambles*, but I had only the small, cheap edition published many years ago by Messrs Nelson, which did not include any of the author's drawings. I think that it was my mother's appreciation of the classic which first directed my attention to it and persuaded me that there was much more in the mountaineering chapters than in those earlier ones on the construction of the Mont Cenis tunnel and the author's theories and observations on the flow of glaciers. Thus, a youthful pre-occupation with engineering and science was transformed by Whymper's epic of the conquest of the Matterhorn into the beginnings of a life-long enthusiasm for the mountains themselves.

Even a rugged individualist like Whymper could become almost lyrical when writing of the uncanny attraction, or even fixation which this mountain exercised over the most unlikely persons—'Men who ordinarily spoke or wrote like rational beings, when they came under its power, seemed to quit their senses and ranted, and rhapsodised, losing for a time all common forms of speech'. As a concluding reflection, a sort of epilogue to the tragedy of the first ascent of the mountain in 1865, he wrote, 'Ages hence, generations unborn will gaze upon its awful precipices and wonder at its unique form. However exalted may be their ideas and however exaggerated their expectations, none will come to return disappointed'.

I made up my mind that I must and would climb it some day; but, as I had also read A. F. Mummery's account of the

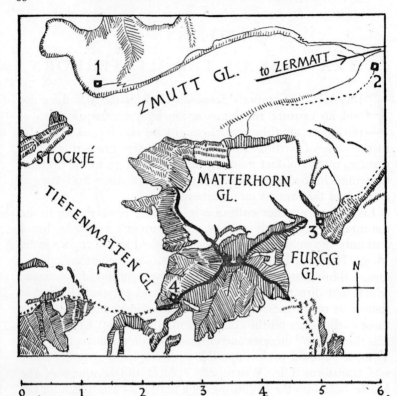

MAP J   MATTERHORN, 14,780 ft.
                 HOTELS AND HUTS
1 Schönbühl Hut   3 Hörnli Hut and Belvedere Hotel
2 Staffelalp Hotel   4 Italian Hut
                      RIDGES
North-East or Hörnli Ridge   South-West or Italian Ridge
North-West or Zmutt Ridge   South-East or Furggen Ridge

first ascent of the Zmutt Ridge of the mountain in 1879, I
decided that I must wait until I had gained sufficient experience
to enable me to climb the Matterhorn by Mummery's route,
without any professional assistance.

My first Alpine holiday was spent in the Tyrol, and it was not
until 1925, when climbing in the Bernese Oberland with Frank
Smythe, that I first saw the Matterhorn. For many hours we

THE MATTERHORN
From the summit of Dent Blanche

were slowly traversing the difficult, spiky ridge from the Schreckhorn to the Lauteraarhorn. The complete chain of the Pennine Alps was in full view, with the truncated pyramid of the Matterhorn in the centre. Can any mountain maintain its influence and reputation as a solitary item in such a vast panorama? There are many lofty peaks among the Pennines. The level ridge connecting the Swiss and Italian summits of the Matterhorn seemed to detract from its dignity by cutting away the apex of the pyramid. There was an indefinable, almost imperceptible sense of anticlimax about it.

In 1926 my impressions of the peak were no more fortunate. I viewed it from the side of Arolla, first from the summit of the Évêque and next from the Col de Bertol, across the lofty snow-fields of the Tête Blanche. Clearly, no mountain can look its best with the whole of its base cut away. A week later I did see it properly from Zermatt, but again the spell was broken, for I climbed Monte Rosa and, sceptic as I remained at bottom, could not forget that I was actually higher than its pointed summit. After these unsatisfactory experiences I resolved to try and climb the mountain at the earliest opportunity. I could not bring myself to believe that level-headed men like Whymper and Mummery were insincere in what they wrote about the Matterhorn. There was a depth of reality in their enthusiasm, and, if I hoped to recapture the subtle essence or vision which I suspected that I had lost, I could only do so by actual contact and struggle with the mountain itself.

The opportunity offered itself during the summer of 1928. Charlie Parry and I sat on the summit of the Dent Blanche and watched a thunderstorm gather about the upper rocks of the Matterhorn. There was no anticlimax on that occasion. All the other peaks around us were in clear sunshine. Only on the Matterhorn was there an inky turmoil of cloud, broken by violet flashes of lightning. We resolved to attempt the Zmutt Ridge at the end of our holiday. We reached Zermatt in an evening of torrential rain and frequent bursts of thunder and lightning. A party told us how they had been benighted on the upper glacier when attempting the traverse of the Dom and Täschhorn. Our prospects were indeed gloomy, as we had only another two days available before the end of our holiday.

Next morning we collected our stock of provisions and started off by the woodland track for the Staffelalp. It was a forenoon of sultry heat and our peak was hidden in dull, grey cloud. However, the hostess at the Inn assured us that the weather was improving, thus encouraging us to proceed along the moraine-covered Zmutt glacier. Our intention was to make a bivouac as high as possible on the rocks below the Zmutt Ridge. We had waterproof sleeping sacks of a light pattern which would secure us against the cold of an average summer night, and a high camp would give us a much better chance of completing the traverse of the mountain. We could only trust that the predictions of the landlady of the Staffelalp as to the probable course of the weather would be as fortunate as those of Mummery before his first ascent, when he insisted that all was well in spite of the gloomy forebodings of his guides, thus acquiring an altogether undeserved reputation for astounding wisdom in this essential branch of Alpine mountaineering.

We were not so fortunate, or at least not at once. A furious squall of rain and snow drove us to shelter under a huge boulder supported by a pillar of ice. Again we progressed, but the ferocity and persistence of the next storm were so unmistakable that we gave in and fled to the shelter and comfort of the Schönbühl Hut. Within was a cheerful group of climbers, German and Austrian. We passed a pleasant evening together, exchanging our adventures and experiences on many mountains. The barometer, meanwhile, was falling steadily, but the Germans were determined to tackle the Dent Blanche. Though without a shred of hope, I mustered up sufficient virtue to rise about 3 a.m. in order to look out at the weather, which was as bad as might have been expected. I then slept soundly for another six hours with a clear conscience. The weather was still as bad as ever, and the Dent Blanche party had returned several hours before, without having got very far.

We were now faced with another problem, as the delay had no corresponding effect on our appetites. We must procure some more bread, butter and cheese at all costs. We decided to return to the Staffelalp for a good meal, and endeavour to coax the required provisions from the good lady of the Inn. The Staffelalp exceeded our expectations, and a full rucksack was an easy and comfortable burden for a pair of lazy, well-fed mountaineers strolling back to the hut in the late afternoon.

The weather was undoubtedly on the mend. We stopped and bathed in a rock-bound tarn, and, while we sunned ourselves on the bank, the clouds parted asunder and the upper crags of the Matterhorn smiled upon us in a dazzling, white garment of new snow. Then the clouds broke up altogether, and, in a perfect evening, Parry and I prospected the crossing of the Zmutt glacier, the first part of our route for the early morning. It was clear to us that the belated efforts of the sun would not avail to clear away the new snow and ice from the most diffi-cult part of our climb: but the mountaineer who does not attempt his peak in an interval of good weather deserves no more than to be caught out by the next tantrums of that fickle goddess. We returned to the hut and prepared to make a very early start.

We were out of bed by 1 a.m. The night was calm and clear, and we lost no time over breakfast. Inside an hour we were crossing the glacier in the starlight, for the moon was very low in the south-west, casting a wan light on the upper snows of our peak, but hardly any illumination in the valleys. We made for a small, tributary glacier which descended from the lower end of the Zmutt Ridge. There was little difficulty as we mounted rapidly over hard snow. Well to our right and above us was a snowy saddle, which we reached at 3.30 a.m. The feeble candle lantern which we had been using guttered out, and we were obliged to proceed rather more slowly. There was still no difficulty, as we were traversing gently upwards over fairly easy ground below the cliffs which fell away towards us from our ridge. We were travelling light and did not carry crampons at all. In the circumstances this did not matter very much, but the night frost was considerable, and several of the snow slopes were rather hard for kicking steps. Parry did not appear to have as sharp nails as I, and I heard him muttering occasional anathemas at the hardness of the surface.

The last snow crossing led us upwards to easy rocks which promised a direct access to the snowy crest of the ridge. Soon we were clambering up the rocks beside a small watercourse Before this disappeared we made a halt for second breakfast and

CC

The North-West Face of the Matterhorn
Dotted line show approx. route up Zmutt Ridge
Left skyline is Swiss Ridge, right skyline Italian Ridge

boiled a small pan of water. It was a short halt, for the cold was intense. The rocks now became slabby, with occasional icicles and an icy crust on many of the ledges. Things were not at all easy for us, and we had to be very careful in picking our route.

We gained the lower end of a long slope of hard snow, and the wind assailed us from behind. Every now and then a terrific gust would envelop us in a cloud of frozen spindrift which stung like a sandblast. We could only cling to our holds until the onslaught ceased and make what progress we could before the next one came. Then we got on to better snow and, for some reason, the gusts ended altogether. Plugging up the hard snow was warm work, and the snow seemed to become harder as we approached the ridge, although we were only forced to cut steps for short distances, now and again. We emerged into the sunshine of the ridge crest at 7.30 a.m. The first part of our ascent was accomplished.

The mountain promptly exacted its tribute of respect, as a fierce gust of wind whirled my hat in the air and sent it sailing far over the Matterhorn glacier on the other side. A thin woolly helmet served me just as well for the rest of the day. The snowy ridge was easy as far as the rocky teeth which are so well seen from the Staffelalp. They, too, were in good condition, and Parry did some rapid and excellent leading. We passed successive teeth on opposite sides, but one traverse on the Tiefenmatten slope required a good deal of care. Then we crossed over again by a gap and traversed above the Matterhorn Gletscher. We were now in shadow, but protected from the high wind. The compensating disadvantage was much drifting of the snow and the need for clearing all the holds in the rock. We also encountered some ice, whereas the crest of the ridge had been swept clear by the wind.

Increasing difficulty forced us backward and upward to the crest of the ridge. We were still a considerable way short of the place where a huge *couloir* drops straight down to the glacier on the left. Interesting and varied climbing continued all the way to the end of the lower ridge, where it abuts against the great, overhanging precipice which is known as the Nose of Zmutt. We had been very fortunate in the dry, bare, windswept condition of the rock, which was perfectly sound and offered very good holds. As we sat down for a short halt from 10.15 to 10.30 a.m. we began to consider that we had a reasonable prospect of success, although we knew that the next section, over the plastered Tiefenmatten slabs, was the crucial one.

There was not much snow on them, to begin with, but all the steeper slabs were partly covered with a thin film of ice, with a profusion of icicles hanging from the cracks and mantelshelves. I do not know whether it could be described as an effect of altitude, but my mind experienced a curious sense of detachment, as if I were merely a casual spectator of our progress. The dreaded Tiefenmatten face which, when seen from the Tête Blanche, looks steeper than any roof of an early Gothic cathedral, seemed to be almost diminutive and to offer no great difficulty. We appeared to be very high up on the mountain and by no means far below the summit. Once again, it was the action of climbing which corrected these fantasies.

We did not wish to traverse too far across the Tiefenmatten face, as we should have to return to our ridge at a higher level. At first, good upward progress could be combined with traversing, but we soon found that we must climb to a steeper shelf which ran across the face. The steeper rocks were festooned and glazed with ice, and we were faced with two very difficult pitches, of which the second was severe and troublesome. After negotiating this icy wall we could expect much easier progress for a long way. I attempted one way up and was repulsed, for there were several holds which were insecure. Parry was no more successful than I, and it seemed that we must tackle the pitch by another way which involved a short overhang. The whole difficulty did not exceed twenty-five feet in height. After a severe struggle, and not without carving numerous holds out of the stumps of icicles, we overcame the problem. It was a nasty place, but I think that the second man was adequately secured.

As we had expected, progress became easier and holds more abundant, although we still had to move very carefully. We were now above the Nose of Zmutt, and it was time to work back towards the upper ridge. This was soon possible by an upward traverse to the left, leading us to a steep slope of hard snow which continued until it lay against the upper ridge. Here, again, we had to cut a good many steps, but the snow was secure, despite the fact that it was a thinnish layer frozen to the slabs beneath. We regained the crest of the ridge without further difficulty, almost at the highest practicable point, beyond which it swung straight up towards the summit with a sheer drop to the slabs which we had just left. The climb did not tally with the accounts which I had read. Where was the famous *galerie* of Carrel, by which the mountain had been first ascended from the Italian ridge? We had not crossed it, so far as we knew, and yet we must be above it.

We proceeded up the crest. There was much more snow than before, but the holds were good. Parry led one awkward traverse on the east side with small, snow-filled holds, and we regained the crest. Then the slope eased off, and at 12.50 p.m. we stood on the Italian summit of the Matterhorn. It was untrodden, and there had been no visitors from the Italian side since the bad weather had sprinkled the mountain with fresh snow. We were alone, and the ambition of many years' standing was gratified. It would be idle to recount the glories of that panorama. There was not a cloud in the sky, and a sea of mountains lay around and beneath. The most striking feature of the Matterhorn is its complete isolation. There were quite a few mountains in that panorama which exceeded ours in height —Mont Blanc, the Weisshorn, the Dom and Monte Rosa—but they did not appear to do so. Zermatt and its valley lay at our feet, very far beneath us and utterly remote. At the other side were Breuil and the Italian Val Tournanche. The Lyskamm of Monte Rosa was, perhaps, the most imposing feature. Again I experienced that peculiar feeling of detachment and unreality. It appeared incredible that such a place could be a part of the material world, and no less so that we ourselves were there.

We passed along the level, narrow ridge to the higher, Swiss summit and found a dry, sheltered spot on the rocks just below it. There we spent an idle, luxurious hour, eating our lunch, enjoying the sun and revelling in the wide prospect. A few, small clouds were hanging over the Italian valleys. No vagaries of mountain or weather could rob us of our achievement. Parry had only one cigarette and I had just enough tobacco to fill one pipe, but that was sufficient, as we had a long descent before us.

At 2 p.m. we moved off downwards, over a steepening slope of snow. We found the footprints of earlier visitors who had come up the Swiss Ridge, but had not proceeded to the

We thought it very courageous of them to have come so far!

Italian summit. About a quarter of an hour below the top we halted, in order to allow a party of two very slow Germans to pass. They were literally crawling up the face on all fours, with an incredible length of loose rope between them in many kinks and coils. They told us that there was much ice lower down, and were very thankful to hear that they were so near the top. We were curious to know where they intended to pass the night, and they assured us that they would reach the Solvay Hut before dark. We hoped they would, and considered that they were just the sort of people that the Refuge Solvay was designed to shelter; although we knew that this small hut was not supposed to be used except in a case of emergency—accident, bad weather or benightment. They were heavily built, and of early middle age. We thought it very courageous of them to have come so far.

Lower down, we came to the uppermost of the fixed ropes and, be it confessed, had no scruples about making use of it. Like *crampons*, with which we were not provided, it was a time saver. This was the steep part of the summit tower of the mountain. There were more fixed ropes below this one, and we used them all. There are actually plenty of holds on this section, but, under the prevailing conditions, everything was masked with snow and ice. The anchorage was generally good enough for one of us to belay the other, even without the wire ropes, but the descent would have taken a long time. Below the steep part was the Shoulder, where the route left the edge above the Matterhorn glacier and kept more to the right. Then came another steep section, and we returned to the northern edge. The Solvay Hut was in a sheltered position, a short distance below, and we had taken a good two hours from the summit to reach it, without wasting any time. The small hut did not look very inviting for a stay during prolonged bad weather.

The irritating feature of the Hörnli (or Swiss) Ridge is the deadening uniformity of its lower half. From the summit one might, in a flight of imagination, deem it possible to fling a stone on to the roof of the Belvedere Hotel, 4,000 feet beneath. In reality it takes hours of steady plodding to reach that hospice. Below the Solvay we found the route more difficult to follow, so that Parry and I wandered too much to the right, towards the Furggen face, making it necessary for us to traverse back to the left in order to regain the ridge. Below this point there was no more snow, and we soon came to the remains of the old *Cabane*. Then we followed occasional nail scratches on the rocks, descending a little subordinate ridge to the right of the true one. Other incidents were a short traverse on the north face and the crossing of several points on the crest before we finally abandoned the ridge altogether and continued obliquely downwards to the right. The last difficulty, really more of a nuisance than a problem, was the descent of a loose and treacherous gully of rotten rock. This may be really dangerous at times, when it acts as a funnel for the debris loosened by other parties higher up on the mountain. We took off the rope and descended in close order. Soon afterwards, at 6.30 p.m., we walked into the Belvedere and drank a bottle of wine.

We did not remain long enough to allow our muscles to set, as we were still 5,000 feet above Zermatt. An easy track led round the north base of the Hörnli rocks, and then past the beautiful Schwartzsee, which reflected the roseate hues of sunset on the snows of Monte Rosa and the Lyskamm. There was little time to spare, and we hurried downwards towards the wooded slopes above the gorge of Zmutt, where we ultimately joined the wider track from the Staffelalp, and were satisfied that we could not lose our way in the forest. I could never forget the story of a friend who had hired a guide to take him up an Alpine peak. After a successful expedition the guide left him to find his own way to his hotel by an ill-marked track through the woods, for the last mile or so. It was both dark and rainy. After a miserable night of aimless wandering he finally emerged from the forest, quite close to the hotel, in the grey light of early morning.

We halted on the bridge over the Zmutt torrent and gazed upward through the trees at the faint outline of our peak. In the half light it emitted a pale, ghostly radiance. Our weary minds could scarcely realise that only a few short hours had passed since we had rested on that ethereal summit. Then the spectre assumed form and substance as the rising moon silvered the mantle of new snow on the uppermost crest of the mountain.

> 'Silent the finger of the summit stood,
> Icy in pure, thin air . . . glittering with snows'.*

The Matterhorn had resumed its moral ascendancy, and all its atmosphere of inaccessibility. By the hard way of a mountaineer I had regained the earlier vision which I feared that I had lost. And yet, there are many active, cultured and intelligent people who continue to ask in wonder why men climb mountains!

* From *The Dauber*, by John Masefield.

SUGGESTIONS FOR FURTHER READING

The literature of mountaineering is, nowadays, so extensive that it would serve no useful purpose to list even a fraction of such books without some comment or discrimination. The selection, which is necessarily the outcome of the author's personal opinion, is meant for the guidance of the novice, who will readily find means of extending it as his experience and interest direct him. The few selected books are grouped in categories, chosen in general on account of their practical value for the purposes of this book, whilst including certain classics with which every serious mountaineer ought to be familiar.

Several books, especially in the latter category, may be out of print, but they should be available in libraries, and some are being reprinted from time to time. Short comments are appended to each group. No books are listed which are concerned with subjects not discussed in this book: e.g., books on mountain travel in a lighter vein, picture books, books on skiing, books on foreign ranges other than the Alps.

TECHNIQUE

Mountaineering Art, by HAROLD RAEBURN, T. Fisher Unwin; 274 pp.
Mountain Craft, by G. WINTHROP YOUNG, Methuen; 591 pp.
Climbing in Britain, by J. E. Q. BARFORD, Penguin Books; 160 pp.
Mountaineering, by T. A. H. PEACOCKE, A. & C. Black; 212 pp.

The first of these, unfortunately out of print, is the best book for the climber who wishes to learn the most of his craft, especially snowcraft, in Scotland before proceeding to the Alps. It deals with and links up both sets of problems, and is unique in this respect. Mr Young's book, much more detailed and comprehensive, ignores Scotland and goes straight to the Alps. It is a book to study after one's first experience of the Alps. Mr Peacocke's is a sound and useful book, mainly on Alpine work and easy to follow. *Climbing in Britain*, the separate chapters due to diverse authors and unified under the editorship of Mr Barford on behalf of the British Mountaineering Council, is very condensed and proceeds rather fast to the more detailed aspects of difficult rock climbing. It has useful information on mountain rescue, British clubs and periodicals etc. For those who are able to consult it, Vol. 21 of the *Scottish Mountaineering Club Journal* contains a useful comparative series of articles on the relation between Scottish and Alpine mountaineering.

British Mountains

Mountaineering in Scotland, by W. H. Murray, J. M. Dent; 252 pp.
British Hills and Mountains, by Bell, Bozman & Blakeborough, B. T. Batsford; 128 pp.
Scottish Mountaineering Club Guide Books, Douglas & Foulis, 9 Castle St., Edinburgh. Several of these are out of print but are being replanned. Those available in 1949 are: *Western Highlands, Island of Skye, Glencoe and Ardgour* (rock climbers' guide) and *Southern Highlands*
Scottish Mountaineering Club Journal, annual issue in April from Douglas & Foulis, Edinburgh
Fell and Rock Climbing Club Guides (rock climbing) *to the English Lake District*, 4 vols., Cloister Press, Heaton Mersey, Manchester
Climbers' Club Guides to North Wales (rock climbing) 7 vols., Cloister Press, Heaton Mersey, Manchester

Mr Murray's is the first book to do justice to the Scottish Bens as a field for difficult mountaineering, both rock climbing and severe climbing on snow and ice. Moreover, it is a fascinating book to read, full of the mountain spirit. *British Hills and Mountains* is well illustrated; it will serve the hillwalker as a guide, and the Scottish section will show him the lie of the land and where the best climbing is available. After that he can be guided by the district Guides published by the Scottish Mountaineering Club. One of these, the *General* Guide, has sections on technique, natural history, meteorology and photography. The English rock-climbing Guides are beautifully clear and detailed.

Alpine Narrative

Scrambles Amongst the Alps, by Edward Whymper, John Murray Blackwell's Mountaineering Library, 7 vols.
   (a) *The Playground of Europe*, by Sir Leslie Stephen
   (b) *My Climbs in the Alps and Caucasus*, by A. F. Mummery
Peaks, Passes and Glaciers, various authors, Dent, Everyman's Library
The Making of a Mountaineer, by G. I. Finch, J. W. Arrowsmith
On High Hills, by G. W. Young, Methuen
Climbs and Ski Runs, by F. S. Smythe, Blackwood
Climbs on Mont Blanc, by J. & T. de Lépiney, E. Arnold
Alpine Pilgrimage, by Julius Kugy, John Murray
Climbs of my Youth, by André Roch, Lindsay Drummond

Edward Whymper's book made history and inspired many a mountaineer, but Mummery has been able, better than any other author, I think, to portray the enthusiasm and jollity of the life of the mountaineer. His last chapter on the pleasures and penalties of mountaineering is unsurpassed and has been translated and quoted extensively. Leslie Stephen writes a prose which is often too polished for the peaks he describes. Winthrop Young is pre-eminently a mountain poet, but one who has done mighty deeds and can describe the struggle in passages of intense and powerful imagery.

Climbs and Ski Runs was Frank Smythe's first book and covers the formative years of his career, culminating in two great climbs on the south face of Mont Blanc. *The Making of a Mountaineer* is, in some ways, a similar book.

No list would be complete which did not contain books by the continental climbers. Julius Kugy's book is wholly delightful. No one has absorbed the soul of the mountains or the finer things of the mountain way more than he. The other two books describe the hardest expeditions in modern Alpine mountaineering, climbs pursued to the limit of human capacity, without any superfluous imagery and in the simplest of language.

ANTHOLOGIES AND POETRY

The Englishman in the Alps, by ARNOLD LUNN, Oxford Univ. Press
The Mountain Way, by R. L. G. IRVING, Dent
Collected Poems, by G. WINTHROP YOUNG, Methuen

Both of the above anthologies are excellent, containing both verse and prose. If one has perused them, the extent and scope of mountain literature will be appreciated, and no recommendation of Young's *Collected Poems* will be necessary.

ALPINE TOPOGRAPHY AND GUIDE BOOKS

The Alps in Nature and History, by W. A. B. COOLIDGE, Methuen
The Alpine Guide (3 vols.), by JOHN BALL, Longmans Green
Club Guides of the Swiss Alpine Club (many volumes)
Guide de la Chaine du Mont Blanc, LOUIS KURZ
Guide Vallot (to the Mont Blanc district), compiled by the Groupe des Hautes Montagnes of the French Alpine Club (many volumes).

Coolidge's book is of great interest in tracing the history of the Alps and relating it to the topography of passes and mountain ranges. Ball's Guide is an invaluable classic, not too detailed about individual peaks but extremely useful in describing the principal Alpine centres, passes and mountain routes. It is now out of print. For more detailed treatment one must go to the individual guides to the districts, published by the Swiss or French Alpine Clubs in the language of the district. They, as well as the appropriate maps, are easily obtainable in the principal centres.

GLOSSARY

Abseil (or Rappel). See Roping Down.

Alp. Originally a high pasture, now also applies to the mountains.

Anchor. A fixed and stable object on a steep face of rock, snow or ice
to which the climber may attach himself by means of his rope.
The anchor may be natural or artificial, e.g. by the use of piton
or ice-axe.

Arête. A ridge on a mountain, usually narrow, sometimes horizontal,
sometimes steeply inclined. The basis is of rock, but the super-
structure may be snow or ice.

Avalanche. A sliding or falling mass, usually of snow but occasionally
of ice, rocks and mud in the Alps. Snow avalanches are, in
general, of two varieties: (*a*) Dry powder snow (*Staub Lawinen*),
frequent in winter in the Alps and less common or dangerous in
summer, not usually dangerous at all in Scotland. (*b*) Wet snow,
which may often occur in the Alps in summer, especially after
bad weather and fresh snowfalls. This kind can be dangerous on
Scottish hills when a thaw follows a heavy snowfall, or in gullies
surmounted by cornices.

Backing-up. Climbing a gully or chimney with the back against one
wall and the knees or feet on the other.

Belay. To fasten a rope round a projection of rock, over a chockstone
in a crack or through a fixed metal ring secured to a rock, in
order to immobilise a climber. As a noun it applies to the object
to which the rope is fastened. It is also commonly used amongst
climbers to describe the same process or object when the rope
runs over the object under the strict control of the climber. In
snow and ice climbing the object may be an ice-axe or spike
firmly embedded in the surface. There are two principal methods
of belaying a moving climber by a fixed climber. When the
Direct Belay is used the rope runs over the fixed object under the
control of the fixed climber. In the case of the Indirect, Body or
Elastic Belay, the fixed climber is anchored to the object and
actually, in his own body, forms the Belay over which the rope
runs, under strict control, to the moving climber. For Running
Belay and Thread Belay, see separate entries.

Bergschrund (Randkluft or Rimaye). This is the large crevasse formed
at a sudden steepening of the upper *névé* or snow-ice, normally
where it abuts against a rock face or even a concealed rock face.
This only occurs in Scotland in a minor form after spring or
summer has shrunk the snowbeds below gullies on the northern
aspects of big, craggy peaks.

Buttress. Term borrowed from architecture, indicating a projecting and supporting mass of rock on a mountain face. The

slope of a buttress is steep, but it is broader and more rounded in contour than a steep ridge, and more massive than a rib.

Chimney. In rock climbing a narrow, steep rift, possibly vertical, which can be spanned during the climbing process.

Chockstone. A block of rock which is fixed and jammed in a narrow part of a chimney, gully or crack. It must often be surmounted directly. Sometimes it can be used as a belay.

Col. Properly speaking a pass, but applicable to a depression in a mountain ridge, usually the lowest between two peaks. Synonyms in the Alps are Sattel, Scharte, Joch, Lücke.

Combined Tactics. Means by which others in the party assist a leader to surmount a difficulty.

Contouring. Traversing the flank of a mountain, more or less horizontally, in order to by-pass bad ground, rocks or an intervening peak.

Cornice. An overhanging mass of snow or ice above a steep slope or at the side of a ridge. A snow ridge may be bounded by a cornice on either, or more seldom, on both sides. Cornices tend to form away from the prevailing wind. They may break down in thaw weather, and are a potential danger, both on Scottish peaks and in the Alps.

Corrie. An upper mountain valley in Scotland—not so large as and higher than a glen.

Couloir. An Alpine gully, usually very steep, and larger than a Scottish gully.

Crack. A narrower form of chimney. It is not always possible to insert a complete limb during climbing. Cracks may be at any angle or of any width. They are useful in slab climbing, as affording finger or toe holds.

Crampons (or climbing irons). A metal framework furnished with sharp spikes. It is fitted with straps to the underside of climbing boots. The best ones have five spikes on each side of the foot, the foremost being directly under the toes.

Crevasse (or *spalte*). A split of any size in a glacier or snowfield. They are not dangerous when the ice is bare, because avoidable. When partly or wholly snow-covered they are difficult to detect and hence dangerous. The depth may amount to several hundred feet.

Crust. A hard surface layer, often thin, overlying softer snow, which, in its turn, may rest on older snow-ice or even ice. It may be necessary to cut steps in the underlying hard surface for safety.

Dead Reckoning. Method of estimating distance traversed in mist, or darkness, by counting paces or, much less accurately, by timing.

Distress Signal. Signal made to attract attention from other parties within range, in the event of an accident. Use whistle, waving flag or flashing light—six signals at intervals during one minute, one-minute's pause and a repetition. Reply is similar, but using only three signals per minute.

Exposure. Accentuated sense of danger rather than increased actual danger, when climbing a very steep face with small holds, which may, however, be both sound and sufficient when properly used. There is usually a clear drop underneath if one falls off. Difficulty is quite a different matter. A climb may be very severe without exposure, but an exposed climb has always some degree of difficulty.

Firn or *Névé*. Upper Alpine snowfields where the snow has been partially transformed into ice, which still holds air-space and in which steps can be cut fairly easily or crampons used.

Föhn or *Foehn*. A warm, southerly Alpine wind. It means bad weather and soft snow conditions on the peaks.

Frost Crystals. A common winter condition on Scottish crags, especially at great heights. Frost or fog crystals grow into the prevailing wind and may encase the rocks to a considerable thickness, but are usually quite easy to detach.

Gendarme. An upstanding rock or tower on a ridge, which may either be climbed over or passed on the side.

Glissade. The descent of steep snow slopes by sliding, either erect on the feet or sitting. The first is the better and more controllable method.

Gully. A cleft in a rock face or craggy mountain side, much wider than a chimney and with an average gradient less than that of the bounding rocks, although it may contain vertical or overhanging sections.

Hitch. Projection over which a rope can be laid for security purposes. See Belay, direct.

Ice-Axe (*Pickel, Piolet*). Spiked shaft with headpiece (with pick and adze), used for security in snow and ice climbing and for cutting steps in ice or hard snow. It is indispensable for controlling a glissade.

Ice-Fall. A steep and broken-up section of a glacier. It occurs where there is a sharp fall in the bed of the glacier. The result is a confusion of crevasses and intervening walls, ridges and towers of ice, the latter, named *séracs*, being usually unstable.

Icing. On rocks this is a thin film of ice, known as *verglas* in the Alps. It is a dangerous condition, usually caused by frost after a wet thaw or rain. It is common on Scottish peaks in winter and less common in the Alps in summer.

Karabiner or Snap-link is an oval, openable spring link of steel, used for threading the rope for several different purposes; e.g. in Roping Down from a *piton* or in using such for a belay.

Layback. Method of climbing a thin, steep crack in a rock face when almost the only holds are finger and toe holds in the crack itself. One hangs back from these holds. Method is useful in an open corner.

Moraine. Accumulation of boulders and finer debris, brought down by a glacier and lying on its surface. There are the long ridges of side and medial moraines and, at the lower end of the glacier, a mound of debris called the terminal moraine.

Naismith's Rule. In order to estimate the time necessary for an expedition, in average good conditions of weather and ground, W. W. Naismith allowed one hour for every three miles on the flat and an extra hour for every 1,500 feet climbed. Add extra time for halts and adverse conditions.

Névé. See under *Firn*.

Orientation. Method of ascertaining one's exact position and the true bearing of surrounding objects.

Pitch. A difficult section in climbing on rock, snow or ice.

Piton (or peg). A strong spike with attached ring for securing the rope. The spike can be hammered into a crack in the rock or, in some cases, into ice. It is often used in association with a *Karabiner* or snap-link.

Rib. A steep, minor ridge on a rock face.

Roping Down (*Abseil* or *Rappel*). Method of descent from an impossible position on a climb by a controlled slide down a doubled rope which is securely fixed to an anchor above. This method is often used on difficult rock peaks in the Alps, and sometimes in an emergency on British climbs.

Running Belay. Method for securing the leader, or occasionally others as well, usually for a difficult traverse on rock (or ice). The rope runs over a belay, or (better) through a ring fixed to an anchor.

Scree. Slope covered with loose stones.

Sérac. Generally unstable towers or rectangular masses or walls of ice found in an icefall. They may consist of hard snow-ice.

Slab. Flattish masses of rock, smooth or rough, inclined at various angles, usually furnished with few positive holds, which constitute climbing problems of all grades of magnitude and difficulty.

Snap-Link. See under *Karabiner*, also called *Mousqueton*.

Snow Bridge. These span crevasses or *bergschrunds* at their narrowest sections. They are of all varieties of firmness and must be carefully tested before use.

Snow-Ice. Snow which has been partly converted into ice by pressure, thawing and refreezing, or both processes. It is not so homogeneous as ice and still holds a proportion of air. It is of all degrees of hardness and toughness, according to conditions. It can be exceedingly tough on the upper slopes of Scottish peaks. It corresponds to hard *névé* in the Alps.

Stance. Secure position for the feet on a rock or snow climb, considered without reference to handholds.

Standard of Difficulty. The conventional standards for British rock climbs are, in ascending order of difficulty, as follows — easy, moderate, difficult, very difficult, severe, very severe. In the

Alps there are usually six grades numbered upwards from (1) to
(6). It is difficult to apply these standards to snow and ice climbs.
They presuppose dry rock and good conditions. Sometimes two
intermediate grades appear; mild severe before severe and hard
severe before very severe. Such discrimination appears to neglect
the subjective factor involved in all such matters. Precision is
unattainable. The grading applies only to the hardest part of the
route. The author's grading is a personal opinion, but intended
to apply to a climber of average skill.

Thread Belay. Where the security rope can be passed round a wedged
stone in a crack, or similarly secured for belaying purposes, the
resulting anchorage is a thread belay. A double rope may be
used and tied back on itself.

Tourmente. An Alpine blizzard.

Traverse. A more or less horizontal passage across rock or snow.
Sometimes there is a short passage without footholds but offering
handholds. This is a Hand Traverse. Traverse also means to cross
a mountain, up one side and down another.

Variation of the Compass (sometimes called magnetic variation or
declination). The angular divergence between the true north
direction and that indicated by the north-seeking pole of the
compass. It varies from place to place on the earth's surface, and
slowly from year to year. (In Scotland in 1948 the compass points
about twelve degrees west of true north, a slowly diminishing
quantity).

Verglas. See under *Icing.*

INDEX

For convenience of reference this index has been compiled in three sections: Names of Persons, Place Names, and Technical and General. The latter, though mainly on technique, also refers to matters in the descriptive part of the book which do not come under the first two categories. Where Map or Fig. appear before a page number they refer to maps and text diagrams or drawings. The letter G signifies that the technical term is explained in the Glossary at the end of the book. Roman numbers refer to entire chapters.

There are a number of cross references and double entries in Sections II and III. Place names have often been conveniently grouped under such general headings as Aiguille, Ben, Coire, Dent, Glacier, Glen, Loch, Mont, Sgurr; and matters of technique under Alpine, Belay, Descent, Equipment, Geology, Huts, Maxims, Rock, Rope, Safety, Snow, etc. The index does not cover Foreword, Appendices or Photographs.

SECTION I — NAMES OF PERSONS

SECTION II — PLACE NAMES

SECTION III — TECHNIQUE AND GENERAL